Essentials of Accounting for Governmental and Not-for-Profit Organizations

Fourteenth Edition

Paul A. Copley,
Ph.D., CPA, CGFM
Professor School of Accounting
James Madison University

Mc Graw Hill

McGraw Hill

ESSENTIALS OF ACCOUNTING FOR GOVERNMENTAL AND NOT-FOR-PROFIT ORGANIZATIONS, FOURTEENTH EDITION

This book is printed on acid-free paper.

1 2 3 4 5 6 7 8 9 LCR 24 23 22 21 20 19

ISBN 978-1-260-20138-3 (bound edition)
MHID 1-260-20138-4 (bound edition)
ISBN 978-1-260-78922-5 (loose-leaf edition)
MHID 1-260-78922-5 (loose-leaf edition)

Portfolio Manager: *Elizabeth Eisenhart*
Product Developer: *Alexandra Kukla*
Marketing Manager: *Katherine Wheeler*
Content Project Managers: *Lori Koetters, Angela Norris*
Buyer: *Laura Fuller*
Design: *Matt Diamond*
Content Licensing Specialist: *Lori Hancock*
Cover Image: *Courtesy of Paul A. Copley*
Compositor: *SPi Global*

Library of Congress Cataloging-in-Publication Data

Names: Copley, Paul A., author.
Title: Essentials of accounting for governmental and not-for-profit organizations / Paul A. Copley, Ph.D., CPA, Professor, School of Accounting, James Madison University.
Description: Fourteenth edition. | New York, NY : McGraw-Hill Education, [2019]
Identifiers: LCCN 2019015283 | ISBN 9781260201383 (alk. paper)
Subjects: LCSH: Administrative agencies—United States—Accounting. | Nonprofit organizations—United States—Accounting.
Classification: LCC HJ9801 .H39 2019 | DDC 657/.83500973—dc23
LC record available at https://lccn.loc.gov/2019015283

mheducation.com/highered

Preface

Thank you for considering the fourteenth edition of *Essentials of Accounting for Governmental and Not-for-Profit Organizations.* The focus of the text is on the preparation of external financial statements. The coverage is effective in preparing candidates for the CPA examination. I have used the text with traditional three-semester-hour classes, with half-semester GNP courses, and as a module in advanced accounting classes. It is appropriate for accounting majors or as part of a public administration program.

Both the FASB and GASB issued major new standards since the previous edition:

1. GASB *Statement No. 84: Fiduciary Activities* (Chapter 7). This standard changes the categories of fiduciary activities and the reporting requirements of custodial (formerly agency) funds.
2. FASB *Accounting Standards Update 2018-08: Clarifying the Scope and the Accounting Guidance for Contributions Received and Contributions Made* (Chapter 10). This standard clarifies a number of issues including distinguishing exchange transactions from contributions. Additionally, the standard distinguishes between donor conditions and donor restrictions and illustrates the accounting for each. Grant accounting, in particular, is affected by this standard.
3. *FASB Accounting Standards Update 2016-14: Presentation of Financial Statements of Not-for-Profit Entities* (Chapter 10). This standard alters the format of the Activity Statement as well as providing new residual equity account titles. The Statement of Functional Expense is required of all not-for-profits while a reconciliation between the Activity Statement and Cash Flows from Operations is no longer required.

Health care entities, in particular, are affected by *FASB Accounting Standards Update 2014-09: Revenue from Contracts with Customers.* Chapter 12 now summarizes the major elements of this comprehensive standard in the context of accounting for hospitals. The standard requires health care entities to estimate implicit price concessions as part of recognition of revenue.

The fourteenth edition has been updated for other new standards, including

- *GASB Statement No. 83: Certain Asset Retirement Obligations (Chapter 6)*
- *GASB Statement Nos. 87: Leases (Chapter 9)*
- *GASB Statement No. 89: Accounting for Interest Costs Incurred before the End of a Construction Period (Chapter 6)*

The text contains a discussion of the *GASB Codification of Financial Reporting Standards.* References are made throughout the text to specific segments of the Codification. With the implementation of *GASB 54* (Fund Balance Reporting), the last vestige of budgetary accounting is phased out of government financial statements. The fourteenth edition continues to provide budget and encumbrance journal entries, but presents these as distinct accounts that are not commingled with the accounts appearing in the basic financial statements. This approach should reduce confusion sometimes experienced by students, particularly with the recording of encumbrances.

Among the more challenging aspects of state and local government reporting is the preparation of government-wide financial statements. The approach demonstrated in the text is similar to that used in practice. Specifically, day-to-day events are recorded at the fund level using the basis of accounting for fund financial statements. Governmental activities are recorded using the modified accrual basis. The fund-basis statements are then used as input in the preparation of government-wide statements. The preparation of government-wide statements is presented in an Excel worksheet. This approach has two advantages: (1) it is the approach most commonly applied in practice, and (2) it is an approach familiar to students who have studied the process of consolidation in their advanced accounting classes. State and local government reporting is illustrated using an ongoing example integrated throughout Chapters 4 through 8 and 13.

Mc Graw Hill connect

Connect: Intuitive and user friendly, Connect is a homework and learning management solution that embeds learning science and award-winning adaptive tools to improve student results.

Supplements and additional features of the text are available in Connect and the eBook, including:

- **New! SmartBook 2.0:** SmartBook identifies and closes knowledge gaps through a continually adapting reading and questioning experience that helps students master the key concepts in the chapter.
    - SmartBook 2.0 is the latest version of SmartBook, with key updates to improve accessibility, to provide mobile functionality, allow a more granular level of content selection, and to provide the ability to assign Recharge activities.
- **Test Bank:** An auto-gradable test bank and chapter-specific quizzes.
- **Continuous Problem Set—City of Monroe:** A Continuous Problem Set—City of Monroe is a continuous homework problem found in Chapters 4 through 8 and Chapter 13 in the text and in the Instructor Library in Connect. The continuous problem is presented to provide an overview of the reporting process, including preparation of fund basis and government-wide statements. The problem assumes the government is using fund accounting for its internal record-keeping and then at year-end makes necessary adjustments to prepare the government-wide statements.

- **Instructor Guide**
- **PowerPoint Slides**
- **Excel-based Assignments**
- **Additional Practice Set**

Acknowledgments

I am indebted to users of the textbook for their helpful suggestions, including Patricia Lopez (Valencia College), Georgia Smedley (University of Missouri–Kansas City), Vandee DeVore (Columbia College), and particularly to Dori Danko (Grand Valley State). I am especially appreciative of Loretta Manktelow for her thorough review and advice. Additional comments and suggestions are welcome and may be addressed to: copleypa@JMU.edu.

Paul A. Copley

Mc Graw Hill connect®

FOR INSTRUCTORS

You're in the driver's seat.

Want to build your own course? No problem. Prefer to use our turnkey, prebuilt course? Easy. Want to make changes throughout the semester? Sure. And you'll save time with Connect's auto-grading too.

65%

Less Time Grading

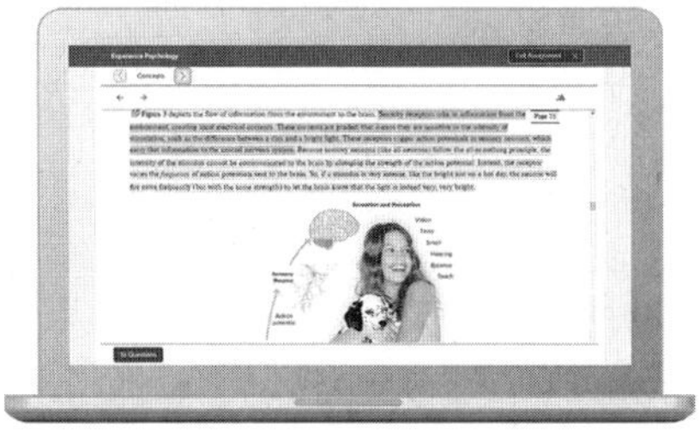

Laptop: McGraw-Hill Education

They'll thank you for it.

Adaptive study resources like SmartBook® 2.0 help your students be better prepared in less time. You can transform your class time from dull definitions to dynamic debates. Find out more about the powerful personalized learning experience available in SmartBook 2.0 at **www.mheducation.com/highered/connect/smartbook**

Make it simple, make it affordable.

Connect makes it easy with seamless integration using any of the major Learning Management Systems—Blackboard®, Canvas, and D2L, among others—to let you organize your course in one convenient location. Give your students access to digital materials at a discount with our inclusive access program. Ask your McGraw-Hill representative for more information.

Padlock: Jobalou/Getty Images

Solutions for your challenges.

A product isn't a solution. Real solutions are affordable, reliable, and come with training and ongoing support when you need it and how you want it. Our Customer Experience Group can also help you troubleshoot tech problems—although Connect's 99% uptime means you might not need to call them. See for yourself at **status.mheducation.com**

Checkmark: Jobalou/Getty Images

SUPPORT AT every step

FOR STUDENTS

Effective, efficient studying.

Connect helps you be more productive with your study time and get better grades using tools like SmartBook 2.0, which highlights key concepts and creates a personalized study plan. Connect sets you up for success, so you walk into class with confidence and walk out with better grades.

Study anytime, anywhere.

Download the free ReadAnywhere app and access your online eBook or SmartBook 2.0 assignments when it's convenient, even if you're offline. And since the app automatically syncs with your eBook and SmartBook 2.0 assignments in Connect, all of your work is available every time you open it. Find out more at **www.mheducation.com/readanywhere**

"I really liked this app—it made it easy to study when you don't have your text-book in front of you."

- Jordan Cunningham, Eastern Washington University

Calendar: owattaphotos/Getty Images

No surprises.

The Connect Calendar and Reports tools keep you on track with the work you need to get done and your assignment scores. Life gets busy; Connect tools help you keep learning through it all.

Learning for everyone.

McGraw-Hill works directly with Accessibility Services Departments and faculty to meet the learning needs of all students. Please contact your Accessibility Services office and ask them to email accessibility@mheducation.com, or visit **www.mheducation.com/about/accessibility** for more information.

Top: Jenner Images/Getty Images, Left: Hero Images/Getty Images, Right: Hero Images/Getty Images

Contents

Chapter Three
MODIFIED ACCRUAL ACCOUNTING: INCLUDING THE ROLE OF FUND BALANCES AND BUDGETARY AUTHORITY 53

Chapter Four
ACCOUNTING FOR THE GENERAL AND SPECIAL REVENUE FUNDS 82

Chapter Eight GOVERNMENT-WIDE STATEMENTS, CAPITAL ASSETS, LONG-TERM DEBT 212

Chapter Nine ADVANCED TOPICS FOR STATE AND LOCAL GOVERNMENTS 260

Chapter Ten ACCOUNTING FOR PRIVATE NOT-FOR-PROFIT ORGANIZATIONS 283

Chapter Eleven
COLLEGE AND UNIVERSITY ACCOUNTING 321

Chapter Twelve
ACCOUNTING FOR HOSPITALS AND OTHER HEALTH CARE PROVIDERS 349

Chapter Thirteen
AUDITING, TAX-EXEMPT ORGANIZATIONS, AND EVALUATING PERFORMANCE 378

Chapter Fourteen
FINANCIAL REPORTING BY THE FEDERAL GOVERNMENT 403

Chapter **One**

Introduction to Accounting and Financial Reporting for Governmental and Not-for-Profit Organizations

No Money shall be drawn from the Treasury, but in Consequence of Appropriations made by Law; and a regular Statement and Account of the Receipts and Expenditures of all public Money shall be published from time to time. Article 1, Section 9: The United States Constitution

If men were angels, no government would be necessary. If angels were to govern men, neither external nor internal controls on government would be necessary. James Madison, fourth president of the United States and principal author of the U.S. Constitution

Learning Objectives

- Obtain an overview of financial reporting for nonbusiness entities.
- Distinguish between private and public sector organizations.
- Identify the sources of authoritative accounting standards for various public and private sector organizations.
- Define the 11 fund types used by state and local governments.

In its relatively short existence, the United States has grown to be the largest and most successful economy in history. Why then would a country founded on the principles of free markets and private investment rely on governments to provide many goods and services? The answer lies in understanding the incentives of a free enterprise economy. There are many services that simply cannot be priced in a way that naturally encourages commercial entrepreneurs to enter the marketplace. Commonly this is because the service is subject to free-riding. For example, public safety and a clean environment benefit all citizens, whether or not they contribute to its cost. In other instances, free market incentives do not align with public interest. For example, society finds it desirable to provide a K–12 education to all its citizens, not just those with the ability to pay. Because there is no practical means for businesses to sell these services, governments are called upon through the political process to provide those services that citizens demand.[1]

Although the majority of products and services are provided by either businesses or governments, in some circumstances private organizations are formed to provide goods or services without the intent of earning a profit from these activities. Examples include public charities, trade associations, and civic groups. Again, the goods or services they provide often cannot be priced in a way that encourages commercial entrepreneurship. For example, a public radio broadcast cannot be effectively restricted to only those individuals choosing to support the public radio station. While this explains why the services are not provided by businesses, why aren't governments called upon to provide them?

In some instances, obstacles exist that prevent government involvement. For example, the U.S. Constitution provides for separation of church and state. Therefore, any group that wishes to promote religious activities must do so through private organizations rather than through government. More commonly the reason is lack of political influence. Support for the arts may be important to a group of individuals but unless that group is sufficiently large to influence the political process, it is unlikely that elected officials will use government funds for that purpose. However, support for the arts could still be provided by forming a charitable foundation with no relationship to the government and having the foundation solicit donations from that segment of the public that finds the arts important.

The organizations introduced in the preceding paragraphs are the focus of this book: governmental and not-for-profit organizations. They are distinguished from commercial businesses by the absence of an identifiable individual or group of individuals who hold a legally enforceable residual claim to the net resources. Throughout the text a distinction will be made between **public** and **private** organizations. Public organizations are owned or controlled by governments. Private organizations are not owned or controlled by governments and include businesses as well as private not-for-profit organizations. **Not-for-profit organizations** lack a residual ownership claim and the organization's purpose is something other than to provide goods and services at a profit.

Because significant resources are provided to governments and not-for-profit organizations, financial reporting by these organizations is important. To paraphrase the James Madison quotation provided at the beginning of the chapter, because humans (not angels) operate governments, controls are necessary. Financial reports that reflect the policies and actions of governmental managers are an effective means to control the actions of those entrusted with public resources. To be effective, external financial reports must be guided by a set of generally accepted

[1] The branch of economics that studies the demand for government services is termed *public choice*.

accounting principles. The generally accepted accounting principles for governmental and private not-for-profit organizations are the subject of this book. The first nine chapters of the text deal with public sector (state and local government) organizations and Chapters 10, 11, and 12 deal primarily with private not-for-profit organizations. Chapter 13 discusses auditing and tax-related issues unique to governments and private not-for-profits and also evaluates performance of these entities. Chapter 14 describes financial reporting by the federal government.

GENERALLY ACCEPTED ACCOUNTING PRINCIPLES

Biologists tell us that organisms evolve in response to characteristics of their environment. Similarly, accounting principles evolve over time as people find certain practices useful for decision making. Further, we expect organisms in different environments to evolve differently. Similarly, if the environments in which governments and not-for-profits operate differ in important ways from that of commercial enterprises, we would expect the accounting practices to evolve differently. It is important to understand how governments and not-for-profit organizations differ from commercial businesses if we are to understand why the accounting practices of these nonbusiness organizations have evolved in the manner we will see throughout the remainder of this text.

The Governmental Accounting Standards Board published a document titled *Why Governmental Accounting and Financial Reporting Is—and Should Be—Different* (http://www.gasb.org/white_paper_full.pdf). This white paper identifies five environmental differences between governments and for-profit business enterprises and describes how those differences manifest in differences in the objectives and practice of financial reporting.

1. **Organizational Purposes.** While the purpose of a commercial business is to generate a profit for the benefit of its owners, governments exist for the well-being of citizens by providing public services—whether or not the services are profitable undertakings. The result is that government accounting practices are not focused on the measurement of net income for the purpose of measuring return to investors. Rather they are intended to satisfy the information needs of a variety of users.

While the purpose of government operations differs greatly from commercial businesses, the purpose of governmental accounting is the same—to provide information that is useful to stakeholders in making decisions. However, governments have vastly different sets of users of accounting information. Like businesses, governments have creditors who are interested in assessing the creditworthiness of the government. Citizens and businesses, both within the government's jurisdiction and those considering relocation to the jurisdiction, are also stakeholders who rely on governmental reporting to make economic decisions. In addition, governments receive resources from other governments and grantors who may require financial reports and audits as a condition of the grant. Since this diverse set of resource providers have varying interests, the information needs of one group may not meet the needs of another. The result is that governments report far more disaggregated information than commercial enterprises.

2. **Sources of Revenues.** Net income is a universally accepted measure of business performance. The calculation of net income begins with sales. A sale occurs when an independent party perceives that the service offered both provides value and is fairly priced. Net income then simply determines whether this measure of demand (sales) exceeds the cost of providing the service and is an accepted measure of performance for business organizations. In contrast, governments derive many of their resources from taxes. Individuals and businesses pay taxes to avoid penalty, not voluntarily because they perceive government services to be of value and fairly priced. Since taxes do not involve an earnings process, the timing of the recognition of tax revenue is not always clear.

3. **Potential for Longevity.** Because the U.S. and state constitutions grant state and local governments the ability to tax, governments very rarely go out of business. This long-term view of operations changes the focus of accounting from one of near-term recovery of amounts invested in assets to a longer-term focus on the sustainability of services and the ability to meet future demand. As a result, governments may elect not to depreciate some capital assets but expense improvements that extend an asset's useful life.

4. **Relationship with Stakeholders.** Taxes are levied through the legislative process by officials elected by the citizens. Because citizens and businesses are then required to pay these taxes, governments have an obligation to demonstrate accountability for these public funds. While a business can use its resources as it deems appropriate, governments frequently receive resources that are restricted to a particular purpose. For example, a city may collect a telephone excise tax legally restricted to operating a 911 emergency service. In an effort to provide assurance that resources are used according to legal or donor restrictions, governments use **fund accounting.** A fund represents part of the activities of an organization that is separated from other activities in the accounting records to more easily demonstrate compliance with legal restrictions or limitations.

5. **Role of the Budget.** Many businesses prepare budgets, but these are for planning and control purposes and are rarely made available to creditors or investors. In contrast, government budgets are expressions of public policy and often carry the authority of law, preventing public officials from spending outside their budgetary authority. The increased importance of budgets is reflected in government financial reports by a required report comparing budgeted and actual amounts.

For these and other reasons, the accounting practices of governmental organizations evolved differently from those of businesses. As you will see in later chapters, the accounting practices of not-for-profit organizations more closely resemble those of commercial businesses. However, the not-for-profit environment shares some important characteristics with governments. Similar to governments, not-for-profits do not have residual owners. "Investors" in not-for-profits are diverse and include donors, volunteers, and members. In addition, as with governments, the excess of revenues over expenses is not an effective measure of organizational performance. Finally, like governments, not-for-profits commonly receive resources with donor-imposed restrictions.

Sources of Generally Accepted Accounting Principles

Further complicating accounting issues is the fact that we have three levels of government (federal, state, and local) and not-for-profits may be either publicly or privately owned. This is important because different standards-setting bodies have authority for establishing reporting standards for these groups. Illustration 1-1 summarizes the various organizational types and the bodies with primary standard-setting authority.

Accounting and financial reporting standards for the federal government are published by the **Federal Accounting Standards Advisory Board (FASAB).** The standards are technically "recommendations" since, as a sovereign nation, the federal government cannot relegate authority to an independent board. Recommendations of the FASAB are reviewed and become effective unless objected to by one of the **principals,** the U.S. Government Accountability Office (GAO), the U.S. Department of the Treasury, or the U.S. Office of Management and Budget. These standards apply to financial reports issued by federal agencies and to the Consolidated Financial Report of the United States Government. Accounting and financial reporting standards for the federal government are illustrated in Chapter 14.

Accounting and financial reporting standards for state and local governments in the United States are set by the **Governmental Accounting Standards Board (GASB).** The GASB also sets accounting and financial reporting standards for governmentally related not-for-profit organizations, such as colleges and universities, health care entities, museums, libraries, and performing arts organizations that are owned or controlled by governments. Accounting and financial reporting standards for profit-seeking businesses and for nongovernmental not-for-profit organizations are set by the **Financial Accounting Standards Board (FASB).**

The GASB and the FASB are parallel bodies under the oversight of the **Financial Accounting Foundation (FAF).** The FAF appoints the members of the two boards and provides financial support to the boards by obtaining contributions from businesses; professional organizations of accountants and financial analysts; CPA firms; debt-rating agencies; and state and local governments. Because of the breadth of support and the lack of ties to any single organization or government, the GASB and the FASB are referred to as "independent standards-setting bodies." Standards set by the FASAB, GASB, and FASB are the primary sources of **generally accepted accounting principles (GAAP)** as the term is used in accounting and auditing literature.

ILLUSTRATION 1-1 **Summary of Standards-Setting Organizations**

Reporting Organization	Standards-Setting Board
Federal government	Federal Accounting Standards Advisory Board (FASAB)
State and local governments	Governmental Accounting Standards Board (GASB)
Public not-for-profits	Governmental Accounting Standards Board (GASB)
Private not-for-profits	Financial Accounting Standards Board (FASB)
Investor-owned businesses	Financial Accounting Standards Board (FASB)

GASB standards are set forth in documents called **Statements** of Financial Accounting Standards. Although no longer used, in the past the GASB also issued **Interpretations** that provided guidance on previously issued statements. From time to time, the Board finds it necessary to expand on standards in **Technical Bulletins** and Implementation Guides. The sources of authoritative GAAP for state and local governments therefore are

- Category A: GASB Statements (and Interpretations)
- Category B: GASB Implementation Guides, GASB Technical Bulletins, and literature of the American Institute of Certified Public Accountants (AICPA) specifically cleared by the GASB

If the accounting treatment for a given transaction is not specified by a statement in Category A, a state and local government should consider whether it is covered by one of the sources identified in Category B. If the accounting treatment is not specified within one of these authoritative sources, the government should consider whether the transaction is sufficiently similar to ones covered by one of the authoritative sources that a similar accounting treatment can be applied. If not, the government may use nonauthoritative sources for guidance, including

- GASB Concept Statements,
- FASB, FASAB, or International Standards Board pronouncements,
- AICPA literature not specifically cleared by the GASB,
- Other sources provided by professional organizations, regulatory agencies, textbooks, and published articles, or
- Prevalent practices that evolved among governments without specific authoritative action.

Both the FASB and FASAB have similar hierarchies of GAAP for entities falling within their jurisdictions. The GASB, FASB, and FASAB publish **codifications** (organized versions) of accounting standards. The GASB also publishes a comprehensive collection of its implementation guides. The advantage of using the codified versions of standards is that all relevant standards for a particular topic are presented together and any superseded segments of standards have been removed. Codification references are presented in two parts: the first (section) identifies a topic and the second identifies a paragraph within the codification. Letters typically give a clue as to the topic (e.g., L for leases and Ho for hospitals). Paragraph numbers may be used to determine the level of authority within the GAAP Hierarchy. These are summarized as follows:

Section #s	Topics
1000–1900	General Principles
2000–2900	Broad Financial Reporting Requirements
Letters (A–Z)	Specific Balance Sheet or Operating Accounts
Double letters	Specialized Industries or Reporting Units

Paragraph #s	Level of Authority
100–499	GASB Statements
500–599	Definitions
600–699	GASB Technical Bulletins and AICPA Audit and Accounting Guides and Statements of Position
700–799	AICPA Practice Bulletins
900–999	Nonauthoritative discussions

For example:

Codification Reference	Section	Paragraph
1000.101	Section 1000 indicates this pertains to general principles (in this case GAAP Hierarchy).	Paragraphs 101–104 present the GAAP Hierarchy and since the paragraph number is <500, it comes from a GASB Statement (in this case Statement No. 76).
1700.601	Section 1700 indicates this pertains to reporting of budgetary information.	Paragraph 601 states what to disclose if a government is not legally required to adopt a budget. Since the paragraph number is 600–699, this is Level B GAAP.
F60.101	The single letter (F) identifies a specific account (in this case Food stamps).	The paragraph number (<500) indicates this standard comes from a GASB Statement.
Co5.902	The double letters (Co) identify a specialized industry (Colleges and universities).	The paragraph number (>900) indicates these are nonauthoritative examples of financial statements for a state university.

Definition of Government

Some organizations possess certain characteristics of both governmental and non-governmental not-for-profit organizations. Since there are different standard-setting boards, it is important to identify which board's standards apply to a given entity. For this reason, the FASB and GASB agreed upon a definition of governmental organizations:

> Public corporations and bodies corporate and politic are governmental organizations. Other organizations are governmental organizations if they have one or more of the following characteristics:
>
> *a.* Popular election of officers or appointment (or approval) of a controlling majority of the members of the organization's governing body by officials of one or more state or local governments;
>
> *b.* The potential for unilateral dissolution by a government with the net resources reverting to a government; or
>
> *c.* The power to enact and enforce a tax levy.

Furthermore, organizations are presumed to be governmental if they have the ability to issue directly (rather than through a state or municipal authority) debt that pays interest exempt from federal taxation.

OBJECTIVES OF ACCOUNTING AND FINANCIAL REPORTING

All three standards-setting organizations—the Federal Accounting Standards Advisory Board, the Financial Accounting Standards Board, and the Governmental Accounting Standards Board—take the position that the establishment of accounting and financial reporting standards should be guided by conceptual considerations so that the body of standards is internally consistent and the standards address broad issues. The cornerstone of a conceptual framework is said to be a statement of the objectives of financial reporting.

Objectives of Accounting and Financial Reporting for State and Local Governmental Units

GASB has issued six concept statements. *Concepts Statement No. 1* identifies three primary user groups of government accounting information: creditors, citizens, and oversight bodies (including granting agencies and the legislature). The information needs of government creditors are not greatly different from their counterparts in the corporate world, namely to evaluate the likelihood the government will continue to make its debt payments as they come due. Citizens and oversight bodies have a very different purpose, which is to determine whether elected officials have raised and expended the public's money in a manner consistent with law and the public's best interest. Satisfying this citizen "right to know" objective is not easily accomplished and commonly requires government financial reports to provide much greater detail than can be found in corporate annual reports.

One difficulty governments have in meeting the information needs of citizens is that traditional financial statements, which measure events in dollars, are not well designed to evaluate the government's effectiveness in delivering services. For example, consider a public school system. A traditional financial report will show the sources of revenues and amounts expended, but does little to tell the reader whether the schools are doing a good job. In many cases nonfinancial measures are better indicators of performance. These might include the number of students advancing to the next grade, graduation rates, and scores on college entrance exams. *Concepts Statements No. 2* and *No. 5* relate to the reporting of nonfinancial measures, called **service efforts and accomplishments** reporting. Service efforts and accomplishments reporting will be more fully described in Chapter 13.

Concepts Statement No. 3 defines methods of presenting information in financial reports and develops the following disclosure hierarchy:

1. When items (assets, liabilities, revenues, etc.) can be measured with sufficient reliability, they should be reported in the **basic financial statements.**
2. The **notes to the financial statements** are intended to enhance the understanding of items appearing in the financial statements but are not a substitute for recognition when a transaction or event can be measured with sufficient reliability.
3. Occasionally the GASB determines that additional information is necessary to provide context and understanding of information in the statements or notes.

In such cases, the GASB requires the presentation of **required supplementary information (RSI).** RSI appears most commonly in the form of schedules or tables. Management's Discussion and Analysis is also an example of RSI.

4. The final level of disclosure includes other supplementary information that is not required by GASB standards but which the reporting government feels is useful in understanding the operations of the government.

Concepts Statement No. 4 provides key definitions of items appearing in financial statements. Not surprisingly, assets, liabilities, and net position (residual equity) are each defined. However, GASB utilizes two additional elements that do not appear in the balance sheets of nongovernmental organizations: deferred inflows and deferred outflows of resources. The most common deferred inflows are taxes that have been deferred to a future period when they are expected to be available for operations. Deferred inflows and outflows are also used by GASB to record events and transactions that appear in Accumulated Other Comprehensive Income (AOCI) in commercial organizations. For example, prior service costs resulting from changes in pension terms and changes in the value of hedging derivatives are recognized as AOCI by business organizations and as deferred inflows and outflows by governments.

Finally, *Concepts Statement No. 6* examines the issue of when it is most appropriate to measure assets and liabilities at historical cost and when it is more appropriate to remeasure assets to fair value or settlement amount. In general, remeasurement is appropriate for assets that will be converted to cash and liabilities where there is uncertainty over the timing and amount of payments.

Objectives of Financial Reporting by the Federal Government

The Federal Accounting Standards Advisory Board (FASAB) was established to recommend accounting and financial reporting standards to the principals—the U.S. Office of Management and Budget, the U.S. Department of the Treasury, and the U.S. Government Accountability Office. The FASAB has issued eight **Statements of Federal Financial Accounting Concepts (SFFACs).** These concepts apply to financial reporting for the federal government as a whole and for individual reporting agencies.

SFFAC 1, *Objectives of Federal Financial Reporting,* outlines four objectives that should be followed in federal financial reporting. The first, budgetary integrity, indicates that financial reporting should demonstrate accountability with regard to the raising and expending of moneys. The second, operating performance, suggests that financial reporting should enable evaluation of the service efforts, costs, and accomplishments of the federal agency. The third, stewardship, reflects the concept that financial reporting should enable an assessment of the impact on the nation of the government's operations and investments. Finally, the fourth, systems and controls, indicates that financial reporting should reveal whether financial systems and controls are adequate.

Other federal government accounting concept statements include

- SFFAC 2—*Entity and Display,*
- SFFAC 3—*Management's Discussion and Analysis,*

- SFFAC 4—*Intended Audience and Qualitative Characteristics for the Consolidated Financial Report of the United States Government,*
- SFFAC 5—*Definitions of Elements and Basic Recognition Criteria for Accrual-Basis Financial Statements,*
- SFFAC 6—*Distinguishing Basic Information, Required Supplementary Information, and Other Accompanying Information,*
- SFFAC 7—*Measurement of the Elements of Accrual Basis Financial Statements in Periods After Initial Recording,* and
- SFFAC 8—*Federal Financial Reporting.*

Objectives of Financial Reporting by Not-for-Profit Entities

FASB has issued eight concepts statements, including one dedicated to nonbusiness entities. In its *Statement of Financial Accounting Concepts No. 4,* the FASB identifies the information needs of the users of nonbusiness financial statements. These include providing information that is useful to present and potential resource providers who are

- Making decisions about the allocation of resources to those organizations,
- Assessing the services that a nonbusiness organization provides and its ability to continue to provide those services,
- Assessing management's stewardship and performance, and
- Evaluating an organization's economic resources, obligations, and effects of changes in those net resources.

STATE AND LOCAL GOVERNMENT FINANCIAL REPORTING

GASB *Concepts Statements* stress that accounting and reporting standards for state and local governments should meet the financial information needs of many diverse groups: citizen groups, legislative and oversight officials, and investors and creditors. The primary report for meeting these diverse needs is the Comprehensive Annual Financial Report.

Comprehensive Annual Financial Report

GASB *Codification* Sec. 2200 sets standards for the content of the Comprehensive Annual Financial Report of a state or local government reporting entity. A **Comprehensive Annual Financial Report (CAFR)** is the government's official annual report prepared and published as a matter of public record. In addition to the basic financial statements and other financial statements, the CAFR contains introductory material, an auditor's report, certain RSI, schedules necessary to demonstrate legal compliance, and statistical tables. Chapter 2 presents an extensive discussion and illustration of the basic financial statements and the other major components of the CAFR.

Illustration 1-2 presents an overview of the financial reporting process for state and local governments. While a business will typically have a single general ledger, the activities of governments are broken down into accounting subunits called *funds.* A typical town or county government could have a dozen funds while cities and states generally have many more. Each fund requires its own general ledger and general journal. These are represented at the bottom of Illustration 1-2. In addition, records are kept of general fixed assets and long-term debt.

ILLUSTRATION 1-2 Financial Reporting Process for State and Local Governments

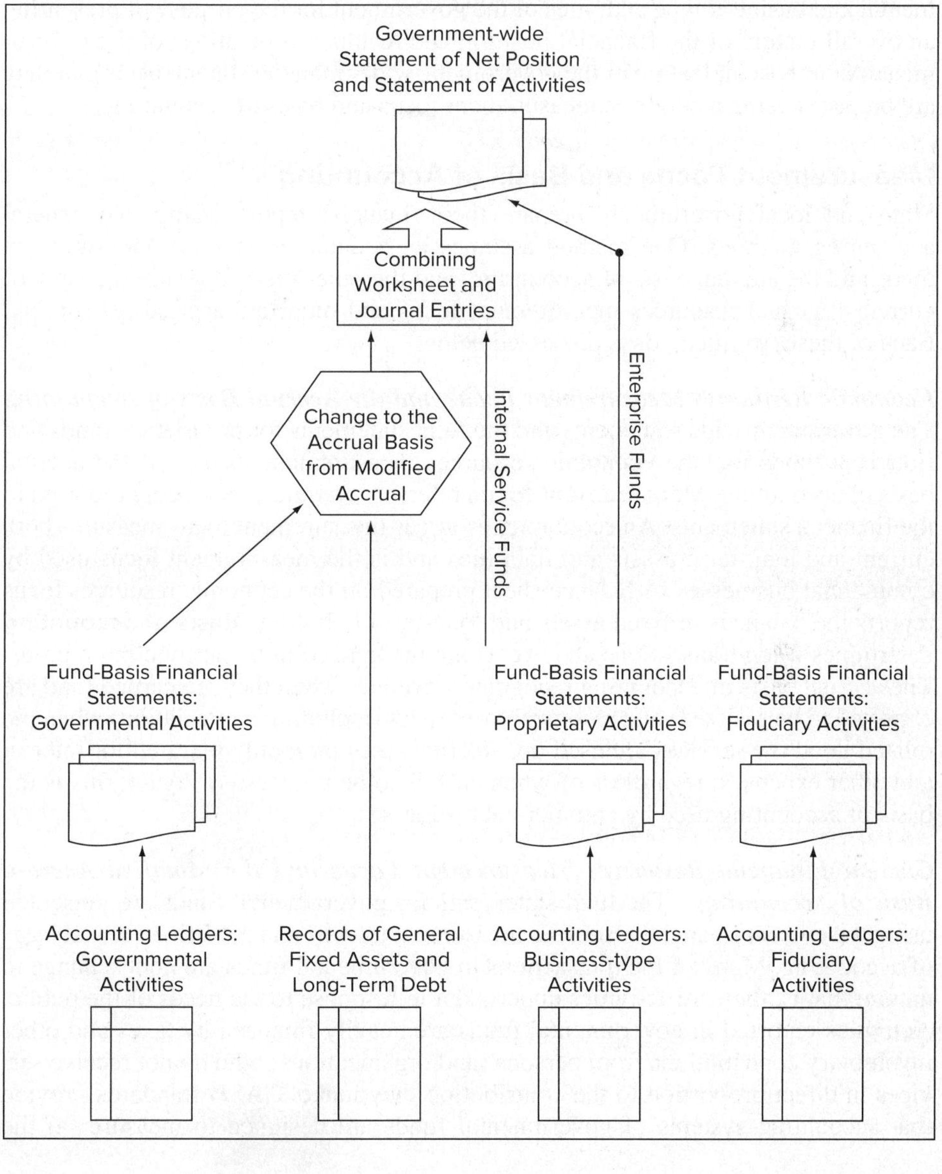

Governments have two levels of financial statement reporting. The first is the fund-basis financial statements. Fund-basis statements are presented for three categories of activities: governmental, proprietary, and fiduciary. These categories and the funds that comprise each category are described in detail later in this chapter. While the fund-basis statements present an in-depth record of individual activities of the government, it is difficult for the financial statement user to pull this disaggregated information together and form an overall view of the government's finances. For that reason, governments are also required to present government-wide financial statements. The government-wide statements combine the governmental and business-type activities of the government for the purpose of presenting an overall picture of the financial position and results of operations of the government. An important feature of the government-wide financial statements is that they are prepared using a common measurement focus and basis of accounting.

Measurement Focus and Basis of Accounting

State and local governments prepare their financial reports using two general accounting methods. One method assumes an economic resources measurement focus and the accrual basis of accounting, and the other method assumes a flow of current financial resources measurement focus and modified accrual accounting. Each of these two methods is discussed below.

Economic Resources Measurement Focus and the Accrual Basis of Accounting The government-wide statements and the fund statements for proprietary funds and fiduciary funds use the economic resources measurement focus and the accrual basis of accounting. **Measurement focus** refers to *what* items are being reported in the financial statements. An economic resources measurement focus measures both current and long-term assets and liabilities and is the measurement focus used by commercial businesses. A balance sheet prepared on the economic resources focus reports the balances in fixed assets and long-term liabilities. **Basis of accounting** determines *when* transactions and events are recognized in the accounting records. The accrual basis of accounting recognizes revenues when they are earned (and are expected to be realized) and recognizes expenses (including depreciation) when the related goods or services are used up. Accruals are commonly required for interest and other expenses, regardless of when cash is to be transferred. Again, this is the basis of accounting used by commercial businesses.

Current Financial Resources Measurement Focus and the Modified Accrual Basis of Accounting The fund statements for governmental funds are presented using the current financial resources measurement focus and modified accrual basis of accounting. Many of the transactions in governmental funds are nonexchange in nature; that is, they are activities undertaken in response to the needs of the public. Activities reported in governmental funds are heavily financed by taxes and other involuntary contributions from persons (and organizations) who do not receive services in direct proportion to the contribution they make. GASB standards provide that accounting systems of governmental funds are designed to measure (a) the extent to which financial resources obtained during a period are sufficient to cover claims incurred during that period against financial resources and (b) the net financial resources available for future periods. Thus, governmental funds are said to have a flow of **current financial resources measurement focus,** as distinguished from the government-wide, proprietary fund, and fiduciary fund statements, which have an **economic resources measurement focus.** Activities of governmental funds are said to be **expendable;** that is, the focus is on the receipt and expenditure of resources. These resources are generally restricted to current assets, investments, and short-term liabilities.

Modified accrual accounting, as the term implies, is a modification of accrual accounting. As will be discussed much more fully in Chapters 3, 4, and 5, revenues are generally recognized when *measurable* and *available* to finance the expenditures of the current period. Expenditures (not expenses) are recognized in the period in which the fund liability is incurred. Long-term assets, with minor exceptions, are not recognized; the same is true of most long-term debt. Capital (fixed) assets and long-term debt are not reported in governmental fund balance sheets. It should be noted that governmental *funds* are reported using the modified accrual basis of accounting; however, governmental-type *activities* are reported in the government-wide statements using the accrual basis of accounting, including fixed assets and long-term debt. As shown in Illustration 1-2, the governmental activities fund-basis financial statements and the records of general fixed assets and long-term debt serve as inputs to the government-wide financial statements. In Chapter 8 we will see that the governmental activities balances are changed through combining worksheets and journal entries to reflect an economic resources measurement focus and the accrual basis of accounting before being presented in the government-wide financial statements.

Fund Structure for State and Local Government Accounting and Reporting

Traditionally, state and local government financial reporting has been based on **fund accounting.** A fund is (1) a self-balancing set of accounts that (2) separately reports the resources and activities of a part of the government and (3) is segregated because of the existence of restrictions or limitations on the use of some resources.

Note that two conditions must be met for a fund to exist: (1) there must be a **fiscal entity**—assets set aside for specific purposes, and (2) there must be a double-entry **accounting entity** created to account for the fiscal entity. This second condition requires that debits equal credits within each fund. Therefore no journal entry may debit an account in one fund and credit an account in another fund. Every journal entry must be within a single fund (debits = credits). If there are transactions between funds, two journal entries are required—one for each of the affected funds.

State and local governments use 11 fund types. These fund types are organized into three categories: governmental funds, proprietary funds, and fiduciary funds. The first issue in recording a transaction is determining where (in which fund) to record the event. Governmental accounting is definition driven; that is, where we account for a transaction is determined by the definition of the 11 fund types.

Governmental Funds Five fund types are classified as **governmental funds:**

1. The **General Fund** accounts for most of the basic services provided by the government. Technically, it accounts for and reports all financial resources not accounted for and reported in another fund.
2. **Capital projects funds** account for and report financial resources that are restricted, committed, or assigned to expenditure for capital outlays. As such, it accounts for the purchase or construction of major capital improvements, except those purchased or constructed by a proprietary (and less commonly, fiduciary) fund.
3. **Debt service funds** account for and report financial resources that are restricted, committed, or assigned to expenditure for principal and interest, other than interest or principal on proprietary or fiduciary activities.
4. **Special revenue funds** account for and report the proceeds of specific revenue sources that are restricted or committed to expenditure for a specified purpose other than debt service or capital projects. These include activities funded by federal or state grants or by taxes specifically restricted to certain activities.
5. **Permanent funds** account for and report resources (typically provided under trust arrangements) that are restricted to the extent that only earnings, and not principal, may be used for purposes that support the reporting government's programs.

Every government will have a single General Fund but may have multiple funds in each of the other categories. Accounting for the General Fund and special revenue funds is discussed in Chapters 3 and 4, while capital project, debt service, and permanent fund accounting is illustrated in Chapter 5.

Proprietary Funds This category of funds is used to account for a government's activities that are businesslike in nature. Specifically they operate to provide services to customers who pay for the services received. **Proprietary funds** are discussed in Chapter 6. There are two types of proprietary funds:

1. **Enterprise funds** are used when resources are provided primarily through the use of sales and service charges to parties external to the government. Examples of enterprise funds include water and other utilities, airports, swimming pools, and transit systems.
2. **Internal service funds** account for services provided by one department of a government to another, generally on a cost-reimbursement basis. In some cases, these services are also provided to other governments. Examples of internal service funds include print shops, motor pools, and self-insurance funds.

Fiduciary Funds **Fiduciary funds** account for resources that are held by the government in a trustee capacity. A fiduciary position exists when one party prudently takes care of money or other assets for another party. Commonly, these funds involve a **trust agreement,** which is a formal agreement through which the government is given custody of assets on behalf of one or more beneficiaries. Under a trust agreement, resources are received and held by the governmental unit as trustee, to be expended or invested in accordance with the conditions of the trust. Fiduciary funds are covered in Chapter 7. Four types of fiduciary funds exist:

1. **Pension (and other employee benefit) trust funds** are used to account for pension and employee benefit funds for which the governmental unit is the trustee.
2. **Investment trust funds** account for the external portion of investment pools governed by a trust agreement in which the sponsoring government is the trustee.
3. **Private-purpose trust funds** report all other fiduciary activities governed by trust arrangements under which principal and income benefit individuals, private organizations, or other governments.
4. **Custodial funds** are used to account for all other fiduciary activities, including activities where a trust agreement is not in effect. An example would be a county tax custodial fund, where the county collects property taxes on behalf of towns located within the county.

Illustration 1-3 summarizes the fund types, basis of accounting, and required fund-basis financial statements for each fund category. The table is presented in reverse order from the earlier presentation to assist in identifying the appropriate fund to record a given transaction. Starting at the top, determine whether a given transaction is a fiduciary activity. If it is, identify which of the four fiduciary fund types is appropriate and do not consider the proprietary or governmental-type funds. If the transaction is not fiduciary, determine whether it is a proprietary activity, and if it is, determine whether it is internal service or enterprise. Any transaction that is not fiduciary or proprietary must be a governmental activity. Again, start at the top of the governmental activity funds and determine first whether the transaction meets the definition of a permanent fund. If it does not, move down through the list. Any transaction that has not been identified as a permanent, debt service, capital projects, or special revenue fund transaction must be accounted for in the General Fund.

ILLUSTRATION 1-3 **Summary of Funds Used by State and Local Governments**

Fund Category	Fund	Basis of Accounting	Fund-Basis Financial Statements
Fiduciary	Private-Purpose Trust Investment Trust Pension Trust Custodial	Accrual	• Statement of Fiduciary Net Position • Statement of Changes in Fiduciary Net Position
Proprietary	Internal Service Enterprise	Accrual	• Statement of Net Position • Statement of Revenues, Expenses, and Changes in Fund Net Position • Statement of Cash Flows
Governmental	Permanent Debt Service Capital Project Special Revenue General	Modified accrual	• Balance Sheet • Statement of Revenues, Expenditures, and Changes in Fund Balances

Number of Funds Required

The GASB Summary Statement of Principles states that *governmental units should establish and maintain those funds required by law and sound financial administration.* If state law and/or agreements with creditors do not require a separate fund for the receipt of revenues that are raised solely for a defined purpose and if administrators do not feel that use of a separate fund is needed to be able to demonstrate that revenues were raised solely for that particular purpose, the General Fund should be used to account for the revenue and related expenditures.

Questions and Exercises

1–1. Obtain a copy of a recent Comprehensive Annual Financial Report (CAFR). These may commonly be obtained from the website of a city or county of your choice. It would be best, but not absolutely necessary, to use a CAFR that has a Certificate of Excellence in Financial Reporting from the Government Finance Officers Association. You will be answering questions related to the CAFR in Chapters 1 through 8. Answer the following questions related to your CAFR.

a. What are the inclusive dates of the fiscal year?

b. Identify the name and address of the independent auditor. Is the auditor's opinion unmodified? If not, describe the modification. Is the opinion limited to the basic financial statements, or does the opinion include combining and individual fund statements?

c. Does the report contain an organization chart? A table of contents? A list of principal officials? A letter of transmittal? Is the letter of transmittal dated and signed by the chief financial officer? List the major items of discussion in the letter of transmittal.

d. Does the report include a Management's Discussion and Analysis? List the major items of discussion.

e. Does the report include the government-wide statements (Statement of Net Position and Statement of Activities)?

f. Does the report reflect fund financial statements for governmental, proprietary, and fiduciary funds? List those statements. List the major governmental and proprietary funds (the funds that have separate columns in the governmental and proprietary fund statements).

1–2. Identify and describe the five environmental differences between governments and for-profit business enterprises as identified in the Governmental Accounting Standards Board's *Why Governmental Accounting and Financial Reporting Is—and Should Be—Different.*

1–3. Identify and briefly describe the three organizations that set standards for state and local governments, the federal government, and nongovernmental not-for-profit organizations.

1–4. What is the definition of a government as agreed upon by the FASB and GASB?

1–5. Describe the "hierarchy of GAAP" for state and local governments.

1–6. Accounting and financial reporting for state and local governments use, in different places, either the economic resources measurement focus and the accrual basis of accounting or the current financial resources measurement focus and the modified accrual basis of accounting. Discuss the differences in measurement focus and basis of accounting related to (*a*) the conceptual differences, (*b*) differences in revenue recognition, (*c*) differences in expense/expenditure recognition, (*d*) differences in recognition of fixed assets, and (*e*) differences in the recording of long-term debt.

1–7. Distinguish between private and public sector organization.

1–8. Go to the GASB website (www.gasb.org). What is the mission of GASB?

1–9. For each of the items below, identify which fund(s) would be used to account for the item and provide a justification for your answer.

a. A city government issued general obligation bonds to finance the construction of a new jail.

b. A tax of $1.00 per residential phone number is collected by a city government from the phone company. This amount is required by state law to be used for the operation of the 911 emergency phone system.

c. A county government expended $1 million to expand the water treatment plant.

d. A donor signed a trust agreement and provided investments totaling $4 million to create an endowment, the earnings of which will be used to provide scholarships.

e. A donor provided $50,000 to be used to purchase newspaper and magazine subscriptions for the public library. There is no requirement that the original principal may not be spent.

f. A city government sold surplus street maintenance trucks for $10,000.

g. A city government contributed $500,000 to a pension trust administered by the city for its teachers, public safety employees, and employees of the water department.

Chapter **Two**

Overview of Financial Reporting for State and Local Governments

Budgets that don't balance, public programs that aren't funded, pension funds that are running out of money, schools that aren't funded—How does that help anyone? Gina Marie Raimondo, a former venture capitalist who was the first woman to serve as the governor of Rhode Island

Detroit's financial challenges—the decline of the American auto industry, the impact of the global economic recession, declining population and an erosion of the municipal tax base—are key to understanding what led this great city to an inability to provide basic city services . . . Ron Dellums, 48th mayor of Oakland, CA, and 13-term congressman from California's 9th Congressional District

Learning Objectives

- Obtain an overview of the contents of a governmental financial report.
- Define the governmental reporting entity.
- Illustrate the basic financial statements for a state or local government.

Chapters 3 through 9 of this text describe and illustrate detailed accounting and financial reporting requirements for state and local governments. The purpose of this chapter is to provide an overview so students may better understand the material that follows. This chapter presents a detailed look at financial statements and certain required schedules.

State and local governments are encouraged to prepare a **Comprehensive Annual Financial Report (CAFR).** In addition to the required financial statements and supplementary information, the CAFR contains additional items, including combining and individual fund statements, schedules, narrative explanations, and a statistical section. While governments are encouraged to prepare a complete CAFR, the GASB has identified a (minimum) set of statements and disclosures that are required to be in compliance with generally accepted accounting principles (GAAP). The required contents of a governmental financial report appear in Illustration 2-1.

ILLUSTRATION 2-1 Required Contents of Governmental Financial Reports

1. Management's Discussion and Analysis
2. Basic Financial Statements
   a. Government-wide Financial Statements

      Government-wide Statement of Net Position—Illustration 2–5
      Government-wide Statement of Activities—Illustration 2–6

   b. Fund-Basis Financial Statements

      <u>Governmental Type Funds</u>
      Balance Sheet—Illustration 2–7b
      Statement of Revenues, Expenditures, and Changes in Fund Balances—Illustration 2–8b
      Reconciliation of governmental statements to government-wide statements—Illustration 2–7a and Illustration 2–8a

      <u>Proprietary Funds</u>
      Statement of Net Position—Illustration 2–9
      Statement of Revenues, Expenses, and Changes in Fund Net Position—Illustration 2–10
      Statement of Cash Flows—Illustration 2–11

      <u>Fiduciary Funds</u>
      Statement of Fiduciary Net Position—Illustration 2–12
      Statement of Changes in Fiduciary Net Position—Illustration 2–13

   c. Notes to the Financial Statements—Illustration 2–14
3. Required Supplementary Information (other than MD&A)

   Information about infrastructure assets using the modified approach—Illustration 2–15
   Budgetary comparison schedule (General and major Special Revenue Funds)—Illustration 2–16
   Funding schedules required for defined benefit pension plans
   Schedules required for external financing pools

The remainder of this chapter presents (1) a discussion of the financial reporting entity, (2) an overview of the CAFR contents, and (3) a detailed presentation of the Comprehensive Annual Financial Report, including illustrative statements.

THE GOVERNMENTAL REPORTING ENTITY

One of the most fundamental issues in accounting for any organization is identifying the accounting entity. This is made more difficult by the fact that general-purpose governments, such as states and large cities and counties, typically are complex organizations that include semiautonomous boards, commissions, and agencies created to accomplish projects or activities that (for one reason or another), may not be carried out by a government as originally constituted. Very often each legal entity issues a separate annual report. But there are times when it is appropriate to combine these entities with a general-purpose government in order to give an overall picture of government operations. For example, state universities issue separate financial statements but also appear as component units within the state government's annual report.

GASB *Codification* Sec. 2100 establishes that the **financial reporting entity** is the primary government together with its component units. The **primary government** can be a state government, a general-purpose local government such as a city or county, or a special-purpose government such as a school district. **Component units** are legally separate organizations for which the elected officials of the primary government are *financially accountable.* In addition, a component unit can be an organization for which the nature and significance of its relationship with a primary government are such that exclusion would cause the reporting entity's financial statements to be misleading or incomplete.

GASB provides guidance for determining when a primary government should include a legally separate organization in its financial report. First, the relationship with the related entity must have one of the following characteristics: (1) the primary government controls a voting majority of the other organization's governing board or otherwise may impose its will on the organization; or (2) the other organization is fiscally dependent upon the primary government. An entity is fiscally dependent on a primary government if that government approves or modifies its budget, sets charges for its services, or if the government's approval is required to issue debt.

Second, the related organization must represent a financial benefit or burden to the primary government. A financial burden exists, for example, if the primary government is responsible for liabilities of the other organization. In contrast, a financial benefit exists if the government is entitled to or may access the other organization's resources.

Governments occasionally acquire a controlling interest in the ownership of a commercial business. A government that holds a controlling equity interest is deemed to be financially accountable for that organization and should report the organization as a component unit. An exception is permitted if the equity interest is an investment (i.e., the purpose is solely to earn income or profit).

Once it is determined that an organization is a component unit of a primary government, the issue becomes how to include its financial information in the primary government's financial reports. GASB standards provide two methods for including component unit financial information with that of the primary government. The first is known as **blending,** because the financial information becomes part of the financial statements of the primary government. Blended organizations are reported as though they were funds of the primary government. Blending is appropriate when the component unit is so intertwined with the primary government that they are in substance the same entity. This may be the case if the two entities have the same governing boards, the primary government is the sole corporate member of the board, or management of the primary government has operational responsibility for the component unit. Additionally, blending is appropriate if the component unit provides services solely to the primary government or if the component unit's debt is expected to be paid by the primary government.

More commonly, component units are reported using **discrete presentation.** In discrete presentation, the financial information of the component is presented in a column, apart from the primary government and not included in the totals reported for the primary government. Most discretely presented component units appear as separate columns in the government-wide statements. Pension plans that are administered through trusts are frequently legally separate entities from the government. If a primary government has a legal obligation to make contributions to the pension plan, the plan is deemed to be a financial burden to the government and is reported as a component unit. Unlike other component units, these pension trusts are reported as separate columns within the fiduciary fund statements.

REPORTING BY MAJOR FUNDS

In addition to the government-wide statement, governments report fund-level financial statements for each of the three categories of funds: governmental, proprietary, and fiduciary. Because governments may have many governmental and proprietary funds, governments are only required to present separate columns for each **major fund.** The General Fund is always considered a major fund. Other governmental funds are considered major when both of the following conditions exist:

1. total assets, liabilities, revenues, *or* expenditures of that individual governmental fund constitute 10 percent of the total for the governmental funds category, *and*
2. total assets, liabilities, revenues, *or* expenditures of that individual governmental fund are 5 percent of the total of the governmental and enterprise categories, combined.

Deferred outflows are included with assets and deferred inflows are included with liabilities for purposes of applying these criteria. Similar tests are applied to determine major enterprise funds. Additionally, a government may designate any fund as a major fund if reporting that fund separately would be useful. Any funds not reported separately are aggregated and reported in a single column under the label *nonmajor funds.* If the reporting government is preparing a complete CAFR, a schedule showing the detail of nonmajor funds is provided in the other supplementary information section.

OVERVIEW OF THE COMPREHENSIVE ANNUAL FINANCIAL REPORT (CAFR)

The Comprehensive Annual Financial Report has three major sections: introductory, financial, and statistical. An outline of the CAFR was presented in Illustration 2-1. Information appearing in the CAFR is described and illustrated in the following sections, beginning with the Introductory Section, Illustration 2-2.

Example Comprehensive Annual Financial Report
Introductory Section

Introductory Section

The Introductory Section of a CAFR includes the table of contents, a letter of transmittal from the preparer (typically the government's finance director), a list of government officials, and an organizational chart. If a government received a *Certificate of Achievement for Excellence in Financial Reporting* from the Government Finance Officers Association in the prior year,[1] the introductory section will include a reproduction of that certificate. The introductory section is not audited.

ILLUSTRATION 2-2 **Introductory Section of CAFR**

Letter of Transmittal from the Finance Director

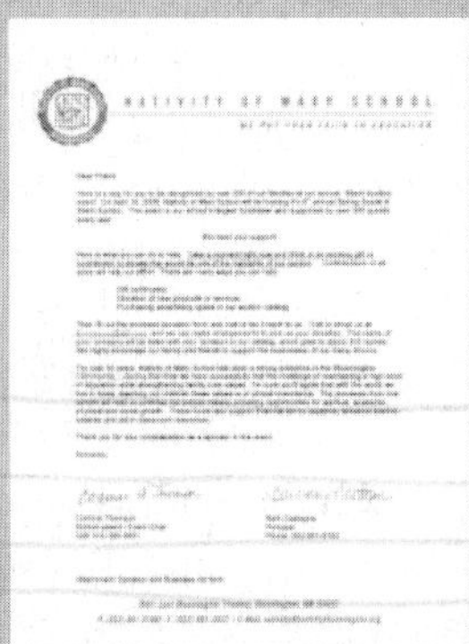

List of Government Officers

CHRISTINE SHADLEY, MAYOR
10 CITY HALL
SALEM CITY

BUTCH KENNEDY, CITY MANAGER
10 CITY HALL
SALEM CITY

CITY COMMISSIONERS
CHARLIE OBAUGH
CHARLENE SHOWALTER
TIM BROWN

Organizational Chart

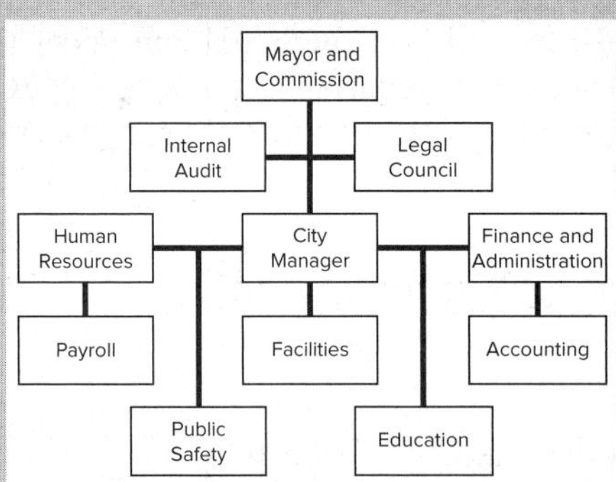

GFOA Certificate (if awarded)

[1] The Government Finance Officers Association of the United States and Canada sponsors a certificate program to encourage and promote excellent financial reporting. To receive that certificate, a government must have an unmodified audit opinion and have its report reviewed, using an extensive checklist, by independent reviewers who are experienced in financial reporting. See www.gfoa.org

Example Comprehensive Annual Financial Report
Financial Section: Auditor's Report

Financial Section: Auditor's Report

The auditor's report (Illustration 2-3), placed at the beginning of the financial section, normally expresses an opinion on the basic financial statements. Like other audits, government audits must be conducted by CPAs according to auditing standards issued by the American Institute of Certified Public Accountants. In addition, specialized governmental auditing standards must be followed. Governmental auditing standards are discussed in more detail in Chapter 13.

ILLUSTRATION 2-3 **Independent Auditor's Report**

Independent Auditors

Report on the Financial Statements

We have audited the accompanying financial statements of the governmental activities, the business-type activities, the aggregate discretely presented component units, each major fund, and the aggregate remaining fund information of the City of Salem as of and for the year ended December 31, 2020, and the related notes to the financial statements, which collectively comprise the City's basic financial statements as listed in the table of contents.

Management's Responsibility for the Financial Statements

Management is responsible for the preparation and fair presentation of these financial statements in accordance with accounting principles generally accepted in the United States of America; this includes the design, implementation, and maintenance of internal control relevant to the preparation and fair presentation of financial statements that are free from material misstatement, whether due to fraud or error.

Auditor's Responsibility

Our responsibility is to express opinions on these financial statements based on our audit. We conducted our audit in accordance with auditing standards generally accepted in the United States of America. Those standards require that we plan and perform the audit to obtain reasonable assurance about whether the financial statements are free from material misstatement.

Additional paragraphs (not presented here) describe the nature of audit procedures and whether the auditor believes they provide an adequate basis.

Opinions

In our opinion, the financial statements referred to above present fairly, in all material respects, the respective financial position of the governmental activities, the business-type activities, the aggregate discretely presented component units, each major fund, and the aggregate remaining fund information of the City of Salem, Any State, as of June 30, 2020, and the respective changes in financial position, and, where applicable, cash flows thereof for the year then ended in accordance with accounting principles generally accepted in the United States of America.

Additional paragraphs (not presented here) address required supplementary information and other information contained in the CAFR. Illustration 13-2 provides an example of a complete (unmodified) opinion.

[Auditor's signature], [address], and [date]

Example Comprehensive Annual Financial Report
Financial Section: Required Supplementary Information
Management's Discussion and Analysis

Management's Discussion and Analysis (MD&A)

The MD&A (Illustration 2-4) provides an opportunity for the government to provide, in plain terms, an overview of the government's financial activities. This section is considered **required supplementary information,** which means that it is required and entails some auditor responsibility, but not as much as the basic financial statements. Auditors review the material to establish that it is not misleading in relation to the basic statements but do not include the MD&A in the scope of the audit. A number of specific items must be included:

1. A brief discussion of the financial statements.
2. Condensed financial information derived from the government-wide financial statements, comparing the current year with the prior year. GASB identifies specific items for discussion.
3. An analysis of the government's overall financial position and results of operations to assist users in assessing whether financial position has improved or deteriorated as a result of the year's operations.
4. An analysis of balances and transactions of individual funds.
5. An analysis of significant variations between original and final budget amounts and between final budget amounts and actual results for the General Fund.
6. A description of significant capital asset and long-term debt activity during the year.
7. A discussion by governments that use the modified approach to report infrastructure assets (discussed in Chapter 8), which includes: discussion of changes in the condition of infrastructure assets, comparison of assessed condition with the condition level established by the government, and disclosure of the difference between the amount needed to maintain infrastructure assets and the amount actually expended.
8. A description of any known facts, decisions, or conditions that would have a significant effect on the government's financial position or results of operations.

GASB *Codification* Sec. 2200.109 makes it clear that MD&A is limited to the preceding eight items. However, governments may expand the discussion of these items if deemed appropriate.

Example Comprehensive Annual Financial Report
Financial Section: Required Supplementary Information
Management's Discussion and Analysis

ILLUSTRATION 2-4 Management's Discussion and Analysis

Financial Highlights

Highlights for the City of Salem's Government-wide Financial Statements

- The City's total net position of governmental activities was $38.4 million at December 31, 2020. Net position for the business-type activities was $47.9 million.
- Total revenues of governmental activities exceeded total expenses by $3.25 million.
- The City's total debt at December 31, 2020, was $62.2 million, a net increase of $6.5 million. The City issued $9.7 million in general obligation bonds during 2020 to renovate the courthouse.

Overview of the Financial Statements

The financial section of this annual report consists of four parts: (1) management's discussion and analysis, (2) the basic financial statements, (3) required supplementary information, and (4) other supplementary information.

The basic financial statements include two kinds of statements that present different views of the City:

- The government-wide financial statements provide readers with a broad overview of the City's finances, including long-term and short-term information about the City's overall financial status.
- The fund financial statements focus on the individual parts of the City government, reporting the City's operations in more detail than the government-wide statements.

Government-wide Financial Statements

The government-wide financial statements report information about the City of Salem as a whole using accounting methods similar to those used by private sector companies. The Statement of Net Position and the Statement of Activities are the government-wide statements. These statements include all of the government's assets and liabilities using the accrual basis of accounting. All revenues and expenses are reported, regardless of when cash is received or paid.

The City's total assets exceeded liabilities by $86 million at December 31, 2020. The largest portion of the City's net position (63 percent) reflects its investments in capital assets, less accumulated depreciation and any related outstanding debt used to acquire those assets. The City uses these assets to provide services to its citizens and customers; therefore these assets are not available for future spending. Presented below is a table comparing the three categories of net position for the City's governmental, business-type, and component unit activities for fiscal years 2019 and 2020.

Management's Discussion and Analysis typically continues for 10 or more pages.

Example Comprehensive Annual Financial Report
Financial Section: Basic Financial Statements
Government-wide Financial Statements: Statement of Net Position

Statement of Net Position

The Statement of Net Position (Illustration 2-5) presents the government-wide asset, liability, and net position balances (measured on the accrual basis and economic resources measurement focus). Notice there are two columns, one for the entity's governmental activities and another for the business-type activities. Together, the governmental and business activities constitute the primary government. Similar information is presented in a separate column for the government's discretely presented component units. Fiduciary activities, however, are not included in the government-wide statements. Prior year balances may be presented but are not required.

Assets are generally reported in order of liquidity. A classified approach (presenting separate totals for current assets and current liabilities) may be used but is not required. Note in particular that capital assets (property and equipment) are presented in the governmental activities column. This will not be the case when we examine the governmental fund-basis financial statements. The capital assets include infrastructure (roads, bridges, sewers, etc.) and are reported net of accumulated depreciation. Similarly, long-term debt is presented in the governmental activities column of the government-wide Statement of Net Position but is not presented for governmental funds in the fund-basis balance sheet.

The difference between assets and liabilities is called *net position* and is reported in three categories. **Net investment in capital assets** is computed by taking the capital assets, less accumulated depreciation, and deducting outstanding debt that is related to the financing of capital assets. Liabilities incurred to finance operations (including long-term liabilities for compensated absences or employee benefits) would not be deducted. **Restricted net position** includes resources that are restricted by (*a*) external parties, including creditors, grantors, contributors, or by laws or regulations of other governments; or (*b*) laws or constitutional provisions of the reporting government. The remaining amount, **unrestricted net position,** is a "plug" figure that is determined by deducting the balances of the other two net position categories from the overall excess of assets over liabilities.

Example Comprehensive Annual Financial Report
Financial Section: Basic Financial Statements
Government-wide Financial Statements: Statement of Net Position

ILLUSTRATION 2-5 **Statement of Net Position**

CITY OF SALEM
Statement of Net Position
As of December 31, 2020

	Primary Government			
Assets	Governmental Activities	Business-type Activities	Primary Government	Component Units
Cash and cash equivalents	$ 8,242,998	$ 4,814,724	$13,057,722	$ 84,733
Investments	3,312,992	10,350,334	13,663,326	____
Inventory	1,072,963	30,779	1,103,742	____
Receivables (net):				
Taxes receivable	2,872,611	____	2,872,611	____
Accounts receivable	722,215	2,657,326	3,379,541	27,085
Due from other governments	1,328,448	____	1,328,448	____
Restricted assets	3,933,126	2,295,043	6,228,169	____
Capital assets (net of accumulated depreciation)	65,690,373	48,894,402	114,584,775	11,170,900
Total assets	87,175,726	69,042,608	156,218,334	11,282,718
Liabilities				
Accounts payable	2,425,447	493,849	2,919,296	710
Accrued liabilities	4,340,108	473,168	4,813,276	____
Bonds payable due within one year	2,164,521	1,342,717	3,507,238	____
Bonds payable due in more than one year	39,834,882	18,858,187	58,693,069	____
Total liabilities	48,764,958	21,167,921	69,932,879	710
Net position				
Net investment in capital assets	23,690,970	30,757,135	54,448,105	11,197,985
Restricted	3,933,126	2,295,043	6,228,169	____
Unrestricted	10,786,672	14,822,509	25,609,181	84,023
Total net position	$38,410,768	$47,874,687	$86,285,455	$11,282,008

Example Comprehensive Annual Financial Report
Financial Section: Basic Financial Statements
Government-wide Financial Statements: Statement of Activities

Government-wide Statement of Activities

Note the general format of the Statement of Activities (Illustration 2-6). Expenses are measured on the accrual basis and reported first. Expenses for governmental activities are reported initially, followed by the business-type activities and the component units (reading from top to bottom). Direct expenses, including depreciation, are required to be reported by function (General Government, Judicial Administration, etc.). Although rarely done, governments may allocate indirect expenses to functions. However, the government is required to show a separate column for these allocated amounts.

Depreciation that relates to assets serving multiple functions may be allocated as an indirect expense, charged in total to general government, or displayed in a separate line. Interest on long-term debt would be included in direct expenses if the interest related to a single function. Most interest, however, cannot be identified with a single function and should be shown separately.

Revenues that can be directly associated with functions are deducted, and a net expense (or revenue) is presented. Examples include garbage collection fees, museum admissions, and parking fines. Charges for services include charges by enterprise funds, such as fees for water used by homeowners and businesses. Grants and contributions are typically resources provided by other governments.

In contrast, general revenues are presented in the lower right-hand section of the statement. General revenues are not associated directly with a particular function or program. All taxes levied by the government, including those restricted to a particular purpose, are reported as general revenues. Contributions to endowments and extraordinary items (items that are both unusual *and* infrequent) are reported separately after general revenues. However, **special items** (items within the control of management but which are unusual in nature *or* infrequent in occurrence) are shown in a separate line within general revenues.

The Statement of Activities is a consolidated statement within columns (governmental activities, business-type activities, and component units), which means that interfund services provided and used and transfers between two governmental funds are eliminated. Transfers between governmental and business-type activities ($615,062) are displayed in the general revenues section and offset. Notice that the bottom line, *Net position, ending,* agrees with the balances appearing in the Statement of Net Position (Illustration 2-5).

Financial Section: Basic Financial Statements
Government-wide Financial Statements: Statement of Activities

ILLUSTRATION 2-6 Statement of Activities

CITY OF SALEM
Statement of Activities
For the Year Ended December 31, 2020

		Primary Government						
		Program Revenues			Net (Expense) Revenue and Change in Net Position			
Functions/Programs	Expenses	Charges for Services	Operational Grants and Contributions	Capital Grants and Contributions	Governmental Activities	Business-type Activities	Total	Component Units
Governmental activities								
General government	$ 3,734,068	$1,144,018	$ 263,178	$ —	($2,326,872)	$ —	($2,326,872)	$ —
Judicial administration	1,433,650	56,497	1,002,525	—	(374,628)	—	(374,628)	—
Public safety	9,265,997	275,492	750,109	277,700	(7,962,696)	—	(7,962,696)	—
Public works	6,167,650	—	2,903,982	1,853,091	(1,410,577)	—	(1,410,577)	—
Health and welfare	4,436,534	—	2,861,389	4,203	(1,570,942)	—	(1,570,942)	—
Education	9,292,427	—	73,300	—	(9,219,127)	—	(9,219,127)	—
Parks and recreation	3,217,236	604,359	302,672	500	(2,309,705)	—	(2,309,705)	—
Community development	1,720,121	51,611	298,495	156,361	(1,213,654)	—	(1,213,654)	—
Interest on long-term debt	1,422,428	—	—	—	(1,422,428)	—	(1,422,428)	—
Total governmental activities	40,690,111	2,131,977	8,455,650	2,291,855	(27,810,629)	—	(27,810,629)	—
Business-type activities								
Water	6,041,987	6,385,233	—	3,109,692	—	3,452,938	3,452,938	—
Solid waste	2,556,633	2,351,433	6,594	2,085,064	—	1,886,458	1,886,458	—
Parking	481,869	261,107	—	—	—	(220,762)	(220,762)	—
Total business-type activities	9,080,489	8,997,773	6,594	5,194,756	—	5,118,634	5,118,634	—
Total primary government	49,770,600	11,129,750	8,462,244	7,486,611	(27,810,629)	5,118,634	(22,691,995)	—
Component units								
Industrial development authority	4,322,849	9,979	20,000	4,193,964	—	—	—	(98,906)
		General revenues						
		Property taxes			15,382,482	—	15,382,482	—
		Sales taxes			5,729,224	—	5,729,224	—
		Hotel and meals taxes			4,998,045	—	4,998,045	—
		Grants			2,724,725	—	2,724,725	—
		Miscellaneous			1,611,886	729,488	2,341,374	1,172
		Transfers			615,062	(615,062)	—	—
		Total general revenues			31,061,424	114,426	31,175,850	1,172
		Change in net position			3,250,795	5,233,060	8,483,855	(97,734)
		Net position, beginning			35,159,973	42,641,627	77,801,600	11,379,742
		Net position, ending			$38,410,768	$47,874,687	$86,285,455	$11,282,008

Example Comprehensive Annual Financial Report
Financial Section: Basic Financial Statements
Governmental Funds Statements: Balance Sheet

Governmental Funds: Balance Sheet

Illustration 2-7b presents a Balance Sheet for the governmental funds, including the General, special revenue, capital projects, and debt service funds. The City of Salem does not have a permanent fund or it would be presented here as well. Each of the city's governmental funds is considered a major fund and is presented separately. If the city had multiple smaller funds, they would be combined and reported in a single column labeled *nonmajor funds.*

The governmental fund statements are prepared using the current financial resources measurement focus and the modified accrual basis of accounting. For this reason, capital assets and long-term debt do not appear on the Balance Sheet. The excess of assets and deferred outflows over liabilities and deferred inflows is labeled *fund balance,* an account title used only in the governmental funds. All other funds and the government-wide statements label residual equity as *net position.*

Several features of the Balance Sheet should be noted. First, a total column is required. Second, fund balance is displayed within the categories of nonspendable, restricted, committed, assigned, and unassigned. These will be more fully described in later chapters, but represent varying degrees of constraint placed on the use of the (net) resources of governmental funds.

Finally, total fund balances reported in the total column ($12,922,626) must be reconciled to total net position ($38,410,768) presented in the governmental activities column of the government-wide Statement of Net Position. The reconciliation is presented separately in Illustration 2-7a. These amounts differ because the two statements have different bases of accounting and because internal service funds are generally included in the governmental activities column on the government-wide statements.

ILLUSTRATION 2-7a Reconciliation to (Government-wide) Statement of Net Position

Fund balance reported in the Governmental Funds Balance Sheet	$12,992,626
Amounts reported for governmental activities in the Statement of Net Position are different because	
• Capital assets used in government operations are not financial resources and therefore are not reported in the funds.	65,690,373
• Some liabilities are not due and payable in the current period and are not reported in fund liabilities.	(41,999,403)
• The assets and liabilities of internal service funds are included in governmental activities for the Statement of Net Position.	436,475
• Accrued liabilities that are not to be paid from current financial resources are not recognized in the funds.	(3,117,390)
• Receivables on the Statement of Net Position that do not provide current financial resources are reported as deferred inflows in the funds.	4,408,087
Net position of governmental activities in the Statement of Net Position	$38,410,768

Example Comprehensive Annual Financial Report
Financial Section: Basic Financial Statements
Governmental Funds Statements: Balance Sheet

ILLUSTRATION 2-7b **Governmental Funds Balance Sheet**

CITY OF SALEM
Balance Sheet
Governmental Funds
As of December 31, 2020

Assets	General Fund	Special Revenue Fund	Courthouse Renovation Fund	Debt Service Fund	Total Governmental Funds
Cash and cash equivalents	$ 6,408,214	$627,837	$ 895,300	$230,000	$ 8,161,351
Investments	3,312,992	—	—	—	3,312,992
Receivables (net)					
Taxes receivable	2,872,611	—	—	—	2,872,611
Accounts receivable	679,215	14,177	—	—	693,392
Due from other governments	1,085,184	—	243,264	—	1,328,448
Supplies inventory	23,747	—	—	—	23,747
Restricted assets	3,933,126	—	—	—	3,933,126
TOTAL ASSETS	$18,315,089	$642,014	$1,138,564	$230,000	$20,325,667
Liabilities					
Accounts payable	2,085,358	70,000	207,134	—	2,362,492
Accrued liabilities	543,064	—	19,398	—	562,462
TOTAL LIABILITIES	2,628,422	70,000	226,532	—	2,924,954
Deferred Inflows of Resources					
Property Taxes	4,408,087	—	—	—	4,408,087
TOTAL DEFERRED INFLOWS	4,408,087	—	—	—	4,408,087
Fund Balance					
Nonspendable					
- Supplies inventory	23,747	—	—	—	23,747
Restricted					
- Intergovernmental grants	—	312,000	500,000	—	812,000
- Bond sinking fund	—	—	—	230,000	230,000
Committed					
- Rainy day fund	4,500,000	—	—	—	4,500,000
- Courthouse renovation	—	—	380,000	—	380,000
Assigned					
- School lunch program	—	260,014	—	—	260,014
- Other capital projects	917,300	—	32,032	—	949,332
Unassigned	5,837,533	—	—	—	5,837,533
TOTAL FUND BALANCE	11,278,580	572,014	912,032	230,000	12,992,626
TOTAL LIABILITIES, DEFERRED INFLOWS AND FUND BALANCE	$18,315,089	$642,014	$1,138,564	$230,000	$20,325,667

Example Comprehensive Annual Financial Report
Financial Section: Basic Financial Statements
Governmental Funds Statements: Statement of Revenues, Expenditures, and Changes in Fund Balance

Governmental Funds: Statement of Revenues, Expenditures, and Changes in Fund Balance

Illustration 2-8b presents the operating statement for the same governmental funds appearing in Illustration 2-7b (the Balance Sheet). Again, the statement is prepared using the current financial resources measurement focus and the modified accrual basis of accounting. Revenues are reported by source, and expenditures (not expenses) are reported by character: current, capital outlay, and debt service. Within the current category, expenditures are presented by function: general government, judicial administration, public safety, and so on. Within the debt service category, expenditures are displayed as interest or principal.

Following revenues and expenses, the statement reports *other financing sources and uses.* These reflect interfund transfers and the proceeds of issuing debt. Most of the items appearing in this section are eliminated when preparing the government-wide financial statements. Like all operating statements, reconciliations to the Balance Sheet are required. In this case, the operating statement is reconciled to total fund balances by adding the beginning of year fund balances.

The excess of revenues and other sources over expenditures and other uses (negative $1,485,357) is reconciled to the change in net position (positive $3,250,795) for the governmental activities column in the government-wide Statement of Activities. This reconciliation would normally appear at the bottom of the Statement of Revenues, Expenditures, and Changes in Fund Balance but is presented in Illustration 2-8a due to space considerations.

ILLUSTRATION 2-8a Reconciliation to (Government-wide) Statement of Activities

Excess of revenues and other sources over expenditures and other uses reported in the Governmental Funds Statement of Revenues, Expenditures, and Changes in Fund Balance.	$(1,485,357)
Amounts reported for governmental activities in the Statement of Activities are different because	
• Governmental funds report the cost of capital assets as expenditures, while they are capital assets in the government-wide statements.	10,924,818
• Debt proceeds provide current financial resources to the governmental funds but are liabilities in the government-wide statements.	(9,675,400)
• Depreciation is not recorded in the governmental funds but is expensed in the Statement of Activities.	(1,691,116)
• Income earned by internal service funds is included in governmental activities on government-wide statements.	23,964
• Payments of principal on long-term debt are expenditures in the governmental funds but reduce the liability in the government-wide statements.	1,155,326
• Property taxes expected to be collected more than 60 days after year-end are deferred in the governmental funds.	3,998,560
Change in net position of governmental activities (government-wide)	$3,250,795

Example Comprehensive Annual Financial Report
Financial Section: Basic Financial Statements
Governmental Funds Statements: Statement of Revenues, Expenditures, and Changes in Fund Balance

ILLUSTRATION 2-8b **Governmental Funds Statement of Revenues, Expenditures, and Changes in Fund Balance**

CITY OF SALEM
Statement of Revenues, Expenditures, and Changes in Fund Balances—Governmental Funds
For the Year Ended December 31, 2020

	General	Special Revenue	Courthouse Renovation	Debt Service	Total Governmental
Revenues					
Property taxes	$15,361,830	$ —	$ —	$ —	$15,361,830
Other local taxes	11,761,522	—	—	—	11,761,522
Charges for services	1,601,435	291,243	—	—	1,892,678
Intergovernmental	7,098,698	3,456,194	441,548	—	10,996,440
Miscellaneous	1,262,549	—	—	—	1,262,549
Total revenues	37,086,034	3,747,437	441,548	—	41,275,019
Expenditures					
Current:					
General government	3,353,502	—	—	—	3,353,502
Judicial administration	1,456,734	1,981,144	—	—	3,437,878
Public safety	8,216,347	—	—	—	8,216,347
Public works	4,602,273	—	—	—	4,602,273
Health and welfare	4,418,294	—	—	—	4,418,294
Education	8,887,834	—	—	—	8,887,834
Parks and recreation	3,055,325	—	—	—	3,055,325
Community development	899,209	1,093,804	—	—	1,993,013
Capital outlay	—	—	10,924,818	—	10,924,818
Debt service:					
Principal	—	—	—	1,155,326	1,155,326
Interest	—	—	—	924,818	924,818
Total expenditures	34,889,518	3,074,948	10,924,818	2,080,144	50,969,428
Revenues over (under) expenditures	2,196,516	672,489	(10,483,270)	(2,080,144)	(9,694,409)
Other financing sources (uses)					
Issuance of debt	—	—	9,675,400	—	9,675,400
Transfers from other funds				2,080,144	2,080,144
Transfers (to) other funds	(3,256,899)	(289,593)	—	—	(3,546,492)
Total other financing sources (uses)	(3,256,899)	(289,593)	9,675,400	2,080,144	8,209,052
Excess of revenues and other sources over (under) expenditures and other uses	(1,060,383)	382,896	(807,870)	—	(1,485,357)
Fund balance—beginning of year	12,338,963	189,118	1,719,902	230,000	14,477,983
Fund balance—end of year	$11,278,580	$572,014	$912,032	$230,000	$12,992,626

Example Comprehensive Annual Financial Report
Financial Section: Basic Financial Statements
Proprietary Funds Statements: Statement of Net Position

Proprietary Funds: Statement of Net Position

Illustration 2-9 presents a Statement of Net Position for the proprietary funds. Again, major funds must be presented in separate columns. An enterprise fund is considered major if (*a*) assets, liabilities, revenues, *or* expenses are 10 percent or more of the total for all enterprise funds, *and* (*b*) its assets, liabilities, revenues, *or* expenses are 5 percent or more of the total of the governmental and enterprise categories, combined. In this case, the parking enterprise fund does not meet the requirements, but the government chooses to display it separately rather than label it a nonmajor fund.

Internal service funds are also presented in a separate column in the proprietary fund Statement of Net Position. However, internal service funds do not follow the procedures described for major funds. Governments with more than one internal service fund combine the funds into one column for the Statement of Net Position. Detailed financial statements for each internal service fund are included in the other supplementary information.

The proprietary funds use the economic resources measurement focus and the accrual basis of accounting. Since this is the same as the government-wide statements, reconciliations between the two sets of statements are typically not needed. In this example, you should be able to trace amounts reported in the total column for the enterprise funds to the business activities column of the Statement of Net Position. The internal service fund, however, is included in the governmental activities column in the government-wide statements since it primarily serves departments reported in the General Fund, such as police, fire, parks, and maintenance.

GASB requires a classified balance sheet where separate totals are reported for current assets and current liabilities. Both noncurrent assets and long-term liabilities are presented. The excess of assets over liabilities is reported as net position, in the same manner as the government-wide Statement of Net Position. In particular, net position is reported as (1) net investment in capital assets, (2) restricted, or (3) unrestricted. Illustration 2-9 uses a "net position" format (assets minus liabilities equal net position), but a balance sheet format is also acceptable (assets equal liabilities plus net position).

Example Comprehensive Annual Financial Report
Financial Section: Basic Financial Statements
Proprietary Funds Statements: Statement of Net Position

ILLUSTRATION 2-9 Proprietary Funds: Statement of Net Position

CITY OF SALEM
Statement of Net Position—Proprietary Funds
As of December 31, 2020

	Business-type Activities—Enterprise Funds				Governmental Activities—Internal Service Fund
Assets	Water	Solid Waste	Parking	Total	
Current assets:					
Cash and cash equivalents	$ 3,801,978	$ 847,889	$ 164,857	$ 4,814,724	$ 81,647
Investments	4,433,039	5,917,295	—	10,350,334	—
Inventory	30,779	—	—	30,779	330,759
Receivables (net)	—	—	—	—	—
Accounts receivable	2,307,643	342,394	7,289	2,657,326	—
Due from other funds	—	—	—	—	28,824
Restricted assets	1,394,787	900,256	—	2,295,043	—
Total current assets	11,968,226	8,007,834	172,146	20,148,206	441,230
Noncurrent assets:					
Capital assets (net of accumulated depreciation)	37,975,852	4,611,754	6,306,796	48,894,402	68,603
Total assets	$49,944,078	$12,619,588	$6,478,942	$69,042,608	$509,833
Liabilities					
Current liabilities:					
Accounts payable	317,131	174,087	2,631	493,849	62,958
Accrued liabilities	437,363	25,854	9,951	473,168	3,309
Total current liabilities	754,494	199,941	12,582	967,017	66,267
Liability for landfill closure and postclosure care costs	—	2,063,637	—	2,063,637	—
Capital leases payable					7,091
Bonds payable	16,114,097	—	2,023,170	18,137,267	—
Total noncurrent liabilities	16,114,097	2,063,637	2,023,170	20,200,904	7,091
Total liabilities	16,868,591	2,263,578	2,035,752	21,167,921	73,358
Net position					
Net investment in capital assets	21,861,755	4,611,754	4,283,626	30,757,135	61,512
Restricted	1,394,787	900,256	—	2,295,043	—
Unrestricted	9,818,945	4,844,000	159,564	14,822,509	374,963
Total net position	$33,075,487	$10,356,010	$4,443,190	$47,874,687	$436,475

Example Comprehensive Annual Financial Report
Financial Section: Basic Financial Statements
Proprietary Funds Statements: Statement of Revenues, Expenses, and Changes in Fund Net Position

Proprietary Funds: Statement of Revenues, Expenses, and Changes in Fund Net Position

Illustration 2-10 presents a Statement of Revenues, Expenses, and Changes in Fund Net Position for the proprietary funds. GASB requires that operating revenues and expenses be reported first, followed by operating income or loss. Note that depreciation expense is separately displayed as an operating expense. Nonoperating revenues and expenses are reported after operating income. Interest revenue and expense are nonoperating.

Capital contributions, additions to endowments, special and extraordinary items, and transfers appear after the nonoperating revenues and expenses. Capital contributions frequently represent contributions of capital assets by neighborhood and commercial property developers. The change in net position is reconciled to the Statement of Net Position by adding the beginning balance of net position for the period.

Note that the $436,475 total net position appearing at the bottom of the Internal Service Fund columns in this statement and the Statement of Net Position (Illustration 2-9) appears in the reconciliation of the Governmental Funds Balance Sheet with the government-wide Statement of Net Position (Illustration 2-7a). That is because the internal service fund's assets and liabilities are reported within governmental activities in the government-wide Statement of Net Position.

Example Comprehensive Annual Financial Report
Financial Section: Basic Financial Statements
Proprietary Funds Statements: Statement of Revenues, Expenses, and Changes in Fund Net Position

ILLUSTRATION 2-10 **Proprietary Funds: Statement of Revenues, Expenses, and Changes in Fund Net Position**

CITY OF SALEM
Statement of Revenues, Expenses, and Changes in Fund Net Position—Proprietary Funds
For the Year Ended December 31, 2020

	Business-type Activities—Enterprise Funds				Governmental Activities—Internal Service Fund
	Water	Solid Waste	Parking	Total	
Operating revenues					
Charges for services	$ 6,335,022	$ 2,292,322	$ 261,088	$ 8,888,432	$663,162
Miscellaneous	45,499	58,827	—	104,326	—
Total revenues	6,380,521	2,351,149	261,088	8,992,758	663,162
Operating expenses					
Personnel services	1,576,088	1,164,629	126,466	2,867,183	591,010
Repairs and maintenance	389,271	50,296	—	439,567	2,698
Contractual services	1,107,169	439,355	—	1,546,524	34,622
Depreciation	1,374,214	353,411	153,097	1,880,722	6,654
Utilities	186,195	1,173	40,619	227,987	100
Other	699,009	332,110	63,766	1,094,885	4,256
Landfill closure costs	—	215,659	—	215,659	—
Total operating expenses	5,331,946	2,556,633	383,948	8,272,527	639,340
Operating income (loss)	1,048,575	(205,484)	(122,860)	720,231	23,822
Nonoperating revenues (expenses)					
Interest income	452,718	279,924	1,558	734,200	700
State aid	23,746	6,878	—	30,624	—
Interest expense	(710,042)	—	(97,901)	(807,943)	(558)
Total nonoperating revenue	(233,578)	286,802	(96,343)	(43,119)	142
Income before contributions and transfers	814,997	81,318	(219,203)	677,112	23,964
Capital contributions	3,085,946	2,085,064	—	5,171,010	—
Transfers in	—	—	179,440	179,440	—
Transfers out	(92,300)	(702,202)	—	(794,502)	—
Change in net position	3,808,643	1,464,180	(39,763)	5,233,060	23,964
Net position—beginning of year	29,266,844	8,891,830	4,482,953	42,641,627	412,511
Net position—end of year	$33,075,487	$10,356,010	$4,443,190	$47,874,687	$436,475

Example Comprehensive Annual Financial Report
Financial Section: Basic Financial Statements
Proprietary Funds Statements: Statement of Cash Flows

Proprietary Funds: Statement of Cash Flows

Proprietary funds are the only funds that report a Statement of Cash Flows, presented here in Illustration 2-11. Several differences exist between the GASB format cash flow statement and the FASB format required of commercial businesses:

1. GASB requires governments to prepare cash flows from operating activities using the direct method.
2. The reconciliation of income to cash flows from operating activities of the proprietary fund, which appears in the bottom section of the statement, begins with operating income, not total change in net position (or net income for a private sector business).
3. The statement has four sections, rather than the three observed in FASB format statements:
   - Operating activities are those associated with operating income. As a result, cash flows from interest expense, interest revenue, and investment income do not appear in the operating activities section.
   - Noncapital-related financing activities involve the borrowing and payment (including interest) of loans for purposes other than financing capital additions, chiefly, borrowing for operations.
   - Capital and related financing include grants and debt transactions (including interest) used to finance capital additions.
   - Investing activities involve the acquisition and sale of investments as well as cash received from investment income.

One purpose of a cash flow statement is to help in explaining changes between the beginning and ending balances of assets and liabilities. Differences resulting in cash inflows and outflows are reflected in the body of the statement. However, some investing, and financing activities may not affect cash. For example, developers commonly install streets and sidewalks in new developments and contribute these to city governments. The contribution is a noncash capital transaction. Noncash activities such as these are disclosed below the cash flow statement.

In some cases, a portion of the government's cash may be classified on the Statement of Net Position as *restricted assets.* Therefore, *cash and cash equivalents* appearing on the Statement of Cash Flows will include several balances. For the City of Salem example, these two statements are reconciled as follows:

	Total Enterprise Funds	
Cash and cash equivalents	$4,814,724	Statement of Net Position
Restricted assets	2,295,043	Statement of Net Position
Cash and cash equivalents	$7,109,767	Statement of Cash Flows

ILLUSTRATION 2-11 Proprietary Funds: Statement of Cash Flows

CITY OF SALEM
Statement of Cash Flows
Proprietary Funds
For the Year Ended December 31, 2020

	Business-type Activities—Enterprise Funds				Governmental Activities—Internal Service Fund
	Water	Solid Waste	Parking	Total	
Cash flows from operating activities					
Cash received from customers	$6,388,018	$2,343,431	$259,946	$8,991,395	$649,426
Cash paid to suppliers	(2,490,241)	(822,363)	(80,137)	(3,392,741)	(630,437)
Cash paid to employees	(948,035)	(764,032)	(99,517)	(1,811,584)	—
Other	(588,974)	(322,472)	(50,430)	(961,876)	—
Net cash provided by operating activities	2,360,768	434,564	29,862	2,825,194	18,989
Cash flows from noncapital financing activities					
Operating grants received	—	6,594	—	6,594	—
Transfers from other funds	—	—	179,440	179,440	—
Transfers to other funds	(92,300)	(702,202)	—	(794,502)	—
Net cash provided by noncapital financing activities	(92,300)	(695,608)	179,440	(608,468)	—
Cash flows from capital and related financing activities					
Acquisition of capital assets	(543,169)	(456,179)	—	(999,348)	—
Principal paid on long-term debt	(1,014,887)	—	(128,420)	(1,143,307)	(3,719)
Interest paid	(535,567)	—	(95,961)	(631,528)	—
Net cash provided from capital and related financing activities	(2,093,623)	(456,179)	(224,381)	(2,774,183)	(3,719)
Cash flows from investing activities					
Interest received	287,725	279,924	1,558	569,207	700
Net cash provided from investing activities	287,725	279,924	1,558	569,207	700
Increase in cash	462,570	(437,299)	(13,521)	11,750	15,970
Cash and cash equivalents—beginning of year	4,734,195	2,185,444	178,378	7,098,017	65,677
Cash and cash equivalents—end of year	$5,196,765	$1,748,145	$164,857	$7,109,767	$ 81,647
Reconciliation of operating income to net cash provided by operating activities:					
Operating income	1,048,575	(205,484)	(122,860)	720,231	23,822
Depreciation	1,374,214	353,411	153,097	1,880,722	6,654
(Increase) decrease in receivables	21,097	122,828	(375)	143,550	(13,736)
(Increase) decrease in inventory	—	—	—	—	(46,535)
Increase (decrease) in accounts payable	(83,118)		—	(83,118)	48,784
Increase in landfill closure liability	—	163,809	—	163,809	—
Net cash provided by operating activities	$2,360,768	$ 434,564	$ 29,862	$2,825,194	$ 18,989
Noncash investing, capital, and financing activities:					
Contributions of capital assets from developers	$3,085,946	$2,085,064	$ —	$5,171,010	$ —

Example Comprehensive Annual Financial Report
Financial Section: Basic Financial Statements
Fiduciary Funds Statements: Statement of Fiduciary Net Position;
Statement of Changes in Fiduciary Net Position

Fiduciary: Statement of Fiduciary Net Position

Illustration 2-12 presents a Statement of Fiduciary Net Position. Fiduciary funds are reported by fund type, rather than individual major funds. GASB requires that fiduciary fund statements be included for all trust and custodial fund types and for component units that are fiduciary in nature. GASB also requires that if separate GAAP basis financial statements are not issued for individual pension and other employee benefit plans, those reports must be included in the notes to the basic financial statements. The fiduciary funds use the economic resources measurement focus and may include noncurrent assets and long-term liabilities. Note in Illustration 2-12 that the excess of assets over liabilities is labeled *net position* and the statement indicates that the resources are restricted for varying purposes.

Fiduciary: Statement of Changes in Fiduciary Net Position

Illustration 2-13 presents a Statement of Changes in Fiduciary Net Position. Although fiduciary funds use accrual accounting, the activity accounts are not labeled Revenues and Expenses. Rather the terms *additions* and *deductions* are used to reflect the fact that the government only has custody of the resources. Recall also that fiduciary funds are not included in the government-wide financial statements.

Custodial funds are a relatively new category (effective in 2019) that include resources held by a government in a fiduciary arrangement but may not have been created through a formal trust agreement. Tax collection funds are a common custodial fund. These are established when one government collects sales or property taxes for another government. Note that the tax collections are reported as additions and the amounts due the other government are reported as deductions in the Statement of Changes in Fiduciary Net Position.

Trust funds frequently have substantial investments activities. GASB requires that investments be reported at fair value. Changes in the value of investments are reflected in the Statement of Changes in Fiduciary Net Position as *increase (decrease) in the fair value of investments.* In the case of the City of Salem, this totals $163,050.

Example Comprehensive Annual Financial Report
Financial Section: Basic Financial Statements
Fiduciary Funds Statements: Statement of Fiduciary Net Position; Statement of Changes in Fiduciary Net Position

ILLUSTRATION 2-12 Statement of Fiduciary Net Position

CITY OF SALEM
Statement of Fiduciary Net Position
As of December 31, 2020

Assets	Employee Pension Trust	Private-Purpose Trust	Custodial Fund
Cash and cash equivalents	$ 172,000	$ 12,500	$21,200
Taxes receivable for other governments	—		50,000
Interest and dividends receivable	13,690	—	—
Investments at fair value			
Corporate bonds	2,725,600	—	—
Corporate stocks	6,852,300	—	—
U.S. government securities	1,325,000	900,256	—
Total assets	$11,088,590	$912,756	71,200
Liabilities			
Accounts payable	$ 105,000	7,600	—
Due to other governments	—		70,000
Total liabilities	105,000	7,600	70,000
Net position			
Restricted for pension benefits	10,983,590	—	—
Restricted for individuals or organizations	—	905,156	1,200
Total net position	$10,983,590	$905,156	$ 1,200

ILLUSTRATION 2-13 Statement of Changes in Fiduciary Net Position

CITY OF SALEM
Statement of Changes in Fiduciary Net Position
For the Year Ended December 31, 2020

Additions	Employee Pension Trust	Private-Purpose Trust	Custodial Funds
Contributions:			
Plan members	$ 912,000	$ —	$ —
Employer	1,600,000	—	—
Gifts and bequests	—	100,000	1,000
Total contributions	2,512,000	100,000	1,000
Tax collections for other governments			512,000
Investment income:			
Interest	18,560	8,500	—
Dividends	63,000	—	—
Increase in fair value of investments	163,050	—	—
Total investment income	244,610	8,500	—
Total additions	2,756,610	108,500	513,000
Deductions			
Payments of taxes to other governments	—	—	512,000
Administrative expenses	12,900	—	—
Benefits	883,600	7,600	—
Refunds of contributions	35,000	—	—
Total deductions	931,500	7,600	512,000
Change in net position	1,825,110	100,900	1,000
Net position—beginning of year	9,158,480	804,256	200
Net position—end of year	$10,983,590	$905,156	$ 1,200

like an income Stmt

Example Comprehensive Annual Financial Report
Financial Section: Basic Financial Statements
Notes to the Financial Statements

Notes to the Financial Statements

The notes to the financial statements are an integral part of the basic financial statements. As presented in Illustration 2-14, the first note is a summary of the significant accounting policies, and the first of these is generally a description of the reporting entity. Any event significant to understanding and interpreting the financial statements should be described in the notes, whether or not it is specifically required by GASB standards. The following items commonly appear among the notes to the financial statements.

1. Summary of significant accounting policies, including
   - A brief description of the component units and their relationship to the reporting entity.
   - A description of the activities reported in each of the following columns presented in the basic financial statements: major funds, internal service funds, and fiduciary fund types.
   - A description of the government-wide statements and the measurement focus and basis of accounting used in the government-wide statements.
   - The revenue recognition policies used in the fund financial statements, including the length of time used to define *available* for purposes of revenue recognition in the governmental fund financial statements.
   - The policy for eliminating internal activity in the government-wide statement of activities.
   - The policy for capitalizing assets and for estimating the useful lives of those assets.
   - A description of the types of transactions included in program revenues and the policy for allocating indirect expenses to functions (if applicable) in the statement of activities.
   - The policy for defining operating and nonoperating revenues of proprietary funds.
   - The definition of cash and cash equivalents used in the statement of cash flows for the proprietary funds.
   - The government's policy with regard to restricted and unrestricted resources when an expense is incurred for purposes for which both restricted and unrestricted resources are available.
2. Description of cash deposits with financial institutions.
3. Investments.
4. Contingent liabilities.
5. Encumbrances outstanding.
6. Effects of events subsequent to the date of the financial statements.

Example Comprehensive Annual Financial Report
Financial Section: Basic Financial Statements
Notes to the Financial Statements

ILLUSTRATION 2-14 **Notes to the Financial Statements**

1. Summary of Significant Accounting Policies

The City of Salem was established as a town in 1861 and incorporated as a city by an act of the State Legislature in 1930. The City has an area of 19.9 square miles and a population of 23,875, according to the 2010 Census. The City provides a full range of services, including general government, judicial administration, public safety, public works, health and welfare, education, parks and recreation, community development, water utility, refuse disposal, and parking facilities.

The financial statements of the City have been prepared in accordance with accounting principles generally accepted (GAAP) in the United States applicable to governmental units as specified by the Governmental Accounting Standards Board. The following is a summary of the more significant accounting policies of the City:

A. The Financial Reporting Entity

As required by GAAP, these financial statements present the City (primary government) and its component unit. The Salem Industrial Development Authority is reported as a separate and discretely presented component unit of the City. The City has no blended component units.

The Salem Industrial Development Authority has the responsibility to promote industry and develop trade by inducing manufacturing, industrial, and other commercial enterprises to locate or remain in the City. The City appoints all seven members of the Authority's Board of Directors. In addition, the City issued $10 million in general obligation bonds in 2004 to provide a capital grant to the Authority. As a result, the Authority imposes a financial burden on the City. Complete financial statements of the Authority may be obtained from the Salem Industrial Development Authority's offices, located at 10 West Main Street.

The notes typically continue for 20 or more pages.

7. Annual pension cost and net pension liability.
8. Violations of finance-related legal and contractual provisions and actions taken to address violations.
9. Debt service requirements.
10. Commitments under noncapitalized (operating) leases.
11. Construction and other significant commitments.
12. Required disclosures about capital leases.
13. Required disclosures about long-term liabilities.
14. Deficit fund balances or net position of individual nonmajor funds.
15. Interfund receivables and payables.
16. Disclosures about donor-restricted endowments.
17. For component units, the nature and amount of significant transactions with other units of the reporting entity.

Of course, the disclosures just listed are not required when they do not apply. For example, lease disclosures are not applicable if the government has no noncancelable leases.

Required Supplementary Information Other Than MD&A

Recall that required supplementary information appears in two parts of the financial section: the MD&A precedes the basic financial statements and certain required supplementary information (RSI) schedules follow the notes. Among the required schedules are the following: information required when using the modified approach to infrastructure, budgetary comparison schedule, pension schedules (illustrated in Chapter 7), and schedules of risk management activities.

Modified Approach for Reporting Infrastructure As an alternative to depreciating streets, sewers, and other infrastructure assets, governments may choose to use a modified approach (described in Chapter 8). Governments that choose to use the modified approach must present a schedule of the assessed condition of infrastructure assets and a schedule comparing the estimated cost to maintain infrastructure assets with the amounts actually expended. These schedules are part of the RSI and are presented in Illustration 2-15.

ILLUSTRATION 2-15 **Required Schedules When Using the Modified Approach for Infrastructure**

CITY OF SALEM
Condition Rating of City's Street System

	Fiscal Years 2014–2017 % of Streets	Fiscal Years 2018–2020 % of Streets
Excellent to Good	35%	85%
Fair	26	13
Poor to Substandard	39	2

Comparison of Needed-to-Actual Maintenance Expenditures for City's Street System

	2017	2018	2019	2020
Needed to maintain	$1,113,851	$1,251,518	$1,406,200	$1,580,000
Actual amount expended	$1,111,346	$1,248,703	$1,403,037	$1,576,446

The City has an ongoing street rehabilitation program, funded in the General Fund, that is intended to improve the condition rating of the City's streets. The rehabilitation program is formulated based on deficiencies identified as part of its Asset Management System.

Budgetary Comparison Schedule Illustration 2-16 presents a budgetary comparison schedule, which is required of the General Fund and each major special revenue fund that has a legally adopted budget. This schedule includes the original budget, the final appropriated budget, and the actual results computed on the same basis as the budget. The variance column is optional. When the basis of accounting used in the budget differs from that in the Statement of Revenues, Expenditures, and Changes in Fund Balance, the two must be reconciled in the schedule or in notes to the RSI. In the case of the City of Salem, the city uses the GAAP basis for budgeting and no reconciliation is required.

Example Comprehensive Annual Financial Report
Financial Section: Required Supplementary Information
Other Than Management's Discussion and Analysis

ILLUSTRATION 2-16 **Schedule of Revenues, Expenditures, and Changes in Fund Balance—Budget and Actual: General Fund**

CITY OF SALEM
Schedule of Revenues, Expenditures, and Changes in Fund Balance—
Budget and Actual: General Fund (Non-GAAP Budgetary Basis)
For the Year Ended December 31, 2020

	Budgeted Amounts		Actual Amounts Budgetary	Variance with Final
Revenues	Original	Final	Basis	Budget
Property taxes	$14,666,000	$14,666,000	$15,361,830	$695,830
Other local taxes	11,562,500	11,562,500	11,761,522	199,022
Charges for services	1,613,011	1,613,011	1,601,435	(11,576)
Intergovernmental	7,892,080	8,047,907	7,098,698	(949,209)
Miscellaneous	1,504,977	1,388,385	1,262,549	(125,836)
Total revenues	37,238,568	37,277,803	37,086,034	(191,769)
Expenditures				
Current				
General Government	3,567,838	3,489,870	3,353,502	136,368
Judicial Administration	1,321,048	1,497,845	1,456,734	41,111
Public Safety	7,753,002	8,325,564	8,216,347	109,217
Public Works	4,541,651	4,984,353	4,602,273	382,080
Health and Welfare	4,823,267	4,440,167	4,418,294	21,873
Education	8,963,248	8,929,725	8,887,834	41,891
Parks and Recreation	2,983,861	3,097,528	3,055,325	42,203
Community Development	872,594	904,168	899,209	4,959
Total expenditures	34,826,509	35,669,220	34,889,518	779,702
Revenues over (under) expenditures	2,412,059	1,608,583	2,196,516	587,933
Other financing sources (uses):				
Transfers (to) other funds	(3,560,000)	(3,257,000)	(3,256,899)	101
	(3,560,000)	(3,257,000)	(3,256,899)	101
Excess of revenues and other sources over (under) expenditures and other uses	(1,147,941)	(1,648,417)	(1,060,383)	588,034
Fund balance—beginning of year	12,338,963	12,338,963	12,338,963	—
Fund balance—end of year	$11,191,022	$10,690,546	$11,278,580	$588,034

Example Comprehensive Annual Financial Report
Financial Section: Other Supplementry Information

Combining Statements

A complete CAFR presents combining statements to reflect its nonmajor funds whenever a nonmajor column is used in one of the fund statements. Any fund that was not large enough to be reported as a major fund will be presented in the combining statement. The total column in the combining statements will be the same as the *nonmajor funds* column in the basic financial statements.

Example Comprehensive Annual Financial Report
Statistical Section

Statistical Information

Governments wishing to present the more complete Comprehensive Annual Financial Report (CAFR) will include a statistical section. This section is not part of the CAFR's financial section and, like the introductory section, is not audited. Governments typically present 10 years of information in each table or schedule. The purpose of the statistical section is to provide historical (trend) information and additional detail to help the financial statement user better understand and assess a government's economic condition. Failure to include the statistical section will not result in a modified or adverse audit opinion.

GASB *Codification* Sec. 2800 provides guidance on the content of the statistical section. Statistical information, when presented, should be presented in five categories:

1. *Financial trends information* assists users in understanding how a government's financial position has changed over time.
2. *Revenue capacity information* is used to assess the government's ability to generate revenue from its own sources (i.e., taxes, service charges, and investments).
3. *Debt capacity information* is used to assess a government's debt burden and ability to take on more debt.
4. *Demographic and economic information* describes a government's socioeconomic environment and is used to interpret comparisons across time and between governments.
5. *Operating information* provides contextual information about a government's operations such as number of government employees, volume and usage of capital assets, and indicators of the demand for government services.

The sources of information and important assumptions must be described. Governments may provide other information as long as it is consistent with the objectives of improving the understanding and assessment of a government's economic condition.

SUMMARY

This chapter provides an overview of the Comprehensive Annual Financial Report for state and local governments. The purpose is to familiarize you with where we are headed before getting into the details of how this report comes together. How the CAFR comes together will be the purpose of the next seven chapters. Chapters 3 through 7 examine the various funds and demonstrate the recording of typical transactions for each, as well as the preparation of fund-basis financial statements. Chapter 8 then takes the fund information and builds the government-wide statements.

Questions and Exercises

2–1. Using the Comprehensive Annual Financial Report obtained for Exercise 1–1, answer the following questions:

a. Compare the items discussed in the MD&A in your CAFR with the list of items in this chapter. Which topics listed in this chapter are not in your CAFR? Which topics are in your CAFR that are not listed in this chapter? Do you think your CAFR has a reasonably complete discussion?

b. From the MD&A in your report, write a short summary of (1) the financial condition of your government, (2) a comparison of revenues compared with the prior year, (3) a comparison of expenses compared with the prior year, and (4) a comparison of budgeted and actual activity.

c. From the Statement of Net Position, identify the following: (1) unrestricted net position—governmental activities; (2) unrestricted net position—business-type activities; (3) restricted net position by restriction—governmental activities; (4) restricted net position by restriction—business-type activities; and (5) unrestricted and restricted net position—component units (if any).

d. From the Statement of Activities, identify the following: (1) net program expense (or revenue)—governmental activities; (2) net program expense (or revenue)—business-type activities; (3) net program expense (or revenue)—component units; (4) change in net position—governmental activities; (5) change in net position—business-type activities; and (6) change in net position—component units. Does the ending net position in this statement agree with the net position figures in the Statement of Net Position?

e. From the Statement of Revenues, Expenditures, and Changes in Fund Balances for Governmental Funds, identify the names of the major governmental funds. List the net change in fund balance for each major fund.

f. From the governmental fund statements, take one major fund (other than the General Fund) and prove, using the 10 percent and 5 percent criteria described in this chapter, that the fund is required to be reported as a major fund.

g. From the Statement of Revenues, Expenses, and Changes in Fund Net Position, list the major enterprise funds. For each, identify: (1) the operating income, (2) the income (loss) before contributions and transfers, and (3) the change in net position.

2–2. With regard to GASB rules for the financial reporting entity, define

a. The financial reporting entity.

b. A primary government; give an example.

c. A component unit; give an example.

d. And describe the two methods of reporting the primary government and component units in the financial reporting entity.

2–3. With regard to the Comprehensive Annual Financial Report (CAFR)

a. What are the three major sections?

b. List the government-wide statements. Indicate the measurement focus and basis of accounting used for the government-wide statements.

c. List the governmental fund statements. Indicate the measurement focus and basis of accounting used for the governmental fund statements.

d. List the proprietary fund statements. Indicate the measurement focus and basis of accounting used for the proprietary fund statements.

e. List the fiduciary fund statements. Describe the measurement focus and basis of accounting used for the fiduciary fund statements.

f. Outline the reports and schedules to be reported as required supplementary information.

2–4. Describe the test for determining whether a governmental fund is a major fund. Describe the test for determining whether an enterprise fund is a major fund.

2–5. Describe how the cash flow statement of an enterprise fund differs in format from the cash flow statements of private sector organizations such as commercial businesses.

2–6. Describe the net position classification appearing on the government-wide Statement of Net Position.

2–7. The following information is available for the preparation of the government-wide financial statements for the city of Southern Springs as of April 30, 2020:

Cash and cash equivalents, governmental activities	$ 4,050,000
Cash and cash equivalents, business-type activities	880,000
Receivables, governmental activities	650,000
Receivables, business-type activities	1,130,000
Inventories, business-type activities	520,000
Capital assets, net, governmental activities	10,600,000
Capital assets, net, business-type activities	11,350,000
Accounts payable, governmental activities	550,000
Accounts payable, business-type activities	659,000

Noncurrent liabilities, governmental activities	5,550,000
Noncurrent liabilities, business-type activities	3,210,000
Net position, net investment in capital assets, governmental activities	5,050,000
Net position, net investment in capital assets, business-type activities	8,140,000
Net position, restricted for debt service, governmental activities	754,000
Net position, restricted for debt service, business-type activities	223,000

From the preceding information, prepare, in good form, a Statement of Net Position for the city of Southern Springs as of April 30, 2020. Calculate and include the unrestricted net position. Include a total column.

2–8. The following information is available for the preparation of the government-wide financial statements for the city of Northern Pines for the year ended June 30, 2020:

Expenses:	
General government	$ 10,000,000
Public safety	23,000,000
Public works	11,890,000
Health and sanitation	6,210,000
Culture and recreation	4,198,000
Interest on long-term debt, governmental type	1,021,000
Water and sewer system	11,550,000
Parking system	419,000
Revenues:	
Charges for services, general government	1,110,000
Charges for services, public safety	1,410,000
Operating grant, public safety	698,000
Charges for services, health and sanitation	2,355,000
Operating grant, health and sanitation	1,210,000
Charges for services, culture and recreation	2,198,000
Charges for services, water and sewer	12,678,000
Charges for services, parking system	298,000
Property taxes	27,112,000
Sales taxes	20,698,000
Investment earnings, business-type	319,000
Special item—gain on sale of unused land, governmental type	1,250,000
Transfer from governmental activities to business-type activities	888,000
Net position, July 1, 2019, governmental activities	12,222,000
Net position, July 1, 2019, business-type activities	22,333,000

From the previous information, prepare, in good form, a Statement of Activities for the city of Northern Pines for the year ended June 30, 2020. Northern Pines has no component units.

2–9. The following General Fund information is available for the preparation of the financial statements for the City of Eastern Shores for the year ended September 30, 2020:

Revenues:	
Property taxes	$27,520,000
Sales taxes	13,816,000
Fees and fines	1,324,000

Licenses and permits	1,721,000
Intergovernmental	2,368,000
Investment earnings	654,000
Expenditures:	
Current:	
General government	11,725,000
Public safety	24,444,000
Public works	6,211,000
Health and sanitation	1,163,000
Culture and recreation	2,154,000
Transfer to capital project fund	1,529,000
Special item—proceeds from sale of land	821,000
Fund balance, October 1, 2019	1,750,000

From the information given above, prepare, in good form, a General Fund Statement of Revenues, Expenditures, and Changes in Fund Balances for the city of Eastern Shores General Fund for the year ended September 30, 2020.

2–10. The following water and sewer fund information is available for the preparation of the financial statements for the City of Western Sands for the year ended December 31, 2020:

Operating revenues—charges for services	$17,387,000
Operating expenses:	
Personnel services	5,877,000
Contractual services	2,995,000
Utilities	888,000
Repairs and maintenance	1,992,000
Depreciation	5,422,000
Interest revenue	29,000
State aid (intergovernmental revenue)	100,000
Interest expense	104,000
Capital contributions	1,632,000
Transfer to General Fund	365,000
Net position, January 1, 2020	1,800,000

From the information given above, prepare, in good form, a Water and Sewer Fund column for the proprietary fund Statement of Revenues, Expenses, and Changes in Fund Net Position for the year ended December 31, 2020.

2–11. Use the CAFR information for the City of Salem (Illustrations 2-2 through 2–16) to find the following items. In your answer, indicate which financial statement contained the information as well as the item and the dollar amount.

	Information Item	**Statement**	**$ Amount**
Ex	Amounts due from other governments to support governmental activities	Balance Sheet—Governmental funds	$1,328,448
A.	Total capital outlay for the courthouse renovation		
B.	Total cash paid for capital additions for the solid waste fund		
C.	Interest paid (not expense) on general long-term debt		
D.	Interest paid (not expense) on water department debt		
E.	Capital asset (net) for the government's component units		
F.	Contributions received for use by the private-purpose trust		
G.	Noncurrent liabilities associated with governmental activities that are due in more than one year.		
H.	Noncash contributions of capital assets for the water department		

2–12. Use the CAFR information for the City of Salem (Illustrations 2-2 through 2–16) to find the following items. Each item will appear in two separate financial statements. In your answer indicate *both* financial statements that contained the information item and the dollar amount.

	Information Item	**Statements**		**$ Amount**
Ex	Investments held by the Enterprise Funds	Statement of Net Position—Proprietary Funds	Government-wide Statement of Net Position	$10,350,334
A.	Total fund balance of the Special Revenue Fund			
B.	Net resources (i.e., net position) available for employee pensions			
C.	Operating income for the Internal Service Funds			
D.	Net resources (i.e., net position) of the primary government			

Continuous Problem

Chapters 2 through 9 deal with specific knowledge needed to understand accounting and financial reporting by state and local governments. A continuous problem is available in additional resources through Connect. The problem assumes the government is using fund accounting for its internal record-keeping and then at year-end makes necessary adjustments to prepare the government-wide statements. The problem covers all of the funds of the City of Monroe. At appropriate stages, beginning in Chapter 4, preparation of the fund and government-wide statements are required. The following funds are included in this series of problems:

General
Special revenue—Street and Highway Fund
Capital projects—City Hall Annex Construction Fund
Debt service—City Hall Annex Debt Service Fund
Debt service—City Hall Debt Service Fund
Internal service—Stores and Services Fund
Enterprise—Water and Sewer Fund
Private-purpose trust—Student Scholarship Fund
Pension trust—Fire and Police Retirement Fund

The continuous problem is available in Connect through the Additional Student Resources in the eBook or instructor library.

Chapter Three

Modified Accrual Accounting: Including the Role of Fund Balances and Budgetary Authority

In New Mexico, I inherited the largest structural deficit in state history, and our legislature is controlled by Democrats. We don't always agree, but we came together in a bipartisan manner and turned that deficit into a surplus. And we did it without raising taxes. Susana Martinez, the first female governor of New Mexico and the first Hispanic governor in the United States

Every family in America knows they have to do a budget. Every small business in America knows they have to do a budget. Every local government, every state, knows they have to do a budget. John Boehner, Republican congressman from Ohio who served as Speaker of the House of Representatives from 2011–2015

Learning Objectives

- Describe the basic accounts used by governmental funds.
- Identify the recognition criteria for revenues and expenditures under the modified accrual basis.
- Apply fund balance classifications for governmental funds.
- Prepare journal entries for the expenditures cycle using both budgetary and activity accounts.

The most distinguishing feature of governmental accounting is the use of the modified accrual basis (and current financial resources measurement focus) of accounting.[1] Although the use of modified accrual accounting is limited to one type

[1] The term *modified accrual* is used throughout this chapter to represent both the current financial resources measurement focus and the modified accrual basis of accounting.

of fund (i.e., governmental funds) and then only to the fund-basis statements, this does not mean it is inconsequential. Recall that every general-purpose government will have (at least) a General Fund, and the General Fund is commonly the largest fund when measured in terms of government expenditures. Further, since most tax revenue is received by the General and other governmental funds, these funds are of particular interest to taxpayers.

Before describing exactly what the modified accrual basis is, it may be useful to describe what it is not. The modified accrual basis is not equivalent to the cash basis. Governmental funds record receivables (e.g., taxes receivable) and recognize revenues before collection, which is not true of a cash-basis system. Similarly, governmental funds record many liabilities (e.g., salaries payable) and accrue expenditures when payable, rather than waiting until payment occurs. Additionally, the modified accrual basis is also not merely a "light" version of the accrual basis, differing only in its failure to recognize long-term assets and liabilities.

The modified accrual basis is a distinct system of accounting that contains financial statement elements that appear nowhere else. Among these are expenditures and fund balances. At the same time, the modified accrual basis contains other elements that are shared with the accrual basis, such as assets and liabilities. Although revenues appear in the financial statements of accrual and modified accrual funds, revenues follow different recognition criteria between the two bases. Finally, there are no expenses in modified accrual funds.

The following sections describe the account structure and recognition criteria for governmental funds. The modified accrual basis evolved from the demand for accountability over public resources and is therefore closely tied to the budget function. Budgetary accounting is illustrated in the appendix to this chapter.

MODIFIED ACCRUAL ACCOUNTS

Balance Sheet Accounts

Illustration 3-1 provides the typical account structure for a governmental fund using modified accrual accounting. Panel 1 displays the Balance Sheet accounts. Because governmental funds report under the current financial resources measurement focus, long-term assets are not presented. Generally speaking, the assets represent cash and assets that may be expected to be converted into cash in the normal course of operations. Similarly, these funds report only those liabilities that will be settled with current financial resources. Therefore, long-term liabilities are not reported in governmental funds.

Deferred Inflows of Resources represent balance sheet accounts with credit balances, similar to liabilities. However these items do not represent obligations and are therefore not liabilities. The most common example in a governmental fund is deferred taxes. **Deferred Outflows of Resources** represent balance sheet accounts with debit balances but are not assets and rarely appear in governmental funds. Only items specifically identified in GASB standards may be reported as deferred inflows or deferred outflows.

ILLUSTRATION 3-1 **Account Structure of Governmental Funds**

Panel 1. Accounts that are not closed at year-end (Balance Sheet)	
Assets	**Liabilities**
Cash and Cash Equivalents	Accounts Payable
Investments	Accrued Liabilities
Receivables:	
Taxes Receivable	**Deferred Inflow of Resources**
Accounts Receivable	Deferred Tax Revenues
Due from Other Governments	
Supplies Inventories	**Fund Balances**
Restricted Assets (typically cash)	Nonspendable
	Restricted
Deferred Outflow of Resources	Committed
	Assigned
	Unassigned
Panel 2. Accounts that are closed at year-end	
Budgetary Accounts	**Activity Accounts**
Estimated Revenues	**Revenues**
	Tax Revenues
	Charges for Services
Appropriations	**Expenditures**
	Current
	Capital Outlay
	Debt Service
Estimated Other Financing Sources	**Other Financing Sources**
	Transfers In
	Debt Proceeds
Estimated Other Financing Uses	**Other Financing Uses**
	Transfers Out
Encumbrances	

The account category **Fund Balance** is unique to governmental funds. Neither property owners nor voters have a legal claim on the excess of fund assets over liabilities; therefore, Fund Balance is not analogous to the capital of an investor-owned entity. However, Fund Balance serves a purpose similar to retained earnings, in that activity accounts are closed to this account at the end of each accounting period. While mathematically comparable to retained earnings, fund balances are very different in interpretation. Because only current financial resources and claims against those resources are recognized in these funds, the difference between assets and liabilities (fund balance) represents the net resources of the fund that are currently available for future spending. However, even current financial resources vary in the extent to which government managers have discretion over their future use, and this is reflected by assigning fund balance to five categories (nonspendable, restricted, committed, assigned, and unassigned).

The fund balance classifications are GASB's response to bond investors and rating agencies who wish to understand the extent to which the net financial resources of governmental funds are constrained and how binding those constraints are. For example, fund resources can be restricted by creditors, donors, or granting agencies. Resources may also be formally committed by elected officials to specific activities. Alternatively, constraints may merely be nonbinding indications of management's intent to use resources for a particular purpose. The five fund balance classifications reflect these varying levels of constraint.

Nonspendable Fund Balances Illustration 3-2 summarizes the reporting requirements for fund balances. The first step is to identify those fund resources that are **nonspendable.** (This is identified as step 1 in the illustration.) Inventories and prepaid items typically appear in governmental funds because they are current assets. However, these resources are nonspendable because they are used in operations rather than converted into cash. The principal (corpus) of a permanent fund that may not be spent, but is required by its donor to be maintained, would also be classified as nonspendable. Other examples include assets held for sale and long-term receivables, which are sometimes reported in governmental funds.

The remaining resources (net of liabilities) of the fund include cash and items expected to be converted into cash in the next period. These "spendable" resources are further classified according to the nature of any constraints imposed on their use, using a hierarchy of constraints. The hierarchy ranges from "restricted" for the most constrained to "unassigned" for the least.

Restricted fund balance (item 2a in the illustration) represents the net resources of a governmental fund that are subject to constraints imposed by external parties or law. Restrictions arising from external parties include debt covenants (such as a requirement for a sinking fund) or constraints imposed by legislation or federal and state agencies on the use of intergovernmental revenues. Restrictions can also result from legally enforceable requirements that resources be used only for specific purposes. For example, some states permit cities and counties to impose taxes on the sale of prepared food and beverages. If approved by the voters, the referendum commonly restricts the use of the tax proceeds (typically to capital projects). The unexpended resources derived from this tax would be displayed as restricted fund balance.

The net position (i.e., equity) section of the government-wide Statement of Net Position classifies net position within three categories, including *restricted net position.* With one exception, those resources classified as restricted net position in the government-wide statements would also be classified as restricted fund balance in the fund-basis statements. The exception is permanent fund principal. These resources are classified as restricted in the government-wide Statement of Net Position and nonspendable fund balance in the (fund-basis) Balance Sheet.

Committed fund balance (item 2b in the illustration) represents the net resources of a governmental fund that the governing body has specified for a particular use. To be classified as committed, the resources should have been designated through ordinance or resolution by the government's highest level of authority (e.g., state legislature, city council, or county board of supervisors). Committed resources

ILLUSTRATION 3-2 Diagram of Fund Balance Classifications

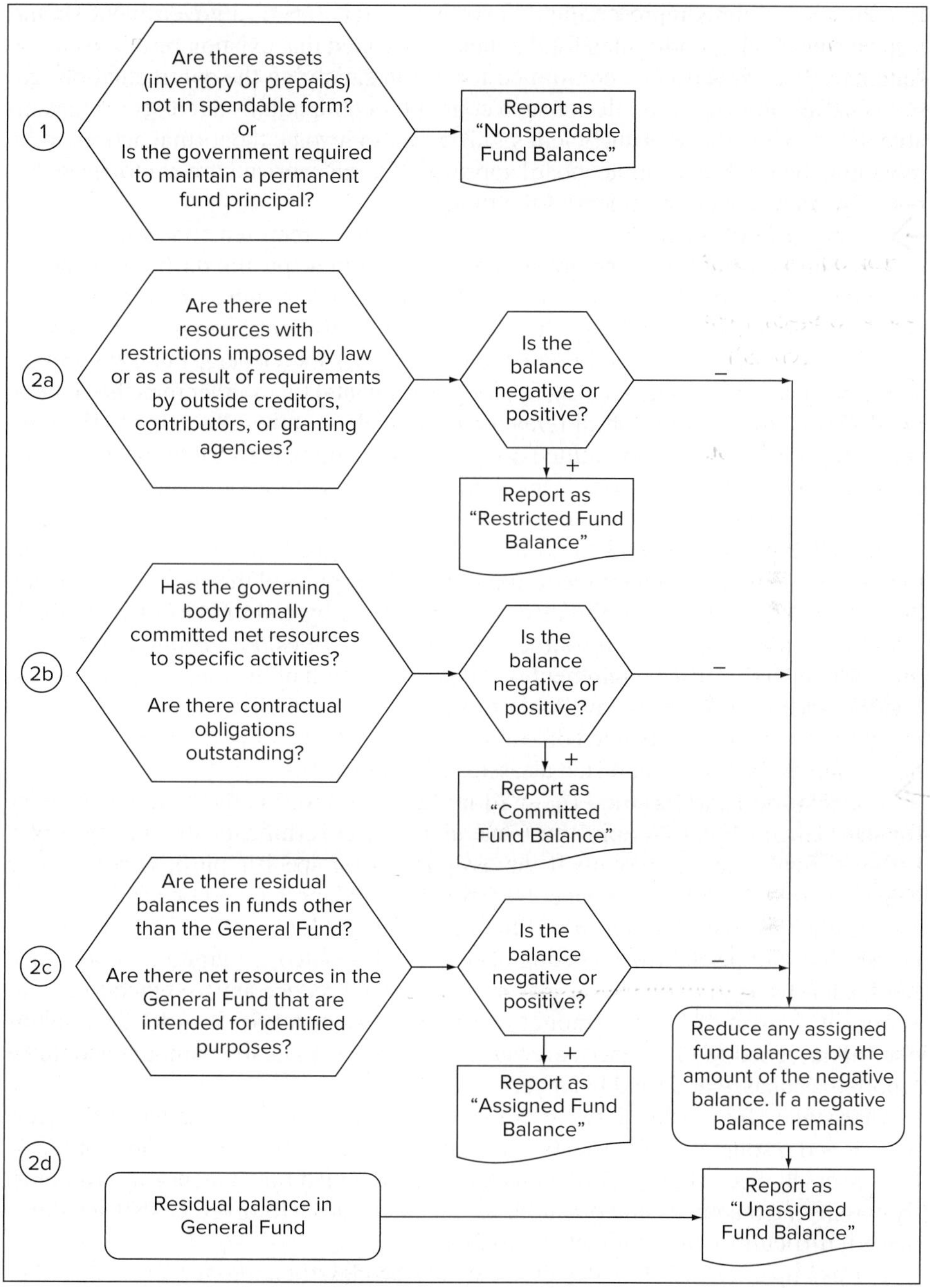

differ from restricted in that the constraint is imposed by a government upon itself. In addition, amounts representing contractual obligations of a government should also be classified as committed fund balance, provided that existing resources in the fund have been specifically committed for use in satisfying the contractual obligation. GASB offers no examples of such contractual obligations, but it seems reasonable that they would be of sufficient significance to involve the formal action of the governing board. For example, board approval of large construction contracts would typically represent commitment of the funds.

Assigned fund balance (item 2c in the illustration) represents the net resources of governmental funds that the government intends for a specific purpose. Assigned resources differ from committed in that the committed resources require a formal action by the governing body of the government. Constraints imposed on assigned resources are more easily modified or removed. Only the General Fund will report (positive) unassigned fund balance. So, for governmental funds other than the General Fund, this is the category for all remaining fund balance after allocating to the nonspendable, restricted, and committed categories. The rationale is that the act of recording resources in special revenue, capital projects, debt service, or permanent funds is evidence of the government's intent to use the resources for a specific purpose.

Resources in the General Fund may also be assigned to a specific purpose if that is the intent of the government. Intent may be expressed through the governing body by means other than ordinance or resolution or by committees or individuals with the authority to assign resources to specific activities. For example, placing a purchase order for office equipment is a clear expression of the intent of the government to use a portion of its available resources for a capital acquisition. Until the resources are actually expended on capital assets, that portion of the General Fund's net resources would be classified as assigned fund balance.

Unassigned fund balance (item 2d in the illustration) is the residual category for the General Fund. Within the General Fund, governments should not report assigned fund balance amounts if the assignment for specific purpose results in a negative unassigned fund balance. Negative fund balances could occur if expenditures for a specific purpose exceed the resources available in the fund. However, GASB does not permit the reporting of negative restricted, committed, or assigned fund balances. If this occurs, the government should reduce any assigned fund balances (in that fund) by the amount of the negative balance. If a deficit remains once all assigned fund balances are zero, the remaining negative amount should be reported as unassigned fund balance.

Unassigned fund balance receives the most attention by citizens who may view unassigned resources as justification for tax relief or spending on favored projects. Government officials may wish to understate unassigned fund balance by temporarily classifying resources into one of the other categories. However, GASB standards make it difficult for governments to do this.

For example, GASB provides guidance on the classification of *budget stabilization* or *rainy day* funds. Rainy day funds are amounts set aside for future periods of economic downturn. Such stabilization amounts that meet certain criteria are classified as committed or (less commonly) restricted, if imposed externally or by law.

GASB standards state that rainy day funds may be classified as committed only if they are created by a resolution or ordinance that identifies the specific circumstances under which the resources may be expended. Rainy day amounts that are available "in emergencies" or in periods of "revenue shortfalls" would not be classified as committed unless the emergency or shortfall condition is specified and of a magnitude to distinguish it from events that occur routinely. Rainy day funds not meeting these conditions are reported as unassigned fund balance in the General Fund.

Illustration 3-3 provides an annotated example of fund balance reporting for the City of Salem example used in Chapter 2. Note that the governmental funds balance sheet is the only financial statement reporting fund balances.

Financial Statement Activity Accounts

Panel 2 of Illustration 3-1 presents activity and budgetary accounts for governmental funds. The activity accounts reflect sources and uses of funds; examples are given in detail in Chapters 4 and 5. *Revenues* and *Other Financing Sources* are sources (or inflows) of financial resources while *Expenditures* and *Other Financing Uses* represent uses (or outflows) of financial resources. **Other Financing Sources** include transfers in from other funds and the proceeds of long-term borrowing. **Revenues** are defined as all other inflows and include taxes, charges for services, and amounts provided by other entities such as the state or federal government. Because taxes and many other revenues do not involve exchange transactions, governments cannot determine the point at which these revenues are earned. Therefore, revenue recognition occurs when the resulting resources are deemed to be both measurable and available to finance expenditures of the current period. Revenue recognition for specific types of nonexchange transactions is described later in this chapter.

Expenditure is a term that replaces both the terms *costs* and *expenses* used in accounting for commercial businesses. **Expenditures** are recognized when a liability is incurred that will be settled with current financial resources. Expenditures may be for salaries (current), land, buildings, or equipment (capital) or for payment of interest and principal on debt (debt service). Transfers of cash out of one fund to other funds are classified as **Other Financing Uses.** An example of the use of transfer accounts occurs when a portion of the taxes recognized as revenue by the General Fund is transferred to a debt service fund that will record payments of interest and principal on general obligation debt. The General Fund would record the taxes as *Tax Revenue* and the amounts transferred to the debt service fund as *Other Financing Uses—Transfers Out.* The debt service fund would record the receipt of the transfer as *Other Financing Sources—Transfer In* and the subsequent payments of interest and principal as *Debt Service Expenditures.* Thus, use of the transfer accounts achieves the desired objective that revenues are recognized in the fund that levied the taxes (i.e., General Fund) and expenditures are recognized in the fund that expends the cash (i.e., debt service fund).

Budgetary Accounts

GASB standards require governments to present a comparison of budgeted and actual results for the General Fund and special revenue funds with legally adopted

ILLUSTRATION 3-3 **Example of Fund Balance Reporting**

CITY OF SALEM
Balance Sheet—Fund Balance Section
Governmental Funds
As of December 31, 2020

	General Fund	Special Revenue Fund	Courthouse Renovation Fund	Debt Service Fund	Total Governmental Funds	
FUND BALANCE						
Nonspendable						
- Supplies inventory	$ 23,747	$ —	$ —	$ —	$ 23,747	← This amount equals the balance of supplies inventories in the asset section of the balance sheet.
Restricted						
- Intergovernmental grants	—	312,000	500,000	—	812,000	← These represent resources which are restricted by outside parties through grant agreements and bond covenants.
- Bond sinking fund	—	—	—	230,000	230,000	
Committed						
- Rainy day fund	4,500,000	—	—	—	4,500,000	← These represent resources which are restricted by City Council as a reserve for revenue shortfalls (General Fund) and by contractual obligation (capital projects fund).
- Courthouse renovation	—	—	380,000	—	380,000	
Assigned						
- School lunch program	—	260,014	—	—	260,014	
- Other capital projects	680,500	—	32,032	—	712,532	← These include the residual balance of the special revenue and capital projects funds. It also includes amounts assigned within the General Fund by expressed intent (e.g., by purchase orders).
- Other purposes	236,800	—	—	—	236,800	
Unassigned	5,837,533	—	—	—	5,837,533	← This is the residual balance of the General Fund.
TOTAL FUND BALANCE	$11,278,580	$572,014	$912,032	$230,000	$12,992,626	

budgets. Although GASB standards guide the format of this comparison, the GASB does not prescribe budgetary accounting practices and does not require governments to maintain budgetary accounts. Budgetary accounts do not appear in the general-purpose financial statements. Nevertheless, governments typically record budgets, and governmental accounting systems are designed to assure compliance with budgets.

The accounts appearing in the left-hand side of Illustration 3-1, Panel 2, serve this budgetary (rather than external reporting) function of the government. A government may raise revenues only from sources allowed by law. Laws commonly establish the maximum amount of a tax or set a maximum tax rate. Revenues to be raised pursuant to law during a budget period are set forth in an **estimated revenues** budget.

Resources raised by the government may only be expended for purposes and in amounts approved by the governing body or legislature. This is known as the appropriations process. An **appropriations** budget, when enacted into law, is the legal authorization for the government to make expenditures for specific purposes. Commonly the amount expended may not exceed the amount appropriated for each purpose. In this manner, a government budget has the effect of law by limiting spending to approved levels. **Estimated Other Financing Sources** and **Estimated Other Financing Uses** are additional budgetary accounts reflecting anticipated inflows and outflows of resources from sources other than revenues and spending.

Encumbrances and the related Reserve for Encumbrances are the final two budgetary accounts. When a purchase order or contract is issued as authorized by an appropriation, the government may recognize this commitment as an **encumbrance.** An encumbrance is not a liability because the goods or services have merely been ordered, not received. The process by which a government moves from budgetary authority to expending fund resources is described in the following section.

EXPENDITURE CYCLE

Illustration 3-4 depicts the expenditure cycle and corresponding journal entries for the General Fund or a special revenue fund with a legally adopted budget. To save space, we demonstrate journal entries using control accounts for activity (Revenues and Expenditures) and budgetary accounts (Estimated Revenues, Appropriations, and Encumbrances). Entries to control accounts would be supported with detailed entries in subsidiary accounts. While many accounting systems have discontinued the use of control accounts, in the interest of space we use summarized postings. You are encouraged to use detailed accounts (for example, revenues by source) when preparing end-of-chapter exercises.

The process begins with the governing board or legislature approving a budget. At first glance the budgetary accounts may appear to have balances opposite what would be expected—*Estimated Revenues* have debit balances and *Appropriations* have credit. However, the entry is designed to reflect the anticipated effect on the

ILLUSTRATION 3-4 **Expenditure Cycle**

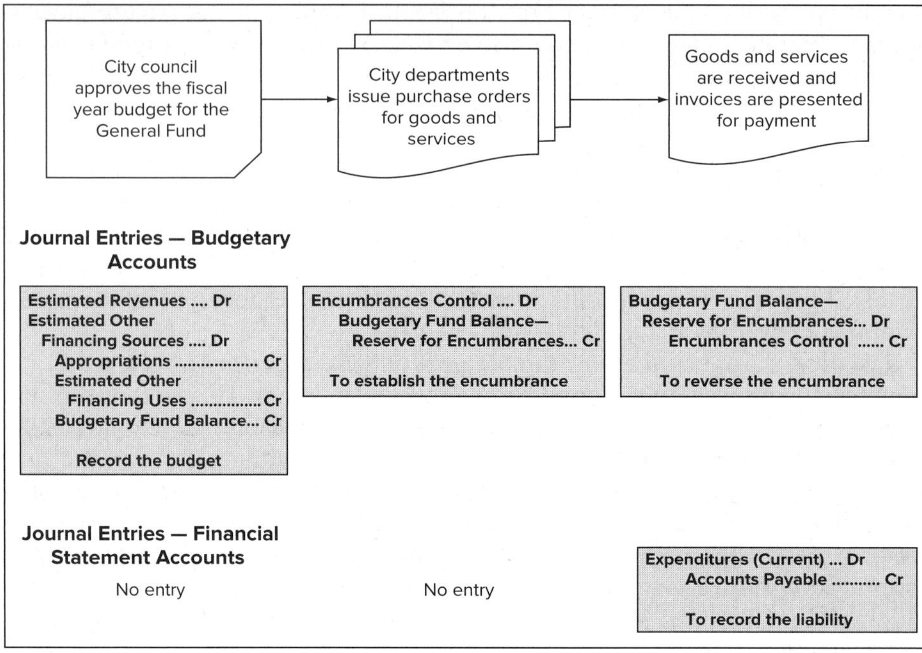

fund's net resources (**Budgetary Fund Balance**) if everything went according to expectations. Because budgeted revenues and other financing sources exceed budgeted expenditures and other uses, fund balance is expected to increase (credit). However, if budgeted expenditures and other uses are expected to exceed budgeted revenues and other financing sources, Budgetary Fund Balance would be debited in the entry. The appendix to this chapter presents more detailed budgetary entries, including budget amendments.

A department (such as police or health) cannot commit the government to expend resources until it is granted budgetary authority through its appropriations. Once that authority exists, departments can begin to commit resources by placing purchase orders or signing contracts. These commitments are reflected in the budgetary accounts through the recording of *Encumbrances* and the corresponding *Budgetary Fund Balance—Reserve for Encumbrances.* GASB requires that significant encumbrances be disclosed in the notes along with required disclosures about other commitments. However, there is no separate reporting of encumbrances within the fund balance section of the governmental funds balance sheet. Rather, encumbered resources should be reported within the restricted, committed, or assigned categories in a manner consistent with the criteria for those classifications.

At the very least, the existence of an encumbrance suggests that the government has expressed an intent to use resources for a particular purpose and therefore these resources should *not* be classified as *unassigned.* Encumbrance accounting may also be used in the case of contractual obligations, such as construction contracts. We will examine the relation of encumbrances to the classification of fund balances in more detail in Chapters 4 and 5.

Once goods or services are received, the government has a liability. At this point, two journal entries are necessary. The first reverses the encumbrance at its original amount. Since the government has incurred an actual liability, it is no longer necessary to reflect a commitment for the outstanding purchase orders or contracts. The second entry records the liability (Accounts Payable) and an Expenditure in the amount of the invoice.

Governments frequently choose not to record encumbrances for some expenditures, particularly those that are relatively predictable in amount. For example, salaries may be initially recorded only as expenditures when due without having been formally encumbered. At the end of the budget period, unencumbered, unexpended appropriations lapse; that is, administrators no longer have the authority to incur liabilities under the expired appropriations. In nearly all cases, administrators continue to have the authority to disburse cash in payment of liabilities legally incurred (and recorded as expenditures) in a prior period. However, appropriations that are encumbered may or may not carry forward to the next accounting period, depending on the government's policy. If they do not carry forward and must be appropriated again in the following year, the encumbrances are said to **lapse.** The entry to record a lapsed encumbrance is the same as the reversal entry when a good or service is received (debit *Budgetary Fund Balance—Reserve for Encumbrances* and credit *Encumbrances—Control*).

REVENUE RECOGNITION FOR NONEXCHANGE TRANSACTIONS

Under modified accrual accounting, revenues are recognized when they are both **measurable** and **available** to finance expenditures of the current period. Many governmental revenues result from nonexchange transactions. **Nonexchange transactions** are transactions in which a government receives resources without directly giving equivalent value in exchange. These are in contrast to exchange transactions, such as the purchase of goods or services. The most common forms of nonexchange transactions are tax revenues and intergovernmental grants. Most of the activities of governmental funds are supported by revenues generated through nonexchange transactions. Before a government may recognize revenue resulting from nonexchange transactions, it must meet a number of **eligibility requirements.** The eligibility requirements are as follows:

1. **Required Characteristics of Recipients.** The recipient must have the qualifying characteristics specified by the provider. For example, a state can provide funding on a per student basis to public schools. In order to recognize this revenue, the entity must be a public school as defined by state laws.

2. **Time Requirement.** If time requirements (for expenditure) are specified, those time requirements must be met. For example, a state can provide funding to support park districts for the next fiscal year. In that case, the revenue would not be recognized by the park districts until that fiscal year. If the resource provider does not specify time requirements, then no condition exists and the revenue would be recognized as soon as other eligibility requirements are met.

3. **Reimbursement.** Many grants require the recipient government to spend money on qualifying items and then request reimbursement. For those grants and gifts that are payable only on a reimbursement basis, revenues would be recognized when the expenditures have been incurred. The government would not have to wait for the payment to be received to recognize this revenue.

4. **Contingencies.** Resources pledged that have a contingency attached are not recognized as revenue until the contingency has been met. For example, if a donor indicates that $100,000 will be donated to build an addition to the city library provided other donors pledge an equal amount, donation revenue would be recognized only after the "matching" $100,000 has been raised from other donors.

Illustration 3-5 identifies the four types of nonexchange transactions and describes when revenues resulting from these transactions are recognized under the modified accrual basis of accounting. The last column of Illustration 3-5 provides representative journal entries, illustrating the application of the *measurable and available* recognition criteria. In some cases, revenues resulting from nonexchange transactions are recognized in different periods in the fund-basis and government-wide financial statements. For this reason, we will revisit this illustration in Chapter 8, which deals with the preparation of government-wide statements.

Imposed nonexchange transactions are taxes and other assessments imposed by governments that are not derived from underlying transactions. Examples include property taxes, special assessments, and fines and forfeits. A special rule applies to property taxes. Property taxes collected within 60 days after the end of the fiscal year may be deemed to be *available* and recorded as revenue in the year assessed, rather than the year collected. Amounts expected to be collected more than 60 days after year-end are not recognized as revenue when assessed, but as deferred revenue. Deferred taxes are not liabilities but are reported as deferred inflows of resources on the Balance Sheet.

Derived tax revenues result from taxes assessed on exchange transactions. Examples include taxes on retail sales, income, and gasoline. The amounts due are recorded in the time period the underlying transaction took place. For example, revenues due from taxes on the sale of gasoline should be recorded along with a receivable (from the retailers) in the month that the gasoline was sold. The revenue is recognized at the time of the exchange transaction provided the cash is expected to be collected shortly after the current fiscal year. If collection is expected to take place after the period considered *available* to pay current period liabilities (e.g., 60 days), it should be credited to deferred inflows of resources.

ILLUSTRATION 3-5 **Classes and Timing of Recognition of Revenue from Nonexchange Transactions**

Type	Description and Examples	Modified Accrual Basis (Governmental Fund-Basis)	Representative Transactions	Example Journal Entry (Governmental Fund-Basis Reporting)
Imposed Nonexchange Revenues	Taxes and other assessments that do not result from an underlying transaction. Examples include property taxes and special assessments imposed on property owners. Also includes fines and forfeits.	Record the receivable (and an allowance for uncollectibles) when an enforceable claim exists. Revenues should be recognized in the period for which the taxes are levied (i.e., budgeted), but are also subject to the availability rule. Property tax revenues expected to be collected > 60 days after year-end are deferred.	1. Property taxes levied. 2. Deferral of portion expected to be collected > 60 days after year-end.	1. Taxes Receivable ....Dr Estimated Uncollectible Taxes ....Cr Revenues Control ....Cr 2. Revenues Control ....Dr Deferred Revenues—Property Taxes ...Cr
Derived Tax Revenues	These are taxes assessed on exchange transactions conducted by businesses or citizens. Examples include sales, income, and excise taxes.	Record the receivable when the taxpayer's underlying transaction takes place. Revenues should be recognized when available and measurable. Revenues not expected to be collected in time to settle current liabilities are deferred (i.e., available and measurable criteria).	1. Income tax withholdings are received. 2. Additional income taxes expected to be received after year-end. Part of this will not be received in time to be available to settle current liabilities.	1. Cash ....Dr Revenues Control ....Cr 2. Taxes Receivable ....Dr Revenues Control ....Cr Deferred Revenues—Income Taxes ...Cr
Government-Mandated Nonexchange Transactions **Voluntary Nonexchange Transactions**	Grants from higher levels of government (federal or state) given to support a program. Since the program is required, the lower-level government has no choice but to participate. Donations and grants given to support a program. Since the program is not required, the receiving government voluntarily agrees to participate.	The recognition rules are the same for mandated and voluntary nonexchange grants. Record the revenue when all eligibility requirements have been met. In the case of reimbursement grants, revenue is recognized only when qualified expenditures have been incurred. In the case of advance funded grants, recognize revenues as qualified expenditures are incurred.	**Reimbursement grant:** 1. Incur qualified expenditures. 2. Recognize revenue. **Advance funded grant:** 3. Receipt of advance funding. 4. Incur expenditures and recognize revenue in an equal amount.	1. Expenditures Control .....Dr Accounts Payable/Cash ....Cr 2. Due from grantor ....Dr Revenues Control ....Cr 3. Cash ....Dr Deferred Revenues—Grants ....Cr 4a. Expenditures Control ...Dr Accounts Payable/Cash ....Cr 4b. Deferred Revenues—Grants ....Dr Revenues Control ....Cr

Government-mandated and **voluntary nonexchange transactions** are recorded as revenue when the eligibility requirements have been met. Generally this is when the receiving government has made qualifying expenditures under the grant agreement. Once qualifying expenditures have been made, the government records the grant revenue. The two types of grants differ in whether or not the receiving government has the ability to refuse to participate. Government-mandated grants are typically from higher levels of government (federal or state) given to support a required program. For example, a state may require school systems to mainstream certain students in the schools and provide funds to carry out this mandate. Because the program is required, the lower-level government has no choice but to accept.

Grants and support received from other governments are recorded as *intergovernmental revenue,* not transfers. Transfers move resources between funds within the same government. Resources received from other governments are inflows to the reporting entity and meet the definition of revenue.

SUMMARY

The current financial resources measurement focus and modified accrual basis of accounting are unique to the governmental funds of state and local governments. The focus is on the flow of financial resources rather than income measurement. Key elements include

- **Revenues.** Inflows of net financial resources from sources other than interfund transfers and debt proceeds. Revenues are recognized when they are both measurable and available to finance current expenditures.
- **Expenditures.** Outflows of net financial resources from sources other than interfund transfers that are recognized when a governmental fund incurs a liability pursuant to budgetary authority provided by appropriation.
- **Fund balance.** The net position (assets less liabilities) of a governmental fund, which can be classified as nonspendable, restricted, committed, assigned, or unassigned.

The General Fund and many special revenue funds record budgets, and their accounting systems are designed to assure compliance with budgets. Budgetary accounting is illustrated in the appendix to this chapter.

APPENDIX: BUDGETARY ACCOUNTING ILLUSTRATED

Budgets and Budgetary Accounts

The fact that budgets are legally binding upon government officials has led to the incorporation of a system of **budgetary accounts** within the General Fund and many special revenue funds. The budgetary accounts include **Estimated Revenues, Appropriations, Estimated Other Financing Sources,** and **Estimated Other**

Financing Uses. These accounts are used to record and amend the budget. Two additional budgetary accounts, ***Encumbrances*** and ***Budgetary Fund Balance—Reserve for Encumbrances,*** are used to record commitments of the government to purchase capital assets, goods, or services. Budgetary accounts are different from others in that they do not appear in the financial statements.

Assume the amounts appearing below have been legally approved as the budget for the General Fund of a city government for the fiscal year ending December 31, 2020. As of January 1, the first day of the fiscal year, the total Estimated Revenues should be recorded in the *Estimated Revenues Control* account, and the amounts that are expected to be recognized during the year from each revenue source, specified in the subsidiary ledger accounts. The account title, *Budgetary Fund Balance,* is used through the text to identify journal entries to establish or amend the budget. Since the budgetary accounts are closed at year-end, the choice of account title has no financial statement effect. If the budget provided for other financing sources, such as transfers, Entry 1 would indicate a debit to Estimated Other Financing Sources. An appropriate entry would be as follows:

	General Ledger		Subsidiary Ledger	
	Debits	**Credits**	**Debits**	**Credits**
1. Estimated Revenues Control.............	1,350,000			
Estimated Other Financing Source Control	0			
Budgetary Fund Balance..............		1,350,000		
Estimated Revenues Ledger:				
Taxes..............................			$ 882,500	
Licenses and permits.................			125,500	
Intergovernmental revenues...........			200,000	
Charges for services			90,000	
Fines and forfeits....................			32,500	
Miscellaneous revenues			19,500	
Total.............................			*$1,350,000*	

Subsidiary ledgers provide for the capture of detailed data specific to a business process. With the development of drop-down menus and other improvements, many accounting information systems have discontinued subsidiary ledgers. To save space throughout future chapters, we will demonstrate journal entries using control accounts to summarize revenue, expenditure, encumbrance, and budgetary accounts as if subsidiary ledgers are in use. These summarized postings are adequate to demonstrate the accounting concepts addressed.

The appropriations legally approved for 2020 for the General Fund of the same city should also be recorded in the *Appropriations Control* account, and the amounts that are appropriated for each function itemized in the budget should be recorded in subsidiary ledger accounts. An appropriate entry would be as follows:

	General Ledger		Subsidiary Ledger	
	Debits	Credits	Debits	Credits
2. Budgetary Fund Balance	1,300,000			
Appropriations Control		1,225,500		
Estimated Other Financing Uses Control		74,500		
Appropriations Ledger:				
General government				$ 129,000
Public safety				277,300
Highways and streets				84,500
Sanitation				50,000
Health				47,750
Welfare				51,000
Culture and recreation				44,500
Education				541,450
Total				*$1,225,500*
Estimated Other Financing Uses Ledger:				
Transfers out				74,500

In this example, the budget also provides for an expected transfer from the General Fund to another governmental fund. The budgetary account, *Estimated Other Financing Uses,* distinguishes transfers from appropriations.

It is acceptable to combine the two entries illustrated and make one General Fund entry to record Estimated Revenues, Appropriations, and Estimated Other Financing Uses; in this case there would be a credit to Budgetary Fund Balance for $50,000 (the amount by which Estimated Revenues exceeds Appropriations and Estimated Other Financing Uses).

Accounting for Revenues

During a fiscal year, actual revenues should be recognized in the general ledger accounts of governmental funds by credits to the Revenues Control account (offset by debits to receivable accounts for revenues susceptible to accrual or by debits to Cash for revenues that are recognized when the cash is collected). The revenue subsidiary ledger accounts are kept in exactly the same detail as the Estimated Revenues subsidiary ledger accounts. For example, assume that the General Fund collected revenues in cash from the following sources in these amounts:

	General Ledger		Subsidiary Ledger	
	Debits	Credits	Debits	Credits
3. Cash	1,314,500			
Revenues Control		1,314,500		
Revenues Ledger:				
Taxes				$ 881,300
Licenses and permits				103,000
Intergovernmental revenues				186,500
Charges for services				91,000
Fines and forfeits				33,200
Miscellaneous revenues				19,500
Total				*$1,314,500*

ILLUSTRATION 3-6 **Revenues Ledger**

NAME OF GOVERNMENT
Revenues Ledger
General Fund: Licenses and Permits Revenue
2020 Fiscal Year

Transaction	Reference	Estimated Revenues	Actual Revenues	Estimated Revenues Not Yet Realized
(1)	Initial budget	$125,500		$125,500
(3)	Collections		($103,000)	22,500
(7)	Budget revision	(22,500)		0
		$103,000	($103,000)	$ 0

$ amounts in ( ) denote credits.

Periodically throughout the year, elected officials and government managers will compare Estimated Revenue subsidiary account balances with actual revenues. If revenues fail to reach the levels anticipated when the budget was enacted, budget revisions may be warranted to prevent the government from deficit spending. Illustration 3-6 shows the Licenses and Permits Revenue subsidiary ledger in a typical spreadsheet format. Because Estimated Revenues are recorded with debits and Actual Revenues with credits, summing the two amounts provides a measure of the variance from expectations. In this case, Licenses and Permits Revenue did not meet expectations and a budget revision was deemed necessary (to be made later through entry 7). Since the budget is recorded at the beginning of the year and actual revenues are recognized throughout the year, the right-hand column, *Estimated Revenues Not Yet Realized,* will commonly have a (net) debit balance.

Accounting for Encumbrances and Expenditures

An appropriation is considered to be **expended** when authorized liabilities are incurred. Purchase orders and contracts are commitments that will result in liabilities when the goods or services are received or the contracts executed. Such expected expenditures are called **encumbrances.** To keep track of purchase orders and contracts outstanding, the Encumbrance Control account is debited and the Budgetary Fund Balance—Reserve for Encumbrances account credited for the amount of each purchase order or contract issued.

The following entries illustrate accounting for Encumbrances and Expenditures for the General Fund. Entry 4 reflects purchase orders issued pursuant to the authority contained in the General Fund appropriations. Amounts chargeable to each function for which purchase orders are issued are shown in the debits to the Encumbrances subsidiary accounts.

When goods or services are received, two entries are necessary: (1) Budgetary Fund Balance—Reserve for Encumbrances is debited, and Encumbrances Control is credited for the amount entered in these accounts when the encumbrance

	General Ledger		Subsidiary Ledger	
	Debits	Credits	Debits	Credits
4. Encumbrances Control	500,100			
Budgetary Fund Balance—Reserve for Encumbrances		500,100		
Encumbrances Ledger:				
General government			$ 73,200	
Public safety			115,100	
Highways and streets			34,600	
Sanitation			29,300	
Health			16,500	
Welfare			18,700	
Culture and recreation			14,800	
Education			197,900	
Total			*$500,100*	

documents were issued; and (2) Expenditures Control is debited and a liability account is credited for the amount to be paid. To accomplish the necessary matching of Appropriations, Encumbrances, and Expenditures, it is necessary that subsidiary ledger classifications of all three correspond exactly.

Entries 5a and 5b illustrate entries required to record the receipt of many of the items for which purchase orders were recorded in entry 4. Note that entry 4 is made for the amounts estimated at the time purchase orders or other commitment documents are issued. When the purchase orders are filled, the actual amount approved by the government for payment to the supplier may differ from the estimated amount recorded in the Encumbrances account. Since the Encumbrances Control account was debited in entry 4 for the estimated amount, the Encumbrances Control account must be credited for the same estimate, to the extent that purchase orders are filled (or canceled). The balance remaining in the Encumbrances Control account, therefore, is the estimated dollar amount of purchase orders that remain outstanding. Entry 5a shows the entry necessary on the assumption that most purchase orders recorded in entry 4 have now been filled but purchase orders for general government and education remain outstanding.

In contrast, expenditures should be recorded at the actual amount the government is obligated to pay the vendors who have filled the purchase orders. Entry 5b shows the entry necessary to record the liability for invoices approved for payment. The fact that estimated and actual amounts differ causes no accounting difficulties as long as goods or services are received in the same fiscal period as ordered.[2] The accounting treatment required when encumbrances outstanding at year-end are filled in a following year is illustrated in Chapter 4.

[2] Governments may require an additional approval (frequently in the form of a revised encumbrance) for amounts in excess of the original purchase order.

	General Ledger		Subsidiary Ledger	
	Debits	**Credits**	**Debits**	**Credits**
5a. Budgetary Fund Balance— Reserve for Encumbrances	492,300			
Encumbrances Control		492,300		
Encumbrances Ledger:				
General government				$ 68,300
Public safety				115,100
Highways and streets				34,600
Sanitation				29,300
Health				16,500
Welfare				18,700
Culture and recreation				14,800
Education				195,000
Total				*$492,300*
5b. Expenditures Control	491,800			
Accounts Payable		491,800		
Expenditures Ledger:				
General government			$ 69,100	
Public safety			115,100	
Highways and streets			34,400	
Sanitation			29,300	
Health			16,600	
Welfare			18,700	
Culture and recreation			14,800	
Education			193,800	
Total			*$491,800*	

Within the General Fund, expenditures are most typically classified by character and function. **Character classification** separates expenditures by the fiscal period they are assumed to benefit and include current, capital outlay, and debt service. **Functional classifications** reflect major activities or programs of the government. These are often performed by more than one department such as public safety, which might include the police and fire departments.

Other classification methods include organizational unit, activity, and object. Reporting expenditures by department is the most common form of classification by organizational unit, such as public safety or education. **Activities** are specific lines of work performed within a department. For example, solid waste collection and waste disposal may be duties of the public works department. Finally, **object** describes the item or service used, such as supplies, personnel services, and contracted services.

The encumbrance procedure is not always needed to make sure that appropriations are not overexpended. For example, although salaries and wages of government employees must be chargeable against valid and sufficient appropriations, many governments do not find it necessary to record encumbrances for recurring, relatively predictable items (such as payroll). Entry 6 shows the recording of expenditures of appropriations for salaries and wages not previously encumbered.

	General Ledger		Subsidiary Ledger	
	Debits	Credits	Debits	Credits
6. Expenditures Control	663,600			
Accounts Payable		663,600		
Expenditures Ledger:				
General government			$ 47,805	
Public safety.			143,295	
Highways and streets.			51,000	
Sanitation			26,950	
Health			27,900	
Welfare			28,100	
Culture and recreation.			26,100	
Education			312,450	
Total.			*$663,600*	

Illustration 3-7 shows a subsidiary ledger for the Education Department that supports all three general ledger control accounts: Appropriations, Encumbrances, and Expenditures. Again the ledger is presented in spreadsheet format. Because Appropriations are recorded as credits and Encumbrances and Expenditures as debits, summing the amounts results in "Unexpended Appropriations Balance." This may be interpreted as how much the Education Department may continue to expend

ILLUSTRATION 3-7 **Subsidiary Ledger for the Education Department**

NAME OF GOVERNMENT
Appropriations, Expenditures, and Encumbrances Ledger
General Fund: Education Department
2020 Fiscal Year

Transaction	Reference	Appropriation	Encumbrances	Expenditures	Unexpended Appropriations Balance
(2)	Budget	($541,450)			($541,450)
(4)	Purchase orders issued		$197,900		(343,550)
(5)	Invoices received and approved for payment		(195,000)	$193,800	(344,750)
(6)	Payrolls			312,450	(32,300)
		($541,450)	$ 2,900	$506,250	($ 32,300)

$ amounts in ( ) denote credits.

and remain within its budget. The purpose of encumbrance accounting is to prevent governments from overspending. This becomes apparent in Illustration 3-7. At the time a purchase order is issued (transaction 4), the encumbrance is recorded in this subsidiary ledger as a debit, thereby reducing the balance appearing in the unexpended appropriation column. The $2,900 appearing at the bottom of the encumbrances column represents purchase orders outstanding at year-end.

Budget Revisions

In most years, governments will prepare and adopt budget revisions. Assume the government in this example decided to revise the Estimated Revenues budget downward by $36,000 and the Appropriations budget upward by $8,000:

	General Ledger		Subsidiary Ledger	
	Debits	**Credits**	**Debits**	**Credits**
7. Budgetary Fund Balance	44,000			
Estimated Revenues Control		36,000		
Appropriations Control		8,000		
Revenues Ledger:				
Licenses and permits				$22,500
Intergovernmental revenues				13,500
Total				*$36,000*
Appropriations Ledger:				
Highways and streets				1,000
Sanitation				7,000
Total				*$ 8,000*

Budget revisions would require adjustments to the budgetary accounts and balances in the subsidiary ledgers (Illustrations 3-6 and 3-7).

Budgetary Comparison Schedule

As indicated earlier, governments report budget-actual comparisons, typically as schedules in Required Supplementary Information. Governments may elect instead to provide those comparisons as one of the basic statements rather than as a schedule. The schedule (or statement) must provide the original budget; the final budget; and the actual amounts of revenues, expenditures, and other financing sources and uses. A variance column between the final budget and actual amounts is encouraged but not required. The format of the schedule may be that of the budget document, or in the form used for the Statement of Revenues, Expenditures, and Changes in Fund Balances (see Illustration 2-16).

Whichever approach is used, the amounts in the Actual column are to be reported on the basis required by law for budget preparation, even if that basis differs from the basis provided in GASB standards. For example, in some states revenues must be budgeted on the cash basis. If the Budget and Actual columns of the budget-actual comparison schedule differ from GASB standards, the heading of the schedule will indicate that the schedule is on a *non-GAAP budgetary basis.* Standards further require that the amounts in the Actual column of the budgetary comparison schedule must be reconciled with the amounts shown in the Combined Statement of Revenues, Expenditures, and Changes in Fund Balances prepared in conformity with GAAP. This may be done either on the face of the budgetary comparison schedule or in a separate schedule.

Illustration 3-8 presents a budgetary comparison schedule as it might be prepared by the government in the example. Assume the government made a transfer out in the amount of $74,500 as provided in the budget. Note that the amounts charged to each department include both expenditures and encumbrances. The Education

ILLUSTRATION 3-8 **Budgetary Comparison Schedule**

NAME OF GOVERNMENTAL UNIT
Budgetary Comparison Schedule
General Fund (Non-GAAP Budgetary Basis)
For the Year Ended December 31, 2020

	Budgeted Amounts		Actual Amounts (Budgetary Basis)	Variance with Final Budget Positive (Negative)
	Original	Final		
Revenues:				
Taxes	$ 882,500	$882,500	$881,300	$ (1,200)
Licenses and permits	125,500	103,000	103,000	—
Intergovernmental revenues	200,000	186,500	186,500	—
Charges for services	90,000	90,000	91,000	1,000
Fines and forfeits	32,500	32,500	33,200	700
Miscellaneous revenues	19,500	19,500	19,500	—
Total revenues	1,350,000	1,314,000	1,314,500	500
Expenditures and encumbrances:				
General government	129,000	129,000	121,805	7,195
Public safety	277,300	277,300	258,395	18,905
Highways and streets	84,500	85,500	85,400	100
Sanitation	50,000	57,000	56,250	750
Health	47,750	47,750	44,500	3,250
Welfare	51,000	51,000	46,800	4,200
Culture and recreation	44,500	44,500	40,900	3,600
Education	541,450	541,450	509,150	32,300
Total expenditures and encumbrances	1,225,500	1,233,500	1,163,200	70,300
Excess (deficiency) of revenues over expenditures and encumbrances	124,500	80,500	151,300	70,800
Other financing sources (uses): transfers out	(74,500)	(74,500)	(74,500)	—
Net change in fund balance	50,000	6,000	76,800	70,800
Fund balance—beginning	350,000	350,000	350,000	—
Fund balance—ending	$ 400,000	$356,000	$426,800	$70,800

Department had actual expenditures of $506,250 ($193,800 + 312,450) and outstanding encumbrances of $2,900 ($197,900 − 195,000). The amount charged to the budget ($509,150) is the sum of these two amounts. This will differ from the amount reported in the Statement of Revenues, Expenditures, and Changes in Fund Balance, which would report only actual expenditures ($506,250).

Prior to issuing a new standard, GASB issues an exposure draft for public comment. In some cases, the Board may issue a preliminary views document, seeking public input before an exposure draft is issued. At the time this book went to publication, the GASB had issued a preliminary views document examining the financial reporting model. Among the changes under consideration is a requirement that the budgetary comparison information appear in the RSI section of the annual report. Additionally the Board is considering requiring the presentation of variances between (1) final budget and actual amounts and (2) original and final budget amounts. The GASB website provides information on the status of this and other projects on the Board's agenda.

Questions and Exercises

3–1. Using the annual report obtained for Exercise 1–1, answer the following questions:

a. Review the Statement of Revenues, Expenditures, and Changes in Fund Balances for the governmental funds. List the revenue source classes. Are expenditures reported by character? List the functional classifications under the current character classification. Are Other Financing Sources and Uses presented separately? Does your report show transfers in? Transfers out? Capital leases? Proceeds of bonds?

b. Review the Budgetary Comparison Schedule in the RSI section of your annual report (or Budgetary Comparison Statement, if that is used by your government) for the General Fund. Is the budgetary format used, or is the schedule in the format used for the Statement of Revenues, Expenditures, and Changes in Fund Balances? Does the report reflect the original budget, revised budget, and actual figures? Are variance columns presented comparing the actual with the revised budget and comparing the original with the revised budget? Is a reconciliation between the budgetary basis of accounting and GAAP presented on the budgetary comparison schedule or in a separate schedule? What are the major differences, if any? Are budgetary comparison schedules (or statements) presented for special revenue funds? Are all special revenue funds included?

c. Review the note that describes the basis of budgeting (usually in the Summary of Significant Accounting Policies). Is the budget prepared on the GAAP basis or some other basis? Are the differences, if any, between the budgetary basis and GAAP clearly explained?

3–2. The City of Oxbow General Fund has the following net resources at year-end:

- $199,000 unexpended proceeds of a state grant required by law to be used for health education.
- $7,000 of prepaid insurance.
- $600,000 rainy day fund approved by city council for use under specified circumstances.
- $200,000 budget stabilization fund to be used in the event of revenue shortfall.
- $275,000 provided for contractual obligations for capital projects.
- $26,000 unexpended proceeds of a tax required by law to be used for emergency 911 services.
- $1,559,000 total fund balance.

Required: Prepare the fund balance section of the Balance Sheet.

3–3. How should rainy day funds be reported?

3–4. Prepare budgetary entries, using general ledger control accounts only, for each of the following unrelated situations:

a. Anticipated revenues are $10.8 million; anticipated expenditures and encumbrances are $9.4 million.

b. Anticipated revenues are $9.7 million; anticipated expenditures and encumbrances are $10.1 million.

c. Anticipated revenues are $10.2 million; anticipated transfers from other funds are $1.3 million; anticipated expenditures and encumbrances are $9.7 million; anticipated transfers to other funds are $0.9 million.

d. Anticipated revenues are $9.9 million; anticipated transfers from other funds are $1.1 million; anticipated expenditures and encumbrances are $10 million; anticipated transfers to other funds are $1.1 million.

3–5. For each of the summarized transactions for the Village of Sycamore General Fund, prepare the general ledger journal entries.

a. The budget was formally adopted, providing for estimated revenues of $1,120,000 and appropriations of $987,000.

b. Revenues were received, all in cash, in the amount of $1,105,000.

c. Purchase orders were issued in the amount of $479,000.

d. Of the $479,000 in (*c*), purchase orders were filled in the amount of $470,500; the invoice amount was $470,000 (not yet paid).

e. Expenditures for payroll not encumbered amounted to $513,000 (not yet paid).

f. Amounts from (*d*) and (*e*) are paid in cash.

3–6. *a.* Distinguish between (1) exchange and (2) nonexchange transactions.

b. Identify and describe the four eligibility requirements for a government to recognize revenue in a nonexchange transaction.

c. GASB classifies nonexchange transactions into four categories. List the four categories, give an example of each, and outline asset and revenue recognition criteria for each.

3–7. *a.* Outline revenue recognition criteria under modified accrual accounting. Include specific requirements for property tax revenue.

b. Outline expenditure recognition criteria under modified accrual accounting.

3–8. Distinguish between the (1) GAAP basis and (2) budgetary basis of reporting for the General Fund.

3–9. The City of South River budget for the fiscal year ended June 30, 2020, included an appropriation for the police department in the amount of $8,900,000. During the month of July 2019, the following transactions occurred (in summary):

Purchase orders were issued in the amount of $520,000.

Of the $520,000 in purchase orders, $480,000 were filled, with invoices amounting to $478,000.

Salaries, not encumbered, amounted to $302,000.

A budget appropriations reduction in the amount of $50,000 was approved by the city council.

Prepare an appropriations, expenditures and encumbrances ledger for the police department for the month of July, in a format similar to Illustration 3-7.

3–10. Appearing below is the subsidiary ledger for the public safety department of the City of Boone. After the first month of the year, five entries have been made to the ledger.

Transaction	Appropriations	Encumbrances	Expenditures	Unexpended Appropriation Balance
1	($300,000)			($300,000)
2		$19,500		(280,500)
3		(16,000)	$15,500	(281,000)
4			11,000	(270,000)
5	18,000			(252,000)
	($282,000)	$ 3,500	$26,500	($252,000)

$ amounts in ( ) denote credits.

Describe the most likely event that led to each of the postings (items 1–5).

3–11. The Budgetary Comparison Schedule for the City of Vienna appears below. Several items of information are missing (denoted with "?").

CITY OF VIENNA
Budgetary Comparison Schedule
General Fund
For the Year Ended December 31, 2020

	Budgeted		Actual Amounts (Budgetary Basis)	Variance with Final Budget
	Original	Final		
Revenues:				
Taxes	$6,500,000	$6,465,000	$6,480,000	$ 15,000
Licenses	230,000	?	225,000	(5,000)
Intergovernmental	1,200,000	1,200,000	1,200,000	0
Miscellaneous	120,000	104,000	?	2,000
Total revenues	8,050,000	?	?	12,000
Expenditures and Encumbrances:				
General Government	2,700,000	2,602,000	?	98,500
Public Safety	4,050,000	4,200,000	4,215,000	(15,000)
Health and Welfare	?	?	1,198,000	22,000
Total expenditures and encumbrances	?	?	?	105,500
Net Change in Fund Balance	70,000	(23,000)	94,500	117,500
Fund Balance—Beginning	350,000	350,000	350,000	0
Fund Balance—Ending	$ 420,000	$ 327,000	$ 444,500	$117,500

Required:

a. Determine the missing amounts.

b. During the year, the City made a single budget revision. Prepare the journal entry to record that revision.

3–12. Following are transactions and events of the General Fund of the City of Springfield for the fiscal year ended December 31, 2020.

1. Estimated revenues (legally budgeted)

Property taxes	$5,641,000
Sales taxes	4,830,000
Licenses and permits	1,500,000
Miscellaneous	500,000

2. Appropriations

General government	$5,285,000
Culture and recreation	4,210,000
Health and welfare	1,000,000

3. Revenues received (cash)

Property taxes	$5,545,000
Sales taxes	4,700,000
Licenses and permits	1,700,000
Miscellaneous	800,000

4. Encumbrances issued (includes salaries and other recurring items)

	Estimated
General government	$5,275,000
Culture and recreation	4,630,000
Health and welfare	905,000

5. Goods and services received (paid in cash)

	Estimated	Actual
General government	$5,275,000	$5,285,000
Culture and recreation	4,630,000	4,610,000
Health and welfare	905,000	890,000

6. Budget revisions

Increase appropriations:	
General government	$140,000
Culture and recreation	110,000

7. Fund balance on January 1, 2020, was $753,000. There were no outstanding encumbrances at that date.
   a. Record the transactions using appropriate journal entries.
   b. Prepare a budgetary comparison schedule for the General Fund.

3–13. The town council of Riverside estimated revenues for 2020 to be $685,000 from property taxes and $165,000 from business licenses. The appropriations budget from the council was as follows:

General government	$395,000
Parks and recreation	110,000
Sanitation	90,000
Streets and sidewalks	160,000

In April, heavy spring rains caused some flooding near the river. As a result, a picnic area at River's Edge Park was ruined and several damaged shops had to shut down. The council adopted an upward revision of $50,000 for the parks and recreation budget and reduced the estimated revenues from business licenses by $30,000.

The General Fund began the year with a balance of $49,000. During the year, tax collections totaled $687,500 and revenues from business licenses were $124,000. Expenditures were $365,000 for general government, $160,500 for parks and recreation, $91,600 for sanitation, and $157,333 for streets and sidewalks. There are no outstanding encumbrances at year-end.

1. Prepare a budgetary comparison schedule for the General Fund for 2020.

Excel-Based Problems

Microsoft Excel templates are available in Connect for use with problems 3–14 and 3–15.

3–14. The Budgetary Comparison Schedule for the City of Salem appears in Illustration 2-16. Assume the general and subsidiary ledgers for the General Fund were lost after a water pipe burst. You are charged with reproducing the journal entries that took place during the year ended December 31, 2020.

Use the Excel file provided to prepare summary journal entries, including subsidiary ledger entries, for the following events:

a. Record the original budget.

b. Record the revisions to the budget.

c. Record the actual revenues.

d. Record the encumbrances, assuming all expenditures originated as encumbrances and the encumbrance and expenditure are equal in amount.

e. Record the actual expenditures and reversal of the associated encumbrance.

You should follow the format of the entries provided in entries 1 to 7 of the appendix to Chapter 3.

3–15. The City of Grafton's records reflected the following budget and actual data for the General Fund for the fiscal year ended June 30, 2020:

1. Estimated revenues:

Taxes (property)	$3,218,000
Licenses and permits	790,000
Intergovernmental revenues	310,000
Miscellaneous revenues	200,000

2. Revenues:

Taxes (property)	$3,215,500
Licenses and permits	792,000
Intergovernmental revenues	299,000
Miscellaneous revenues	212,000

3. Appropriations:

General government	$ 920,000
Public safety	2,090,000
Health and welfare	1,400,000

4. Expenditures:

General government	$ 878,000
Public safety	2,005,000
Health and welfare	1,398,000

5. Encumbrances outstanding as of June 30, 2019:

General government	$33,000
Public safety	82,000

6. Transfer to debt service fund:

Budget	$120,000
Actual	120,000

7. Budget revisions approved by the city council:

Estimated revenues:	
Decrease intergovernmental revenues	$10,000
Increase miscellaneous revenues	3,000
Appropriations:	
Decrease general government	2,000

8. Total fund balance at July 1, 2019, was $695,000.

Required: Use the Excel file provided to prepare a budgetary comparison schedule for the City of Grafton for the fiscal year ended June 30, 2020. Include outstanding encumbrances with expenditures.

Chapter **Four**

Accounting for the General and Special Revenue Funds

When the burdens of the presidency seem unusually heavy, I always remind myself it could be worse. I could be a mayor. Lyndon B. Johnson, 36th president of the United States

Winning the election is a good-news, bad-news kind of thing. Okay, now you're the mayor. The bad news is, now you're the mayor. Clint Eastwood, American actor and filmmaker, elected mayor of Carmel-by-the-Sea, California, in 1986

Learning Objectives

- Apply the modified accrual basis of accounting in the recording of a typical transaction of a General or special revenue fund.
- Prepare closing entries and classify fund balances.
- Prepare the fund-basis financial statements for a General or special revenue fund.

Modified accrual accounting is illustrated in Chapter 3 along with the use of budgetary accounts. This chapter applies that knowledge by recording common transactions and events in the operation of the General Fund and a special revenue fund of a hypothetical local government, the Village of Riverside. We will continue with the Village of Riverside in Chapters 5 through 8, demonstrating governmental, proprietary, and fiduciary fund accounting. Chapters 4 through 7 present the required fund-basis financial statements, and Chapter 8 illustrates the preparation of government-wide financial statements. In the interest of clarity of presentation, subsidiary ledgers are not illustrated throughout this chapter for the budgetary and operating statement accounts, but keep in mind that more detailed general ledger accounts for revenues, expenditures, and budgetary accounts would be required in actual situations.

Recall from Chapter 1 the following fund definitions:

- **Permanent funds** Account for resources provided under trust agreements that are restricted so that only earnings may be expended for purposes that benefit the public.
- **Capital projects funds** Account for and report financial resources that are *restricted, committed, or assigned* to expenditure for capital outlays.
- **Debt service funds** Account for and report financial resources that are *restricted, committed, or assigned* to expenditure for principal and interest.
- **Special revenue funds** Account for and report the proceeds of specific revenue sources that are *restricted or committed* to expenditure for a specified purpose other than debt service or capital projects.
- **General Fund** Accounts for and reports all financial resources not accounted for and reported in another fund.

The purpose of fund accounting is to segregate those financial resources that have constraints or limitations on their use so that the government may demonstrate compliance with those limitations. However, many resources have no limitations on their use and do not require segregation. The General Fund accounts for any resources not reported in one of the other (limited-use) funds. Every general-purpose government will have one, and only one, General Fund. Special revenue funds are an example of a fund established because of constraints placed on the use of government resources. Note, however, that special revenue funds are not used if the resources are required to be used to acquire capital assets or for the payment of interest and principal on long-term debt.

GASB standards provide particular guidance for the use of special revenue funds. Specifically, the standards require that special revenue funds be used only if a substantial portion of the resources are provided by one or more *restricted* or *committed* (but not *assigned*) revenue sources. Although a government may use resources to supplement a special revenue fund, assignment of resources is not sufficient for the establishment of a special revenue fund. In this respect, special revenue funds are notably different from debt service and capital project funds. Further, if the government expects that a substantial portion of the resources supporting a special revenue fund's activities will no longer be derived from restricted and committed revenue sources, the government should discontinue the use of a special revenue fund and report the fund's remaining resources in the General Fund.

OVERVIEW OF MODIFIED ACCRUAL ACCOUNTING

The financial statements of governmental funds are prepared on the **modified accrual basis of accounting.** Under modified accrual accounting, revenues are recognized when they are both **measurable** and **available** to finance expenditures of the current period. The term *measurable* means that the government is able to determine or reasonably estimate the amount. For example, property taxes are measurable before collection because the government determines the amount assessed and estimates any portion that will ultimately prove to be uncollectible. The term *available* means the amount is expected to be collected within the current period or soon enough thereafter to be used to pay liabilities of the current period.

The term *expenditure* rather than *expense* is used in modified accrual accounting. **Expenditures** are decreases in net financial resources and are generally recognized when the related liability is incurred. Expenditures may be for current purposes (such as salaries or electricity), for capital outlay, or for debt service (principal or interest). GASB *Interpretation 6, Recognition and Measurement of Certain Liabilities and Expenditures in Governmental Fund Financial Statements* (Sec. 1600.116), clarifies when expenditures should be recognized when using modified accrual accounting.

Generally, expenditures are recorded and fund liabilities are recognized when goods and services are received, regardless of whether resources are available in the fund. As a result, many expenditures are accrued, even in governmental funds. Expenditures for claims and judgments, compensated absences, pensions, and landfill closure and postclosure care costs of governmental funds should be recognized to the extent that the liabilities are going to be paid with available resources; additional amounts are reported as (long-term) liabilities in the government-wide statements. The most important exception is that debt service expenditures for principal and interest are recorded when *due*. This means that debt service expenditures are not accrued, but are recognized and fund liabilities are recorded on the maturity date.

INTERFUND TRANSACTIONS

Interfund transactions are transactions between individual funds. Interfund transactions are of particular interest to financial statement preparers and users because failure to properly report these transactions results in two funds being misstated. Additionally, because most of these transactions are eliminated in the government-wide statements, it is particularly important they be identified in the accounts of the affected funds.

Like related party transactions, transactions between funds of the same government may not be assumed to be arm's length in nature. An arm's-length transaction is one in which both parties act in their own self-interest and are not subject to pressure or influence. GASB standards require that interfund transactions be classified into two categories, each with two subcategories. Journal entries to record interfund transactions are based on these classifications. **Reciprocal interfund transactions** are the internal counterpart to exchange and exchange-like transactions and include **interfund loans** and **interfund services provided and used. Nonreciprocal interfund transactions** include **interfund transfers** and **interfund reimbursements.** The accounting for interfund transactions is described below and summarized in Illustration 4-1.

Interfund Loans

Interfund loans are resources provided from one fund to another with the understanding that they will be repaid in the future. The fund providing the resources records an interfund receivable (*Due from Other Funds*) and the fund receiving the resources records an interfund payable (*Due to Other Funds*). Long-term loans use the terms *Advance to Other Funds* and *Advance from Other Funds.* Interfund loan receivables and payables are reported separately on the balance sheets of the affected funds.

ILLUSTRATION 4-1 **Summary of Interfund Transactions**

Interfund Transaction	Description	Example Journal Entry: Fund Making the Payment	Example Journal Entry: Fund Receiving the Payment
Interfund Loans	In an interfund loan, resources are provided from one fund to another with the expectation they will be repaid.	Due from Other Fund ... Dr Cash .... Cr If the loan is long term, *Advance to Other Funds* is used in place of *Due from Other Funds.*	Cash .... Dr Due to Other Fund .... Cr If the loan is long-term, *Advance from Other Funds* is used in place of *Due to Other Funds.*
Interfund Services	The most common examples are services purchased by a governmental fund from an internal service (or enterprise) fund.	Expenditures .... Dr Cash .... Cr If the fund receiving the service is a proprietary fund, *Expense* is used in place of *Expenditure.*	Cash .... Dr Operating Revenue — Charges for Services ...... Cr
Interfund Transfers	In an interfund transfer, resources are provided from one fund to another **without** the expectation they will be repaid.	Other Financing Uses— Transfers Out .... Dr Cash .... Cr	Cash .... Dr Other Financing Sources— Transfers In .... Cr
Interfund Reimbursement	In an interfund reimbursement, one fund initially records a purchase that belongs in another fund.		Expenditures .... Dr Cash .... Cr
	The fund where the purchase correctly belongs reimburses the fund that made the payment, and the paying fund reverses its initial entry.	Expenditures .... Dr Cash .... Cr If the fund is a proprietary fund, *Expense* is used in place of *Expenditure.*	Cash .... Dr Expenditures .... Cr If the fund is a proprietary fund, *Expense* is used in place of *Expenditure.*

Interfund Services Provided and Used

Interfund services provided and used represent transactions involving sales and purchases of goods and services between funds. An example is the sale of water from a water utility (enterprise) fund to the General Fund. In these transactions, one fund records a revenue (enterprise, in this example) and the other fund records an expenditure or expense (the General Fund). Sometimes called *quasi-external transactions,* these transactions are reported as if they were transactions with parties outside the government.

Interfund Transfers

Interfund transfers represent flows of cash or other assets from one fund to another without a requirement for repayment. An example would be an annual transfer of resources from the General Fund to a debt service fund. Interfund transfers are classified as other financing sources (the debt service fund) and other financing uses (the General Fund).

Interfund Reimbursements

Interfund reimbursements represent repayments to the funds that initially recorded expenditures or expenses by the fund actually responsible for the payment. For example, assume the General Fund had previously debited expenditures to acquire postage, but the postage should have been charged to a special revenue fund. The reimbursement entry would have one fund (the special revenue fund) debit an expenditure and credit Cash. The other fund (the General Fund) would debit Cash and credit the expenditure, with the result that the expenditure would net to zero in the General Fund.

ILLUSTRATIVE CASE—GENERAL FUND

The following example illustrates typical transactions of a General Fund. The accounts follow the Governmental Fund Account Structure presented in Illustration 3-1 (in Chapter 3). Assume that at the beginning of fiscal year 2020, the Village of Riverside's General Fund had the following balances in its accounts:

	Debits	Credits
Cash	$100,000	
Taxes Receivable	400,000	
Estimated Uncollectible Taxes		$ 40,000
Interest and Penalties Receivable on Taxes	25,000	
Estimated Uncollectible Interest and Penalties		10,000
Accounts Payable		135,000
Deferred Inflows—Property Taxes		20,000
Due to Federal Government		30,000
Fund Balance		290,000
Totals	$525,000	$525,000

Two items appearing in the opening trial balance require particular note. The Deferred Inflows—Property Taxes account reflects the portion of the $400,000 in taxes receivable outstanding at year-end that management estimates will not be collected within the first 60 days of 2020. This amount was not recognized as revenue in 2019 but will need to be recognized in the current year.

The second item to note is Fund Balance. Within the trial balance, no distinction is made between the various categories of fund balance. To determine these, we will need to look to the December 31, 2019, balance sheet. Assume that total fund balance was reported as follows in last year's balance sheet:

Assigned for Other Purposes	$ 45,000
Unassigned	245,000

Assume the Village had outstanding purchase orders totaling $45,000 at the end of 2019 and it is the government's policy to honor those commitments. By issuing purchase orders that were unfilled at the end of the year, the Village had effectively expressed its intent to use $45,000 of the General Fund's net resources for a particular purpose, and this amount is classified as *Assigned Fund Balance.*

Use of Budgetary Accounts

GASB does not require governments to record budgets or encumbrances, and budgetary accounts do not appear in the general purpose financial statements. Nevertheless, governments commonly record these items because they are viewed as important elements of budgetary control and they facilitate the preparation of the Budgetary Comparison Schedule.

The approach we will use throughout this chapter is to record events in the budgetary accounts (Illustration 3-1) but not to intermix budgetary accounts with those accounts appearing in the general-purpose financial statements. Budgetary accounts will be closed at the end of each period. Should a government choose to carryover budgetary authority to the next fiscal year (as is commonly the case with outstanding encumbrances), we will re-establish that authority by reversing the prior period's closing entry in the new fiscal year. The first two entries for the Village of Riverside are made within the budgetary accounting system.

Recording the Budget

At the beginning of fiscal year 2020, the Village records the General Fund budget. Assume estimated revenues total $6,200,000, appropriations are $5,200,000, a planned transfer to the debt service fund is $204,000, and a planned transfer to establish an internal service fund is $596,000. The entry to record the budget would be as follows (keeping in mind that appropriate subsidiary ledger detail would be required in actual situations):

	Debits	Credits
1. Estimated Revenues Control	6,200,000	
Appropriations Control		5,200,000
Estimated Other Financing Uses Control		800,000
Budgetary Fund Balance		200,000

Re-establishment of Encumbrances

Assuming the $45,000 in purchase orders outstanding at the beginning of the year will be honored, it is necessary to re-establish the encumbrances. As we will see later in this chapter (entry 29b), outstanding encumbrances are closed at year-end. Re-establishing the encumbrance in the following year can be accomplished by reversing the effect of that entry.

2. Encumbrances Control (*prior year*)	45,000	
Budgetary Fund Balance—Reserve for Encumbrances		45,000

Recording Prior-Year Property Taxes as Revenues

Sometimes taxpayers are late in paying their property taxes, with the result that taxes may be collected in the year following the one in which they were assessed. GASB standards require property taxes expected to be collected within 60 days of year-end to be included in revenues of the year assessed. Taxes expected to be collected later than 60 days after year-end are deferred and recognized as revenue in the following year. At the end of last year, the Village of Riverside deferred $20,000 in property taxes, and that amount is reflected in the beginning trial balance as a deferred inflow of resources. Since these taxes will be available for 2020 expenditures, entry 3 recognizes that amount as a revenue for 2020 (see entry 27 for the current year deferral):

3. Deferred Inflows—Property Taxes	20,000	
Revenues Control		20,000

Tax Anticipation Notes Payable

In the trial balance of the General Fund of the Village of Riverside, liabilities (Accounts Payable and Due to Federal Government) total $165,000. Cash of the General Fund on the date of the trial balance amounts to $100,000. Although some collections of 2019 taxes receivable are expected early in the year, payrolls and other liabilities are incurred and must be paid before substantial amounts of cash will be collected. Accordingly, it may be desirable to arrange a short-term loan. The taxing power of the Village is ample security for a short-term loan. Local banks customarily meet the working capital needs of governmental units by accepting a "tax anticipation note" (a short-term note) from the government officials. Assume $200,000 is borrowed and recorded as follows:

4. Cash	200,000	
Tax Anticipation Notes Payable		200,000

Because the loan is short term, it is reflected as a liability of the fund, even though the fund uses modified accrual accounting.

Payment of Liabilities as Recorded

Checks were drawn to pay the accounts payable and the amount due to the federal government as of the end of the previous year:

5. Accounts Payable	135,000	
Due to Federal Government	30,000	
Cash		165,000

Issue Purchase Orders

In addition to the $45,000 encumbrance outstanding at the beginning of the year, purchase orders for materials and supplies are issued in the amount of $826,000. The general ledger entry to record encumbrances for the purchase orders is as follows:

6. Encumbrances Control	826,000	
Budgetary Fund Balance—Reserve for Encumbrances		826,000

Recording Property Tax Levy

Assume the gross amount of the current property tax levy is $3,265,306. After considering local economic conditions and the Village's tax collection policies, it is estimated that 2 percent of these taxes will be uncollectible. Therefore, the following entry is made at the time of the tax levy:

7. Taxes Receivable	3,265,306	
Estimated Uncollectible Taxes		65,306
Revenues Control		3,200,000

Keep in mind that Revenues Control and Taxes Receivable are control accounts and would be supported by subsidiary ledgers.

Collection of Delinquent Taxes

Delinquent taxes are subject to interest and penalties that must be paid at the time the tax bill is paid. The government should accrue the amount of penalties and interest at the time that the taxes become delinquent. Interest was accrued at year-end in 2019 and must also be accrued for the period from the date of last recording to the date when a taxpayer pays the delinquent taxes.

In the current year, the Village of Riverside collected delinquent taxes in the amount of $330,000, on which interest and penalties of $20,000 had been accrued at the end of 2019; further, $3,000 additional interest was collected for the period from the first day of 2020 to the dates on which the delinquent taxes were collected. Entry 8a records the additional interest as revenue; entry 8b records the collection of the delinquent taxes and the total interest and penalties owed on them.

	Debit	Credit
8a. Interest and Penalties Receivable	3,000	
Revenues Control		3,000
8b. Cash	353,000	
Taxes Receivable		330,000
Interest and Penalties Receivable		23,000

Collection of Current Taxes

Collections of property taxes levied are $2,700,000. Since the revenue was recognized at the time the receivable was recorded, Taxes Receivable (rather than revenue) is credited.

	Debit	Credit
9. Cash	2,700,000	
Taxes Receivable		2,700,000

Other Revenues

At the time of sale, sales taxes are paid to retailers who then submit them to the state government. Although the entire amount collected is paid to the state, typically only a portion of the tax is revenue to the state government and the remaining portion is revenue to the local government. Assume that retailers must submit sales taxes by the 10th of the following month to the state government and the state pays the local governments their share within 30 days. During the year, $1,350,000 of sales taxes resulting from 2020 sales are received by the Village from the state government. An additional $60,000 resulting from sales during the final week of 2020 are expected to be received in January 2021.

	Debit	Credit
10. Cash	1,350,000	
Due from State Government	60,000	
Revenues Control		1,410,000

Revenues from licenses and permits, fines and forfeits, intergovernmental revenue, charges for services, and other sources not susceptible to accrual are recognized on the cash basis. Collections for the year are $1,450,000.

11. Cash	1,450,000	
Revenues Control		1,450,000

Repayment of Tax Anticipation Notes

As tax collections begin to exceed current disbursements, it becomes possible for the Village of Riverside to repay the local bank for the money borrowed in tax anticipation notes (entry 4). Just as borrowing money did not involve the recognition of revenue, the repayment of the principal is merely the extinguishment of short-term debt of the General Fund and not an expenditure. Payment of interest, however, must be recognized as an expenditure. Assuming the interest is $5,000, the entry is as follows:

12. Tax Anticipation Notes Payable	200,000	
Expenditures Control	5,000	
Cash		205,000

Recognition of Expenditures for Encumbered Items

Some of the materials and supplies ordered last year and this year (see entries 2 and 6) were received. Invoices for the items received totaled $820,300; related purchase orders totaled $821,000. After inspection of the goods and supplies, the invoices were approved for payment. Since the purchase orders had been recorded as encumbrances against the appropriations, it is necessary to reverse the encumbered amount and to record the expenditure in the amount of the actual liability:

13a. Budgetary Fund Balance—Reserve for Encumbrances	821,000	
Encumbrances Control		821,000
13b. Expenditures Control (*prior year*)	45,000	
Expenditures Control	775,300	
Accounts Payable		820,300

The designation of expenditures (by notation) as relating to a prior year is desirable, since expenditures arising from 2019 encumbrances would typically not be reflected in the Budgetary Comparison Schedule for fiscal year 2020. Instead, they would have been reflected in the previous year's Budgetary Comparison Schedule.

Payrolls and Payroll Taxes

The gross pay of employees of General Fund departments amounted to $3,345,000. The Village of Riverside does not use the encumbrance procedure for payrolls. The gross pay is charged against the appropriations of the individual departments through a subsidiary ledger (not presented). Deductions from gross pay for the period amounted to $78,000 for employees' state income tax withholdings and $686,000 due to the federal government ($430,000 for federal income tax withholdings and $256,000 for the employees' share of Social Security and Medicare taxes). The entries to record the payroll and subsequent payment are as follows:

	Debits	Credits
14a. Expenditures Control	3,345,000	
Due to Federal Government		686,000
Due to State Government		78,000
Wages Payable		2,581,000
14b. Wages Payable	2,581,000	
Cash		2,581,000

The Village is liable for the employer's share of Social Security tax and Medicare tax ($256,000) and for contributions to additional retirement funds established by state law (assumed to amount to $167,000 for the year). The Village's liabilities for its contributions are recorded:

	Debits	Credits
15. Expenditures Control	423,000	
Due to Federal Government		256,000
Due to State Government		167,000

Payment on Account and Other Items

Payment is made on $770,000 of the outstanding accounts payable, and the amounts due the state and federal governments are paid in full:

	Debits	Credits
16. Accounts Payable	770,000	
Due to Federal Government	942,000	
Due to State Government	245,000	
Cash		1,957,000

Correction of Errors

No problems arise in the collection of current taxes if they are collected as billed; the collections are debited to Cash and credited to Taxes Receivable. Sometimes, even in a well-designed and well-operated system, errors occur and must be corrected. If, for example, duplicate tax bills totaling $1,200 were sent out for the same piece of property, the following entry would be required. (The error also caused a slight overstatement of the credit to Estimated Uncollectible Taxes in entry 7, but the error in that account is not considered material enough to correct.)

	Debit	Credit
17. Revenues Control	1,200	
Taxes Receivable		1,200

Audit procedures may disclose errors in the recording of expenditures during the current year or during a prior year. If the error occurred during the current year, the Expenditures Control account and the proper subsidiary ledger account can be debited or credited as needed to correct the error. If the error occurred in a prior year, however, the Expenditures account in error has been closed to Fund Balance, so theoretically the correcting entry should be made to that account. As a practical matter, immaterial changes resulting from corrections of prior period errors may be recorded in the current period Revenues or Expenditures accounts.

Amendment of the Budget

Comparisons of budgeted and actual revenues by sources and comparisons of departmental or program appropriations with expenditures and encumbrances may indicate the desirability or necessity of amending the budget during the fiscal year. For example, assume that the revenues budget was increased by $50,000 in the Charges for Services source category and that the appropriation for the public works department was increased by $100,000. The amendments to the budget would be recorded when they were legally approved, as follows:

	Debit	Credit
18. Estimated Revenues Control	50,000	
Budgetary Fund Balance	50,000	
Appropriations Control		100,000

Interfund Transactions

Interfund Services Provided and Used Interfund services provided and used are recognized as revenues or expenditures (or expenses in the case of proprietary funds) of the funds involved in the same manner as transactions with outside organizations.

Water utilities ordinarily provide a city with fire hydrants and water service for fire protection at a flat annual charge. A government-owned water utility expected to support the cost of its operations by user charges should be accounted for as an enterprise fund. Fire protection is logically budgeted as an activity of the fire department, a General Fund department. Assuming that the amount charged by the water utility to the General Fund for hydrants and water service was $80,000, the General Fund entry would be as follows:

19. Expenditures Control	80,000	
Due to Other Funds (Water Utility Fund).		80,000

The account *Due to Other Funds* is a current liability. The enterprise fund would also record this transaction (see enterprise fund entry 1 in Chapter 6).

Another common transaction for the General Fund is the receipt of supplies or services from an internal service fund established to centralize purchasing and distribution services among government departments. Assume that the General Fund received $377,000 in supplies from the Supplies Fund and later made a partial payment of $322,000 in cash. The entries would be as follows:

20a. Expenditures Control	377,000	
Due to Other Funds (Supplies Fund)		377,000
20b. Due to Other Funds (Supplies Fund)	322,000	
Cash		322,000

The internal service fund would also record this (see internal service fund entries 5b and 7 in Chapter 6).

Interfund Transfers Assuming that the General Fund made the budgeted transfer to a debt service fund for the payment of interest and principal, the General Fund entry would be as follows:

21a. Other Financing Uses—Transfers Out Control.	204,000	
Due to Other Funds (Debt Service Fund).		204,000

Note that transfers are identified as *other financing uses* rather than *expenditures.* Other financing uses are reported in a different section of the activity statement than expenditures. When the cash is transferred, the entry would be as follows:

21b. Due to Other Funds (Debt Service Fund).	204,000	
Cash		204,000

The debt service fund will make a corresponding entry to record the transfer. See debt service entry 19 in Chapter 5.

Other transfers are nonroutine transactions, often made to establish or discontinue a fund. Assume that the General Fund made a permanent transfer of $596,000 to establish an internal service fund. The General Fund entry would be as follows:

22. Other Financing Uses—Transfers Out Control.	596,000	
Cash		596,000

See internal service fund entry 1 in Chapter 6.

Interfund Reimbursements Assume that \$20,000 of the expenditures in entry 13b related to supplies used for road maintenance should have been charged to the Motor Fuel Tax Fund, a special revenue fund. To correct this, \$20,000 cash is moved from the Motor Fuel Tax Fund to reimburse the General Fund. Accordingly, \$20,000 is charged to the Motor Fuel Tax Fund (see entry 3 in the special revenue fund section of this chapter) and General Fund expenditures are reduced by \$20,000.

23. Cash.	20,000	
Expenditures Control		20,000

Write-off of Uncollectible Delinquent Taxes

Government officials should review aged schedules of receivables periodically to determine the adequacy of allowance accounts and to authorize the write-offs of items judged to be uncollectible. Although the levy of property taxes creates a lien against the underlying property in the amount of the tax, accumulated taxes may exceed the market value of the property, or in the case of personal property (e.g., cars), the property may be removed from the jurisdiction of the government. When delinquent taxes are deemed to be uncollectible, the related interest and penalties must also be written off. If the treasurer of the Village of Riverside received approval to write off delinquent taxes totaling \$30,000 and related interest and penalties of \$3,000, the entry would be as follows:

24. Estimated Uncollectible Taxes	30,000	
Taxes Receivable		30,000
25. Estimated Uncollectible Interest and Penalties.	3,000	
Interest and Penalties Receivable		3,000

When delinquent taxes are written off, the tax bills are retained in the files, although they are no longer subject to general ledger control, because changes in conditions may make it possible to collect the amounts in the future. If collections of write-off taxes are made, the amounts should be returned to general ledger control by making an entry that is the reverse of the write-off entry, so that the procedures described in entries 8a and 8b may be followed.

Accrual of Interest and Penalties

Delinquent taxes are subject to interest and penalties. The amount of interest and penalties earned by the General Fund of the Village of Riverside and not yet recognized is $56,410, but it is expected that only $39,490 of that can be collected. The entry would be as follows:

26. Interest and Penalties Receivable	56,410	
Estimated Uncollectible Interest and Penalties		16,920
Revenues Control		39,490

Deferral of Property Tax Revenue

A review of the taxes receivable subsidiary ledger indicated that approximately $40,000 would probably be received more than 60 days beyond the end of the fiscal year. The 60-day rule requires that the $40,000 be deferred and classified as a deferred inflow of resources on the Balance Sheet.

27. Revenues Control	40,000	
Deferred Inflows—Property Taxes		40,000

Special Item

GASB standards require that extraordinary items and special items be reported separately after other financing sources and uses. Extraordinary items are significant transactions or other events that are both unusual and infrequent. **Special items** are significant transactions or other events that are *either* unusual or infrequent but *within* the control of management. Assume the Village sold land for $300,000.

28. Cash	300,000	
Special Item—Proceeds from Sale of Land		300,000

The reduction in the land account would be reported in the government-wide financial statements. Because governmental funds report only current financial resources, land does not need to be removed from the General Fund's assets.

Preclosing Trial Balance

Illustration 4-2 presents the general ledger control accounts after all journal entries have been posted. Note that only Balance Sheet accounts have beginning balances (denoted *bb*). Budgetary accounts appear in the shaded portion of the illustration. It is often useful to prepare a trial balance before proceeding with the year-end closing entries and financial statements. Illustration 4-3 presents the preclosing trial balance for the General Fund at December 31, 2020.

ILLUSTRATION 4-2 General Ledger Control Accounts

CASH

Ref	Debit	Credit	Ref
*bb	100,000		
(4)	200,000	165,000	(5)
(8)	353,000	205,000	(12)
(9)	2,700,000	2,581,000	(14)
(10)	1,350,000	1,957,000	(16)
(11)	1,450,000	322,000	(20)
(23)	20,000	204,000	(21)
(28)	300,000	596,000	(22)
	443,000		

TAXES RECEIVABLE

Ref	Debit	Credit	Ref
bb	400,000		
(7)	3,265,306	330,000	(8)
		2,700,000	(9)
		1,200	(17)
		30,000	(24)
	604,106		

ESTIMATED UNCOLLECTIBLE TAXES RECEIVABLE

Ref	Debit	Credit	Ref
		40,000	bb
		65,306	(7)
(24)	30,000		
		75,306	

INTEREST AND PENALTY RECEIVABLE

Ref	Debit	Credit	Ref
bb	25,000		
(8)	3,000	23,000	(8)
(26)	56,410	3,000	(24)
	58,410		

ESTIMATED UNCOLLECTIBLE INTEREST AND PENALTY REC.

Ref	Debit	Credit	Ref
		10,000	bb
(24)	3,000	16,920	(26)
		23,920	

DUE FROM STATE GOVERNMENT

Ref	Debit	Credit	Ref
bb	-		
(10)	60,000		
	60,000		

ACCOUNTS PAYABLE

Ref	Debit	Credit	Ref
		135,000	bb
(5)	135,000	820,300	(13)
(14)	2,581,000	2,581,000	(14)
(16)	770,000		
		50,300	

TAX ANTICIPATION NOTES PAYABLE

Ref	Debit	Credit	Ref
		-	bb
(12)	200,000	200,000	(4)
		-	

DUE TO STATE GOVERNMENT

Ref	Debit	Credit	Ref
		-	bb
(16)	245,000	78,000	(14)
		167,000	(15)
		-	

DUE TO FEDERAL GOVERNMENT

Ref	Debit	Credit	Ref
		30,000	bb
(5)	30,000	686,000	(14)
(16)	942,000	256,000	(15)
		-	

DEFERRED INFLOWS: PROPERTY TAXES

Ref	Debit	Credit	Ref
		20,000	bb
(3)	20,000	40,000	(27)
		40,000	

DUE TO OTHER FUNDS

Ref	Debit	Credit	Ref
		-	bb
(20)	322,000	80,000	(19)
(21)	204,000	377,000	(20)
		204,000	(21)
		135,000	

REVENUES CONTROL

Ref	Debit	Credit	Ref
(17)	1,200	20,000	(3)
(27)	40,000	3,200,000	(7)
		3,000	(8)
		1,410,000	(10)
		1,450,000	(11)
		39,490	(26)
		6,081,290	

EXPENDITURES CONTROL

Ref	Debit	Credit	Ref
(12)	5,000	20,000	(23)
(13)	820,300		
(14)	3,345,000		
(15)	423,000		
(19)	80,000		
(20)	377,000		
	5,030,300		

TRANSFERS OUT CONTROL

Ref	Debit	Credit	Ref
(21)	204,000		
(22)	596,000		
	800,000		

SPECIAL ITEM PROCEEDS SALE LAND

Ref	Debit	Credit	Ref
		300,000	(28)
		300,000	

FUND BALANCE

Ref	Debit	Credit	Ref
		290,000	bb
		290,000	

BUDGETARY FUND BALANCE

Ref	Debit	Credit	Ref
(18)	50,000	200,000	(1)
		150,000	

ESTIMATED REVENUE CONTROL

Ref	Debit	Credit	Ref
(1)	6,200,000		
(18)	50,000		
	6,250,000		

APPROPRIATIONS CONTROL

Ref	Debit	Credit	Ref
		-	
		5,200,000	(1)
		100,000	(18)
	5,300,000		

ESTIMATED OTHER FIN. USES CONTROL

Ref	Debit	Credit	Ref
		-	
		800,000	(1)
		800,000	

BFB RESERVE FOR ENCUMBRANCES

Ref	Debit	Credit	Ref
		45,000	(2)
		826,000	(6)
(13)	821,000		
		50,000	

ENCUMBRANCES CONTROL

Ref	Debit	Credit	Ref
(2)	45,000		
(6)	826,000		
		821,000	(13)
	50,000		

* bb indicates balance at January 1.

ILLUSTRATION 4-3 Preclosing Trial Balance

VILLAGE OF RIVERSIDE General Fund Trial Balance As of December 31, 2020		
	Debits	**Credits**
FINANCIAL STATEMENT ACCOUNTS		
Cash	$ 443,000	
Taxes Receivable	604,106	
Estimated Uncollectible Taxes		$ 75,306
Interest and Penalties Receivable	58,410	
Estimated Uncollectible Interest and Penalties		23,920
Due from State Government	60,000	
Accounts Payable		50,300
Due to Water Utility Fund		80,000
Due to Supplies Fund		55,000
Deferred Inflows—Property Taxes		40,000
Fund Balance		290,000
Revenues Control		6,081,290
Expenditures Control	5,030,300	
Other Financing Uses—Transfers Out	800,000	
Special Item—Proceeds from Sale of Land		300,000
Totals	$6,995,816	$6,995,816
BUDGETARY ACCOUNTS		
Budgetary Fund Balance		$ 150,000
Estimated Revenues Control	$6,250,000	
Appropriations Control		5,300,000
Estimated Other Financing Uses Control		800,000
Budgetary Fund Balance—Reserve for Encumbrances		50,000
Encumbrances Control	50,000	
Totals	$6,300,000	$6,300,000

Similar to Illustration 4-2, the budgetary accounts appear in the shaded area at the bottom of the illustration. Since this is a preclosing trial balance, the amount appearing in Fund Balance is the beginning of year balance.

Closing Entries

The essence of the closing process is the reclassification of the operating statement accounts for the year to the Fund Balance account. Additionally, all budgetary accounts are closed. Note that the first entry (entry 29a) has the effect of reversing the entry to record the budget entry (entry 1) and the entry to amend the budget (entry 18). The second entry closes the outstanding encumbrances.

29a. Appropriations Control	5,300,000	
Estimated Other Financing Uses Control	800,000	
Budgetary Fund Balance	150,000	
Estimated Revenues Control		6,250,000
29b. Budgetary Fund Balance—Reserve for Encumbrances	50,000	
Encumbrances Control		50,000

At the end of a fiscal year, outstanding encumbrances may or may not carry forward to the following year, depending on the policy of the government. If they do not carry forward, encumbrances are said to *lapse*. If it is the policy to carry forward encumbrances from one year to the next, the $50,000 encumbrance would be re-established in 2021 with a journal entry similar to entry 2.

Although the general-purpose financial statements are unaffected by whether the encumbrance is carried forward or lapses, a government's policy with respect to this issue commonly affects the Budgetary Comparison Schedule. If the government chooses to carry forward the outstanding encumbrance, the $50,000 would appear with expenditures in the 2020 Budgetary Comparison Schedule. However, if encumbrances lapse at year-end, any resulting expenditure would appear in the 2021 schedule.

Within governmental funds, activity accounts (sources and uses of funds) are closed to *Fund Balance.*

30. Revenues Control	6,081,290	
Special Items—Proceeds from Sale of Land	300,000	
Expenditures Control		5,030,300
Other Financing Uses—Transfer Out Control		800,000
Fund Balance		550,990

After this closing entry is posted, the Fund Balance account represents the net resources of the General Fund that are available for future appropriation and has a balance of $840,990 ($290,000 beginning balance plus $550,990 from the closing entry 30). The Balance Sheet of the General Fund must report fund balance within the five categories described in Chapter 3.

The General Fund has no unused supplies or prepaid expenses, so there are no *nonspendable* resources in this example. Assume that the Village received a grant of $350,000 from the state that is restricted to qualifying expenditures associated with public works. At year-end, $75,000 of this grant remained unexpended and is reported as *Restricted Fund Balance.* Assume also that the Village Council has formally *committed* $100,000 of the remaining fund balance to capital projects improving the communication equipment of the police, fire, and EMT programs. The (preclosing) balance of Reserve for Encumbrances represents purchase orders outstanding at year-end that will be paid next year from the General Fund. For purposes of fund balance reporting, these purchase commitments reflect an expressed intent by the government to use $50,000 of the General Fund's net resources for specific purposes and should be reported as *Assigned Fund Balance.* The residual amount of the fund's net resources ($615,990) is reported as *Unassigned Fund Balance.* These amounts are summarized as follows:

Fund Balance Category	Amount	Explanation
Nonspendable	$ 0	The General Fund has no supplies or prepaid items.
Restricted	75,000	Unexpended portion of a state grant for use to support public works.
Committed	100,000	Funds formally committed by Village Council to the purchase of communications equipment.
Assigned	50,000	Purchase orders outstanding at year-end.
Unassigned	615,990	Residual value (i.e., plug) of the General Fund.
Total Fund Balance	$840,990	

Some governments may choose to allocate these amounts to individual fund balance accounts through journal entry. Our approach will be to determine the components of fund balance in the manner illustrated above and present the totals directly in the balance sheet. In this way we reduce the number of accounts necessary to record changes in overall fund balance.

Year-End Financial Statements

The Balance Sheet for the General Fund of the Village of Riverside as of the end of 2020 is shown in Illustration 4-4. Trace specific account balances back to the T-accounts appearing in Illustration 4-2. If the General Fund has both a due from and a due to another fund, it is permissible to offset these amounts, provided they are with the same fund. (It should be emphasized, however, that it is not acceptable to offset a receivable from one fund against a payable to a different fund.)

The General Fund is also required to report a Statement of Revenues, Expenditures, and Changes in Fund Balance. Illustration 4-5 presents the actual revenues and expenditures that resulted from transactions illustrated in this chapter, including the expenditure of $45,000 relating to a 2019 encumbrance (entry 13). Note that the expenditures do not include the $50,000 encumbrance outstanding at the end of 2020.

For governments with more than one governmental fund, the information shown in Illustration 4-5 would be presented in columnar form with other government-type funds in the Statement of Revenues, Expenditures, and Changes in Fund Balances for governmental funds (see Chapter 5).

Illustration 4-6 presents the Budgetary Comparison Schedule for the General Fund that would appear in the required supplementary information (detailed amounts are assumed for purposes of the illustration). Note the required reconciliation between the budgetary basis and GAAP basis reporting of expenditures appearing at the bottom of the schedule. Additional differences may exist and would require similar explanation.

ILLUSTRATION 4-4 Balance Sheet for the General Fund

VILLAGE OF RIVERSIDE General Fund Balance Sheet As of December 31, 2020		
Assets		
Cash		$ 443,000
Taxes Receivable	$604,106	
Less Estimated Uncollectible Accounts	(75,306)	
Net Taxes Receivable		528,800
Interest and Penalties Receivable	58,410	
Less Estimated Uncollectible Accounts	(23,920)	
Net Interest and Penalties Receivable		34,490
Due from State Government		60,000
Total Assets		$1,066,290
Liabilities, Deferred Inflows, and Fund Balances		
Liabilities:		
Accounts Payable	$ 50,300	
Due to Water Utility Fund	80,000	
Due to Supplies Fund	55,000	
Total Liabilities		$ 185,300
Deferred Inflows of Resources:		
Property Taxes		40,000
Fund Balance:		
Restricted for Public Works	75,000	
Committed to Capital Projects	100,000	
Assigned for Other Purposes	50,000	
Unassigned	615,990	
Total Fund Balance		840,990
Total Liabilities, Deferred Inflows, and Fund Balances		$1,066,290

ILLUSTRATIVE CASE—SPECIAL REVENUE FUND

Special revenue funds are used when it is desirable to provide separate reporting of resources that are *restricted or committed* to expenditure for a specified purpose other than debt service or capital projects. Resources appropriately reported within proprietary or fiduciary funds are also excluded from special revenue funds. Governments should attempt to keep the number of special revenue and other funds to a reasonable number. Often a functional classification in the General Fund is adequate to meet the information needs of users interested in assuring compliance with resource limitations.

Commonly, special revenue funds are used for intergovernmental grants in which the federal or state government provides resources to local governments. The legislation providing these resources typically imposes restrictions on the use of

ILLUSTRATION 4-5 Statement of Revenues, Expenditures, and Changes in Fund Balance

VILLAGE OF RIVERSIDE
General Fund
Statement of Revenues, Expenditures, and Changes in Fund Balance
For the Year Ended December 31, 2020

Revenues (amounts assumed):		
Property taxes	$3,178,800	
Interest and penalties	42,490	
Sales taxes	1,410,000	
Licenses and permits	540,000	
Fines and forfeits	430,000	
Intergovernmental revenue	350,000	
Charges for services	100,000	
Miscellaneous revenues	30,000	
Total revenues		$6,081,290
Expenditures (amounts assumed):		
General government	810,000	
Public safety	2,139,500	
Public works	630,000	
Health and welfare	480,100	
Parks and recreation	527,400	
Contribution to retirement funds	423,000	
Miscellaneous expenditures	20,300	
Total expenditures		(5,030,300)
Excess of revenues over expenditures		1,050,990
Other financing uses:		
Transfers out		(800,000)
Special item:		
Proceeds from sale of land		300,000
Net change in fund balance		550,990
Fund balance, January 1, 2020		290,000
Fund balance, December 31, 2020		$ 840,990

intergovernmental revenues. Special revenue funds may also be necessary in the case of taxes that require the government to use the tax proceeds to support specific activities. An example is the emergency 911 surcharge commonly paid by consumers to phone service providers. These taxes are collected by the phone company and paid to city or county governments. The taxes are required by law to be used for the support of the 911 emergency phone network.

As an illustration, assume the Village of Riverside maintains a Motor Fuel Tax Fund, as required by state law. Revenues include state motor fuel tax receipts and state reimbursement grants. Expenditures are incurred for road repairs and maintenance. A legally adopted annual budget is not required or used. Assume, at the beginning of 2020, the Motor Fuel Tax Fund has cash of $212,500 and (restricted) fund balance in the same amount.

ILLUSTRATION 4-6 **Budgetary Comparison Schedule**

VILLAGE OF RIVERSIDE
Budgetary Comparison Schedule
General Fund
For the Year Ended December 31, 2020

	Budgeted Amounts		Actual Amounts (BUDGETARY BASIS)*	Variance with Final Budget Positive (Negative)
	Original	FINAL		
Revenues:				
Property taxes	$3,000,000	$3,000,000	$3,178,800	$178,800
Interest and penalties	30,000	30,000	42,490	12,490
Sales taxes	1,763,000	1,763,000	1,410,000	(353,000)
Licenses and permits	550,000	550,000	540,000	(10,000)
Fines and forfeits	420,000	420,000	430,000	10,000
Intergovernmental	350,000	350,000	350,000	—
Charges for services	50,000	100,000	100,000	—
Miscellaneous	37,000	37,000	30,000	(7,000)
Total revenues	6,200,000	6,250,000	6,081,290	(168,710)
Current Expenditures and Encumbrances:				
General government	821,000	821,000	765,000	56,000
Public safety	2,240,000	2,240,000	2,139,500	100,500
Public works	540,000	640,000	630,000	10,000
Health and welfare	528,000	528,000	480,100	47,900
Parks and recreation	628,000	628,000	577,400	50,600
Contribution to retirement funds	423,000	423,000	423,000	—
Miscellaneous	20,000	20,000	20,300	(300)
Total expenditures and encumbrances	5,200,000	5,300,000	5,035,300	264,700
Excess (deficiency) of revenues Over expenditures & encumbrances	1,000,000	950,000	1,045,990	95,990
Other financing sources (uses)				
Special item: sale of land			300,000	300,000
Transfers to other funds	(800,000)	(800,000)	(800,000)	—
Net change in fund balance	200,000	150,000	545,990	395,990
Fund balance, beginning	290,000	290,000	290,000	—
Fund balance, ending	$ 490,000	$ 440,000	$ 835,990	$395,990

Budget to GAAP Differences*	**General Government Expenditures**	**Parks and Recreation Expenditures**	**Total Fund Balance Dec. 31, 2020**
Budgetary Basis	$765,000	$577,400	$835,990
Encumbrances outstanding 12-31-2019	45,000		(45,000)
Encumbrances outstanding 12-31-2020		(50,000)	50,000
GAAP Basis	810,000	527,400	840,990

**Explanation:* Encumbrances for goods and services ordered but not received are reported in the year the orders are placed for budgetary purposes, but they are reported in the year received for GAAP purposes.

Motor Fuel Tax Revenues

During 2020, the State notified the Village that it would be granted $650,000 in motor fuel taxes. Records show $575,000 was received in cash; the remainder is accrued as a receivable (and revenue) because it will be received within 60 days of the end of the fiscal year. Motor fuel taxes are a derived tax revenue; under modified accrual accounting, revenues are recognized in the same year that the underlying transactions (sales of fuel by gas stations) take place. Note that control accounts are not used since there is a limited number of revenues and expenditures.

	Debits	Credits
1. Cash	575,000	
Due from State Government	75,000	
Motor Fuel Tax Revenues		650,000

Expenditures for Road Repairs

Expenditures for road repairs amounted to $605,000, of which $540,000 was paid during the year. Note that encumbrance accounting may be used but is omitted for the sake of brevity.

	Debits	Credits
2. Current Expenditures—Public Works	605,000	
Cash		540,000
Accounts Payable		65,000

Reimbursement to General Fund

Entry 23 in the General Fund example related to supplies, originally charged to expenditures by the General Fund, that were for road repairs and should be charged to the Motor Fuel Tax Fund. The corresponding interfund reimbursement entry charges the expenditure to the Motor Fuel Tax Fund and reimburses cash to the General Fund.

	Debits	Credits
3. Current Expenditures—Public Works	20,000	
Cash		20,000

Reimbursement Grant Accounting

Assume the State awarded the Village a grant of $450,000 for major repairs to three Village intersections. The funds will be released by the State only as work is completed, as a reimbursement. This represents an eligibility requirement under

GASB revenue recognition standards. Accordingly, grant revenues and receivables would be recognized at the same time that expenditures are incurred. During 2020, expenditures in the amount of $350,000 were incurred, of which $280,000 was paid. The Village billed the State $350,000 and received $300,000 cash before the end of the year.

	Debit	Credit
4. Current Expenditures—Public Works	350,000	
Cash		280,000
Accounts Payable		70,000
5. Due from State Government	350,000	
State Reimbursement Grant Revenue		350,000
6. Cash	300,000	
Due from State Government		300,000

Closing Entry

At year-end, the Motor Fuel Tax Fund would prepare the following closing entry:

	Debit	Credit
7. Motor Fuel Tax Revenues	650,000	
State Reimbursement Grant Revenue	350,000	
Current Expenditures—Public Works		975,000
Fund Balance		25,000

After the closing entries are posted to the general ledger, the fund balance is $237,500 ($212,500 beginning balance plus $25,000 from the closing entry 7). As with the General Fund, these amounts must be reported within the five categories of fund balance.

The Motor Fuel Tax Fund has no unused supplies or prepaid expenses, so there are no *Nonspendable* resources in this example. All of the resources in this fund are required by state law to be used for road repairs and maintenance under the public works department. This represents a restriction imposed by an outside entity, and the net resources are reported as *Restricted Fund Balance*. Had the Village supplemented the Motor Fuel Tax Fund with resources that were not restricted or committed, the residual balance would be reported as *Assigned Fund Balance*. Recall, only the General Fund may report a positive *Unassigned Fund Balance*.

Year-End Financial Statements

Illustrations 4-7 and 4-8 reflect the Balance Sheet and the Statement of Revenues, Expenditures, and Changes in Fund Balances for the Motor Fuel Tax Fund.

ILLUSTRATION 4-7 Balance Sheet for Motor Fuel Tax Fund

VILLAGE OF RIVERSIDE
Motor Fuel Tax Fund Balance Sheet
As of December 31, 2020

Assets	
Cash	$247,500
Due from State Government	125,000
Total Assets	$372,500
Liabilities and Fund Balance	
Liabilities:	
Accounts Payable	$135,000
Fund Balance:	
Restricted for Road Repair	237,500
Total Liabilities and Fund Balance	$372,500

ILLUSTRATION 4-8 Statement of Revenues, Expenses, and Changes in Fund Balances

VILLAGE OF RIVERSIDE
Motor Fuel Tax Fund
Statement of Revenues, Expenditures, and Changes in Fund Balances
For the Year Ended December 31, 2020

Revenues:	
Motor Fuel Taxes	$ 650,000
State Reimbursement Grant	350,000
Total Revenues	1,000,000
Expenditures:	
Public Works	975,000
Net Change in Fund Balance	25,000
Fund Balance, January 1, 2020	212,500
Fund Balance, December 31, 2020	$ 237,500

RECOGNITION OF INVENTORIES IN GOVERNMENTAL FUNDS

In most cases, supplies inventories are small relative to governmental fund expenditures. Perhaps because of this, generally accepted accounting principles permit two methods of accounting for inventories. The most familiar alternative is the method used by commercial businesses, the **consumption method.** Under this method, Supplies Inventory is debited when inventories are acquired. When supplies are consumed, the Expenditures account is debited and Supplies Inventory credited, with the result that the expenditure equals the amount of supplies used during a period.

Assume that the public works department began the year with $4,500 of supplies, purchased $50,000, and ended the year with unused supplies of $2,000. The entries under the consumption method would be as follows:

Consumption method	**Debits**	**Credits**
Supplies Inventories	50,000	
Accounts Payable		50,000
Public Works Expenditures*	52,500	
Supplies Inventories (see calculation below)		52,500

$ 4,500	Beginning supplies inventory (and nonspendable fund balance)
50,000	Supplies purchased
(2,000)	Less: ending inventory
$52,500	Supplies used = Expenditure*

In this case a portion of the ending fund balance (equal to the unused Supplies Inventory) is classified as *Nonspendable Fund Balance* in the fund balances section of the Balance Sheet.

Under the alternative **purchases method,** Expenditures are debited when supplies are received. At the beginning of the year, the *Supplies Inventory* and *Nonspendable Fund Balance* accounts are equal ($4,500). The accounts remain unchanged throughout the year and expenditures (rather than supplies inventories) are charged for any purchases. At year-end, the balances in the *Supplies Inventory* and *Nonspendable Fund Balance* are adjusted to reflect the amount of unused supplies on hand.

Purchases method		
Public Works Expenditures	50,000	
Accounts Payable		50,000
Nonspendable Fund Balance	2,500	
Supplies Inventories* (see calculation below)		2,500

$ 4,500	Beginning supplies inventory (and nonspendable fund balance)
(2,000)	Less: ending inventory
$ 2,500	Decrease in supplies inventory*

The difference between the two methods is in the amount of expenditures reported. Expenditures under the consumption method equal the amount of supplies *used,* whereas under the purchases method expenditures equal the amount of supplies *purchased.* The consumption method is preferable since it requires no adjustment to supplies expense when preparing the government-wide statements.

SUMMARY

Every government will have a single General Fund to account for resources not reported in other funds. Special revenue funds are established to account for resources whose use is restricted or committed to specific purposes. The General Fund and special revenue funds report using the modified accrual basis of accounting and the current financial resources measurement focus and include the following:

- Revenues—inflows of resources that are measurable and available (i.e., will be collected in time to settle current obligations),
- Expenditures—outflows of resources that are recognized when the government incurs a liability, and
- Fund Balance—the excess of fund assets over fund liabilities.

As governmental-type funds, the General Fund and special revenue funds record receivables expected to be collected in the short term but do not record capital or other long-term assets. These funds record short-term liabilities, including notes payable, but do not record long-term obligations. The excess of assets over liabilities is termed *fund balance,* and all operating statement accounts (sources and uses of funds) are closed to this account. Fund balance is reported on the fund Balance Sheet within five categories representing varying degrees to which the net resources of the fund are available for future expenditure.

Questions and Exercises

4–1. Using the annual financial report obtained for Exercise 1–1, answer the following questions:

a. Review the General Fund column of the Balance Sheet for governmental funds. What are the major assets? Liabilities? What categories of Fund Balances are reported?

b. Review the General Fund column of the governmental funds Statement of Revenues, Expenditures, and Changes in Fund Balances. Prepare a schedule showing percentages of revenues by source. Prepare a schedule showing percentages of expenditures by function. Does your government have significant transfers in or out? Can you identify the fund that provides or receives these resources? Does your government have any other financing sources or uses? Special and/or extraordinary items?

c. Does your government report any special revenue funds as major funds in the governmental fund statements? What are they? What are the major revenue sources? Expenditure functions?

d. Review the notes to the financial statements to determine the measurement focus and basis of accounting used to prepare the governmental fund financial statements. Do the notes describe modified accrual accounting in a manner consistent with this book? Which revenue sources are subject to accrual? Are expenditures generally recognized when goods and services are received? Which specific modifications to accrual accounting are mentioned in the notes?

e. Review the General Fund column of the governmental fund statements from the point of view of a financial analyst. Is the Fund Balance as of the balance sheet date larger or smaller than at the beginning of the year? Are reasons for the change apparent from the statements? Compute a ratio of Fund Balance/General Fund Revenues and compare it with your class members' ratios.

4–2. The Village of Seaside Pines prepared the following General Fund Trial Balance as of December 31, 2020, the last day of its fiscal year. Control accounts are used for budgetary entries.

	Debits	Credits
Accounts Payable		$ 19,000
Allowance for Uncollectible Taxes		12,000
Appropriations (Control)		490,000
Budgetary Fund Balance		9,000
Cash	$ 175,000	
Deferred Inflows—Property Taxes		38,000
Due from Capital Projects Fund	5,000	
Due to Debt Service Fund		17,000
Encumbrances	63,000	
Estimated Revenue (Control)	534,000	
Estimated Other Financing Uses (Control)		35,000
General Government Expenditures	138,000	
Other Revenues		55,000
Property Tax Revenue		491,000
Public Safety Expenditures	295,000	
Budgetary Fund Balance—Reserve for Encumbrances		63,000
Supplies Inventory	24,000	
Tax Anticipation Note Payable		100,000
Taxes Receivable	205,000	
Transfer Out (to Internal Service Fund)	30,000	
Fund Balance		140,000
Totals	$1,469,000	$1,469,000

1. Prepare the closing entries for December 31. (It is not necessary to use control accounts and subsidiary ledgers.)
2. Prepare the Statement of Revenues, Expenditures, and Changes in Fund Balance for the General Fund for the year ended December 31.
3. Prepare the Fund Balance section of the December 31 Balance Sheet assuming there are no restricted or committed net resources and the outstanding encumbrances are for capital additions.

4–3. On January 1, 2020, the first day of its fiscal year, Carter City received notification that a federal grant in the amount of $560,000 was approved. The grant was restricted for the payment of wages to teenagers for summer employment. The terms of the grant permitted reimbursement only after qualified expenditures have been made; the grant could be used over a two-year period. The following data pertain to operations of the *Summer Employment Grant Fund*, a special revenue fund of Carter City, during the year ended December 31, 2020:

Show entries in general journal form to record the following events and transactions in the accounts of the *Summer Employment Grant Fund:*

1. The budget was recorded. It provided for Estimated Revenues for the year in the amount of $270,000, and for Appropriations in the amount of $270,000.
2. A temporary loan of $270,000 was received from the General Fund.
3. During the year, teenagers earned and were paid $261,000 under terms of the Summer Employment program. An additional $8,000 is accrued as payable on December 31. Recognize the receivable and revenue (include the $8,000 of wages payable).
4. Each month a properly documented request for reimbursement was sent to the federal government; checks for $267,000 were received.
5. $250,000 was repaid to the General Fund.
6. Necessary closing entries were made.

4–4. The Town of Quincy's fiscal year ends on June 30. The following data relate to the property tax levy for the fiscal year ended June 30, 2020. Prepare journal entries for each of the dates as indicated.

a. The balance in Deferred Inflows—Property Taxes was $48,000 at the end of the previous year. This was recognized as revenue in the current year in a reversing journal entry.

b. On July 1, 2019, property taxes in the amount of $8,200,000 were levied. It was estimated that 0.5 percent would be uncollectible. The property taxes were intended to finance the expenditures for the year ended June 30, 2020.

c. October 31, $4,200,000 in property taxes were collected.

d. December 31, $3,700,000 in additional property taxes were collected.

e. Receivables totaling $8,700 were deemed to be uncollectible and written off.

f. On June 30, $37,000 was moved from Revenues Control to Deferred Inflows, because it was not expected to be collected within 60 days.

4–5. Prepare journal entries in the General Fund of the Brownville School District.

a. The District had outstanding encumbrances of $9,200 for band instruments from the previous year. It is the District's policy to re-establish those encumbrances in the subsequent year.

b. The District ordered textbooks at an estimated cost of $57,000.

c. The band instruments arrived at an invoice price of $8,800 plus $290 shipping.

d. Textbooks originally estimated to cost $49,000 were received with an invoice price of $48,500. The remaining portion of the order is back-ordered.

e. A contract was signed with a CPA to provide the annual audit in the amount of $5,200.

4–6. The following information was abstracted from the accounts of the General Fund of the City of Rome after the books had been closed for the fiscal year ended June 30, 2020.

	Postclosing Trial Balance June 30, 2019	Transactions July 1, 2019, to June 30, 2020		Postclosing Trial Balance June 30, 2020
		Debits	**Credits**	
Cash	$490,000	$1,274,000	$1,310,400	$453,600
Taxes Receivable	28,000	1,316,000	1,279,600	64,400
	$518,000			$518,000
Allowance for Uncollectible Taxes	5,600	5,600	7,000	7,000
Accounts Payable	92,400	1,296,400	1,278,000	74,000
Fund Balance	420,000		17,000	437,000
	$518,000			$518,000

There were no transfers into the General Fund, but there was one transfer out. Prepare journal entries to record the transactions for the fiscal year ended June 30, 2020. Include closing entries.

4–7. The following transactions relate to the General Fund of the City of Buffalo Falls for the year ended December 31, 2020:

1. Beginning balances were: Cash, $80,000; Taxes Receivable, $185,000; Accounts Payable, $50,000; and Fund Balance, $215,000.
2. The budget was passed. Estimated revenues amounted to $1,200,000 and appropriations totaled $1,196,000. All expenditures are classified as General Government.
3. Property taxes were levied in the amount of $902,000. All of the taxes are expected to be collected before February 2021.
4. Cash receipts totaled $870,000 for property taxes and $275,000 from other revenue.
5. Contracts were issued for contracted services in the amount of $90,000.
6. Contracted services were performed relating to $82,000 of the contracts with invoices amounting to $80,000.
7. Other expenditures amounted to $950,000.
8. Accounts payable were paid in the amount of $1,070,000.
9. The books were closed.

Required:

a. Prepare journal entries for the above transactions.

b. Prepare a Statement of Revenues, Expenditures, and Changes in Fund Balance for the General Fund.

c. Prepare a Balance Sheet for the General Fund assuming there are no restricted or assigned net resources and outstanding encumbrances are committed by contractual obligation.

4–8. Lincoln County's General Fund had two interfund transactions:

1. The General Fund paid $225,000 to the Housing and Urban Development Fund, a special revenue fund that is supported by grants from the federal government on a cost reimbursement basis. The amount is to be repaid to the General Fund as grant proceeds are received from the federal government.
2. The General Fund paid $162,000 to the Tourism Fund, a special revenue fund that is supported by hotel and restaurant taxes. The amount is intended to supplement the taxes raised, and there is no expectation that it will be repaid to the General Fund.

Required:

Prepare the journal entries in the General Fund and affected special revenue funds for the interfund transactions above. Describe the effect of these transactions on the fund balance of the General and special revenue funds.

4–9. The following transactions relate to Newport City's special revenue fund.

1. In 2020, Newport City created a special revenue fund to help fund the 911 emergency call center. The center is to be funded through a legally restricted tax on cellular phones. No budget is recorded.
2. During the first year of operations, revenues from the newly imposed tax totaled $489,000. Of this amount, $444,000 has been received in cash and the remainder will be received within 60 days of the end of the fiscal year.
3. Expenditures (salaries) incurred through the operation of the 911 emergency call center totaled $449,000. Of this amount, $422,000 was paid before year-end.
4. During the year the state government awarded Newport City a grant to reimburse the City's costs (not to exceed $150,000) for the purpose of training new 911 operators. During the year, the City paid $146,500 (not reflected in the expenditures above) to train new operators for the 911 emergency call center and billed the state government.
5. $138,000 of the amount billed to the State had been received by year-end.

Required:

a. Prepare the journal entries for the above transactions. It is not necessary to use control accounts and subsidiary ledgers. Prepare closing entries for year-end.

b. Prepare a Statement of Revenues, Expenditures, and Changes in Fund Balance for the special revenue fund.

c. Prepare a Balance Sheet assuming there are no committed or assigned net resources.

4–10. Assume at the beginning of 2020 the Village of Ashlawn *Street and Highway Fund* (a special revenue fund) has cash of $336,000 offset by assigned fund balance in the same amount.

1. During the year, the State notified the Village that $500,000 for the Street and Highway Fund will be awarded for work performed on several bridges over the next two years. The grant is a cost reimbursement arrangement (no budget entry is necessary).
2. During the year, the Village signed contracts for bridge repairs that amounted to $440,000.
3. The bridge repairs were completed and an invoice was received for $435,000, of which $362,000 was paid in cash.
4. The special revenue fund reimbursed the General Fund for a payment the General Fund made on behalf of the Street and Highway Fund in the amount of $2,500. This amount is not related to the bridge repairs under the state grant.
5. The state government paid the Village $412,000 on work completed under the grant before year-end.

Required:

a. Prepare the journal entries for the above transactions. Prepare Closing entries for year-end.

b. Prepare a Statement of Revenues, Expenditures, and Changes in Fund Balance for the special revenue fund.

c. Prepare a Balance Sheet.

Excel-Based Problems

4–11. Jefferson County's General Fund began the year 2020 with the following account balances:

	Debits	**Credits**
Cash	$146,348	
Taxes Receivable	32,220	
Allowance for Uncollectible Taxes		$ 1,900
Supplies	1,660	
Deferred Inflows—Property Taxes		21,000
Wages Payable		570
Fund Balance		156,758
Totals	$180,228	$180,228

During 2020, Jefferson experienced the following transactions:

1. The budget was passed by the County Commission, providing estimated revenues of $286,500 and appropriations of $233,000 and estimated other financing uses of $40,000.

2. Encumbrances totaling $4,800 outstanding at December 31, 2019, were re-established.
3. The Deferred Inflows—Property Taxes at December 31, 2019, is recognized as revenue in the current period.
4. Property taxes in the amount of $288,000 were levied by the County. It is estimated 0.5 percent (1/2 of 1 percent) will be uncollectible.
5. Property tax collections totaled $263,400. Accounts totaling $1,850 were written off as uncollectible.
6. Encumbrances were issued for supplies in the amount of $37,100.
7. Supplies in the amount of $40,500 were received. Jefferson County records supplies as an asset when acquired. The related encumbrances for these items totaled $41,000 and included the $4,800 encumbered last year. The County paid $38,100 on accounts payable during the year.
8. The County contracted to have alarm systems (capital assets) installed in the administration building at a cost of $42,900. The systems were installed and the amount was paid.
9. Paid wages totaling $135,900, including the amount payable at the end of 2019. (These were for general government operations.)
10. Paid other general government operating items of $7,600.
11. The General Fund transferred $39,800 to the debt service fund in anticipation of bond interest and principal payments.
12. Wages earned but unpaid at the end of the year amounted to $890.
13. Supplies of $350 were on hand at the end of the year. (Supplies are used for general government operations.)
14. A review of property taxes receivable indicates that $23,000 of the outstanding balances would likely be collected more than 60 days after year-end and should be deferred.

Required:

Use the Excel template provided on the textbook website to complete the following requirements. A separate tab is provided in Excel for the following items:

a. Prepare journal entries to record the information described in items 1 to 14. Classify expenditures in the General Fund as either General Government Operations or Capital Outlay. Make entries directly to these and the individual revenue accounts; do not use subsidiary ledgers.

b. Post these entries to T-accounts.

c. Prepare closing journal entries; post to the T-account provided. Classify fund balances assuming there are no restricted or committed net resources and the only assigned net resources are the outstanding encumbrances.

d. Prepare a Statement of Revenues, Expenditures, and Changes in Fund Balance for the General Fund for the year ending 2020. Use Excel formulas to calculate the cells shaded in blue.

e. Prepare a Balance Sheet for the General Fund as of December 31, 2020.

4–12. The state government administers a special revenue fund, the *Fish and Game Fund.* By legislation, revenue in this fund can be used only for the purpose of protection, propagation, and restoration of sport fish and game resources and the expenses of administering sport fish and wildlife programs. Revenues are received from the sale of state sport fishing and hunting licenses and special permits as well as money received from fines imposed on individuals violating state hunting and fishing laws. The fund began in 2020 with the following balances:

	Debits	**Credits**
Accounts Payable		$ 68,000
Cash	$200,000	
License Fees Receivable	129,000	
Supplies	5,000	
Fund Balance		265,000
Wages Payable		1,000
Total	$334,000	$334,000

1. The State adopted a budget for the Fish and Game Fund providing estimated revenues of $1,450,000, appropriations of $1,680,000, and anticipated transfers from the State's General Fund of $300,000. All expenditures, other than capital expenditures, are to be charged to *Current Expenditures—Wildlife Management.*
2. At the end of 2019, there were outstanding purchase orders for hatchery supplies totaling $26,000 that will be received in the current year. It is the State's policy to honor outstanding purchase orders from the previous year.
3. Hunting and fishing licenses are sold by outfitters and outdoor equipment retailers and are remitted to the State by the 15th of the following month. During 2020, the State received $1,268,000 in cash for licenses, which includes the amount accrued at the end of the previous year. In addition, it is estimated $102,000 will be received in January 2021 for December 2020 sales.
4. During the year, the State received an additional $212,000 for fines levied against individuals violating state hunting and fishing laws.
5. The State operates fish hatcheries for its stocking program. During the year, the State placed orders totaling $281,000 for hatchlings, feed, and other supplies. These are in addition to the outstanding purchase orders from 2020.
6. The State received supplies at an invoice cost totaling $288,200 for hatchery supplies. The related encumbrances for these items totaled $289,000 (this includes the $26,000 issued in 2019).
7. Payments of accounts payable totaled $312,000 in 2020.

8. The General Fund provided $300,000 to the Fish and Game Fund for the acquisition of a new fish hatchery. This amount was received in 2020.
9. A purchase order was awarded to Aquatics Construction Company for the new hatchery in the amount of $300,900. The contract was completed and capital expenditures for the new hatchery were paid in the amount of $300,900.
10. Wages were paid during the year in the amount of $981,000. This includes the unpaid amounts accrued at the end of the previous year.
11. Unpaid wages related to the last pay period of 2020 totaled $2,500 and will be paid in January 2021.
12. At December 31, the unused hatchery supplies on hand totaled $15,000.

Required:

Use the Excel template provided. A separate tab is provided in Excel for each of these steps.

a. Prepare journal entries to record the information described in items 1 to 12.

b. Post these entries to T-accounts.

c. Prepare closing journal entries; post to the T-account provided. Classify fund balances assuming all spendable net resources are classified as Restricted.

d. Prepare a Statement of Revenues, Expenditures, and Changes in Fund Balance for the special revenue fund for the year ending 2020.

e. Prepare a Balance Sheet for the special revenue fund as of December 31, 2020.

Continuous Problem

The continuous problem is available in Connect through the Additional Student Resources in the eBook or instructor library. Complete the assignment for Chapter 4.

Chapter Five

Accounting for Other Governmental Fund Types: Capital Projects, Debt Service, and Permanent

For an economy built to last we must invest in what will fuel us for generations to come. This is our history—from the Transcontinental Railroad to the Hoover Dam, to the dredging of our ports and building of our most historic bridges—our American ancestors prioritized growth and investment in our nation's infrastructure. Cory Booker, U.S. senator from New Jersey and former mayor of Newark

You know, if you look back in the 1930s, the money went to infrastructure. The bridges, the municipal buildings, the roads, those were all built with stimulus money spent on infrastructure. This stimulus bill has fundamentally gone wrong. Started out with a $500 rebate check, remember. That went to buy flat-screen TVs made in China. Michael Bloomberg on the 2017 stimulus program. Bloomberg, a businessman, author, and philanthropist, served as the 108th mayor of New York City.

Learning Objectives

- Apply the modified accrual basis of accounting in the recording of typical transactions of capital projects, debt service, and permanent funds.
- Prepare the fund-basis financial statements for governmental funds.
- Classify and identify appropriate fund reporting for trust agreements.

Chapter 4 describes accounting and financial reporting for the General Fund and special revenue funds. This chapter describes and illustrates the accounting for the remaining governmental funds: capital projects, debt service, and permanent.

Representative transactions and fund-basis financial statements are presented for the Village of Riverside.

Illustration 5-1 provides a summary of governmental funds. Many of the practices described in Chapter 4 apply to capital projects, debt service, and permanent funds. All of the governmental funds use the modified accrual basis of accounting and the current financial resources measurement focus. Budgets are typically not recorded for capital projects, debt service, and permanent funds. Similarly, encumbrance accounting is typically not used for debt service and permanent funds.

Governmental fund types account for revenues, other financing sources, expenditures, and other financing uses that are for capital outlay and debt service purposes, as well as for current purposes. General fixed assets that are acquired with governmental fund resources are recorded as expenditures in the governmental funds but are displayed as capital assets in the government-wide financial statements. Similarly, the proceeds of general long-term debt incurred for governmental activities are recorded as other financing sources in governmental funds, but the liability is displayed as long-term debt in the government-wide statements. The term *general fixed asset* indicates that these are capital assets that are not associated with a proprietary or fiduciary fund. Similarly, *general long-term debt* is used to describe obligations that are expected to be paid from general (tax) revenues rather than from the activities of proprietary funds.

Since long-term liabilities are not recorded in the governmental funds, payments of principal are recorded as expenditures, rather than reductions of outstanding liabilities. Capital projects funds and debt service funds, in particular, are used to acquire major capital assets and to issue and service long-term debt. Adjustments needed to record the general fixed assets and long-term debt transactions prior to preparing the government-wide statements are illustrated in Chapter 8 of this text.

State governments sometimes establish permanent funds with the proceeds from the sale of land or mineral rights. The amounts are invested permanently and earnings are used to benefit public schools or (in the case of Alaska) are paid directly to state residents. In this chapter, a cemetery perpetual care fund is used to illustrate permanent funds of a local government. Permanent funds reflect resources that are restricted so that principal may not be expended and earnings are used to benefit the government or its citizenry. If both earnings and principal may be expended, the activities should be reported in a special revenue fund.

CAPITAL PROJECTS FUNDS

A major source of funding for capital projects funds is the issuance of long-term debt. In addition to debt proceeds, capital projects funds may receive grants from other governmental units, proceeds of dedicated taxes, transfers from other funds, gifts from individuals or organizations, or a combination of several of these sources.

Capital projects funds differ from General Funds in that a capital projects fund exists only for the duration of the project for which it is created. In some jurisdictions, governments are allowed to account for all capital projects within a single capital projects fund. In other jurisdictions, laws require each project to be accounted for by a separate capital projects fund. Even in jurisdictions that permit the use of a single

ILLUSTRATION 5-1 Summary of Governmental-Type Funds

Fund Name	Modified Accrual Basis	Current Financial Resource Focus	Record Budgets	Record Encumbrances	Fund Description	Fund Term
General Fund	✓	✓	✓	✓	Accounts for all financial resources not required to be reported in another fund.	Indefinite life.
Special Revenue	✓	✓	✓	✓	Accounts for legally restricted revenue sources, other than those restricted for capital projects or debt service.	For each period that a substantial portion of the resources are provided by one or more *restricted* or *committed* revenue sources.
Capital Projects	✓	✓		✓	Accounts for financial resources to be used for acquisition or construction of major capital facilities (other than those financed by proprietary or fiduciary funds).	From the period resources are first provided until the capital facility is complete.
Debt Service	✓	✓*			Accounts for financial resources to be used for payment of interest and principal on general long-term debt (not needed for debt paid from proprietary or fiduciary funds).	From the period funds are first accumulated until the final interest and principal payment is made.
Permanent	✓	✓			Accounts for resources that are legally restricted to the extent earnings (but not principal) may be used to support government programs.	Indefinite life, beginning with the initial contribution.

*Debt service funds are required to report only *matured* interest and principal payments as current liabilities. Unmatured principal installments and accrued interest, although due shortly after year-end, are not required to be reported as liabilities in the debt service fund until due.

fund, managers may prefer to use separate funds to enhance control over individual projects. In such cases, a fund is created when a capital project or a series of related projects is legally authorized; it is closed when the project or series is completed.

GASB standards require capital project fund-basis statements to be reported using the modified accrual basis of accounting. Proceeds of debt issues are recorded as **Proceeds of Bonds** or **Proceeds of Long-Term Notes** rather than as Revenues and are reported in the Other Financing Sources section of the Statement of Revenues, Expenditures, and Changes in Fund Balances. Similarly, revenues raised by the General Fund or other funds and transferred to a capital projects fund are recorded as Transfers In and reported in the Other Financing Sources section of the operating statement. Taxes or other revenues raised specifically for a capital project are recorded as revenues of the capital projects fund. Grants, entitlements, or shared revenues received by a capital projects fund from another governmental unit are considered revenues of the capital projects fund, as is interest earned on temporary investments of the capital projects fund.

Expenditures of capital projects funds are reported in the capital outlay character classification in the Governmental Funds Statement of Revenues, Expenditures, and Changes in Fund Balances. Capital outlay expenditures result in additions to the general fixed assets reported in the government-wide Statement of Net Position. Even though budgetary reporting is not required for capital projects funds, encumbrance accounting is commonly used.

Illustrative Case

The following case illustrates representative transactions of a capital projects fund. Assume that early in 2020 the Village Council of the Village of Riverside authorized an issue of $1,200,000 of 8 percent, 10-year regular serial tax-supported bonds to finance construction of a fire station addition. The total cost of the fire station addition was expected to be $2,000,000, with $600,000 to be financed by grants from the state government and $200,000 to be transferred from an enterprise fund of the Village of Riverside. The project would utilize land already owned by the Village. Completion of the project was expected within the year. Transactions and entries are illustrated next.

The $1,200,000 bond issue, which had received referendum approval by taxpayers, was officially approved by the Village Council. Proceeds of debt issues should be recognized by a capital projects fund at the time the debt is actually incurred, rather than at the time it is authorized, because authorization of an issue does not guarantee its sale.

The sum of $100,000 was borrowed from the National Bank for engineering and other preliminary costs incurred before bonds could be sold. The notes will be repaid in the current period and are recorded as a liability in the capital project fund.

	Debits	Credits
1. Cash	100,000	
Bond Anticipation Notes Payable		100,000

Assume the legislature passes a bill authorizing the grant from the state government. In response the Village Council approves the transfer from the enterprise fund. Amounts to be received from other funds within the Village government are reported as other financing sources. In contrast, amounts to be received from other governments (e.g., federal or state) are reported as intergovernmental revenues. The distinction here is that intergovernmental grants increase the overall resources of the Village, but transfers within the Village do not.

	Debit	Credit
2. Due from Other Funds	200,000	
Due from Other Governmental Units	600,000	
Other Financing Sources—Transfers In		200,000
Revenues Control (*Intergovernmental revenue*)		600,000

Total purchase orders for supplies, materials, items of minor equipment, and contracted services required for the project amounted to $247,698.

	Debit	Credit
3. Encumbrances Control	247,698	
Budgetary Fund Balance—Reserve for Encumbrances		247,698

A contract was issued for the major part of the work to be done by a private contractor in the amount of $1,500,000.

	Debit	Credit
4. Encumbrances Control	1,500,000	
Budgetary Fund Balance—Reserve for Encumbrances		1,500,000

Special engineering and miscellaneous preliminary costs that had not been encumbered were paid in the amount of $97,500.

	Debit	Credit
5. Expenditures—Capital Outlay	97,500	
Cash		97,500

When the project was approximately half-finished, the contractor submitted billing for a payment of $750,000. The following entry converts a commitment (Encumbrances) to a liability, eligible for payment upon proper authentication.

6a. Expenditures—Capital Outlay	750,000	
Contracts Payable		750,000
6b. Budgetary Fund Balance—Reserve for Encumbrances	750,000	
Encumbrances Control		750,000

The transfer of $200,000 was received from the enterprise fund, and $300,000 was received from the state government.

7. Cash	500,000	
Due from Other Funds		200,000
Due from Other Governmental Units		300,000

The bonds were issued at a premium of $12,000 on January 2. As is generally the case, the premium must be used for debt service and is not available for use by the capital projects fund. Therefore, the premium is transferred to the debt service fund. Entry 8a records the receipt by the capital projects fund of the proceeds of the bonds, and 8b records the transfer of the premium amount to the debt service fund.

8a. Cash	1,212,000	
Other Financing Sources—Proceeds of Bonds		1,200,000
Other Financing Sources—Premium on Bonds		12,000
8b. Other Financing Uses—Transfers Out	12,000	
Cash		12,000

If bonds were sold at a discount, either the difference would be made up by a transfer from another fund, or the capital projects fund would have fewer resources available for the project. Generally, bond issue costs would be involved and would be recorded as expenditures.

If bonds were sold between interest dates, the government would collect from the purchaser the amount of interest accrued to the date of sale, because a full six months' interest would be paid on the next interest payment date. Interest payments are made from debt service funds; therefore, cash in the amount of accrued interest sold at the time of bond issuance should be recorded in the debt service fund.

The Village of Riverside's capital projects fund pays the bond anticipation notes and interest (assumed to amount to $2,500), and records the following journal entry:

9. Bond Anticipation Notes Payable	100,000	
Expenditures—Capital Outlay (Interest)	2,500	
Cash		102,500

The contractor's initial claim (see entry 6) is paid, less a 5 percent retention. Retention of a contractually stipulated percentage from payments to a contractor is common until the construction is completed and has been inspected for conformity with specifications and plans.

	Debit	Credit
10. Contracts Payable	750,000	
Cash		712,500
Contracts Payable—Retained Percentage		37,500

Upon final acceptance of the project, the retained percentage will be paid. In the event that the government finds it necessary to spend money correcting deficiencies in the contractor's performance, the payment is charged to Contracts Payable—Retained Percentage.

Disbursements for items ordered at an estimated cost of $217,000 (included in the amount recorded by entry 3) amounted to $216,500.

	Debit	Credit
11a. Expenditures—Capital Outlay	216,500	
Cash		216,500
11b. Budgetary Fund Balance—Reserve for Encumbrances	217,000	
Encumbrances Control		217,000

Assume the contractor completes construction of the fire station and bills the Village for the balance on the contract:

	Debit	Credit
12a. Expenditures—Capital Outlay	750,000	
Contracts Payable		750,000
12b. Budgetary Fund Balance—Reserve for Encumbrances	750,000	
Encumbrances Control		750,000

Assume the amount due from the state government was received:

	Debit	Credit
13. Cash	300,000	
Due from Other Governmental Units		300,000

Invoices for goods and services previously encumbered in the amount of $30,698 were received and approved for payment in the amount of $30,500. Additional construction expenditures, not encumbered, amounted to $116,500. The entire amount was paid in cash.

	Debit	Credit
14a. Expenditures—Capital Outlay	147,000	
Cash		147,000
14b. Budgetary Fund Balance—Reserve for Encumbrances	30,698	
Encumbrances Control		30,698

Assume that inspection revealed only minor problems in the contractor's performance, and upon correction of these, the contractor's bill and the amount previously retained were paid:

	Debit	Credit
15. Contracts Payable—Retained Percentage	37,500	
Contracts Payable	750,000	
Cash		787,500

After entry 15 is recorded, $36,500 in cash remained in the capital projects fund. That amount was transferred to a debt service fund for the payment of bonds:

	Debit	Credit
16. Other Financing Uses—Transfers Out	36,500	
Cash		36,500

Upon completion of the project and disposition of any remaining cash, the following closing entry was made:

	Debit	Credit
17. Revenues Control (*Intergovernmental revenue*)	600,000	
Other Financing Sources—Transfers In	200,000	
Other Financing Sources—Proceeds of Bonds	1,200,000	
Other Financing Sources—Premium on Bonds	12,000	
Expenditures—Capital Outlay		1,963,500
Other Financing Uses—Transfers Out		48,500

Financial statements for the Fire Station Addition Capital Projects Fund are presented as part of the Governmental Funds Balance Sheet (Illustration 5-3) and the Governmental Funds Statement of Revenues, Expenditures, and Changes in Fund Balances (Illustration 5-4) provided near the end of this chapter. Because the Village's fire station project was completed and the remaining resources were transferred to the debt service fund, there are no balances remaining in the fund and it does not appear in the governmental funds Balance Sheet (Illustration 5-3). However, the assets, liabilities, and fund balances of major capital projects continuing into the next period would appear in governmental fund Balance Sheets.

Fund balances of capital projects funds are classified among the categories identified in GASB *Statement 54:* Nonspendable, Restricted, Committed, or Assigned. In the case of capital projects funds, it is common for net resources to be classified as *Restricted.* For example, the bond issue may be the result of a referendum in which the voters both approved the debt issue and established its intended use. Intergovernmental grants and taxes dedicated to capital improvements are also likely to be classified as *Restricted.* Resources not meeting the definition of restricted are likely to be reported as Committed Fund Balance. GASB requires that resources intended to fulfill contractual obligations (such as long-term construction contracts) be reported as Committed. Any remaining net resources would be reported as Assigned, the residual classification for funds other than the General Fund.

The addition to the fire station, excluding interest, will be capitalized and shown as an addition to the capital assets in the government-wide financial statements. In addition, the $1,200,000 in bonds will be recorded as a liability in the government-wide statements. See Chapter 8 for the adjustments necessary as a result of this project.

DEBT SERVICE FUNDS

As we just observed, major capital additions are commonly financed through bond or other debt issues. Another fund type, the **debt service fund,** is used to account for financial resources that are intended to provide payments of interest and principal as they come due. Debt service funds are not created for debt issues where the activities of proprietary funds are intended to generate sufficient cash to make interest and principal payments.

If taxes and/or special assessments are levied specifically for payment of interest and principal on long-term debt, those taxes are recognized as revenues of the debt service fund. More commonly, undesignated taxes are levied by the General Fund and transferred to a debt service fund to repay debt. In that case, the taxes are recorded as revenues by the General Fund and as transfers to the debt service fund. Because the amounts of bond issues and the associated capital projects are often approved by the voters, bond premiums and unexpended capital project resources are generally required to be transferred to debt service funds.

The Modified Accrual Basis—As Applied to Debt Service Funds

Like other governmental funds, debt service funds record transactions using the modified accrual basis of accounting. One peculiarity of the modified accrual basis as applied to debt service accounting is that interest on long-term debt is generally not accrued; it is recognized as an expenditure in the year in which the interest is legally due.

For example, if the fiscal year of a government ends on December 31, and the interest on its bonds is payable on April 1 and October 1 of each year, interest payable would *not* be reported as a liability in the Balance Sheet of the debt service fund prepared as of December 31. The rationale is that, since interest is not legally due until April 1 of the following year, resources need not be expended in the current year. The same reasoning applies to principal amounts that mature in the next fiscal year; expenditures and liabilities are recognized in the debt service fund in the year that the principal is legally due. The only exception permitted by GASB is that if a government has resources available for payment in a debt service fund and the period of time until interest or principal payment is due is no more than one month after year-end, then the interest or principal payment *may* be accrued.

Additional Uses of Debt Service Funds

Debt service funds may be used to service term and serial bonds, notes, capital leases, or warrants. Although each issue of long-term debt is a separate obligation, all debts to be serviced from tax revenues may be accounted for by a single debt service fund, if permitted by state laws and covenants with creditors.

In some jurisdictions, there are no statutes that require the debt service function to be accounted for by a debt service fund. Whether required by statute or local ordinance or not, bond indentures or other agreements with creditors are often construed as requiring the use of a debt service fund. Unless the debt service function is very simple, it may be argued that good financial management would dictate the establishment of a debt service fund even when it is not legally required. If neither law nor sound financial administration requires the use of debt service funds, the function may be performed within the accounting and budgeting framework of the General Fund. In such cases, the accounting and financial reporting standards discussed in this chapter should be followed for the debt service activities of the General Fund.

Debt Service Accounting for Serial Bonds

Serial bonds are the most common form of bonds issued by state and local governments. Serial bonds require principal payments to be made throughout the life of the bond, rather than waiting until the end. Usually the government designates a bank as fiscal agent to handle interest and principal payments for each debt issue. The assets of a debt service fund may, therefore, include Cash with Fiscal Agent, and the expenditures and liabilities may include amounts for the service charges of fiscal agents.

There are four types of serial bonds: regular, deferred, annuity, and irregular. If the total principal of an issue is repayable in a specified number of equal installments over the life of the issue, it is a *regular* serial bond issue. If the first installment is delayed for two or more years after the date of the issue, but thereafter installments fall due on a regular basis, the bonds are known as **deferred serial bonds.** If the amount of annual principal repayments is scheduled to increase each year by approximately the same amount that interest payments decrease (interest decreases, of course, because the amount of outstanding bonds decreases) so that the annual debt service payments remain relatively uniform over the term of the issue, the bonds are called **annuity** serial bonds. *Irregular* serial bonds may have any pattern of repayment that does not fit the other three categories.

Illustrative Case—Regular Serial Bonds

Accounting for regular serial bonds is illustrated by a debt service fund created to pay principal and interest for the fire station project for the Village of Riverside discussed earlier in this chapter. Recall that, early in 2020, the Village Council of the Village of Riverside authorized an issue of $1,200,000 of 8 percent tax-supported bonds. At the time of authorization, no formal entry is required in the capital projects fund; at that time, a memorandum entry may be made in the capital projects fund and provision made to account for debt service of the new debt issue in a debt service fund.

Assume that the bonds in this example are dated January 2, 2020; that interest payment dates are June 30 and December 31; and that the first of the 10 equal annual principal payments will be on December 31, 2020.

The bonds were sold at a premium of $12,000, which was recorded in the capital projects fund (see entry 8a of this chapter). The premium was transferred to the debt service fund (see entry 8b):

	Debits	Credits
18. Cash	12,000	
Other Financing Sources—Transfers In		12,000

While GASB standards do not require the reporting of budget-actual schedules for debt service funds, prudence would dictate internal budgetary planning. Assuming the $12,000 amount was known at the time of budgetary planning, the following would reflect debt service needs related to this project:

Semiannual Interest, June 30 ($1,200,000 × .08 × 6/12)	$ 48,000
Semiannual Interest, December 31 ($1,200,000 × .08 × 6/12)	48,000
Principal, December 31 ($1,200,000/10)	120,000
Total Cash Needed	216,000
Less: Premium	12,000
Cash Needs (Net) for 2020	$204,000

Assume cash was transferred from the General Fund in the amount of $204,000 (see entries 21a and 21b of Chapter 4):

	Debits	Credits
19. Cash	204,000	
Other Financing Sources—Transfers In		204,000

Organizations, such as banks or trust companies, act as fiscal agents for commercial businesses or governments. In the case of commercial businesses, fiscal agents commonly are responsible for making dividend payments to shareholders of record. In the case of state and local governments, fiscal agents receive cash from governments with outstanding bonds and distribute interest and principal payments to bondholders. When a government uses a fiscal agent for this purpose, the government first records its payment to the agent as *Cash with Fiscal Agent* and then records debt service expenditures for any interest or principal that is due.

Assume the Village paid $48,000 to a local bank on June 30 to make the first interest payment.

20a. Cash with Fiscal Agent	48,000	
Cash		48,000
20b. Expenditures—Bond Interest	48,000	
Matured Interest Payable		48,000

When the fiscal agent reports that checks have been issued to all bondholders, entry 21 is made:

21. Matured Interest Payable	48,000	
Cash with Fiscal Agent		48,000

On December 31, the next interest payment of $48,000 is due; also on that date, a principal payment of $120,000 is due. The debt service fund pays $168,000 to the local bank for payment and records the expenditures and liabilities for principal and interest:

22a. Cash with Fiscal Agent	168,000	
Cash		168,000
22b. Expenditures—Bond Principal	120,000	
Expenditures—Bond Interest	48,000	
Matured Bonds Payable		120,000
Matured Interest Payable		48,000

The bank reported that all payments had been made as of December 31, 2020:

23. Matured Bonds Payable	120,000	
Matured Interest Payable	48,000	
Cash with Fiscal Agent		168,000

It should be noted that, if principal and/or interest payment dates were other than at the end of the fiscal year, for example, May 1 and November 1, accruals would *not* be made in the debt service fund financial statements. However, accruals for interest would be made when preparing the government-wide financial statements.

Entry 16 of the capital projects fund illustration in this chapter reflected a transfer of $36,500 to the debt service fund, representing the unused construction funds. The corresponding entry is made in the debt service fund:

24. Cash	36,500	
Other Financing Sources—Transfers In		36,500

At year-end, the debt service fund would reflect the following closing entry:

25. Other Financing Sources—Transfers In	252,500	
Expenditures—Bond Principal		120,000
Expenditures—Bond Interest		96,000
Fund Balance		36,500

Financial statements for the Fire Station Addition Debt Service Fund are presented as part of the Governmental Funds Balance Sheet (Illustration 5-3) and the Governmental Funds Statement of Revenues, Expenditures, and Changes in Fund Balances (Illustration 5-4) provided near the end of this chapter. Unexpended resources transferred to the debt service fund from the General Fund would typically be classified as *Restricted* or *Assigned Fund Balance.* In the case of term bonds, debt agreements may require a government to set aside cash in a sinking fund. If a sinking fund is required by creditors or law, the unexpended resources would be classified as *Restricted.*

OTHER ISSUES INVOLVING PAYMENT OF LONG-TERM DEBT

Debt Service Accounting for Deferred Serial Bonds

If a government issues bonds other than regular serial bonds, debt service fund accounting is somewhat more complex than just illustrated. A government that issues deferred serial bonds will normally have several years without principal repayment during which, if it is fiscally prudent, amounts will be accumulated in the debt service fund for payment when the bonds mature. If this is the case, debt service fund cash should be invested in order to earn interest revenues. Material amounts of interest receivable on investments should be accrued at year-end.

Debt Service Accounting for Term Bonds

Term bond issues mature in their entirety on a given date, in contrast to serial bonds, which mature in installments. It may be desirable to fund term bonds throughout their life to produce level annual payments to the debt service fund. The annuity tables used to determine the annual funding assume that the amounts are invested and earn interest. Interest on investments would be accrued at year-end.

Bond Refundings

Governments occasionally refund bonds, that is, issue new debt to replace old debt. This may be done to obtain better interest rates, to get away from onerous debt covenants, or to change the maturity of the debt. A **current refunding** exists when new debt is issued and the proceeds are used to call the existing debt. Assume a government wishes to refund debt with a new bond issue of $10,000,000. The entries to record the replacement of the old debt with new would be

	Debits	Credits
Cash	10,000,000	
Other Financing Sources—Refunding of Existing Debt		10,000,000
Other Financing Uses—Refunding of Existing Debt	10,000,000	
Cash		10,000,000

Alternatively, an **advance refunding** exists when the proceeds are placed in an escrow account pending the call date or the maturity date of the existing debt. In this case, the debt is said to be **defeased** for accounting purposes. That means the old debt is not reported in the financial statements and is replaced by the new debt. Extensive note disclosures are required for both current and advance refundings.

PERMANENT FUNDS

Governments sometimes receive donations or other resources from individuals, estates, and private or public organizations. Commonly these donations take the form of trusts. A trust is a formal agreement in which a donor gives resources to a government to manage. The government is required to follow the stipulations of the trust and cannot unilaterally change the purpose. Trusts are accounted for in a number of different funds, depending on the nature and terms of the agreement.

Illustration 5-2 summarizes accounting for trusts. Initially, it is important to determine whether the trust benefits the government or its citizenry. Second, it is important to determine whether the trust principal is to be maintained or may be expended. Trusts that generate income for the benefit of the government or its citizens and require the principal to be maintained are reported in permanent funds. (Similar funds whose earnings benefit individuals, private organizations, or other governments are *private-purpose trust funds,* discussed in Chapter 7.) An example of a permanent fund is a cemetery perpetual care fund, which provides resources for the ongoing maintenance of a public cemetery.

ILLUSTRATION 5-2 Summary of Government Trust Accounting

Purpose of Trust	Trust Description	Appropriate Fund
Trust is to be used to benefit the government or its citizenry. *Examples:* Cemetery perpetual care or funds established to support libraries, museums, or zoos.	*Expendable:* Trust does not distinguish between earnings and principal. Both may be expended for the purpose provided.	Special revenue fund
	Nonexpendable: Trust stipulates that earnings only (not principal) may be expended for the purpose provided.	Permanent fund
Trust is to benefit individuals, private organizations, or other governments. *Examples:* Scholarship funds or funds intended to benefit families of police or firefighters killed on duty.	Although these are most commonly nonexpendable, there is no requirement that they be so.	Private-purpose trust fund

Assume that, early in 2020, Richard Lee, a citizen of the Village of Riverside, drove by the Village Cemetery and was distressed by the poor level of maintenance. He entered into an agreement with Village officials on April 1 to provide $300,000 to the Village, with the stipulation that the $300,000 be invested, the principal never be expended, and the earnings be used to maintain the Village Cemetery. Accordingly, the Lee Cemetery Perpetual Care Fund was established, and the following entry was made:

	Debits	Credits
26. Cash	300,000	
Revenues—Additions to Permanent Endowments		300,000

The funds were immediately invested in ABC Company bonds, which were selling at par. The bonds carried an annual interest rate of 8 percent and paid interest on April 1 and October 1:

27. Investments—Bonds	300,000	
Cash		300,000

On October 1, $12,000 interest was received:

28. Cash	12,000	
Revenues—Investment Income—Interest		12,000

During 2020, $11,000 was expended for cemetery maintenance:

29. Expenditures—Cemetery	11,000	
Cash		11,000

Modified accrual accounting requires interest revenues to be accrued at year-end. The amount is $6,000 ($\$300,000 \times .08 \times 3/12$):

30. Accrued Interest Receivable	6,000	
Revenues—Investment Income—Interest		6,000

GASB (Sec. I50.105) requires that investments with determinable fair values be recorded at fair value. On December 31, 2020, the ABC Company bonds had a fair value of $302,000, excluding accrued interest:

31. Investments—Bonds	2,000	
Revenue—Net Increase in Fair Value of Investments		2,000

As of December 31, the books were closed for the Lee Cemetery Perpetual Care Fund:

	Debits	Credits
32. Revenues—Additions to Permanent Endowments	300,000	
Revenues—Investment Income—Interest	18,000	
Revenues—Investment Income—		
Net Increase in Fair Value of Investments	2,000	
Expenditures—Cemetery		11,000
Fund Balance		309,000

Financial statements for the Lee Cemetery Perpetual Care Fund are presented as part of the Governmental Funds Balance Sheet (Illustration 5-3) and the Governmental Funds Statement of Revenues, Expenditures, and Changes in Fund Balances (Illustration 5-4). Like other governmental funds, the fund balances of permanent funds are classified among the categories identified in GASB *Statement 54:* Nonspendable, Restricted, Committed, or Assigned. Since the principal (also called corpus) of permanent funds must be maintained, it is classified as *Nonspendable Fund Balance.* In most cases the remaining unexpended resources would be classified as *Restricted* or *Assigned Fund Balance.*

FINANCIAL REPORTING FOR GOVERNMENTAL FUNDS

GASB standards require two financial statements for the General Fund and other governmental funds. Each major fund is reported in a separate column. There is also a single column for all nonmajor funds (if any) and a "total" column reporting the sum of all the governmental funds.

Financial Statements—Governmental Funds

Illustration 5-3 presents the Balance Sheet for the governmental funds for the Village of Riverside. This Balance Sheet includes the General Fund and special revenue fund illustrated in Chapter 4 as well as the debt service and permanent funds illustrated in this chapter. Note that the capital projects fund does not have a column because the remaining resources (cash) were transferred to the debt service fund when the project was completed. Major capital projects funds continuing into future periods would be included in this statement.

Recall that only current financial resources and obligations appear in the governmental funds Balance Sheet. The net position of each fund is displayed within the five categories of fund balances, but each fund balance has a separate line within those categories. Only the General Fund has an *Unassigned Fund Balance.* The government's decision to record resources in special revenue, capital projects, debt service, or permanent funds is an indication that the resources are at least assigned to a particular purpose. In this example, only the principal of the permanent fund appears as *Nonspendable Fund Balance.* If any of the funds had unused supplies or prepaid expenses, those resources would also have been classified as *Nonspendable Fund Balance.*

Illustration 5-4 presents the Statement of Revenues, Expenditures, and Changes in Fund Balances. This statement includes the funds in Illustration 5-3 plus the capital project fund illustrated in this chapter. Note that the ending fund balance agrees with the amount reported on the Balance Sheet.

ILLUSTRATION 5-3 **Governmental Funds Balance Sheet**

VILLAGE OF RIVERSIDE
Balance Sheet
Governmental Funds
As of December 31, 2020

Assets	**General**	**Motor Fuel Tax**	**Fire Station Addition Debt Service**	**Cemetery Pepetual Care**	**Total Governmental Funds**
Cash	$ 443,000	$247,500	$36,500	$ 1,000	$ 728,000
Investments				302,000	302,000
Taxes receivable (net)	528,800				528,800
Interest receivable (net)	34,490			6,000	40,490
Due from state government	60,000	125,000			185,000
Total Assets	$1,066,290	$372,500	$36,500	$309,000	$1,784,290
Liabilities, Deferred Inflows, and Fund Balances					
Liabilities:					
Accounts payable	$ 50,300	$135,000			$ 185,300
Due to other funds	135,000				135,000
Total Liabilities	185,300	135,000	-0-	-0-	320,300
Deferred Inflows of Resources:					
Property taxes	40,000				40,000
Fund Balances:					
Nonspendable:					
Permanent fund principal				300,000	300,000
Restricted for:					
Road repair and maintenance		237,500			237,500
Public works	75,000				75,000
Committed to capital projects	100,000				100,000
Assigned for:					
Debt service			36,500		36,500
Cemetery care				9,000	9,000
Other purposes	50,000				50,000
Unassigned fund balance	615,990				615,990
Total Fund Balance	840,990	237,500	36,500	309,000	1,423,990
Total Liabilities, Deferred Inflows, and Fund Balance	$ 1,066,290	$372,500	$36,500	$309,000	$1,784,290

ILLUSTRATION 5-4 Governmental Funds Statement of Revenues, Expenditures, and Changes in Fund Balances

VILLAGE OF RIVERSIDE
Statement of Revenues, Expenditures, and Changes in Fund Balances
Governmental Funds
For the Year Ended December 31, 2020

	General	Motor Fuel Tax	Fire Station Addition Debt Service	Fire Station Addition Capital Projects	Cemetery Perpetual Care	Total Governmental Funds
Revenues						
Property taxes	$3,178,800					$3,178,800
Motor fuel taxes		$ 650,000				650,000
Sales taxes	1,410,000					1,410,000
Interest and penalties	42,490					42,490
Licenses and permits	540,000					540,000
Fines and forfeits	430,000					430,000
Intergovernmental revenue	350,000	350,000		$600,000		1,300,000
Charges for services	100,000					100,000
Addition to permanent endowment					$300,000	300,000
Investment income—interest					18,000	18,000
Investment income—net increase in fair value of investments					2,000	2,000
Miscellaneous	30,000					30,000
Total revenues	$6,081,290	$1,000,000	–0–	$600,000	$320,000	$8,001,290

Expenditures						
Current:						
General government	$ 810,000					$ 810,000
Public safety	2,139,500					2,139,500
Public works	630,000	$975,000				1,605,000
Health and welfare	480,100					480,100
Cemetery					$11,000	11,000
Parks and recreation	527,400					527,400
Contribution to retirement funds	423,000					423,000
Miscellaneous	20,300					20,300
Debt service						
Principal			$120,000			120,000
Interest			96,000			96,000
Capital outlay				$1,963,500		1,963,500
Total expenditures	5,030,300	975,000	216,000	1,963,500	11,000	8,195,800
Excess (deficiency) of revenues over expenditures	1,050,990	25,000	(216,000)	(1,363,500)	309,000	(194,510)
Other financing sources (uses)						
Proceeds of bonds				1,200,000		1,200,000
Premium on bonds				12,000		12,000
Transfers in			252,500	200,000		452,500
Transfers out	(800,000)			(48,500)		(848,500)
Total other financing sources (uses)	(800,000)	–0–	252,500	1,363,500	–0–	816,000
Special item						
Proceeds from sale of land	300,000					300,000
Net change in fund balances	550,990	25,000	36,500	–0–	309,000	921,490
Fund balances—beginning	290,000	212,500	–0–	–0–	–0–	502,500
Fund balances—ending	$ 840,990	$237,500	$ 36,500	$ –0–	$309,000	$1,423,990

SUMMARY

This chapter illustrates representative transactions and the resulting financial statements for capital projects, debt service, and permanent funds. Like the General and special revenue funds, these governmental funds use the modified accrual basis and current financial resources measurement focus in the fund-basis financial statements. Unlike the General Fund, these funds do not typically record budgets, and debt service and permanent funds do not record encumbrances. Characteristics of these funds are as follows:

- **Capital projects funds.** These funds commonly account for resources provided by long-term debt issues or dedicated taxes. The capital projects typically involve significant construction contracts, which may take months or years to complete. All the expenditures of a capital project fund are for capital assets, but the assets are not recorded in the fund-basis statements. Instead, they are reported only in the government-wide financial statements.
- **Debt service funds.** Typically resources are provided through transfers from the General or other funds. There are two types of debt service expenditures: interest and principal. In most cases, liabilities for interest and principal payments are not recorded until payment is due.
- **Permanent funds.** These funds are created when resources are provided to a government with the intent they be used to generate income to support a particular purpose. The trust agreement stipulates that the earnings are intended for purposes that benefit the government or citizens and the principal may not be expended. Principal of permanent funds is classified as *Nonspendable Fund Balance.*

Questions and Exercises

5–1. Using the annual financial report obtained for Exercise 1–1, answer the following questions:

a. Examine the governmental fund financial statements. Are any major capital projects funds included? If so, list them. Attempt to find out the nature and purpose of the projects from the letter of transmittal, the notes, or MD&A. What are the major sources of funding, such as bond sales, intergovernmental grants, and transfers from other funds? Were the projects completed during the year?

b. Again looking at the governmental fund financial statements, are any major debt service funds included? If so, list them. What are the sources of funding for these debt service payments?

c. Does your report include supplemental information including combining statements for nonmajor funds? If so, are any capital projects and debt service funds included? If so, list them. Indicate the major revenue and other financing source categories for these funds.

d. Review the governmental fund Statement of Revenues, Expenditures, and Changes in Fund Balances, specifically the expenditure classification. Compute a ratio of capital outlay/total expenditures. Again, compute a ratio of debt service/total expenditures. Compare those with your classmates' ratios. Comment on the possible meaning of these ratios.

e. Review the notes to the financial statements, specifically the note (in the summary of significant accounting policies) regarding the definition of modified accrual accounting. Does the note specifically indicate that modified accrual accounting is used for capital projects and debt service funds? Does the note indicate that debt service payments, both principal and interest, are recorded as an expenditure when due?

f. Does your government report capital leases payable in the government-wide Statement of Net Position? If so, can you determine if new capital leases were initiated during the year? Can you trace the payments related to capital leases?

g. Does your government report any permanent funds, either major or nonmajor? If so, list them. What are the amounts of the permanent resources available for governmental purposes? What is/are the governmental purpose(s)?

5–2. A concerned citizen provides resources and establishes a trust with the local government. What factors should be considered in determining in which fund to report the trust activities?

5–3. What are the major sources of funds for capital project and debt service funds, and how are the sources classified in the Statement of Revenues, Expenditures, and Changes in Fund Balance?

5–4. A government has outstanding bonds payable. Interest is payable on a date other than the fiscal year-end. What is the appropriate method of accounting for interest accruals by debt service funds?

5–5. The citizens of Spencer County approved the issuance of $2,000,000 in 6 percent general obligation bonds to finance the construction of a courthouse annex. A capital projects fund was established for that purpose. The preclosing trial balance of the courthouse annex capital project fund follows:

Trial Balance—December 31, 2020	Debits	Credits
Cash	$ 400,000	
Contract payable		$ 250,000
Due from state government	75,000	
Encumbrances	120,000	
Expenditures—capital	2,160,000	
Intergovernmental grant		385,000
OFS: premium on bonds		25,000
OFS: proceeds sale of bonds		2,000,000
Budgetary fund balance— Reserve for encumbrances		120,000
OFU: Transfer out	25,000	
	$2,780,000	$2,780,000

Required:

a. Prepare any closing entries necessary at year-end.

b. Prepare a Statement of Revenues, Expenditures, and Changes in Fund Balance for the courthouse annex capital project fund.

c. Prepare a Balance Sheet for the courthouse annex capital project fund, assuming all unexpended resources are restricted to construction of the courthouse annex.

5–6. A citizen group raised funds to establish an endowment for the Eastville City Library. Under the terms of the trust agreement, the principal must be maintained, but the earnings of the fund are to be used to purchase database and periodical subscriptions for the library. A preclosing trial balance of the library permanent fund follows:

Trial Balance—December 31, 2020	Debits	Credits
Cash	$ 7,500	
Investments	630,000	
Additions to permanent endowments		$625,000
Investment income		48,000
Expenditures—subscriptions	39,500	
Net increase in fair value of investments		5,000
Accrued interest receivable	2,000	
Accounts payable		1,000
	$679,000	$679,000

Required:

a. Prepare any closing entries necessary at year-end.

b. Prepare a Statement of Revenues, Expenditures, and Changes in Fund Balance for the library permanent fund.

c. Prepare a balance sheet for the Library Permanent Fund (Use *Restricted to Library* for any spendable fund balance).

5–7. Armstrong County established a County Office Building Construction Fund to account for a project that was expected to take less than one year to complete. The County's fiscal year ends on June 30.

1. On July 1, 2019, bonds were sold at par in the amount of $8,000,000 for the project.
2. On July 5, a contract was signed with the Sellers Construction Company in the amount of $7,890,000.
3. On December 30, a progress bill was received from Sellers in the amount of $5,000,000. The bill was paid, except for 5 percent retained upon final inspection.
4. On June 1, a final bill was received in the amount of $2,890,000 from Sellers, which was paid, except for the 5 percent retained. An appointment was made between the county engineer and Bill Sellers to inspect the building and to develop a list of items that needed to be corrected.

5. On the day of the meeting, the county engineer discovered that Sellers had filed for bankruptcy and moved out of the state. The City incurred a liability in the amount of $497,000 to have the defects corrected by the Baker Construction Company. (Charge any excess over the balance of Contracts Payable—Retained Percentage to Capital Expenditures.)
6. All accounts (from 5 above) were paid; remaining cash was transferred to the debt service fund.
7. The accounts of the County Office Building Construction Fund were closed.

Required:

a. Record the transactions in the County Office Building Construction Fund for the fiscal year ended June 30, 2020.

b. Prepare a separate Statement of Revenues, Expenditures, and Changes in Fund Balances for the County Office Building Construction Fund.

5–8. The Village of Hawksbill issued $4,000,000 in 5 percent general obligation, tax-supported bonds on July 1, 2019, at 102. A fiscal agent is not used. Resources for principal and interest payments are to come from the General Fund. Interest payment dates are December 31 and June 30. The first of 20 annual principal payments is to be made June 30, 2020. Hawksbill has a calendar fiscal year.

1. A capital projects fund transferred the premium (in the amount of $40,000) to the debt service fund.
2. On December 31, 2019, funds in the amount of $100,000 were received from the General Fund and the first interest payment was made.
3. The books were closed for 2019.
4. On June 30, 2020, funds in the amount of $220,000 were received from the General Fund, and the second interest payment ($100,000) was made along with the first principal payment ($200,000).
5. On December 31, 2020, funds in the amount of $95,000 were received from the General Fund and the third interest payment was made (also in the amount of $95,000).
6. The books were closed for 2020.

Required:

a. Prepare journal entries to record the events above in the debt service fund.

b. Prepare a Statement of Revenues, Expenditures, and Changes in Fund Balance for the debt service fund for the year ended December 31, 2019.

c. Prepare a Statement of Revenues, Expenditures, and Changes in Fund Balance for the debt service fund for the year ended December 31, 2020.

5–9. The Village of Burksville, which has a fiscal year July 1 to June 30, sold $2,500,000 in 5 percent tax-supported bonds at par to construct an addition to its police station. The bonds were dated and issued on July 1, 2019. Interest is payable semiannually on January 1 and July 1, and the first of 10 equal annual principal payments will be made on July 1, 2020. The Village used a capital projects fund to account for the project, and a debt service fund was created to make interest and principal payments.

1. The bonds were sold on July 1, 2019.
2. The General Fund transferred an amount equal to the first interest payment on December 31, 2019. The debt service fund made the payment as of January 1, 2020.
3. The project was completed on June 15, 2020. Expenditures totaled \$2,497,000. You may omit encumbrance entries.
4. The remaining balance was transferred to the debt service fund from the capital projects fund for the eventual payment of principal.

Required:

a. Prepare journal entries for the capital projects fund based on the aforementioned information. Include a closing entry.

b. Prepare journal entries for the debt service fund based on the information presented above. Include a closing entry.

c. Prepare a Statement of Revenues, Expenditures, and Changes in Fund Balance for the year ended June 30, 2020, for the governmental funds (i.e., use separate columns for the General, capital projects, and debt service funds). Assume the General Fund reports the following: property tax revenues \$512,000, other revenues \$200,000, public safety expenditures \$450,000, general government expenditures \$149,000, capital expenditures \$75,000, other financing uses—transfers out \$50,000, and beginning fund balance \$175,000.

5–10. The Town of McHenry has \$10,000,000 in general obligation bonds outstanding and maintains a single debt service fund for all debt service transactions. On July 1, 2020, a current refunding took place in which \$10,000,000 in new general obligation bonds were issued. Record the transaction on the books of the debt service fund.

5–11. The City of Sharpesburg received a gift of \$1,800,000 from a local resident on June 1, 2020, and signed an agreement that the funds would be invested permanently and that the income would be used to maintain the city wildlife preserve and nature center. The following transactions took place during the year ended December 31, 2020:

1. The gift was recorded on June 1.
2. On June 1, ABC Company bonds were purchased as investments in the amount of \$1,800,000 (par value). The bonds carry an annual interest rate of 3.5 percent, payable semiannually on December 1 and June 1.
3. On December 1, the semiannual interest payment was received.
4. From December 1 through December 31, \$28,900 in maintenance costs were incurred; full payment was made in cash.
5. On December 31, an accrual was made for interest.
6. Also on December 31, a reading of the financial press indicated that the ABC bonds had a fair value of \$1,810,000, exclusive of accrued interest.
7. The books were closed.

Required:

a. Record the transactions on the books of the Wildlife Preserve Permanent Fund.

b. Prepare a separate Statement of Revenues, Expenditures, and Changes in Fund Balances for the Wildlife Preserve Permanent Fund for the year ended December 31, 2020.

c. How would the permanently invested resources be classified in the fund balance section of the governmental funds Balance Sheet and net position section of the government-wide Statement of Net Position?

Excel-Based Problems

5–12. Jefferson County established a capital project fund in 2019 to build low-income housing with the transfer of $100,000 from the General Fund. A portion of that was expended on engineering studies in 2019. The following transactions occurred during 2020:

Capital Project Fund Trial Balance:
December 31, 2019

	Debits	Credits
Cash	$72,000	
Fund Balance		$72,000

1. April 1, 2020, 4 percent bonds with a face value of $800,000 were issued in the amount of $817,000. The bond premium was transferred to the debt service fund.
2. The County received notice that it had met eligibility requirements for a federal government grant intended to support the capital project in the amount of $265,000. The grant (cash) will be received when the project is completed in February 2021.
3. The County issued a contract for the construction in the amount of $1,030,000.
4. The contractor periodically bills the County for construction completed to date. During the year, bills totaling $680,000 were received. By year-end, a total of $605,000 had been paid.

Jefferson County established a debt service fund to make interest and principal payments on the bonds issued in item 1 above. Bond payments are made on October 1 and April 1 of each year. Interest is based on an annual rate of 4 percent. A principal payment of $27,000 is due in 2020. The following transactions occurred during 2020:

5. The bond premium was received by the debt service fund through transfer from the capital project fund.

6. September 30, $43,000 was transferred from the General Fund for the October 1 bond payment.
7. The first debt service payment was made on October 1, 2020.

The Elwood Family Reading Enrichment Fund was established in December 2019, funded by a bequest with the legal restriction that only earnings, and not principal, can be used for the purchase of books for the James K. Polk Library in Jefferson County. The principal amount that must be maintained is $500,000. The following transactions occurred during 2020:

Permanent Fund Trial Balance:
December 31, 2019

	Debits	Credits
Receivable from Grantor	$500,000	
Nonspendable Fund Balance—Library Purchases		$500,000

8. The Elwood family pledge of $500,000 was received in donated corporate bonds with a fair value of $370,000 and the balance in cash.
9. $130,000 was invested in U.S. government securities.
10. Interest in the amount of $16,500 was received in cash during the year.
11. During the year, books totaling $11,500 were ordered for the library.
12. During the year, the library reported receiving books with an invoice amount totaling $11,500; $10,700 of the amounts due for book purchases had been paid by year-end.
13. An additional $700 of interest had accrued on the investments at December 31 and will be received in January of next year.
14. The corporate bonds had a market value of $372,500 and the U.S. securities had a market value of $129,800 as of December 31.

Required:

Using the Excel template provided (a separate tab is provided for each of the requirements):

a. Prepare journal entries recording the events 1 to 14 for the capital projects, debt service, and permanent funds.

b. Post the journal entries to T-accounts.

c. Prepare closing entries.

d. Prepare a Statement of Revenues, Expenditures, and Changes in Fund Balance for the Governmental Funds (the General Fund financial statements have already been prepared).

e. Prepare a Balance Sheet for the Governmental Funds, assuming that unexpended spendable resources in the capital projects and permanent funds are classified as *restricted* and unexpended spendable resources in the debt service fund are classified as *assigned.*

5–13. The state government established a capital project fund in 2019 to build new highways. The fund is supported by a 5 percent tax on diesel fuel sales in the state. The tax is collected by private gas stations and remitted in the following month to the State. The following transactions occurred during 2020:

Capital Project Fund Trial Balance:
December 31, 2019

	Debits	Credits
Cash	$8,550,000	
Taxes Receivable	2,700,000	
Contracts Payable		$1,950,000
Fund Balance		9,300,000

1. $2,100,000 of encumbrances outstanding at December 31, 2019, were re-established.
2. During the year, fuel taxes were remitted to the State totaling $23,600,000, including the amount due at the end of the previous year. In addition, $2,870,000 is expected to be remitted in January of next year for fuel sales in December 2020.
3. The State awarded new contracts for road construction totaling $23,650,000.
4. During the year, contractors submitted invoices for payment totaling $23,970,000. These were all under the terms of contracts (i.e., same $ amounts) issued by the State.
5. The State made payments on outstanding accounts of $23,375,000.

The state government operates a debt service fund to service outstanding general obligation bonds. The following transactions occurred during 2020:

Debt Service Fund Trial Balance:
December 31, 2019

	Debits	Credits
Cash	$210,000	
Fund Balance		$210,000

6. The state General Fund provided cash of $4,850,000 through transfer to the debt service fund.
7. Payments for matured interest totaled $2,985,000 and payments for matured principal totaled $1,850,000 during the year.
8. In December, the State refunded bonds to obtain a better interest rate. New bonds were issued providing proceeds of $25,000,000, which was immediately used to retire outstanding bonds in the same amount.

Required:

Use the Excel template provided. A separate tab is provided in Excel for each of the requirements:

a. Prepare journal entries recording the events 1 to 8 (above) for the capital projects and debt service funds.

b. Post the journal entries to T-accounts.

c. Prepare closing entries.

d. Prepare a Statement of Revenues, Expenditures, and Changes in Fund Balance for the Governmental Funds (the General Fund and special revenue fund financial statements have already been prepared).

e. Prepare a Balance Sheet for the Governmental Funds assuming all unexpended spendable net resources in the capital projects fund are classified as *restricted* and in the debt service fund are classified as *assigned.*

Continuous Problem

The continuous problem is available in Connect through the Additional Student Resources in the eBook or instructor library. Complete the assignments for Chapter 5.

Chapter Six

Proprietary Funds

For every $1 billion we invest in public transportation, we create 30,000 jobs, save thousands of dollars a year for each commuter, and dramatically cut greenhouse gas emissions. Bernie Sanders, senator from Vermont

People in Oklahoma, or in New Hampshire, don't need to be paying for [a stadium] in Nevada. Steven Russell, retired Army officer and Oklahoma congressman, commenting on the use of tax-exempt bonds to finance the construction of a new football stadium in Las Vegas for the NFL Raiders

Learning Objectives

- Apply the accrual basis of accounting in the recording of typical transactions of internal service and enterprise funds.
- Prepare the fund-basis financial statements for proprietary funds.
- Identify when an activity is required to be reported as an enterprise fund.
- Contrast statements of cash flow prepared under GASB guidelines with those prepared under FASB guidelines.

The funds discussed in previous chapters (General, special revenue, capital projects, debt service, and permanent) are classified as governmental funds. They exist to raise revenue and other resources to provide services or acquire facilities to aid in the provision of public services. Funds discussed in previous chapters record only current financial resources and liabilities that will be settled with current financial resources. Capital assets and long-term debt are not reported in governmental funds, but are presented in government-wide statements. Governmental funds recognize encumbrances and expenditures, not expenses.

In contrast, **proprietary funds** are used to account for activities similar to those often engaged in by commercial businesses. That is, users of goods or services are charged amounts at least sufficient to cover the costs of providing the goods or services. Thus, in the pure case, proprietary funds are intended to be self-supporting and may return profits to the government.

The accounting for proprietary funds is summarized in Illustration 6-1. Proprietary funds use the economic resources measurement focus and the accrual basis of accounting. Because revenues and *expenses* (not expenditures) are recognized on

ILLUSTRATION 6-1 Summary of Proprietary Funds

Fund Name	Accrual Basis	Economic Resources Focus	Record Budgets	Encumbrances	Fund Description	Fund Term
Internal Service Fund	✓	✓			Funds used to report activities that provide goods and services to other funds, departments, or agencies on a cost-reimbursement basis. They are used when the government is the predominant user of the goods or services.	Indefinite life. Internal service funds are created by the government and exist at the discretion of the government.
Enterprise Fund	✓	✓			Funds used to report activities in which users are charged a fee for goods or services. They are appropriate when individuals or businesses external to the government are the predominant users.	Indefinite life. Enterprise funds must be maintained if debt is secured solely by user charges, laws require that costs be recovered through user charges, or government policy requires setting charges to cover the costs of providing the goods or service.

the accrual basis, financial statements of proprietary funds are similar in many respects to those of business organizations. Capital assets used in fund operations and long-term debt serviced from fund revenues are recorded in the accounts of each proprietary fund. Depreciation on capital assets is recognized as an expense, and accruals and deferrals common to business accounting are recorded in proprietary funds. Budgets may be prepared for proprietary funds to facilitate management of fund activities, but GASB standards do not require budget-actual reporting.

The use of accrual accounting permits financial statement users to observe whether proprietary funds are operated at a profit or a loss. The accrual basis of accounting requires revenues to be recognized when earned and expenses to be recognized when goods and services are used. Two types of funds are classified as proprietary funds: internal service funds and enterprise funds. Internal service funds provide services to other government departments and charge those departments for the services received. Enterprise funds provide services to the public.

Three financial statements are required for proprietary funds: a Statement of Net Position (or Balance Sheet); a Statement of Revenues, Expenses, and Changes in Fund Net Position; and a Statement of Cash Flows. As is true for governmental funds, enterprise funds are reported by major fund, with nonmajor funds presented in a separate column. However, internal service funds are combined and reported in a single column. These statements will be discussed in more detail and illustrated later in this chapter.

Because proprietary funds use the accrual basis of accounting, governments historically used FASB standards to provide guidance in accrual-based financial statements for items not specifically covered by GASB statements. The GASB clarified this practice by incorporating specific FASB standards into the GASB codification. Among the more common topics incorporated from FASB standards are the following:

- Error corrections and changes in accounting principles and estimates
- Contingencies
- Foreign currency transactions
- Current asset and liability classification
- The equity method for investments in common stock

As we discussed in Chapter 1, if the accounting treatment for a given transaction is not specified by a GASB pronouncement, a government may use nonauthoritative sources for guidance, including FASB standards dealing with similar events.

INTERNAL SERVICE FUNDS

As governments become more complex, efficiency can be improved if services used by several departments or funds or even by several governmental units are combined in a single department. Purchasing, printing services, garages, janitorial services, and risk management activities are common examples. Activities that produce goods or services to be provided to *other departments* on a cost-reimbursement basis are accounted for by internal service funds.

Internal service funds recognize revenues and expenses on the accrual basis. They report capital assets used in their operations and long-term debt to be serviced from revenues generated from their operations, as well as for all current assets and current liabilities. Net position (fund equity) is reported in three categories: (1) net investment in capital assets; (2) restricted; and (3) unrestricted.

Establishment and Operation of Internal Service Funds

The establishment of an internal service fund is normally subject to legislative approval. The original allocation of resources to the fund may be derived from a transfer of assets of another fund, such as the General Fund or an enterprise fund, intended as a **transfer** not to be repaid or as a loan that is in the nature of a long-term **advance** to be repaid by the internal service fund over a period of years.

Because internal service funds are established to improve the management of resources, they should be operated and accounted for on a businesslike basis. For example, assume that administrators request the establishment of a fund for the purchasing, warehousing, and issuing of supplies used by a number of funds and departments. A budget should be prepared for the internal service fund (but not recorded in the accounts) to demonstrate that fund management has realistic plans to generate sufficient revenues to cover the cost of goods issued and such other expenses, including depreciation.

Departments and units expected to purchase goods and services from internal service funds should include in their budgets the anticipated outlays for goods and services. During the year, as supplies are issued or services are rendered, the internal service fund records operating revenues (*Charges for Services* is an account title commonly used instead of Sales). Since the customer is another department of the government, a journal entry to record the purchase is recorded at the same time the internal service fund records revenue. If the other fund is a governmental fund, the purchase is recorded as an expenditure. Periodically and at year-end, an operating statement should be prepared for each internal service fund to compare revenues and related expenses; these operating statements, called Statements of Revenues, Expenses, and Changes in Fund Net Position, are similar to income statements prepared for investor-owned businesses.

Illustrative Case—Supplies Fund

Assume that the administrators of the Village of Riverside obtain approval from the Village Council in early 2020 to centralize the purchasing, storing, and issuing of maintenance, office, and cleaning supplies in an internal service fund, the Supplies Fund. A payment of $596,000 cash is made from the General Fund that is not to be repaid by the Supplies Fund. Of the $596,000, $290,000 is to finance capital acquisitions and $306,000 is to finance noncapital acquisitions. Additionally, a long-term advance of $200,000 is made from the Water Utility Fund for the purpose of acquiring capital assets. The advance is to be repaid in 20 equal annual installments, with no interest. The receipt of the transfer and the liability to the Water Utility Fund would be recorded in the Supplies Fund accounts in the following manner.[1]

[1] The corresponding entry in the General Fund is entry 22 in Chapter 4. The corresponding entry in the Water Utility Fund is entry 5 in the "Illustrative Case—Water Utility Fund" section later in this chapter.

	Debits	Credits
1. Cash	796,000	
Transfers In		596,000
Advance from Water Utility Fund		200,000

To provide some revenue on funds not needed currently, $50,000 is invested in marketable securities:

2. Investments	50,000	
Cash		50,000

Assume that early in 2020, a satisfactory warehouse building is purchased for $350,000; $80,000 of the purchase price is considered as the cost of the land. Necessary warehouse machinery and equipment are purchased for $100,000. Delivery equipment is purchased for $40,000. If the purchases are made for cash, the acquisition of the assets would be recorded in the books of the Supplies Fund as follows:

3. Land	80,000	
Building	270,000	
Machinery and Equipment—Warehouse	100,000	
Equipment—Delivery	40,000	
Cash		490,000

Supplies are ordered to maintain inventories at a level sufficient to meet expected usage. No entry is needed because proprietary funds are not required to record encumbrances. During the year, supplies are received and related invoices are approved for payment in the amount of $523,500; the entry needed to record the asset and the liability is as follows:

4. Inventory of Supplies	523,500	
Accounts Payable		523,500

The Supplies Fund accounts for its inventories on the perpetual inventory basis because the information is needed for proper performance of its primary function. Accordingly, when supplies are issued, the Inventory account must be credited for the cost of the supplies issued. However the amount charged the fund purchasing the supplies includes a markup, with the result that the Receivable and Revenue accounts reflect the selling price. The markup above cost should be determined on the basis of budgeted expenses and other items to be financed from net income. If the budget for the Village of Riverside's Supplies Fund indicates that a markup of 30 percent on cost is needed, issues to General Fund departments of supplies costing $290,000 would be recorded by the following entries:

5a. Operating Expenses—Cost of Sales and Services	290,000	
Inventory of Supplies		290,000
5b. Due from General Fund	377,000	
Operating Revenues—Charges for Sales and Services ($290,000 * 130%)		377,000

During the year, purchasing expenses totaling $19,000, warehousing expenses totaling $12,000, delivery expenses totaling $13,000, and administrative expenses totaling $11,000 are incurred. The government has chosen to separate operating expenses into three categories: (1) costs of sales and services, (2) administration, and (3) depreciation. If all liabilities are vouchered before payment, the entry would be as follows:

6. Operating Expenses—Costs of Sales and Services	44,000	
Operating Expenses—Administration	11,000	
Accounts Payable		55,000

If collections from the General Fund during the year total $322,000, the entry would be as follows (see Chapter 4, entries 20a and 20b for General Fund entries corresponding to entries 5b and 7):

7. Cash	322,000	
Due from General Fund		322,000

Assuming that payment of vouchers during the year totals $567,500, the following entry is made:

8. Accounts Payable	567,500	
Cash		567,500

The advance from the Water Utility Fund is to be repaid in 20 equal annual installments; repayment of one installment at the end of the current year is recorded as follows:

9. Advance from Water Utility Fund	10,000	
Cash		10,000

At the time depreciable assets are acquired, the warehouse building has an estimated useful life of 20 years; the warehouse machinery and equipment have an estimated useful life of 10 years; and the delivery equipment has an estimated useful life of 10 years. Further, none of the assets have any expected salvage value. Under these assumptions, straight-line depreciation of the building would be $13,500 per year; depreciation of machinery and equipment, $10,000 per year; and depreciation of delivery equipment, $4,000 per year.

10. Operating Expense—Depreciation	27,500	
Accumulated Depreciation—Building		13,500
Accumulated Depreciation—Warehouse Equipment		10,000
Accumulated Depreciation—Equipment—Delivery		4,000

Organizations that keep perpetual inventory records must adjust the records periodically to reflect shortages, overages, and out-of-condition stock disclosed by physical inventories. Adjustments to the Inventory account are considered to be adjustments to the warehousing expenses of the period. In this illustrative case, it is assumed that no adjustments are found to be necessary at year-end.

Interest income is earned and received in cash on the investments purchased at the beginning of the year:

11. Cash	3,000	
Nonoperating Revenues—Interest		3,000

Assuming that all revenues, expenses, and transfers have been properly recorded by the entries illustrated, the nominal accounts should be closed as of December 31:

12. Operating Revenues—Charges for Sales and Services	377,000	
Nonoperating Revenues—Interest	3,000	
Transfers In	596,000	
Operating Expenses—Costs of Sales and Services		334,000
Operating Expenses—Administration		11,000
Operating Expenses—Depreciation		27,500
Net Position		603,500

Recall that the net position of governmental funds is termed *Fund Balance* and is classified within five categories. In contrast, the excess of assets over liabilities of proprietary funds is termed *Net Position* and classified within three categories:

1. Net Investment in Capital Assets
2. Restricted Net Position
3. Unrestricted Net Position

Net investment in capital assets is computed as capital assets less accumulated depreciation minus the balance of any debt associated with the acquisition of capital assets. **Restricted net position** is defined as net resources whose use is restricted by external parties (creditors, grantors, or other governments) or law. **Unrestricted net position** is the residual account for any net resources that are not classified in either of the other two categories. For the Village of Riverside example, the net position balances to be reported in the December 31, 2020, Statement of Net Position are calculated as follows:

	Net Investment in Capital Assets	Restricted	Unrestricted	Total
Net Investment in Capital Assets				
Capital Assets	$490,000			$490,000
Less Accumulated Depreciation	(27,500)			(27,500)
Less Advance from Enterprise Fund	(190,000)			(190,000)
Restricted		-0-		-0-
Unrestricted (plug)			$331,000	$331,000
Total Net Position	$272,500	-0-	331,000	$603,500

The category *Net Investment in Capital Assets* is calculated using end of period balances in capital assets, accumulated depreciation, and debt. Borrowings for operations (if any) would not be subtracted here. In most cases, internal service funds will not have *restricted net position. Unrestricted net position* is the residual balance calculated after the other two categories. Similar to fund balances, some governments choose to allocate these amounts to individual net position accounts through journal entry. Our approach will be to determine the components of net position in the aforementioned manner and present the totals directly in the Statement of Net Position. In this way we reduce the number of accounts necessary to record changes in overall fund net position. These amounts appear only in the Statement of Net Position (Illustration 6-3, presented later in the chapter). In addition to the Statement of Net Position, internal service funds report a Statement of Revenues, Expenses, and Changes in Fund Net Position (Illustration 6-4) and a Statement of Cash Flows (Illustration 6-5).

OTHER ISSUES INVOLVING INTERNAL SERVICE FUNDS

Risk Management Activities

In recent years, governments have been turning to self-insurance for part or all of their risk financing activities. If a government decides to use a single fund to accumulate funds and make payments for claims, it must use either the General Fund or an internal service fund. Many use the internal service fund type.

When using internal service self-insurance funds, interfund premiums are treated as interfund services provided and used. Thus, revenues are recognized in the internal service fund for interfund charges, and an expenditure or expense, as appropriate, is recognized in the contributing fund. When claims are paid or accrued, an operating expense is recorded in the internal service fund.

Charges should be based on anticipated claims or on a long-range plan to break even over time, such as an actuarial method. Payments by contributing funds in excess of the amount required to break even are recorded as transfers. If an internal service fund has a material deficit at year-end, that deficit should be made up over a reasonable period of time and should be disclosed in the notes to the financial statements.

Implications for Other Funds

The operation of internal service funds has important implications for other funds. As we have seen, charges for services (i.e., revenues) of the internal service fund are recorded as expenditures in the governmental fund purchasing the services (or expenses if enterprise funds are the purchaser). Since the internal service fund records the costs of providing services as operating expenses, the costs of these services are recorded in two funds in the same set of fund-basis financial statements.

Additional problems arise if the internal service fund has significant positive (or negative) operating income. Operating income is the excess of service revenues over the costs of providing the service (i.e., operating expenses). Consider the case of an internal service fund servicing police, fire, and other vehicles used in departments reported in the General Fund. If the internal service fund has positive operating income, the expenditures reported in the General Fund exceed the true cost of operating the government. If these amounts are significant over periods of time, some of the accumulated surplus (fund balance) of the General Fund is effectively shifted to the internal service fund. The opposite is true if internal service funds have negative operating income: the General Fund understates the true cost of operating the government and assets are effectively shifted from the internal service fund to the General Fund.

Compounding these problems is the fact that GASB standards do not require the use of internal service funds. Some governments choose to use internal service funds and others choose to account for the same activities in other funds. This makes comparisons between governments difficult. The problems that internal service funds create in the fund-basis financial statements were a major consideration when the GASB designed the government-wide financial statements. As we will see in detail in Chapter 8, the problems of duplicate recording of costs, potential over- or understatement of governmental expenditures, and lack of comparability between governments are resolved in the government-wide financial statements.

ENTERPRISE FUNDS

Enterprise funds are appropriate when a government offers services *to the public* on a user-charge basis. GASB only rarely dictates when a government must account for activities in a separate fund. Enterprise funds are one example. GASB standards require the use of an enterprise fund under the following circumstances:

- When debt is backed solely by fees and charges.
- When a legal requirement exists that the cost of providing services for an activity, including capital costs, be recovered through fees or charges.
- When a government has a policy to establish fees and charges to cover the cost of providing services for an activity.

The most common examples of governmental enterprises are public utilities, notably water and sewer utilities. Electric and gas utilities, mass transit systems, airports, landfills, hospitals, toll bridges, municipal golf courses, parking lots, parking garages, lotteries, municipal sports stadiums, and public housing projects are other examples.

Enterprise funds are to be reported using the economic resources measurement focus and accrual basis of accounting. Capital assets and long-term debt are included in the accounts. As a result, accounting is similar to that for business enterprises and includes depreciation, accrual of interest payable, amortization of discounts and premiums on debt, and so on.

Governmental enterprises often issue debt, called **revenue bonds,** that is payable solely from the revenues of the enterprise. These bonds are recorded directly in the accounts of the enterprise fund. On the other hand, **general obligation bonds** are sometimes issued for governmental enterprises. General obligation bonds provide greater security by pledging the full faith and credit of the government in addition to enterprise revenues. If payment is to be paid from enterprise revenues, these general obligation bonds would also be reflected in the accounts of enterprise funds.

Budgetary accounts are used only if required by law. Debt service and construction activities of a governmental enterprise are accounted for within an enterprise fund, rather than by separate debt service and capital project funds. Thus, the reports of enterprise funds are self-contained; and creditors, legislators, or the general public can evaluate the performance of a governmental enterprise by the same criteria used to evaluate commercial businesses in the same industry.

Unlike internal service funds, it is frequently desirable for enterprise funds to operate at a profit (increase in net position). Like commercial businesses, operating profits are necessary to establish adequate working capital, provide for expansion of physical facilities, and retire debt. Additionally, governments may find it desirable to use enterprise fund profits to support general government expenditures that would otherwise require increased taxes. State lotteries, for example, are established with the intent to operate at significant profits. The profits are then typically transferred from the lottery (enterprise fund) to the state General Fund in support of public education.

By far the most numerous and important enterprise services rendered by local governments are public utilities. In this chapter we examine typical transactions of a water utility fund.

Illustrative Case—Water Utility Fund

Assume that as of December 31, 2019, the accountants for the Village of Riverside prepared the postclosing trial balance shown here:

VILLAGE OF RIVERSIDE Water Utility Fund Postclosing Trial Balance December 31, 2019		
	Debits	**Credits**
Cash	$ 467,130	
Customer Accounts Receivable	72,500	
Allowance for Uncollectible Accounts		$ 2,175
Materials and Supplies	37,500	
Restricted Assets	55,000	
Utility Plant in Service	4,125,140	
Accumulated Depreciation Utility Plant		886,500
Construction Work in Progress	468,125	
Accounts Payable		73,700
Revenue Bonds Payable		2,700,000
Net Position		1,563,020
Totals	$5,225,395	$5,225,395

It is common for governmental enterprises, especially utilities, to report "restricted assets." In this example, the restricted assets include $55,000 set aside for future debt service payments as required by a revenue bond indenture agreement.

Budgets are not recorded in enterprise funds. When utility customers are billed during the year, appropriate revenue accounts are credited. Assuming that during 2020 the total bills to nongovernmental customers amounted to $975,300, bills to the Village of Riverside General Fund amounted to $80,000, and all revenue was from sales of water, the following entry summarizes the results (see entry 19 in Chapter 4 for the corresponding entry in the General Fund):

	Debits	Credits
1. Customer Accounts Receivable	975,300	
Due from General Fund	80,000	
Operating Revenues—Charges for Sales and Services		1,055,300

Assume collections from nongovernmental customers totaled $968,500 for water billings:

2. Cash	968,500	
Customer Accounts Receivable		968,500

Customers owing bills totaling $1,980 left the Village and could not be located. The unpaid balances of their accounts receivable were written off to the allowance for uncollectible accounts as follows:

3. Allowance for Uncollectible Accounts	1,980	
Customer Accounts Receivable		1,980

Governments commonly impose impact fees on developers or builders to pay for capital improvements, such as increased water and sewer facilities, that are necessary to service new developments. Increasingly, governments are using impact fees to limit sprawl and to create incentives for developers to refurbish existing commercial properties rather than create new ones. Assume the Village of Riverside imposes impact fees on commercial developers in the amount of $12,500 and that these fees are not associated with specific projects or improvements.

4. Cash	12,500	
Capital Contributions		12,500

Note that Capital Contributions is an activity account that will increase Net Position but is reported separately in the Statement of Revenues, Expenses, and Changes in Fund Net Position (see Illustration 6-4). Hookup fees for new customers are not capital contributions but are exchange transactions and are included in operating revenues. If the impact fees had been restricted to a specific project, the cash would have been reported as a restricted asset.

During 2020, the Village of Riverside established a Supplies Fund, and the Water Utility Fund advanced $200,000 to the Supplies Fund as a long-term receivable. The entry by the Supplies Fund is illustrated in entry 1 in the "Illustrative Case—Supplies Fund" section of this chapter. The following entry should be made by the Water Utility Fund:

5. Long-Term Advance to Supplies	200,000	
Cash		200,000

Materials and supplies in the amount of $291,500 were purchased during the year by the Water Utility Fund, and vouchers in that amount were recorded as a liability:

6. Materials and Supplies	291,500	
Accounts Payable		291,500

When materials and supplies are issued to the departments of the Water Utility Fund, operating expenses are charged for the cost of materials and supplies. Materials and supplies issued for use for construction projects are capitalized temporarily as Construction Work in Progress. (Entry 10 illustrates the entry required when a capital project is completed in an enterprise fund.)

	Debits	Credits
7. Operating Expenses—Costs of Sales and Services	110,400	
Operating Expenses—Administration	60,000	
Construction Work in Progress	127,600	
Materials and Supplies		298,000

Payrolls for the year were chargeable to the accounts in the following entry. Taxes were accrued and withheld in the amount of $90,200, and the remainder was paid in cash.

	Debits	Credits
8. Operating Expenses—Costs of Sales and Services	253,600	
Operating Expenses—Administration	92,900	
Operating Expenses—Selling	17,200	
Construction Work in Progress	58,900	
Payroll Taxes Payable		90,200
Cash		332,400

Enterprise funds commonly undertake large capital projects financed through bond offerings (e.g., water treatment plants or municipal stadiums). Unlike those construction projects studied in Chapter 5, enterprise funds do not use capital projects funds. Both the bonds and the capital assets are recorded directly on the books of the enterprise funds.

It is common for governments to incur interest during the construction phase of a major capital addition. In a recent standard, GASB clarified the accounting for interest incurred during the construction phase by requiring such interest to be expensed, rather than capitalized. Assume bond interest in the amount of $189,000 was paid:

	Debits	Credits
9. Nonoperating Expenses—Interest	189,000	
Cash		189,000

Construction projects on which costs totaled $529,300 were completed and the assets placed in service. The cost of the asset is reclassified from *Construction Work in Progress* (which is not depreciated) to *Utility Plant in Service* (which is subject to depreciation).

	Debits	Credits
10. Utility Plant in Service	529,300	
Construction Work in Progress		529,300

Payment of accounts totaled $275,600, and payments of payroll taxes amounted to $81,200.

11. Accounts Payable	275,600	
Payroll Taxes Payable	81,200	
Cash		356,800

The Water Utility Fund received $10,000 cash from the Supplies Fund as partial payment of the long-term advance (see Supplies Fund, entry 9).

12. Cash	10,000	
Long-Term Advance to Supplies Fund		10,000

During the year, the Water Utility Fund made a transfer of $200,000 to the Fire Station Addition Capital Projects Fund (see entries 2 and 7 in Chapter 5):

13. Transfers Out	200,000	
Cash		200,000

At year-end, several adjustments are necessary. First, depreciation is recorded as an operating expense:

14. Operating Expenses—Depreciation	122,800	
Accumulated Depreciation—Utility Plant		122,800

Provision is made for bad debts from utility customers. Consistent with guidance provided by a GASB, the bad debt provision is a revenue reduction not an expense:

15. Operating Revenues—Charges for Sales and Services	2,200	
Allowance for Uncollectible Accounts		2,200

Following a provision in the revenue bond indenture, $55,000 was transferred from operating cash to the Restricted Assets category.

16. Restricted Assets	55,000	
Cash		55,000

Illustration 6-2 presents the general ledger account balances after posting the Water Utility Fund journal entries.

ILLUSTRATION 6-2 Water Utility General Ledger

Cash

Ref	Debit	Credit	Ref
*bb	467,130		
2	968,500	200,000	5
4	12,500	332,400	8
12	10,000	189,000	9
		356,800	11
		200,000	13
		55,000	16
	124,930		

Customer Accounts Receivable

Ref	Debit	Credit	Ref
bb	72,500		
1	975,300	968,500	2
		1,980	3
	77,320		

Allowance for Uncollectible Accounts

Ref	Debit	Credit	Ref
		2,175	bb
3	1,980	2,200	15
		2,395	

Due from General Fund

Ref	Debit	Credit	Ref
1	80,000		
	80,000		

Materials & Supplies

Ref	Debit	Credit	Ref
bb	37,500		
6	291,500	298,000	7
	31,000		

LT Advance to Other Funds

Ref	Debit	Credit	Ref
5	200,000	10,000	13
	190,000		

Restricted Assets

Ref	Debit	Credit	Ref
bb	55,000		
17	55,000		
	110,000		

Utility Plant in Service

Ref	Debit	Credit	Ref
bb	4,125,140		
10	529,300		
	4,654,440		

Accumulated Depreciation – Plant

Ref	Debit	Credit	Ref
		886,500	bb
		122,800	14
		1,009,300	

Construction Work in Process

Ref	Debit	Credit	Ref
bb	468,125		
7	127,600	529,300	10
8	58,900		
	125,325		

Accounts Payable

Ref	Debit	Credit	Ref
		73,700	bb
11	275,600	291,500	6
		89,600	

Payroll Taxes Payable

Ref	Debit	Credit	Ref
11	81,200	90,200	8
		9,000	

Revenue Bonds Payable

Ref	Debit	Credit	Ref
		2,700,000	bb
		2,700,000	

Net Position

Ref	Debit	Credit	Ref
		1,563,020	bb
		1,563,020	

Operating Revenue Charges for Services

Ref	Debit	Credit	Ref
15	2,200	1,055,300	1
		1,053,100	

Cost of Sales & Services

Ref	Debit	Credit	Ref
7	110,400		
8	253,600		
	364,000		

Administrative Expense

Ref	Debit	Credit	Ref
7	60,000		
8	92,900		
	152,900		

Depreciation Expense

Ref	Debit	Credit	Ref
14	122,800		
	122,800		

Selling Expense

Ref	Debit	Credit	Ref
8	17,200		
	17,200		

Nonoperating Expenses Interest

Ref	Debit	Credit	Ref
9	189,000		
	189,000		

Capital Contributions

Ref	Debit	Credit	Ref
		12,500	4
		12,500	

Transfers Out

Ref	Debit	Credit	Ref
13	200,000		
	200,000		

* bb indicates balance at January 1.

Revenue, expense, transfers, and capital contributions accounts for the year were closed to the Net Position account:

	Debit	Credit
17. Operating Revenues—Charges for Sales and Services	1,053,100	
Capital Contributions	12,500	
Operating Expenses—Costs of Sales and Services		364,000
Operating Expenses—Administration		152,900
Operating Expenses—Selling		17,200
Operating Expenses—Depreciation		122,800
Transfers Out		200,000
Nonoperating Expenses—Interest		189,000
Net Position		19,700

After posting the closing entry, Net Position has a balance of $1,582,720 ($1,563,020 beginning balance plus $19,700 from the closing entry). The Net Position balances to be reported in the December 31, 2020, Statement of Net Position are calculated as follows:

	Net Investment in Capital Assets	**Restricted**	**Unrestricted**	**Total**
Net Investment in Capital Assets:				
Construction Work in Process	$ 125,325			$ 125,325
Utility Plant in Service	4,654,440			4,654,440
Less Accumulated Depreciation	(1,009,300)			(1,009,300)
Less Revenue Bonds Payable	(2,700,000)			(2,700,000)
Restricted: Restricted Assets		$110,000		110,000
Unrestricted (plug)			$402,255	402,255
Total Net Position	$1,070,465	$110,000	$402,255	$1,582,720

Note that the capital assets included in Net Investment in Capital Assets are composed of both the Utility Plant in Service and the Construction Work in Process. Restricted Net Position equals the balance of the Restricted Assets that are required to be maintained by debt covenant. Unrestricted Net Position is the residual, computed as total net position less the balance in the other two net position categories ($1,582,720 – $1,070,465 – $110,000 = $402,255).

PROPRIETARY FUND FINANCIAL STATEMENTS

Governments are required to report the following proprietary fund financial statements: (1) Statement of Net Position; (2) Statement of Revenues, Expenses, and Changes in Fund Net Position; and (3) Statement of Cash Flows. As was true for governmental funds, *major* enterprise funds are to be presented separately, along with columns for nonmajor funds and total enterprise funds, where appropriate. On the other hand, a single column is to include all internal service funds. Illustrations 6-3, 6-4, and 6-5 reflect the proprietary funds statements for the Village of Riverside, which is assumed to have only one enterprise fund and one internal service fund.

ILLUSTRATION 6-3 Statement of Net Position

VILLAGE OF RIVERSIDE
Statement of Net Position
Proprietary Funds
December 31, 2020

	Business-type Activities—Enterprise Funds—Water Utility	Governmental Activities—Internal Service Funds
Assets		
Current assets:		
Cash	$ 124,930	$ 3,500
Investments		50,000
Accounts receivable (net)	74,925	
Due from General Fund	80,000	55,000
Materials and supplies	31,000	233,500
Total current assets	310,855	342,000
Noncurrent assets:		
Restricted assets	110,000	
Long-term advance to supplies fund	190,000	
Capital assets, net of accumulated depreciation	3,770,465	462,500
Total noncurrent assets	4,070,465	462,500
Total assets	4,381,320	804,500
Liabilities		
Current liabilities:		
Accounts payable	89,600	11,000
Payroll taxes payable	9,000	
Total current liabilities	98,600	11,000
Noncurrent liabilities:		
Advance from Water Utility Fund		190,000
Revenue bonds payable	2,700,000	
Total noncurrent liabilities	2,700,000	190,000
Total liabilities	2,798,600	201,000
Net Position		
Net investment in capital assets	1,070,465	272,500
Restricted for debt service	110,000	
Unrestricted	402,255	331,000
Total net position	$1,582,720	$603,500

ILLUSTRATION 6-4 Statement of Revenues, Expenses, and Changes in Fund Net Position

VILLAGE OF RIVERSIDE
Statement of Revenues, Expenses, and Changes in Fund Net Position
Proprietary Funds
For the Year Ended December 31, 2020

	Business-type Activities— Enterprise Funds— Water Utility	Governmental Activities— Internal Service Funds
Operating revenues:		
Charges for sales and services	$1,053,100	$377,000
Operating expenses:		
Cost of sales and services	364,000	334,000
Administration	152,900	11,000
Selling	17,200	
Depreciation	122,800	27,500
Total operating expenses	656,900	372,500
Operating income	396,200	4,500
Nonoperating revenues (expenses):		
Interest revenue		3,000
Interest expense	(189,000)	
Total nonoperating revenues (expenses)	(189,000)	3,000
Income before contributions and transfers	207,200	7,500
Capital contributions	12,500	
Transfers in		596,000
Transfers out	(200,000)	
Change in net position	19,700	603,500
Net position—January 1, 2020	1,563,020	–0–
Net position—December 31, 2020	$1,582,720	$603,500

Statement of Net Position

The Statement of Net Position for the proprietary funds for the Village of Riverside is presented as Illustration 6-3. GASB permits either this statement (Assets – Liabilities = Net Position) or a Balance Sheet where Assets = Liabilities + Net Position. GASB requires a classified format, where current assets, noncurrent assets, current liabilities, and noncurrent liabilities are presented separately. Net Position is segregated into the same three categories used for the government-wide Statement of Net Position. Restricted net position represents resources with constraints that are

1. Externally imposed by creditors (such as through debt covenants), grantors, contributors, or laws or regulations of other governments, or
2. Imposed by law through constitutional provisions or enabling legislation.

ILLUSTRATION 6-5 Statement of Cash Flows

VILLAGE OF RIVERSIDE Statement of Cash Flows Proprietary Funds For the Year Ended December 31, 2020	Business-type Activities—Enterprise Funds—Water Utility	Governmental Activities—Internal Service Funds
Cash flows from operating activities:		
Cash received from customers and departments	$968,500	$ 322,000
Cash paid to suppliers and employees	(502,700)	(567,500)
Net cash provided (used) by operating activities	465,800	(245,500)
Cash flows from noncapital financing activities:		
Transfer from General Fund for working capital		306,000
Transfer to capital projects fund	(200,000)	
Net cash provided (used) by noncapital financing activities	(200,000)	306,000
Cash flows from capital and related financing activities:		
Advance from Water Utility Fund		200,000
Transfer from General Fund for capital assets		290,000
Acquisition and construction of capital assets	(186,500)*	(490,000)
Interest paid on long-term debt	(189,000)	
Contributed capital	12,500	
Partial repayment of advance from Water Utility Fund		(10,000)
Net cash (used) by capital and related financing activities	(363,000)	(10,000)
Cash flows from investing activities:		
Advance to supplies fund	(200,000)	
Partial repayment of advance by supplies fund	10,000	
Purchase of investments		(50,000)
Interest received		3,000
Net cash (used) by investing activities	(190,000)	(47,000)
Net increase (decrease) in cash and cash equivalents	(287,200)	3,500
Cash and cash equivalents—beginning of year	522,130	0
Cash and cash equivalents—end of year	$234,930	$ 3,500
Reconciliation of operating income to net cash provided (used) by operating activities		
Operating income (loss)	396,200	4,500
Adjustments to reconcile operating income (loss) to net cash provided (used) by operating activities:		
Depreciation expense	122,800	27,500
Changes in assets and liabilities:		
Increase in customer accounts receivable	(4,600)	
Increase in interfund receivables	(80,000)	(55,000)
(Increase) decrease in inventory	6,500	(233,500)
Increase (decrease) in accounts payable	15,900	11,000
Increase in accrued liabilities	9,000	
Net cash provided (used) by operating activities	$465,800	$(245,500)

* Assume that the supplies used for capital additions in entry 7 are all paid for in entry 11 and none of the amount due for those supplies remains in Accounts Payable [$127,600 (entry 7) + $58,900 (entry 8)].

In the Village of Riverside example, the various fixed asset and accumulated depreciation accounts were combined to present a single net figure for each fund. It was assumed that all long-term debt was for capital assets. In the Water Utility Fund of the Village of Riverside, it is assumed that the $110,000 was restricted through a bond covenant.

It is worth noting that the balances appearing in an enterprise fund's Statement of Net Position appear in much the same manner in the government-wide Statement of Net Position. Compare the enterprise fund column in Illustration 6-3 with the *business-type activities* column in Illustration 8-6 found in Chapter 8. Note also that the internal service fund balances in Illustration 6-3 are labeled "Governmental Activities." This is because the internal service fund provides services primarily to other government departments, which are reported in the General Fund. Through a process that will be described in Chapter 8, the internal service fund's assets and liabilities are combined with those of the governmental funds and are reported in the *governmental activities* column of the government-wide Statement of Net Position (Illustration 8-6).

Statement of Revenues, Expenses, and Changes in Fund Net Position

The Statement of Revenues, Expenses, and Changes in Fund Net Position for the proprietary funds of the Village of Riverside is presented as Illustration 6-4. GASB requires that operating revenues and operating expenses be shown separately from and prior to nonoperating revenues and expenses. Operating income must be displayed. Operating revenues should be displayed by source. Operating expenses may be reported by function, as shown in Illustration 6-4, or may be reported by object classification, such as personal services, supplies, travel, and so forth.

Capital contributions, extraordinary and special items, and transfers should be shown separately, after nonoperating revenues and expenses. GASB requires the all-inclusive format, which reconciles to the ending net position. Note that the ending net position figure shown in Illustration 6-4 is the same as the total net position shown in the Statement of Net Position (Illustration 6-3).

The last three amounts appearing in Illustration 6-4 (change in net position $19,700, beginning net position $1,563,020, and ending net position $1,582,720) for the enterprise fund may be found at the bottom of the business-type activities column of the government-wide Statement of Activities in Illustration 8-7. In contrast to the detailed asset and liability balances, enterprise fund expense information is shown only as a total ($656,900 + $189,000 = $845,900) in the government-wide Statement of Activities.

Statement of Cash Flows

The Statement of Cash Flows for the proprietary funds for the Village of Riverside is presented as Illustration 6-5. Note that the figure for cash and cash equivalents includes the restricted assets, as is customary in practice. From Illustration 6-3, cash of $124,930 plus restricted assets of $110,000 equals the cash and cash equivalents of $234,930 (Illustration 6-5). GASB requires the direct method of reporting cash flows from operating activities. Other differences exist between GASB requirements and the requirements by FASB for businesses and nongovernmental not-for-profit organizations.

First, cash flow statements for proprietary funds have four categories, rather than the three presented under FASB standards. The four categories are

1. *Operating Activities:* Cash flows from **operating activities** include receipts from customers, payments to suppliers, payments to employees, and receipt and payment of cash for quasi-external transactions (interfund services provided and used) with other funds.
2. *Noncapital Financing Activities:* Cash flows from **noncapital financing activities** include proceeds and repayment of debt not clearly related to capital outlay, grants received from and paid to other governments for noncapital purposes, transfers to and from other funds, and the payment of interest associated with noncapital debt. Illustration 6-5 makes the assumption that $306,000 of the initial contribution from the General Fund to the internal service fund was for working capital.
3. *Capital and Related Financing Activities:* Cash flows from **capital and related financing activities** include proceeds and repayment of debt related to capital acquisition, the receipt of and payment of grants related to capital acquisition, the payment of interest on debt related to capital acquisition, and the purchase or construction of capital assets.
4. *Investing Activities:* Cash flows from **investing activities** include cash used to acquire investments, whether directly or through investment pools; the interest received on such investments; and cash received from the sale or redemption of investments. Note that cash flows from investing activities do not include acquisition of capital assets, as is the case with FASB requirements.

A reconciliation is required between the Statement of Revenues, Expenses, and Changes and Fund Net Position and the Cash Flow Statement. The reconciliation should be between operating income and cash flows from operating activities. This also is different from FASB format cash flow statements, which reconcile overall net income (or total change in net assets) to cash flows from operations.

Governments are required to disclose noncash investing, capital-related financing, and noncapital-related financing activities. These disclosures generally appear below the reconciliation of operating income and cash flows from operating activities at the bottom of the Statement of Cash Flows. As the heading suggests, these are activities that do not affect cash but change the balance of nonoperating asset and liability accounts. A capital lease is an example of a transaction that affects a nonoperating asset (e.g., equipment) and a long-term liability. Capital leases entered during the year would be disclosed and the amount (present value of minimum lease payments) reported as part of the Statement of Cash Flows. Sometimes developers contribute capital assets, such as water lines, to the local government. Since these do not involve cash, such contributions would also be disclosed as noncash items in a cash flow statement (see bottom of Illustration 2-11 for an example). A similar requirement exists for cash flow statements prepared for commercial businesses and private not-for-profit organizations.

ENVIRONMENTAL LIABILITIES

Accounting for Municipal Solid Waste Landfills

Many of the solid waste landfills in the United States are operated by local governments and reported as enterprise funds. GASB standards require that certain postclosure costs be estimated and accrued during the period the landfills receive solid waste.

The federal government requires that owners and operators of solid waste landfills be responsible for the landfill after it closes. Governments must assume the cost of closure, including the cost of equipment used, the cost of the landfill cover, and the cost of caring for the site for a period of 30 years as required by regulations. These costs are measured in current costs, in that the costs are estimated as if they were incurred at the time of estimate.

GASB standards require that a portion of those future estimated costs be charged as an expense and a liability of the landfill operation on a units-of-production method (based on capacity used divided by total capacity) as waste is accepted. For example, if the total estimated costs for closure and postclosure were $10 million, and the landfill accepted 10 percent of its anticipated capacity (cubic yards) in a given year, the charge and liability for that year would be $1 million. Each year, revisions would be made, if necessary, for changes in cost estimates, landfill capacity, and inflation.

If the landfill is operated as an enterprise fund, the entries would be made directly in the enterprise fund, following accrual accounting. If the landfill is operated as a governmental fund, then modified accrual principles would apply, and the fund expenditure and liability would be limited to the amount to be paid with available financial resources. The remainder would be reflected as a liability in the government-wide financial statements.

For example, assume a landfill is operated as an enterprise fund. The total estimated closure and postclosure costs are $30 million. Total estimated capacity of the landfill is 100 million tons. During 2020, the first year of operations, the landfill accepted 2 million tons, or 2 percent of its capacity. A $600,000 charge would be made during 2020:

	Debits	Credits
Operating Expenses—Estimated Landfill Closure and Postclosure Costs	600,000	
Accrued Liability for Estimated Landfill Closure and Postclosure Costs		600,000

The purpose of the charge is to match the estimated costs with the revenues during the period of time waste is accepted. Adjustments should be made yearly or whenever estimates for capacity or costs change. When the landfill is closed, and closure and postclosure costs are incurred, those costs will be charged to the liability account.

Pollution Remediation Costs and Asset Retirement Obligations

Increasingly, landfill and other waste storage sites are being identified by the U.S. Environmental Protection Agency or similar state agencies as requiring pollution remediation (cleanup and control). In 1980, Congress passed the Comprehensive Environmental Response, Compensation, and Liability Act (generally referred to as the Superfund Act), which places responsibility for pollution remediation on current and past owners and users of waste sites. State and local governments are increasingly finding they are responsible for the cleanup of sites failing to comply with federal and state standards. Even in cases where they did not operate a site, but merely used the facility, local governments can be held responsible for the cleanup. In response, GASB requires governments to accrue the cost of pollution remediation as a liability in the basic financial statements.

If the site is operated as an enterprise fund, the entries would be made in the enterprise fund, following accrual accounting. Otherwise, fund expenditures equal to the amount to be paid with available resources would appear in a governmental fund and the long-term portion of the liability in the government-wide Statement of Net Position. In addition, note disclosure is required describing the nature and scope of the government's responsibility, the estimated liability, the methods and assumptions used to estimate the liability, and any estimates of recoveries that might reduce the liability.

A recent GASB standard establishes reporting of **asset retirement obligations.** Laws, regulations, or contractual terms may require governments to retire certain assets at the end of their useful lives. For example, governments may be responsible for the costs of decommissioning nuclear power plants or shutting down sewage treatment facilities. GASB standards require financial statements prepared on the economic resource measurement focus (enterprise funds and government-wide statements) to reflect estimates of these liabilities on the Statement of Net Position.

Once it is determined that a government has an asset retirement obligation, the government should record its best estimate of the costs as a liability and a deferred outflow of resources. The liability will be reduced by payments for retirement-related activities. The deferred outflow will be amortized to expense (in a manner similar to depreciation) over the estimated useful life of the asset.

SUMMARY

This chapter examines accounting and reporting for proprietary funds. These funds account for those activities of the government that are businesslike in nature; that is, they charge other entities for goods and services with the purpose of measuring income. Enterprise funds provide goods and services to individuals and businesses and include water utilities, transit systems, airports, and recreational facilities. Internal service funds provide goods and services to other departments within the government and include centralized supplies, motor pools, printing centers, and risk management activities. These funds report using the accrual basis of accounting and the economic resources measurement focus. Significant aspects of proprietary fund accounting include the following:

- The required financial statements of proprietary funds include a Statement of Net Position; a Statement of Revenues, Expenses, and Changes in Fund Net Position; and a Statement of Cash Flows.
- The net position (i.e., fund equity) section of the Statement of Net Position is displayed within three categories: (1) Net Investment in Capital Assets, (2) Restricted, and (3) Unrestricted Net Position.
- The Statement of Cash Flows must be prepared using the direct method and includes cash flows from operating activities, investing activities, capital and related financing activities, and noncapital-related financing activities.

Questions and Exercises

6–1. Using the annual financial report obtained for Exercise 1–1, answer the following questions:

a. Review the Statement of Net Position for the proprietary funds. Is the Net Position or the Balance Sheet format used? List the major enterprise funds from that statement. Is the statement classified between current and noncurrent assets and liabilities? Is net position broken down into the three classifications shown in your text? Is a separate column shown for internal service funds?

b. Review the Statement of Revenues, Expenses, and Changes in Net Position for the proprietary funds. Is the "all-inclusive" format used? Are revenues reported by source? Are expenses (not expenditures) reported by function or by object classification? Is depreciation reported separately? Is operating income, or a similar title, displayed? Are nonoperating revenues and expenses shown separately after operating income? Are capital contributions, extraordinary and special items, and transfers shown separately? List any extraordinary and special items.

c. Review the Statement of Cash Flows for the proprietary funds. List the four categories of cash flows. Are they the same as shown in the text? Are interest receipts reported as cash flows from investing activities? Are interest payments shown as financing activities? Is the direct method used? Is a reconciliation shown from operating income to net cash provided by operations? Are capital assets acquired from financing activities shown as decreases in cash flows from financing activities? Does the ending cash balance agree with the cash balance shown in the Statement of Net Position (note that restricted assets may be included)?

d. If your government has a CAFR, look to any combining statements and list the nonmajor enterprise funds. List the internal service funds.

e. Examine the financial statements from the point of view of a financial analyst. Write down the unrestricted net position balances for each of the major enterprise funds and (if you have a CAFR) the nonmajor enterprise funds and internal service funds. Look at the long-term debt of major enterprise funds. Can you tell from the statements or the notes whether the debt is general obligation or revenue in nature? Write down the income before contributions, extraordinary items, special items, and transfers for each of the funds. Compare these numbers with prior years, if the information is provided in your financial statements. Look at the transfers. Can you tell if the general government is subsidizing or is subsidized by enterprise funds?

6–2. What accounting problem arises if an internal service fund is operated at a significant profit? What accounting problem arises if an internal service fund is operated at a significant loss?

6–3. Why might it be desirable to operate enterprise funds at a profit?

6–4. The Village of Seaside Pines prepared the following enterprise fund Trial Balance as of December 31, 2020, the last day of its fiscal year. The enterprise fund was established this year through a transfer from the General Fund.

	Debits	**Credits**
Accounts payable		$ 96,000
Accounts receivable	$ 32,000	
Accrued interest payable		28,000
Accumulated depreciation		45,000
Administrative and selling expenses	47,000	
Allowance for uncollectible accounts		12,000
Capital assets	712,000	
Cash	89,000	
Charges for sales and services		550,000
Cost of sales and services	479,000	
Depreciation expense	45,000	
Due from General Fund	17,000	
Interest expense	40,000	
Interest revenue		4,000
Transfer in from General Fund		119,000
Bank note payable		625,000
Supplies inventory	18,000	
Totals	$1,479,000	$1,479,000

Required:

a. Prepare the closing entries for December 31.

b. Prepare the Statement of Revenues, Expenses, and Changes in Fund Net Position for the year ended December 31.

c. Prepare the Net Position section of the December 31 balance sheet. (Assume that the revenue bonds were issued to acquire capital assets and there are no restricted assets.)

6–5. Using the information provided in Exercise 6–4, prepare the reconciliation of operating income to net cash provided by operating activities that would appear at the bottom of the December 31 Statement of Cash Flows. Recall that the beginning balance of all assets and liabilities is zero.

6–6. The Town of Weston has a Water Utility Fund with the following trial balance as of July 1, 2019, the first day of the fiscal year:

	Debits	Credits
Cash	$ 250,000	
Customer accounts receivable	200,000	
Allowance for uncollectible accounts		$ 30,000
Materials and supplies	120,000	
Restricted assets (cash)	250,000	
Utility plant in service	7,000,000	
Accumulated depreciation—utility plant		2,600,000
Construction work in progress	180,000	
Accounts payable		120,000
Accrued expenses payable		75,000
Revenue bonds payable		3,600,000
Net position		1,575,000
Totals	$8,000,000	$8,000,000

During the year ended June 30, 2020, the following transactions and events occurred in the Town of Weston Water Utility Fund:

1. Accrued expenses at July 1 were paid in cash.
2. Billings to nongovernmental customers for water usage for the year amounted to $1,380,000; billings to the General Fund amounted to $96,000.
3. Liabilities for the following were recorded during the year:

Materials and supplies	$185,000
Costs of sales and services	345,000
Administrative expenses	202,000
Construction work in progress	220,000

4. Materials and supplies were used in the amount of $275,000, all for costs of sales and services.
5. After collection efforts were unsuccessful, $9,000 of old accounts receivable were written off.
6. Accounts receivable collections totaled $1,459,000 from nongovernmental customers and $48,400 from the General Fund.
7. $1,035,000 of accounts payable were paid in cash.
8. One year's interest in the amount of $175,000 was paid.
9. Construction was completed on plant assets costing $250,000; that amount was transferred to Utility Plant in Service.
10. Depreciation was recorded in the amount of $260,000.
11. The Allowance for Uncollectible Accounts was increased by $9,900.
12. As required by the loan agreement, cash in the amount of $100,000 was transferred to Restricted Assets for eventual redemption of the bonds.

13. Accrued expenses, all related to costs of sales and services, amounted to $83,000.
14. Nominal accounts for the year were closed.

Required:

a. Record the transactions for the year in general journal form.

b. Prepare a Statement of Revenues, Expenses, and Changes in Fund Net Position.

c. Prepare a Statement of Net Position as of June 30, 2020.

d. Prepare a Statement of Cash Flows for the year ended June 30, 2020. Assume all debt and interest are related to capital outlay. Assume the entire construction work in progress liability (see item 3) was paid in entry 7. Include restricted assets as cash and cash equivalents.

6–7. The City of Sandwich purchased a swimming pool from a private operator as of April 1, 2020, for $400,000, of which $200,000 was provided by a one-time contribution from the General Fund, and $200,000 was provided by a loan from the First National Bank, secured by a note. The loan has an annual interest rate of 6 percent, payable semiannually on October 1 and April 1; principal payments of $100,000 are to be made annually, beginning on April 1, 2021. The City has a calendar year as its fiscal year. During the year ended December 31, 2020, the following transactions occurred related to the City of Sandwich Swimming Pool:

1. The amounts were received from the City General Fund and the First National Bank.
2. A loan was provided in the amount of $125,000 from the Water Utility Fund to provide working capital.
3. The purchase of the pool was recorded. Based on an appraisal, it was decided to allocate $100,000 to the land, $200,000 to improvements other than buildings (the pool), and $100,000 to the building.
4. Charges to patrons during the season amounted to $242,000, all received in cash.
5. Salaries paid to employees amounted to $115,000, all paid in cash, of which $75,000 was cost of services and $40,000 was administration.
6. Supplies purchased amounted to $40,000; all but $5,000 was used. Cash was paid for the supplies, all of which was for cost of sales and services.
7. Administrative expenses amounted to $16,500, paid in cash.
8. The first interest payment was made to the First National Bank.
9. The short-term loan was repaid to the Water Utility Fund.
10. Depreciation of $18,500 for the pool and $6,000 on the building was recorded for the nine months they were in operation.
11. Interest was accrued for the year.
12. Closing entries were prepared.

Required:

a. Prepare entries to record the transactions.

b. Prepare a Statement of Revenues, Expenses, and Changes in Fund Net Position for the year ended December 31, 2020, for the City of Sandwich Swimming Pool Fund.

c. Prepare a Statement of Net Position as of December 31, 2020, for the City of Sandwich Swimming Pool Fund.

d. Prepare a Statement of Cash Flows for the year ended December 31, 2020, for the City of Sandwich Swimming Pool Fund.

6–8. The Village of Parry reported the following for its Print Shop Fund for the year ended April 30, 2020.

VILLAGE OF PARRY—PRINT SHOP FUND
Statement of Revenues, Expenses, and Changes in Net Position
For the Year Ended April 30, 2020

Operating revenues:		
Charges for services		$1,118,000
Operating expenses:		
Salaries and benefits	$495,000	
Depreciation	260,000	
Supplies used	200,000	
Utilities	72,000	
Total operating expenses		1,027,000
Income from operations		91,000
Nonoperating income (expenses):		
Interest revenue	3,000	
Interest expense	(5,000)	
Total nonoperating expenses		(2,000)
Income before transfers		89,000
Transfers in		180,000
Changes in net position		269,000
Net position—beginning		1,120,000
Net position—ending		$1,389,000

The Print Shop Fund records also revealed the following:

1. Contribution from General Fund for working capital needs	$ 70,000
2. Contribution from General Fund for purchase of equipment	110,000
3. Loan (interest-free) from Water Utility Fund for purchase of equipment	300,000
4. Purchase of equipment	(500,000)
5. Purchase of one-year investments	(50,000)
6. Paid off a bank loan outstanding at May 1, 2019. The loan was for short-term operating purposes and was the only interest-bearing debt outstanding	(51,000)
7. Signed a capital lease on April 30, 2020	$ 36,780

The following balances were observed in current asset and current liability accounts. ( ) denote credit balances:

	5/1/2019	4/30/2020
Cash	$151,000	$368,800
Accrued interest receivable	300	500
Due from other funds	40,000	55,000
Supplies	0	0
Accrued salaries and benefits	(20,000)	(30,000)
Utility bills payable	(4,000)	(5,000)
Accounts payable (for supplies only)	(30,000)	(25,000)
Accrued interest payable	(1,000)	0
Bank loan payable	(51,000)	0

Prepare a Statement of Cash Flows for the Village of Parry Print Shop Fund for the year ended April 30, 2020. Include the reconciliation of operating income to net cash provided by operating activities.

6–9. The following is a Statement of Cash Flows for the risk management internal service fund of the City of Wrightville. An inexperienced accountant prepared the statement using the FASB format rather than the format required by GASB. All long-term debt was issued to purchase capital assets. The transfer from the General Fund was to establish the internal service fund and provide the initial working capital necessary for operations.

CITY OF WRIGHTVILLE
Risk Management Internal Service Fund
Statement of Cash Flows
For the Year Ended June 30, 2020

Cash flows from operating activities:	
Cash received from other departments	$905,000
Cash paid for suppliers and employees	(120,000)
Cash paid on insurance claims	(700,000)
Transfer from General Fund	250,000
Investment income received	25,000
Interest paid on long-term debt	(15,000)
Cash flows from operating activities	345,000
Cash flows from investing activities:	
Acquisition of property, plant, and equipment	(290,000)
Purchase of investments	(170,000)
Sale of property, plant, and equipment	42,000
Cash flows from investing activities	(418,000)
Cash flows from financing activities:	
Proceeds from issuance of long-term debt	300,000
Payments on long-term debt	(14,000)
Cash flows from financing activities	286,000
Net increase in cash and cash equivalents	213,000
Cash and cash equivalents, July 1, 2019	118,000
Cash and cash equivalents, June 30, 2020	$331,000

Prepare a statement of cash flows using the appropriate format as required by GASB. You do not need to prepare the reconciliation of operating income to cash flow from operations.

6–10. The Town of Frostbite self-insures for some of its liability claims and purchases insurance for others. In an effort to consolidate its risk management activities, the Town recently decided to establish an internal service fund, the Risk Management Fund. The Risk Management Fund's purpose is to obtain liability coverage for the Town, to pay claims not covered by the insurance, and to charge individual departments in amounts sufficient to cover current-year costs and to establish a reserve for losses.

The Town reports proprietary fund expenses by object classification using the following accounts: Personnel Services (salaries), Contractual Services (for the expired portion of prepaid service contracts), Depreciation, and Insurance Claims. The following transactions relate to the year ended December 31, 2020, the first year of the Risk Management Fund's operations.

1. The Risk Management Fund is established through a transfer of $400,000 from the General Fund and a long-term advance from the water utility enterprise fund of $200,000.
2. The Risk Management Fund purchased (prepaid) insurance coverage through several commercial insurance companies for $180,000. The policies purchased require the Town to self-insure for $25,000 per incident.
3. Office equipment is purchased for $25,000.
4. $380,000 is invested in marketable securities.
5. Actuarial estimates were made in the previous fiscal year to determine the amount necessary to attain the goal of accumulating sufficient funds to cover current-year claims and to establish a reserve for losses. It was determined that the General Fund and water utility be assessed a fee of 6 percent of total wages and salaries (interfund premium). Wages and salaries by department are as follows:

Public Safety	$ 5,000,000
General Administrative Operations	1,500,000
Education	1,500,000
Water Utility	2,500,000
Total	$10,500,000

6. Cash received in payment of interfund premiums from the General Fund totaled $380,000, and cash received from the water utility totaled $150,000.
7. Interest and dividends received totaled $18,000.
8. Salaries for the Risk Management Fund amounted to $172,000 (all paid during the year).
9. Claims paid under self-insurance totaled $207,000 during the year.

10. The office equipment is depreciated on the straight-line basis over five years.
11. At year-end, $165,000 of the insurance policies purchased in January had expired.
12. The market value of investments at December 31 totaled $391,000 (*Hint:* credit *Nonoperating Revenue—Net Increase in Fair Market Value of Investments*).
13. In addition to the claims paid in entry 9 above, estimates for the liability for the Town's portion of known claims since the inception of the Town's self-insurance program totaled $190,000.

Required:

a. Prepare the journal entries (including closing entries) to record the transactions.

b. Prepare a Statement of Revenues, Expenses, and Changes in Fund Net Position for the year ended December 31, 2020, for the Risk Management Fund.

c. Prepare a Statement of Net Position as of December 31, 2020, for the Risk Management Fund.

d. Prepare a Statement of Cash Flows for the year ended December 31, 2020, for the Risk Management Fund. Assume $25,000 of the transfer from the General Fund was for the purchase of the equipment. Further, assume the remainder of the transfer from the General Fund and all of the advance from the enterprise fund are to establish working capital (noncapital-related financing).

e. Comment on whether the interfund premium of 6 percent of wages and salaries is adequate.

6–11. The City of Evansville operated a summer camp program for at-risk youth. Businesses and nonprofit organizations sponsor one or more youth by paying the registration fee for program participants. The following Schedule of Cash Receipts and Disbursements summarizes the activity in the program's bank account for the year.

1. At the beginning of 2020, the program had unrestricted cash of $18,000.

	Cash Basis 12 months
Cash receipts:	
Registration fees	$100,000
Borrowing from bank	75,000
Total deposits	175,000
Cash disbursements:	
Wages	46,575
Payroll taxes	7,000
Insurance (paid monthly)	8,000
Purchase of bus	80,000
Interest on bank note	2,250
Total checks	143,825
Excess of receipts over disbursements	$ 31,175

2. The loan from the bank is dated April 1 and is for a five-year period. Interest (6 percent annual rate) is paid on October 1 and April 1 of each year, beginning October 1, 2020.
3. The bus was purchased on April 1 with the proceeds provided by the bank loan and has an estimated useful life of five years (straight-line basis—use monthly depreciation).
4. All invoices and salaries related to 2020 had been paid by close of business on December 31, except for the employer's portion of December payroll taxes, totaling $800.
   a. Prepare the journal entries, closing entries, and a Statement of Revenues, Expenses, and Changes in Fund Net Position assuming the City intends to treat the summer camp program as an enterprise fund.
   b. Prepare the journal entries, closing entries, and a Statement of Revenues, Expenditures, and Changes in Fund Balance assuming the City intends to treat the summer camp program as a special revenue fund.

6–12. The Town of Thomaston has a Solid Waste Landfill Enterprise Fund with the following trial balance as of January 1, 2020, the first day of the fiscal year:

	Debits	Credits
Cash	$2,330,000	
Supplies: diesel fuel	80,000	
Equipment	7,190,000	
Accumulated depreciation		$2,790,000
Accounts payable		130,000
Accrued closure and postclosure care costs payable		2,080,000
Net position		4,600,000
Totals	$9,600,000	$9,600,000

During the year, the following transactions and events occurred:

1. Citizens and trash companies dumped 513,000 tons of waste in the landfill, which charges $5.55 a ton payable in cash.
2. Diesel fuel purchases totaled $347,000 (on account).
3. Accounts payable totaling $430,000 were paid.
4. Diesel fuel used in operations amounted to $368,000.
5. Depreciation was recorded in the amount of $685,000.
6. Salaries totaling $165,000 were paid.
7. Future costs to close the landfill and postclosure care costs are expected to total $81,250,000. The total capacity of the landfill is expected to be 25,000,000 tons of waste.

Prepare the journal entries, closing entries, and a Statement of Revenues, Expenses, and Changes in Fund Net Position for the year ended December 31, 2020.

Excel-Based Problems

6–13. Jefferson County operates a centralized motor pool to service county vehicles. At the end of 2019, the Motor Pool Internal Service Fund had the following account balances:

	Debits	Credits
Due from General Fund	$ 7,000	
Cash	17,500	
Capital assets	35,000	
Supplies inventory	4,000	
Accounts payable		$ 5,500
Accrued wages payable		300
Accumulated depreciation		6,500
Advance from enterprise fund		25,000
Net position		26,200
Total	$63,500	$63,500

The following events took place during 2020:

1. Additional supplies were purchased on account in the amount of $37,500.
2. Services provided to other departments on account totaled $96,000. A total of $66,000 was for departments in the General Fund and $30,000 for enterprise fund departments.
3. Supplies used amounted to $36,700.
4. Payments made on accounts payable amounted to $38,800.
5. Cash collected from the General Fund totaled $62,000, and cash collected from the enterprise fund totaled $30,000.
6. Salaries were paid in the amount of $47,900. Included in this amount is the accrued wages payable at the end of 2019. All of these are determined to be part of the cost of services provided.
7. In a previous year, the enterprise fund loaned the motor pool money under an advance for the purpose of purchasing garage equipment. In the current year, the motor pool repaid the enterprise fund $8,000 of this amount.
8. On July 1, 2020, the Motor Pool Fund borrowed $12,000 from the bank, signing a 12 percent note that is due in two years with annual interest payments on June 30. The borrowings are not related to capital asset purchases but were made to provide working capital.

Additional information includes:

9. Depreciation for the year amounted to $6,900.
10. The payment of interest on the note is payable on June 30, 2021.
11. Unpaid wages relating to the final week of the year totaled $980.

Required:

Using the Excel template provided (a separate tab is provided for each of the requirements):

a. Prepare journal entries and post entries to the T-accounts.

b. Prepare closing entries.

c. Prepare a Statement of Revenues, Expenses, and Changes in Fund Net Position.

d. Prepare a Statement of Net Position.

e. Prepare a Statement of Cash Flows for the year.

6–14. Rural County is an agricultural community located hundreds of miles from any metropolitan center. The County established a Television Reception Improvement Fund to serve the public interest by constructing and operating television translator stations. TV translator stations serve communities that cannot receive the signals of free over-the-air TV stations because they are too far away from a broadcasting TV station. Because of the large distances between customers, commercial cable TV providers are also not inclined to serve rural communities. The fund charges TV owners a monthly fee of $15. The fund was established on December 20, 2019, with a transfer of cash from the General Fund of $125,000. On December 31, 2019, the fund acquired land for its translator stations in the amount of $40,000. The remaining cash and the land are the only resources held by the fund at the beginning of 2020.

1. Other than beginning account balances, no entries have been made in the general ledger.
2. The County prepared a budget for 2020 with estimated customer fees of $32,000, operating costs of $28,000, capital costs of $66,000, and estimated loan proceeds of $55,000.
3. The following information was taken from the checkbook for the year ended December 31, 2020:

	Cash Basis 12 months
Cash Receipts:	
Fees from customers	$35,100
Borrowing from bank	52,000
Total deposits	87,100
Cash Disbursements:	
Supplies	7,300
Labor	12,000
Utilities	7,500
Equipment	64,000
Interest on bank note	2,080
Total checks	92,880
Beginning Cash Balance	85,000
Ending Cash Balance	$79,220

4. The loan from the bank is dated April 1 and is for a five-year period. Interest (8 percent annual rate) is paid on October 1 and April 1 of each year, beginning October 1, 2020. The County has elected not to establish a debt service fund but will pay the interest on this note from the Television Reception Improvement Fund.
5. The machinery was purchased on April 1 with the proceeds provided by the bank loan and has an estimated useful life of 10 years (straight-line basis).
6. In January 2021, customers remitted fees totaling $2,850 for December service.
7. Supplies of $750 were received on December 29 and paid in January 2021.
8. Unused supplies on hand amounted to $760 at December 31, 2020.
9. Utilities are paid in the following month. The utility bill for December 2020 was received on January 4, 2021 in the amount of $550. (Utility bills are recorded through accounts payable.)
10. On December 21, the company placed an order for a new computerized control switch in the amount of $1,500 to be delivered and paid in January 2021.

Required:

You have been asked to provide financial statements for the upcoming County Board meeting for the Television Reception Improvement Fund.

Part 1: Assume the County chooses to report the Television Reception Improvement Fund as a special revenue fund following modified accrual basis statements. Using the Excel template provided,

a. Prepare journal entries recording the events above for the year ending December 31, 2020.

b. Post the journal entries to T-accounts.

c. Prepare closing entries.

d. Prepare a Statement of Revenues, Expenditures, and Changes in Fund Balance.

e. Prepare a Balance Sheet, assuming there are no restricted or committed fund net resources.

Part 2: Assume the County chooses to report the Television Reception Improvement Fund as an enterprise fund following accrual basis statements. Using the Excel template provided,

a. Prepare journal entries recording the events above for the year ending December 31, 2020.

b. Post the journal entries to T-accounts.

c. Prepare closing entries.

d. Prepare a Statement of Revenues, Expenses, and Changes in Fund Net Position.

e. Prepare a Statement of Net Position, assuming the bank note is related to capital asset acquisitions.

The Excel template contains separate tabs for (1) special revenue fund journal entries and T-accounts, (2) special revenue fund closing entries, (3) special revenue fund financial statements, (4) enterprise fund journal entries and T-accounts, (5) enterprise fund closing entries, and (6) enterprise fund financial statements. Both the T-accounts and financial statements contain accounts you will not need under either the modified accrual or accrual bases. Similarly, you may not need to record some of the events, depending on the basis of accounting.

Continuous Problem

The continuous problem is available in Connect through the Additional Student Resources in the eBook or instructor library. Complete the assignments for Chapter 6.

Chapter **Seven**

Fiduciary Funds

I don't recall anyone—I don't remember a single solitary soul in the legislature—expressing any criticism of it. Douglas Wilder, 66th governor of Virginia, defending the state retirement system's investment in property that he subsequently offered to the Washington Redskins for the site of a new stadium. The acquisition was investigated by the state legislature, which instituted reforms designating the retirement system as a constitutionally protected independent trust.

Oak Ridge Monitoring Private-Purpose Trust Fund*—this fund is used to account for monies paid by the federal government to the state for future expenses at the Environmental Management Waste Management Facility at Oak Ridge. After the federal landfill is closed, the income generated from the corpus is to be used for monitoring and maintenance of the facility to ensure there is no radioactive leakage.* State of Tennessee Comprehensive Annual Financial Report—fund descriptions

Learning Objectives

- Identify the fiduciary funds and describe when each is appropriate.
- Apply the accrual basis of accounting in the recording of typical transactions of private-purpose trust, investment trust, pension (and other employee benefit) trust, and custodial funds.
- Prepare the fund-basis financial statements for fiduciary funds.
- Apply GASB standards for the measurement and reporting of investments.

Governments commonly are given custody of assets to be held for the benefit of third parties, including individuals, organizations, and other governmental units. Frequently these activities are reported in Fiduciary Funds. Fiduciary activities are reported in two fund basis financial statements: the **Statement of Fiduciary Net Position** and the **Statement of Changes in Fiduciary Net Position.** Because the resources of fiduciary activities are *not* held for the benefit of the reporting entity, fiduciary activities are excluded from the government-wide financial statements.

Fiduciary activities may be performed through a legally separate component unit of the government. This is commonly the case with employee benefit (pension) plans. Legally separate pension plans are deemed to be fiduciary component units if there is a financial benefit or burden relationship and either a majority of the pension board is appointed by the primary government or the pension plan is fiscally dependent on the primary government. A financial burden exists when the primary government is responsible for making contributions to the pension plan.

In other cases fiduciary activities may be governed by formal trust agreements. A trust is established when assets are entrusted to a government through a formal agreement that specifies the purpose of the trust, the beneficiaries, and the powers and limitations of the trustee. Regardless of the varying forms of a fiduciary relationship (component unit, formal trust, or other agreement) fiduciary resources and activities are reported in the two fund-basis financial statements.

A recent GASB pronouncement identifies fiduciary activities and defines four fund types to be used to report such activities. Generally speaking, fiduciary activities meet the following criteria:

- A government either has custody of certain assets or has the ability to direct the use of the assets for the benefit of others outside the government.
- The assets are *not* derived from the government's own-source revenue, such as charges for services or taxes.
- The assets are held for the benefit of another party through
  - A trust agreement in which the government is *not* the beneficiary and the assets are protected from the government's creditors or
  - Another agreement in which the government does *not* have direct administrative or financial involvement. Examples of such agreements include pass-through grants or tax collections for other governments.

Activities meeting these criteria are reported within four types of fiduciary funds:

1. **Pension (or other employee benefit) trust funds** are used to report pension and other employee benefit plans that are held in a trust in which the reporting government is the trustee.
2. An **investment trust fund** exists when the government is the sponsor of a multi-government investment pool. It is used to report the external portion of investment pools that are governed by a trust agreement.
3. **Private-purpose trust funds** are used when the government is in a fiduciary relationship governed by a formal trust agreement other than those reported in pension or investment trust funds.
4. **Custodial funds** report fiduciary activities that are *not* governed by formal trust arrangements.

Fiduciary funds use the economic resources measurement focus and accrual basis of accounting. The residual equity of fiduciary funds is termed "restricted net position" and generally indicates the nature of the restriction (e.g., pensions, investment pool participants, etc.) The terms **additions** and **deductions** are used in fiduciary fund reporting in lieu of revenues and expenses. However, additions and deductions are measured on the accrual basis. The accounting for fiduciary funds is summarized in Illustration 7-1. Recall that fiduciary funds are *not* included in the government-wide financial statements.

ILLUSTRATION 7-1 **Summary of Fiduciary-type Funds**

Fund Name	Accrual Basis	Economic Resources Focus	Record Budgets	Encumbrances	Fund Description	Fund Term
Pension (and other employee benefit) Trust Fund	✓	✓			Accounts for assets held and invested on behalf of government employee pension (or other benefit) plans in which the reporting government acts as trustee.	Indefinite term: While pension benefits continue.
Investment Trust Fund	✓	✓			Accounts for assets held and invested on behalf of other governments under a trust agreement in a multi-government investment pool in which the reporting government is the trustee.	Indefinite term: While other parties (e.g., governments) continue to participate in the investment pool.
Private Purpose Trust Fund	✓	✓			Accounts for assets held according to a trust agreement other than a trust reported in pension or investment trust funds.	Indefinite term: While assets continue to be held in trust.
Custodial Fund	✓	✓			Accounts for assets held in a fiduciary capacity *not* governed by a trust agreement.	Indefinite term: While assets continue to be collected or held for others.

Pensions require two types of reporting: plan and employer. This chapter illustrates reporting by the plan and Chapter 9 describes employer reporting. In addition to the two required financial statements, schedules are required for pension (and other employee benefit) trust funds as Required Supplementary Information (RSI).

PRIVATE-PURPOSE TRUST FUNDS

We will start by illustrating the accounting for a private-purpose trust fund since it is perhaps the least complex and because it illustrates the general principles of trust accounting. Recall that when a fiduciary activity exists and is governed by a trust agreement other than a pension or investment trust fund, it should be reported as a private-purpose trust fund. A common example of such a trust agreement is the establishment of an endowment.

Endowments are created when individuals or organizations contribute resources with the agreement that principal and/or income will be used to benefit others. For example, a government may agree to be trustee for a community foundation, where awards are made to not-for-profit organizations. In some cases, the principal of those gifts may be *nonexpendable,* in which case an **endowment** has been created. In other cases, the principal of those gifts may be expendable.

In either case, management of the trust may involve significant investments. Therefore, before we begin to illustrate the accounting for a private-purpose trust fund, a review of investment accounting is presented below.

Accounting for Investments

GASB standards require (1) interest-earning investment contracts (CDs, time deposits, etc.), (2) external investment pools, (3) open-end mutual funds, (4) debt securities, and (5) equity securities that have readily determinable fair values to be reported in the balance sheet at fair value. GASB standards also require investments of pension funds to be reported at fair value with the result that most investments are reported at fair value, regardless of which fund holds the investment.

GASB developed a hierarchy to assist in identifying the most appropriate measure of fair value. The highest level are quoted prices from an active market in which buyers and sellers are acting in their own best interest. Market prices are not adjusted for transaction costs associated with a purchase or sale. There are a few exceptions to the fair value requirement. For example, investments in bonds without determinable fair values would be reported at amortized cost. Also, if a government has sufficient investments in a company to justify the equity method of accounting (see an intermediate accounting text), then the equity method of accounting would be followed.

Additionally, investment income, including changes in the fair value of investments, should be recognized as revenue. When identified separately as an element of investment revenue, the change in the fair value of investments should be captioned *net increase (decrease) in the fair value of investments.* GASB does not permit separate display of the realized and unrealized components of the change in fair value, with the exception of external investment pools. However, GASB does permit note disclosure of the amount of realized gains. Other major disclosures include (1) methods and assumptions used to determine fair value, if other than quoted market prices, and (2) the policy for determining which investments would be accounted for at amortized cost.

Similarly, GASB standards require that endowments with investments in real estate report those assets at fair value rather than historical cost. Any resulting changes in fair value (e.g., gains or losses) are to be reported as investment income. The standard applies to land and other real estate held in endowments for investment purposes, including investments held in permanent funds. The standard ensures similar accounting treatment for real estate investments between endowments and other investment activities (e.g., pensions or external investment pools).

Another GASB standard[1] establishes reporting requirements for governments entering into derivative instruments. Derivative instruments are financial contracts whose fair value is derived from the price of an underlying asset or obligation. For example, a government may enter into a derivative contract to protect against increases in natural gas costs. In this case, the fair value of the derivative is derived from the level and volatility of natural gas prices. Derivatives include swaps, options, forward contracts, and futures contracts. Regardless, derivative instruments are to be reported at fair value. However, the reporting of the change in value (i.e., gains or losses) depends on the type of derivative.

- **Hedging derivatives.** Governments can enter derivative contracts to mitigate the risk of economic loss arising from changes in the underlying asset or obligation. This activity is known as *hedging*. For example, a government purchasing equipment from a Japanese manufacturer enters a forward (currency) exchange contract to protect against an unfavorable change in exchange rates. If the derivative is effective in reducing a government's exposure to identifiable risks, then the changes in the value of that derivative are deferred. This means the changes in value are reported in the Statement of Net Position, not the activity statement. The deferred gains or losses typically continue to be reported as deferred outflows or deferred inflows until the hedged transaction occurs (e.g., when payment is made for the equipment).
- **Investment derivatives.** Less commonly, governments may enter derivative contracts for the purpose of earning a return. Changes in the value of derivatives classified as investment purpose are reflected as investment gains or losses in the period that the value changes.

GASB provides additional guidance for determining whether a hedge is effective. These are beyond the scope of this text. However, derivative instruments that are deemed to be ineffective hedges are classified as investment purpose, and the gains and losses are recognized in each period's activity statement. The treatment described above applies to government financial statements prepared using the accrual basis of accounting, including government-wide statements, proprietary

[1] *Codification* § D40.101.

funds, and fiduciary funds. In the case of governmental funds engaged in derivative activities, the requirements apply only to reporting at the government-wide level, not the fund-basis statements.

In the example that follows, we examine the accounting for investments in the context of a private-purpose trust fund. However, it should be noted that the concepts are applicable to any fund type with investment activity.

Illustrative Case—Private-Purpose Trust Funds

Assume that on January 2, 2020, a wealthy individual contributed $500,000 to the Village of Riverside and signed a trust agreement specifying that the principal amount be held intact and invested. The income is to be used to provide college scholarships to selected graduates from the Village's two high schools.

Private-purpose trust funds account for endowment trust agreements where principal and/or income benefit individuals, private organizations, or other governments. The distinguishing characteristic of a private-purpose trust fund is that the benefit is limited to specific private, rather than general public, purposes (see Illustration 5-2 for a summary of trust types). Since the beneficiaries are limited to students receiving scholarships, this endowment would be reported as a fiduciary (rather than permanent) fund.

On January 2, the gift was recorded in the newly created Scholarship Fund:

	Debits	Credits
1. Cash	500,000	
Additions—Contributions		500,000

On the same day, Village administrators purchased AB Company bonds as an investment in the amount of $480,000 plus accrued interest. The bonds carry an annual rate of interest of 6 percent, payable semiannually on May 1 and November 1. As of that date, accrued interest amounted to $4,800 ($480,000 × .06 × 2/12):

	Debits	Credits
2. Investment in AB Bonds	480,000	
Accrued Interest Receivable	4,800	
Cash		484,800

On May 1, the Scholarship Fund received interest in the amount of $14,400, of which $4,800 was accrued at the time of purchase (item 2 above).

	Debits	Credits
3. Cash	14,400	
Accrued Interest Receivable		4,800
Additions—Investment Earnings—Interest		9,600

On May 31, $9,000 in scholarships were awarded:

	Debits	Credits
4. Deductions—Scholarship Awards	9,000	
Cash		9,000

On November 1, interest in the amount of $14,400 was received:

	Debit	Credit
5. Cash	14,400	
Additions—Investment Earnings—Interest		14,400

As of December 31, an interest accrual was made for two months, November and December ($480,000 × .06 × 2/12):

	Debit	Credit
6. Accrued Interest Receivable	4,800	
Additions—Investment Earnings—Interest		4,800

GASB standards require that investments with determinable market values be reported at fair value. It was determined that the AB Company bonds had a fair value of $482,000 on December 31, exclusive of accrued interest:

	Debit	Credit
7. Investment in AB Bonds	2,000	
Additions—Investment Earnings—Net Increase in Fair Value of Investments		2,000

Finally, a closing entry was prepared for the Scholarship Fund:

	Debit	Credit
8. Additions—Contributions	500,000	
Additions—Investment Earnings—Interest	28,800	
Additions—Investment Earnings—Net Increase in Fair Value of Investments	2,000	
Deductions—Scholarship Awards		9,000
Fiduciary Net Position: Restricted		521,800

Financial statements for the Scholarship Private-Purpose Trust Fund are included in the Village of Riverside Statement of Fiduciary Net Position (Illustration 7-3,) and Statement of Changes in Fiduciary Net Position (Illustration 7-4), presented later in this chapter.

PUBLIC EMPLOYEE RETIREMENT SYSTEMS (PENSION TRUST FUNDS)

The U.S. government first began to provide pension benefits to veterans of the Revolutionary War and continued with Union veterans of the Civil War. Following the Civil War, some southern state governments offered pensions to Confederate veterans. Beginning in the late 1800s other government employees began to receive pensions, and today most full-time public sector employees have retirement benefits. Pension plans for governments are often called **Public Employee Retirement Systems (PERS).**

A pension plan may be either *contributory* or *noncontributory,* depending on whether employees are required to contribute. A plan also may be defined benefit or defined contribution. A **defined benefit (pension or retirement) plan** is one in which the plan is required to pay out a certain level of benefit (for example, 2 percent times the average salary over the past four years times the number of years worked), regardless of the amount available in the plan. **Defined contribution (pension or retirement) plans** provide an individual retirement account for each participating employee, and no obligation exists for pension benefits beyond what has been accumulated in each individual's account. As a result, defined benefit plans may have unfunded actuarial liabilities, whereas defined contribution plans do not.

While some larger cities have their own defined benefit pension plans, the majority of local governments participate in the pension plans administered by their state governments. Statewide plans often exist for teachers, police and fire department employees, legislators, and other state and local government employees. Hundreds of individual governments may participate in a single statewide pension system. These statewide multiemployer plans may be either an agent plan or a cost-sharing plan.

An **agent multiple-employer defined benefit pension plan** is one in which each participating employer, such as a city government, has a separate account and each government is responsible for keeping its own contributions up to date. In such a plan, a given city government may have fully funded its pension obligation, while a neighboring city's pension plan could be significantly underfunded because it failed to make required contributions. A **cost-sharing multiple-employer defined benefit pension plan** is a statewide plan in which separate accounts are not kept for each employer. Instead each participating government shares proportionally in the resources and obligations of the pension system. In such cases, all participating governments are equally over- or underfunded.

There are two categories of pension reporting. Employer reporting involves measurement of the pension liability and annual expense. These are reported in financial statements using the economic resources measurement focus and accrual basis of accounting (i.e., the government-wide statements and enterprise fund statements). Employer reporting is described in Chapter 9. The second category of pension reporting is "reporting for the plan." This applies only to governments that act as trustees for a retirement plan. Because of the trust relationship, the resources managed on behalf of current and future government retirees are reported in fiduciary funds. Pension plan reporting is illustrated in the following section.

Accounting and Reporting for Defined Benefit Pension Plans

Pension trust funds receive contributions from other funds within the government and from contributions by the employees themselves. These resources are invested to earn a return. When they retire, employees receive benefits from the plan based on their salary upon retirement and the number of years they worked for the government. The difficulty for the government is determining how much to contribute to the plan to ensure there are adequate resources available in the future to fulfill its obligation to retiring employees. This involves estimation in the presence of many variables that cannot be known in advance, such as the level of future benefits that will be paid, the life expectancy of retiring employees, and the investment income that will ultimately be realized on the plan's assets. Governments commonly engage the assistance of actuaries who are trained to mathematically evaluate the probability of future events and determine the necessary level of contributions.

Consistent with other fiduciary funds, pension trust funds are reported in two financial statements prepared using the accrual basis of accounting:

- The Statement of Fiduciary Net Position reports assets, liabilities, and net position of the pension trust fund. Pension plan assets include cash, receivables (typically contributions due from employers and employees), and investments. Investments are reported at fair value. Liabilities consist principally of pension benefits currently due to retired employees. The Statement of Fiduciary Net Position does *not* report a liability for unfunded pension obligations—that is, amounts expected to be paid to employees in the future in excess of resources currently available.
- The Statement of Changes in Fiduciary Net Position reports additions and deductions from plan resources. Additions include contributions and investment income. Deductions include benefit payments and administrative expenses. The excess of additions over deductions is reported as the *net increase in fiduciary net position.*

In addition to these statements, extensive note disclosures are required describing the plan, the components of the pension liability, and significant assumptions underlying measurement of the liability. Required supplementary information must also be presented displaying annual pension information over 10-year intervals. The information contained in the notes and required supplementary information is complex and likely involves consultation with trained actuaries. In contrast, the recording of events in the pension trust fund is straightforward.

Assume the Village of Riverside is trustee for the Public Employees Retirement Trust Fund. The Statement of Fiduciary Net Position as of the end of the previous year appears in Illustration 7-2. During the year ended December 31, 2020, the following events and transactions took place:

ILLUSTRATION 7-2 **Statement of Fiduciary Net Position**

VILLAGE OF RIVERSIDE Public Employees Retirement Trust Fund Statement of Fiduciary Net Position December 31, 2019	
Assets	
Cash	$ 30,500
Accrued Interest Receivable	50,000
Investments, at Fair Value:	
Bonds	3,200,000
Common Stocks	2,100,000
Commercial Paper and Repurchase Agreements	500,000
Total Assets	5,880,500
Liabilities	
Accounts Payable and Accrued Expenses	30,000
Net Position Restricted for Pensions	$5,850,500

Accrued interest receivable at the beginning of the year was collected:

	Debits	Credits
1. Cash	50,000	
Accrued Interest Receivable		50,000

Member contributions in the amount of $210,000 and employer contributions in the amount of $210,000 were received in cash:

	Debits	Credits
2. Cash	420,000	
Additions—Contributions—Plan Members		210,000
Additions—Contributions—Employer		210,000

Annuity benefits in the amount of $110,000 and disability benefits in the amount of $15,000 were recorded as liabilities:

	Debits	Credits
3. Deductions—Annuity Benefits	110,000	
Deductions—Disability Benefits	15,000	
Accounts Payable and Accrued Expenses		125,000

Accounts payable and accrued expenses paid in cash amounted to $140,000:

	Debits	Credits
4. Accounts Payable and Accrued Expenses	140,000	
Cash		140,000

Terminated employees whose benefits were not vested were refunded $50,000 in cash:

	Debits	Credits
5. Deductions—Refunds to Terminated Employees	50,000	
Cash		50,000

Investment income received in cash amounted to $410,000, of which $210,000 was dividends and $200,000 was interest; additionally, $70,000 interest income was accrued at year-end:

	Debits	Credits
6. Cash	410,000	
Accrued Interest Receivable	70,000	
Additions—Investment Earnings—Interest		270,000
Additions—Investment Earnings—Dividends		210,000

Commercial paper and repurchase agreements carried at a cost of $200,000 matured, and cash in that amount was received:

	Debits	Credits
7. Cash	200,000	
Commercial Paper and Repurchase Agreements		200,000

Common stock carried at a fair value of $1,250,000 was sold for $1,300,000. New investments included $500,000 in common stock and $1,600,000 in bonds.

	Debits	Credits
8a. Cash	1,300,000	
Investments in Common Stock		1,250,000
Additions—Investment Earnings—Net Increase in Fair Value of Investments		50,000
8b. Investments in Bonds	1,600,000	
Investments in Common Stock	500,000	
Cash		2,100,000

Administrative expenses for the year totaled $80,000, all paid in cash:

	Debits	Credits
9. Deductions—Administrative Expenses	80,000	
Cash		80,000

During the year, the fair value of common stock increased $40,000; the fair value of bonds decreased $30,000:

	Debits	Credits
10. Investments in Common Stock	40,000	
Investments in Bonds		30,000
Additions—Investment Earnings—Net Increase in Fair Value of Investments		10,000

Nominal accounts for the year were closed:

	Debits	Credits
11. Additions—Contributions—Plan Members	210,000	
Additions—Contributions—Employer	210,000	
Additions—Investment Earnings—Interest	270,000	
Additions—Investment Earnings—Dividends	210,000	
Additions—Investment Earnings—Net Increase in Fair Value of Investments	60,000	
Deductions—Annuity Benefits		110,000
Deductions—Disability Benefits		15,000
Deductions—Refunds to Terminated Employees		50,000
Deductions—Administrative Expenses		80,000
Net Position Restricted for Pensions		705,000

ILLUSTRATION 7-3 Statement of Fiduciary Net Position

VILLAGE OF RIVERSIDE Statement of Fiduciary Net Position Fiduciary Funds December 31, 2020	Public Employees Retirement Trust Fund	Private-Purpose Trust Fund
Assets		
Cash	$ 40,500	$ 35,000
Accrued Interest Receivable	70,000	4,800
Investments, at Fair Value:		
Bonds	4,770,000	482,000
Common Stock	1,390,000	
Commercial Paper and Repurchase Agreements	300,000	
Total Investments	6,460,000	482,000
Total Assets	6,570,500	521,800
Liabilities		
Accounts Payable and Accrued Expenses	15,000	–0–
Net Position		
Net Position Restricted for Scholarships		$521,800
Net Position Restricted for Pensions	$6,555,500	

Illustration 7-3 reflects the Statement of Fiduciary Net Position for the fiduciary funds, including the private-purpose trust fund and the Public Employees Retirement Trust Fund, as of December 31, 2020.

Illustration 7-4 presents the Statement of Changes in Fiduciary Net Position for the fiduciary funds, including the private-purpose trust fund and the Public Employee Retirement System for the year ended December 31, 2020.

Additional Disclosures

The way pension systems should work is that governments set aside money throughout the period that employees are working. These amounts are invested and grow over time so that there will be adequate resources to pay pension benefits when the employees retire and stop working. The key question is whether the amount a government is setting aside will be enough. If the amount contributed and earned through investment is not adequate to pay future benefits, the pension is said to be underfunded.

Determining whether a pension plan is sufficiently funded *cannot* be determined from the fiduciary fund statements. The Statement of Fiduciary Net Position reports the excess of currently available resources over benefits *currently payable* to retired employees (net position of $6,555,500 for the Village of Riverside). The statement does *not* report a liability for amounts expected to be paid to current employees when they retire in the future.

To determine whether a pension plan is adequately funded, we need to compare the net position of the pension fund to an estimate of the government's total

ILLUSTRATION 7-4 **Statement of Changes in Fiduciary Net Position**

VILLAGE OF RIVERSIDE Statement of Changes in Fiduciary Net Position Fiduciary Funds For the Year Ended December 31, 2020		
Additions	**Public Employees Retirement Trust Fund**	**Private-Purpose Trust Fund**
Contributions:		
Employer	$210,000	
Plan members	210,000	
Individuals		$500,000
Total contributions	420,000	500,000
Investment earnings:		
Interest	270,000	28,800
Dividends	210,000	
Net increase in fair value of investments	60,000	2,000
Total investment earnings	540,000	30,800
Total additions	960,000	530,800
Deductions		
Annuity benefits	110,000	
Refunds to terminated employees	50,000	
Administrative expenses	80,000	
Disability benefits	15,000	
Scholarship awards		9,000
Total deductions	255,000	9,000
Net increase in fiduciary net position	705,000	521,800
Net position—beginning of year	5,850,500	–0–
Net position—end of year	$6,555,500	$521,800

obligation. Assume that a government provides a pension to its schoolteachers equal to 2 percent of their salary upon retirement for each year of service. Each year of service adds 2 percent to the government's obligation. An employee with 26 years of service would receive a pension payment each month of 52 percent of her monthly salary at the time of retirement. The future obligation for this pension that is attributable to years of service already performed is termed the **total pension liability.** Like most long-term liabilities, it is measured at present value.

Every year, two factors serve to increase the amount of the total pension liability. First, employees complete another year of service and add 2 percent to their level of future benefits. The increase in the total pension liability attributable to this effect is termed service cost. Secondly, since the total pension liability represents a present value of pension benefits to be provided in the future and each year brings employees closer to retirement, the balance of the liability increases with the passage of time. This is termed the *interest cost component.* Another factor serves to reduce the total pension liability each year. Like other liabilities, the balance of the total pension liability is reduced as payments are made to currently retired employees.

The balance in the total pension liability may change as a result of other, less predictable events. Sometimes governments change the terms of the pension plan. For example, a government may change the plan so that instead of basing the monthly benefit on an employee's salary at retirement, it is based on her average salary over the last five years preceding retirement. In most cases, this would reduce the monthly benefit and the liability.

Another change comes about when governments deem it appropriate to change one or more assumptions used in calculating the liability. Key assumptions include projections of the rate of inflation and salary increases, as well as employee mortality. The discount rate (interest rate) used in the present value calculation is an especially important assumption. The larger the discount rate, the smaller the reported liability. Finally, changes in the total pension liability commonly arise when governments experience differences between projected and actual returns on pension plan investments.

GASB standards provide guidance on the actuarial method, frequency of actuarial evaluations, and the determination of appropriate discount rates. To assist financial statement users in evaluating the adequacy of pension funding, GASB standards require extensive note disclosures and required supplementary information. Among the required supplementary schedules is a 10-year schedule displaying changes in the net pension liability. The **net pension liability** is the difference between the total pension liability and the net position of the pension fund reported in the Statement of Fiduciary Net Position. Illustration 7-5 provides a partial illustration (only 2 of the required 10 years are presented) of a Schedule of Changes in Net Pension Liability and Related Ratios for the Village of Riverside.

The schedule has four distinct segments (separated by horizontal lines in the illustration). The first computes the total pension liability, separately displaying the various sources of the change. Below that, the schedule summarizes information contained in the Statement of Fiduciary Net Position and displays the plan's net fiduciary position. The difference between the total pension liability and the net fiduciary position of the pension plan is the net pension liability ($8,740,600 – $6,555,500 = $2,185,100). This is the amount by which the pension is currently underfunded. The final section provides ratios for interpreting the magnitude of the underfunding. GASB standards call for additional schedules of required supplementary information. These include a 10-year schedule of employer contributions and another of investment returns.

Other Postemployment Benefit Trust Funds

Many governments offer other benefits to their retired employees, with the most significant being health care benefits. Other benefits may include death benefits, life insurance, disability income, and long-term care. These postemployment benefits share many characteristics with pensions. Notably, the right to these benefits arises during the service lives of employees, but most of the costs occur after retirement. As with pensions, measuring the future costs of such benefits involves the

ILLUSTRATION 7-5 **Required Supplementary Information: Schedule of Changes in Net Pension Liability and Related Ratios**

VILLAGE OF RIVERSIDE
Schedule of Changes in Net Pension Liability and Related Ratios
Public Employees Retirement Trust Fund
For the Year Ended December 31, 2020

	2020	2019	
Total Pension Liability			
Service cost	$ 268,900	$ 242,000	
Interest	626,000	599,200	
Change in benefit terms	—	—	Additional columns would appear for a total of 10 years.
Differences between expected and actual experience	(40,000)	(20,000)	
Changes of assumptions	—	50,000	
Benefit payments (including refunds)	(240,000)	(215,000)	
Net change in total pension liability	614,900	656,200	
Total pension liability—beginning of year	8,125,700	7,469,500	
Total pension liability—end of year (a)	$8,740,600	$8,125,700	
Plan Fiduciary Net Position			
Contributions—Employer	$ 210,000	$ 190,000	
Contributions—Plan members	210,000	190,000	
Net investment earnings	540,000	505,000	
Benefit payments (including refunds)	(175,000)	(215,000)	
Administrative expenses	(80,000)	(12,000)	
Net increase in fiduciary net position	705,000	658,000	
Fiduciary net position—beginning of year	5,850,500	5,192,500	
Fiduciary net position—end of year (b)	$6,555,500	$5,850,500	
Pension plan net pension liability—ending (a) – (b)	$2,185,100	$2,275,200	
Plan fiduciary net position as a percentage of the total pension liability	75%	72%	
Covered-employee payroll	$1,456,700	$1,318,000	
Net pension liability as a percentage of covered-employee payroll	150%	173%	

use of estimates and actuarial assumptions. The cost of future health care benefits is particularly difficult to estimate. Traditionally, these benefits have been less well funded than pensions.

Like pensions, other postemployment benefits involve two categories of reporting: (1) employer reporting of the liability and related expense/expenditure and (2) reporting by the plan itself. As with pensions, governments may establish trust funds to manage the accumulation and distribution of resources set aside for employee postemployment benefits. Contributions to the plan come from the General and enterprise funds, and the assets of the plan include cash, investments, prepaid insurance, and receivables from other funds.

The reporting of these plans is very similar to that illustrated for pensions. A Statement of Fiduciary Net Position reports the fair value of resources available for payment to retirees and obligations for benefits currently due. The Statement of Changes in Fiduciary Net Position reports additions (contributions and investment income) and deductions (retiree benefits and administrative costs) for the period.

A Note about IRS 457 Deferred Compensation Plans

Many governments have established **IRS 457 Deferred Compensation Plans** for their employees. If legal requirements are met, these represent tax-deferred compensation plans in which employees are not required to pay taxes on the amounts withheld until distributed to them after retirement. If the plans are administered by an entity outside a government, which is the most common case, then no accounting is required by the government, other than to account for funds withheld and distributed. If a government administers the plan, the resources are held in trust and accounted for as a pension (and other employee benefit) trust fund.

INVESTMENT POOLS

Sometimes governments place excess cash from multiple funds into a single investment pool. *Internal* investment pools are not separate funds and the resources continue to be reported by the funds providing the resources. For example, assume a state government has $900 million in investments, which are pooled for management purposes, and those investments came one-third each from the General, an enterprise, and a private-purpose trust fund. Because the resources came from sources internal to the government, each fund would report $300 million of investments in the Balance Sheet or Statement of Net Position and none of these amounts would be reported in a fiduciary fund. Likewise, income earned on the investments would be reported directly in the funds that contributed the resources.

State governments frequently open their investment pools to cities, counties, or school districts within the state who wish to participate. In these cases, the state government that manages the multigovernment investment pool should report the *external portion* in a fiduciary fund. If the investment pool is governed by a trust agreement, the cash deposited by the local governments for investment would be reported in an investment trust fund. If there is not a trust agreement, the invested amounts would be reported in a custodial fund. The accounting is the same regardless of the fund type.

Like other fiduciary funds, investment trust funds use the economic resources measurement focus and accrual basis of accounting. Investments are reported at their fair values. Investment trust funds are reported in the fiduciary funds Statement of Fiduciary Net Position and Statement of Changes in Fiduciary Net Position. A simplified example follows:

Assume a state government with a June 30 year-end operates an investment trust fund with investments totaling $905,000, no liabilities, and Restricted Net Position of $905,000 at July 1, 2019. Local governments collect property taxes early in the year and deposit $2,500,000 of excess cash in the state investment pool, which is immediately invested:

	Debits	Credits
1. Cash	2,500,000	
Pool Participant Deposits		2,500,000

2. Investment in Short-Term Securities	2,500,000	
Cash		2,500,000

In much the same manner as a commercial bank maintains subsidiary account ledgers for its depositors, states sponsoring multigovernment investment pools would maintain separate ledgers for each of the participating local governments.

Throughout the year, interest and dividends totaling $64,000 are received:

3. Cash	64,000	
Additions—Investment Earnings—Interest and Dividends		64,000

Investment expenses of $3,000 are paid on behalf of participating local governments:

4. Deductions—Investment Expenses	3,000	
Cash		3,000

The investment earnings after deducting expenses ($64,000 – 3,000) are allocated among the accounts of the participating local governments and reinvested:

5. Deductions—Distributions to Pool Participants	61,000	
Reinvested Distributions to Pool Participants		61,000

During the year, local governments draw $2,450,000 of cash from the investment pool to meet expenditures. (Assume that an equal amount of short-term investments were converted to cash—not presented.)

6. *Pool Participant Withdrawals*	2,450,000	
Cash		2,450,000

The accounts appearing in italics in entries (1), (5), and (6) will appear in the Statement of Changes in Fiduciary Net Position but are not additions nor deductions as we customarily think of those. Rather, they are increases or decreases in depositor account balances. The Statement of Changes in Fiduciary Net Position for the state government appears in Illustration 7-6. Note that these accounts appear in a section of the statement titled *Pool Participant Account Transactions.*

CUSTODIAL FUNDS

Any activity meeting the criteria as a fiduciary activity that is not reported in a pension, private-purpose, or investment trust fund should be reported within a custodial fund. Custodial funds are commonly used when a government holds assets temporarily that belong to another party. These include

- Student activity funds of a school district
- Tax collection funds, where one government collects taxes on behalf of another government
- Jail inmate accounts
- Nursing home patient accounts
- Section 529 college savings plans (offered by state governments)

In the past many of the activities included in the custodial fund category reported only a Statement of Fiduciary Net Position. More recent standards now also require all custodial funds to report a Statement of Changes in Fiduciary Net Position. Within that statement, custodial funds report additions by source and deductions by type, with the difference increasing or decreasing net position. Determining the timing and amount of additions to a custodial fund is relatively straightforward since they normally include the receipt of cash. GASB provides guidance regarding the recognition of a liability (and associated deduction) in fiduciary funds. Specifically, a liability should be recognized when an event has occurred that compels the government to disburse resources held in a fiduciary fund. In the following two sections, we illustrate two common examples of custodial funds.

Section 529 College Savings Plans

Most states offer Section 529 college savings plans. These plans provide tax benefits to encourage savings for college expenses. Although contributions to these plans are not deductible by the donor in determining federal income taxes, some states provide state income tax deductions for all or part of the contribution. The main advantage, however, is that the invested amounts grow tax-deferred and distributions for the beneficiary's college expenses are exempt from tax.

Assume a state government with a June 30 year-end operates a § 529 savings plan. At July 1, 2019, the plan reported cash and investments totaling $4,790,000, $90,000 of liabilities, and Restricted Net Position of $4,700,000. During the year, citizens contributed $3,300,000 to the plan.

	Debits	Credits
1. Cash	3,300,000	
Additions—Receipts from Depositors		3,300,000

Following GASB guidelines, a liability would not be recognized upon receipt of cash from depositors because there is no event that compels the state to disburse cash at this time.

Typically state governments engage a mutual fund company to invest amounts received from depositors and keep records of individual investor balances. Assume investment earnings (interest and dividends) for the year totaled $149,000.

2. Cash	149,000	
Additions—Investment Earnings—Interest and Dividends		149,000

Investment expenses of $5,000 are paid on behalf of participating local governments.

3. Deductions—Investment Expenses	5,000	
Cash		5,000

At the point that the children of donor families enter college, they may begin to withdraw funds from the § 529 plan to pay college expenses. When a depositor requests a withdrawal, the custodial fund should recognize a liability because an event has now occurred that compels the state to make a payment. Assume depositors withdrew $2,100,000 during the year.

4. Deductions—Distributions to Depositors	2,100,000	
Amounts Payable to Depositors		2,100,000

Tax Collection Funds

An activity that often results in the creation of a custodial fund is the collection of taxes or other revenues by an official of one government for other governmental units. At the local government level, it is common for an elected county official to serve as collector for all property taxes within the county. For example, a county school district may be a separate government from the county in which it is located. Similarly, towns and villages located within a county are distinct governmental reporting units. Commonly property taxes levied by varying units within the county are paid to a single office within the county. The county collector then makes periodic distributions to the appropriate government. Similarly, state governments commonly collect sales taxes, gasoline taxes, and many other taxes that are apportioned between state agencies and local governments within the state.

Assume that the state imposes a sales tax of seven percent on retail sales. Retail merchants are given until the 10th day of the month following the sale to remit these taxes to the state government. Although the state government collects all the sales taxes, only 5 percent is retained as a General Fund revenue. The state has 30 days to pay the remaining 2 percent of the tax to the local county government in which the sale occurred. The portion due to the local governments is reported in a tax collection custodial fund.

Sales taxes received from retail merchants for the first 11 months of the year totaled $14,000,000 and an additional $1,750,000 for June 2020 sales will be received in July 2020. The entry to record the sales tax revenue in the General Fund is

(General Fund)	**Debits**	**Credits**
Sales Taxes Receivable (5/7 × $1,750,000)	1,250,000	
Cash (5/7 × $14,000,000)	10,000,000	
Revenues—Sales Taxes.		11,250,000

The portion of sales taxes to be paid to the local governments is recorded in a custodial fund as follows:

(Custodial Fund)		
1. Sales Taxes Receivable (2/7 × $1,750,000)	500,000	
Cash (2/7 × $14,000,000)	4,000,000	
Additions—Sales Tax Collections for Other Governments		4,500,000

Recall that the general rule for recognizing a liability in a fiduciary fund is that an event has occurred that compels the government to disburse resources. In the case of tax collection activities, the final recipient is not required to submit a request for payment. GASB guidelines provide a rule of thumb that simplifics this proccss for tax collection activities. If a government is expected to hold funds for three months or less, a liability may be recognized immediately for the amounts that will be paid to the final recipient. The following entry records the liability and related deduction.

(Custodial Fund)		
2. Deductions—Payment of Sales Taxes to Other Governments. . . .	4,500,000	
Amounts Payable to County Governments		4,500,000

The result is that for tax collection custodial funds, additions equal deductions and the residual equity (Net Position) is zero. In contrast, the Section 529 custodial fund has a nonzero net position. This is because there is typically a long period of time between when parents first contribute money to the fund and their child begins to incur college expenses.

The state custodial funds would report a Statement of Fiduciary Net Assets and a Statement of Changes in Fiduciary Net Assets. The Statement of Changes in

ILLUSTRATION 7-6 **Statement of Changes in Fiduciary Net Position**

EXAMPLE STATE GOVERNMENT Statement of Changes in Fiduciary Net Position Fiduciary Funds For the Year Ended June 30, 2020		
Additions	**Investment Trust Fund**	**Custodial Funds**
Contributions:		
Receipts from § 529 depositors	$ -0-	$3,300,000
Total contributions	-0-	3,300,000
Investment earnings:		
Interest and dividends	64,000	149,000
Less investment expenses	3,000	5,000
Net investment earnings	61,000	144,000
Pool Participant Account Transactions		
Deposits by investment pool participants	2,500,000	
Reinvestment of investment pool distributions	61,000	
Withdrawals by investment pool participants	(2,450,000)	-0-
Total participant account transactions	111,000	-0-
Sales tax collections for other governments		4,500,000
Total additions	172,000	7,944,000
Deductions		
Distributions to § 529 depositors		2,100,000
Payment of sales taxes to other governments		4,500,000
Distributions to investment pool participants	61,000	-0-
Total deductions	61,000	6,600,000
Net increase in fiduciary net position	111,000	1,344,000
Net position—beginning of year	905,500	4,700,000
Net position—end of year	$1,016,000	$6,044,000

Fiduciary Net Assets for the example state government is presented in Illustration 7-6. The Section 529 and tax collection custodial funds are combined in a single column but amounts can be readily attributed to the appropriate fund.

A Note about Escheat Property

In many cases, state governments obtain property in the absence of legal claimants or heirs. For example, if property is abandoned or if legal owners cannot be found, the property is turned over to state governments until the legal owners can be contacted. This property is known as **escheat property.** Some escheat property is ultimately claimed by rightful owners; other escheat property never is claimed and is eventually used by the government in some way.

Escheat property generally should be reported as an asset in the governmental or proprietary fund to which the property ultimately reverts. For example, a state might have legislation that requires the residual value of unclaimed property be dedicated to supporting public schools. In this case, the resources might be reported in a special revenue fund dedicated to education. The value of unclaimed property expected to be paid out to claimants would either be reported as a liability in that fund or in a fiduciary fund.

A FINAL COMMENT ON FUND ACCOUNTING AND REPORTING

Chapters 4 to 7 presented accounting and fund-basis financial reporting requirements for governmental, proprietary, and fiduciary fund types. These are summarized for the Village of Riverside example in Illustration 7-7. Governmental fund reports for the General and major governmental funds include the Balance Sheet and the Statement of Revenues, Expenditures, and Changes in Fund Balances. Finally, a Budgetary Comparison Schedule is required as an RSI schedule and is presented in Illustration 4-6. Proprietary fund reports for major enterprise funds and the internal

ILLUSTRATION 7-7 Summary of Fund-Basis Reporting for Village of Riverside

Fund-Basis Financial Statements

Governmental Funds
Balance Sheet—Illustration 5-3
Statement of Revenues, Expenditures, and Changes in Fund Balances—Illustration 5-4

Proprietary Funds
Statement of Net Position—Illustration 6-3
Statement of Revenues, Expenses, and Changes in Fund Net Position—Illustration 6-4
Statement of Cash Flows—Illustration 6-5

Fiduciary Funds
Statement of Fiduciary Net Position—Illustration 7-3
Statement of Changes in Fiduciary Net Position—Illustration 7-4

Notes to the Financial Statements (not presented)

Required Supplementary Information (other than MD&A)

Governmental Funds
Budgetary Comparison Schedule (General and major special revenue funds)—Illustration 4-6

Pension Funds
Schedule of Changes in Net Pension Liability and Related Ratios—Illustration 7-5
Schedule of Employer Contributions (not presented)
Schedule of Investment Returns (not presented)

service fund type include the Statement of Net Position; the Statement of Revenues, Expenses, and Changes in Fund Net Position; and the Statement of Cash Flows.

Fiduciary fund reporting, by fund type, includes the Statement of Fiduciary Net Position and the Statement of Changes in Fiduciary Net Position. In addition, GASB requires several RSI schedules for governments with defined benefit pension and other employee benefit trust plans.

As indicated in Chapter 2, GAAP require the presentation of government-wide financial statements: a Statement of Net Position and a Statement of Activities. These are *consolidated* statements, presented using the economic resources measurement focus and accrual basis of accounting. Fiduciary funds are not included in the government-wide statements because governments merely have custody, not ownership, of fiduciary resources. The process of converting the fund-basis statements to government-wide statements is described in Chapter 8. The fund-basis statements prepared in Chapters 5 and 6 serve as inputs to the government-wide statements. Our approach will be similar to the approach most commonly taken in practice. That is, governments record events on a day-to-day basis in a manner that leads directly to preparation of the fund-basis statements. At year-end, worksheet adjustments are made to those balances to comply with the requirements for government-wide statements.

Questions and Exercises

7–1. Using the annual report obtained for Exercise 1–1, answer the following questions:

a. Examine the Statement of Fiduciary Net Position. Which fund types are included? Look at the Statement of Changes in Fiduciary Net Position. Are increases and decreases shown as additions and deductions, rather than revenues and expenses? What are the main additions? What are the main deductions?

b. Are custodial funds included in the Statement of Fiduciary Net Position and Statement of Changes in Fiduciary Net Position? If so, list them. Describe the purposes for which they exist.

c. Does the government have private-purpose trust funds? If so, list them. Describe the purposes for which they exist. Can you tell if any of those funds are endowments, and have resources permanently restricted? How much income was generated by each of the private-purpose funds, and how much was released for use? Does the government report escheat property as private-purpose funds? If so, indicate the nature of the process by which property is released and for what purposes.

d. Does the government report investment trust funds? If so, describe the nature of the external investment pool. Which other governments are included? Has your government refrained from including its own investments in the investment trust funds?

e. List the pension funds included in the financial statements. From the notes, list the other pension plans that are available to employees of your governmental unit. Are those plans multiemployer plans? If so are they agent plans or cost-sharing plans? Defined contribution or defined benefit? Are required disclosures made in the notes for all pension plans, whether or not the plans are included as trust funds? Look at the actuarial status of the plans and comment about the potential impact of pensions on the financial condition of the government.

f. Review the note disclosures regarding investments. Are investments reported at fair value? Do the notes disclose the realized gains or losses on investments? Do the notes categorize investments based on risk? When the government creates internal investment pools for management purposes, does the government report the individual investments and income from those investments in the funds that provided the resources?

Custodial Funds

7–2. Answer the following questions regarding custodial funds:

a. When is it appropriate to account for an activity in a custodial fund?

b. What are the required financial statements of a custodial fund?

c. What are common examples of activities reported in custodial funds?

7–3. Benton County includes an independent school district and two individually chartered towns within the County. Benton County's Treasurer assesses and collects property taxes on behalf of itself, the school district, and the towns. The County uses a tax collection custodial fund to record tax collections for the school district and towns. During the year ended December 31, 2020, the following transactions took place:

1. The County levied taxes as follows:

Benton County General Fund	$25,000,000
School District	12,500,000
Towns	2,500,000
Total	$40,000,000

2. The property taxes levied in part (a) were collected.
3. The amounts collected were paid to the school district and towns.

Required:

a. Prepare journal entries for Benton County and the Benton County Independent School District—identify the funds.

b. Will tax collection funds typically report a non-zero net position? Explain.

c. Are there other custodial funds that typically report a positive net position? Give an example.

Private-Purpose Trust Funds

7–4. A concerned citizen provides resources and establishes a trust with the local government. What factors should be considered in determining which fund to report the trust activities?

7–5. Presented below is the preclosing trial balance for the Scholarship Fund, a private-purpose trust fund of the Algonquin School District.

Trial Balance—December 31, 2020	Debits	Credits
Accounts Payable		$ 2,500
Accrued Interest Receivable	$ 3,000	
Administrative Expense	4,000	
Cash	52,000	
Increase in Fair Value of Investments		5,400
Distributions—Scholarships	62,000	
Interest Income		71,000
Investment in Bonds	1,214,000	
Net Position—Restricted for Scholarships		1,256,100
	$1,335,000	$1,335,000

Prepare the year-end closing entries and a Statement of Changes in Fiduciary Net Position for the year ended December 31, 2020.

7–6. On July 1, 2019, the City of Belvedere accepted a gift of cash in the amount of $3,500,000 from a number of individuals and foundations and signed an agreement to establish a private-purpose trust. The $3,500,000 and any additional gifts are to be invested and retained as principal. Income from the trust is to be distributed to community nonprofit groups as directed by a Board consisting of city officials and other community leaders. The agreement provides that any increases in the market value of the principal investments are to be held in trust; if the investments fall below the gift amounts, then earnings are to be withheld until the principal amount is re-established.

The following events and transactions occurred during the fiscal year ended June 30, 2020. Record them in the Belvedere Community Trust Fund:

1. On July 1, the original gift of cash was received.
2. On August 1, $2,500,000 in XYZ Company bonds were purchased at par plus accrued interest ($20,833). The bonds pay an annual rate of 5 percent interest semiannually on April 1 and October 1.
3. On August 2, $900,000 in ABC Company common stock was purchased. ABC normally declares and pays dividends semiannually, on January 31 and July 31.
4. On October 1, the first semiannual interest payment ($62,500) was received from XYZ Company. Note that part of this is for accrued interest due at the time of purchase; the remaining part is an addition that may be used for distribution.

5. On January 31, a cash dividend was received from ABC Company in the amount of $25,000.
6. On March 1, the ABC stock was sold for $921,000. On the same day, DEF Company stock was purchased for $945,000.
7. On April 1, the second semiannual interest payment was received from XYZ Company.
8. During the month of June, distributions were approved by the Board and paid in cash in the amount of $82,500.
9. Administrative expenses were recorded and paid in the amount of $5,500.
10. An accrual for interest on the XYZ bonds was made as of June 30, 2020.
11. As of June 30, 2020, the fair value of the XYZ bonds, exclusive of accrued interest, was determined to be $2,503,000. The fair value of the DEF stock was determined to be $941,000.
12. Closing entries were prepared.

Required:

Prepare, in good form, (1) a Statement of Changes in Fiduciary Net Position for the Belvedere Community Trust Fund and (2) a Statement of Fiduciary Net Position.

7–7. On July 1, 2019, the Morgan County School District received a $40,000 gift from a local civic organization with the stipulation that, on June 30 of each year, $2,500 plus any interest earnings on the unspent principal be awarded as a college scholarship to the high school graduate with the highest academic average. A private-purpose trust fund, the Civic Scholarship Fund, was created.

Required:

a. Record the following transactions on the books of the Civic Scholarship Fund:
   1. On July 1, 2019, the gift was received and immediately invested.
   2. On June 30, 2020, $2,500 of the principal was converted into cash. In addition, $1,000 of interest was received.
   3. On June 30, the $3,500 was awarded to a student who had maintained a 4.0 grade point average throughout each of her four years.
   4. The nominal accounts were closed.

b. Prepare a Statement of Changes in Fiduciary Net Position for the Civic Scholarship Fund for the year ended June 30, 2020.

Investment Trust Funds

7–8. Describe GASB requirements for accounting for investment pools. Include (*a*) a discussion of when the use of investment trust fund or a custodial fund is appropriate; (*b*) the portion of the investment pool to be included and excluded from fiduciary funds; (*c*) the basis at which investments are to be reported; (*d*) reporting of realized and unrealized gains and losses on investments; and (*e*) financial reporting (i.e., financial statements).

7–9. The City of St. John operates an investment trust fund for neighboring governments, including St. John County and the independent school district. Assume the investment trust fund began the year 2020 with investments in U.S. government securities totaling $1,200,000, no liabilities, and Restricted Net Position of $1,200,000.

Required:

a. Record the following transactions on the books of the Civic Scholarship Fund:

1. The County and school district deposited $3,400,000 in the investment pool.
2. The investment trust fund invested $1,000,000 in corporate bonds and $2,400,000 in US government securities.
3. Interest received by the investment trust fund totaled $50,000 for the year.
4. At year-end, the fair value of the corporate bonds had increased by $4,000.
5. The earnings of the fund (there are no expenses) are allocated among the accounts of the participating governments.
6. Throughout the year, the participating governments withdrew $3,200,000 of funds from the investment trust fund. Assume that an equal amount of short-term investments were converted to cash as they matured.

b. Prepare a Statement of Changes in Fiduciary Net Position for the Civic Scholarship Fund for the year ended June 30, 2020.

c. How would the reporting differ if the investment pool was not governed by a formal trust agreement?

Pension Trust Funds

7–10. What are the required financial statements for a pension trust fund? What are the required supplementary information schedules?

7–11. With regard to current GASB standards for pension reporting, do the following:

a. Distinguish between (1) defined contribution plans and (2) defined benefit plans.

b. Distinguish between (1) agent and (2) cost-sharing multiemployer plans.

c. Define the following terms: (1) plan fiduciary net position and (2) net pension liability.

7–12. Assume that a local government is the trustee for the pension assets for its police and fire department employees and participates in a statewide plan for all of its other employees. Individual accounts are maintained for all local governments in the statewide plan. Discuss the financial reporting requirements related to pensions for (*a*) police and fire department employees and (*b*) all other employees.

7–13. The City of Sweetwater maintains an Employees' Retirement Fund, a single-employer defined benefit plan that provides annuity and disability benefits. The fund is financed by actuarially determined contributions from the city's General Fund and by contributions from employees. Administration of the retirement fund is handled by General Fund employees, and the retirement fund does not bear any administrative expenses. The Statement of Fiduciary Net Position for the Employees' Retirement Fund as of July 1, 2019, is shown here:

CITY OF SWEETWATER
Employees' Retirement Fund
Statement of Fiduciary Net Position
As of July 1, 2019

Assets	
Cash	$ 145,000
Accrued Interest Receivable	40,000
Investments, at Fair Value:	
Bonds	4,500,000
Common Stocks	1,300,000
Total Assets	5,985,000
Liabilities	
Accounts Payable and Accrued Expenses	400,000
Fiduciary Net Position Restricted for Pensions	$5,585,000

During the year ended June 30, 2020, the following transactions occurred:

1. The interest receivable on investments was collected in cash.
2. Member contributions in the amount of $260,000 were received in cash. The city's General Fund also contributed $830,000 in cash.
3. Annuity benefits of $740,000 and disability benefits of $172,000 were recorded as liabilities.
4. Accounts payable and accrued expenses in the amount of $990,000 were paid in cash.
5. Interest income of $235,000 and dividends in the amount of $40,000 were received in cash. In addition, bond interest income of $45,000 was accrued at year-end.
6. Refunds of $68,000 were made in cash to terminated, nonvested participants.
7. Common stocks, carried at a fair value of $500,000, were sold for $475,000. That $475,000, plus an additional $305,000, was invested in stocks.

8. At year-end, it was determined that the fair value of stocks held by the pension plan had decreased by $42,000; the fair value of bonds had increased by $33,000.
9. Nominal accounts for the year were closed.

Required:

a. Record the transactions on the books of the Employees' Retirement Fund.

b. Prepare a Statement of Changes in Fiduciary Net Position for the Employees' Retirement Fund for the year ended June 30, 2020.

c. Prepare a Statement of Fiduciary Net Position for the Employees' Retirement Fund as of June 30, 2020.

Other Postemployment Benefits

7–14. Presented below is the preclosing trial balance for the Retiree Health Benefit Plan of the Alger County School District.

Trial Balance—December 31, 2020	Debits	Credits
Accrued Interest Receivable	$ 15,500	
Cash	10,200	
Accounts Payable		$ 4,500
Contributions—Employee		355,000
Contributions—Employer		637,000
Deductions: Benefit Payments	590,000	
Deductions: Administrative Expense	28,000	
Increase in Fair Value of Investments		359,000
Investment Income—Dividends		77,000
Investment Income—Interest Income		150,300
Investments—Corporate Bonds	1,222,000	
Investments—Corporate Stocks	2,272,000	
Investments—U.S. Treasury Securities	650,000	
Fiduciary Net Position Restricted—for other postemployment benefits		3,417,200
Receivables—Employee	22,300	
Receivables—Employer	190,000	
	$5,000,000	$5,000,000

Required:

Prepare (1) the year-end closing entries, (2) a Statement of Changes in Fiduciary Net Position, and (3) a Statement of Fiduciary Net Position for the year ended December 31, 2020.

Excel-Based Problems

7–15. In December 2019, the Hamilton County Board of Commissioners established the Hamilton County OPEB Trust Fund. Retired employees of

Hamilton County can participate in postemployment benefits through the Trust. The Trust is a single-employer defined benefit plan. The benefits provided are health insurance and life insurance.

In December 2019, the County made a one-time contribution to the fund of $15,000,000. No other events took place in 2019.

Fiscal year 2020 transactions were as follows:

1. The County paid its actuarially determined annual contribution of $8,750,000.
2. Member (employee) contributions totaled $4,500,000. Of this, $4,350,000 was collected by December 31 and the remainder will be collected in January 2021.
3. Cash totaling $20,000,000 was invested in U.S. government securities.
4. Interest totaling $1,407,000 was earned on these securities. Of this amount, $1,346,000 was collected during the year.
5. Because the County offers a drug plan to retired employees, the federal government Medicare program provides a subsidy to the County. The County received $712,000 from this subsidy.
6. Benefit claims from employees totaled $11,722,000 for the year. By year-end, $9,460,000 had been paid to employees.
7. Administrative expenses totaled $147,000 (all paid in the current year).

Required:

Use the Excel template provided to complete the following requirements; a separate tab is provided in Excel for each of these steps.

a. Prepare journal entries to record the information described in items 1 to 7.

b. Post these entries to T-accounts.

c. Prepare closing journal entries. Post to the T-account provided.

d. Prepare a Statement of Changes in Fiduciary Net Position for the year ending 2020.

e. Prepare a Statement of Fiduciary Net Position as of December 31, 2020.

7–16. A successful businessman in the community has contacted the Moose County Board of Commissioners about donating income-producing securities to the County to support a particular activity. Under the agreement, the County would be required to maintain the principal amount of the gift but could use the resulting earnings. The following events occurred in 2020:

1. Securities, which had an original cost of $4,250,000 were donated to the County on January 1. The fair value of the securities at that date was $5,839,000, including
   - Corporate equities of $2,825,000.
   - Corporate bonds of $3,000,000.
   - Accrued interest receivable on the bonds of $14,000.
2. During the year, the fund received $180,000 in interest payments on the bonds. At the end of the year, accrued interest on the bonds totaled $16,500.

3. During the year, the fund received dividends on the corporate equities of $98,000.
4. During the year, the fund paid $230,000 supporting activities identified in the trust agreement and had outstanding bills to be paid of $6,000.
5. The fair value of the securities at December 31 was
   - Corporate equities of $2,785,000.
   - Corporate bonds of $3,060,000.

Required:

You are to prepare financial statements for the fund. In Part 1, the activities supported by the fund benefit the citizenry in general. In Part 2, the activities benefit only selected individuals.

Part 1: Assume it is appropriate to report the gift and related transactions in a permanent fund following modified accrual basis statements. Using the Excel template provided

a. Prepare journal entries recording the events above.

b. Post the journal entries to T-accounts.

c. Prepare closing entries.

d. Prepare a Statement of Revenues, Expenditures, and Changes in Fund Balance and a Balance Sheet (assume spendable net resources are to be classified as *restricted for other purposes*).

Part 2: Assume it is appropriate to report the gift and related transactions in a private-purpose trust fund following the accrual basis. Using the Excel template provided

a. Prepare journal entries recording the events above.

b. Post the journal entries to T-accounts.

c. Prepare closing entries.

d. Prepare a Statement of Changes in Fiduciary Net Position and a Statement of Fiduciary Net Position.

The Excel template contains separate tabs for (1) permanent fund journal entries and T-accounts, (2) private-purpose trust fund journal entries and T-accounts, (3) closing entries, (4) permanent fund financial statements, and (5) private-purpose trust fund financial statements. Both the T-accounts and financial statements may contain accounts you will not need.

Continuous Problem

The continuous problem is available in Connect through the Additional Student Resources in the eBook or instructor library. Complete the assignments for Chapter 7.

Chapter **Eight**

Government-wide Statements, Capital Assets, Long-Term Debt

Christmas is the time when kids tell Santa what they want and adults pay for it. Deficits are when adults tell government what they want and their kids pay for it. Richard Lamm, governor of Colorado, 1975–1987

Deficits mean future tax increases, pure and simple. Deficit spending should be viewed as a tax on future generations, and politicians who create deficits should be exposed as tax hikers. Ron Paul, M.D., U.S. House of Representatives from Texas's 14th district

Learning Objectives

- Perform the steps necessary to prepare government-wide financial statements, including
  1. Prepare worksheet entries to convert the governmental fund records to the economic resources measurement focus and the accrual basis of accounting.
  2. Prepare worksheet entries to include internal service funds with governmental activities.
  3. Prepare required schedules reconciling the government-wide and fund-basis financial statements.
- Record events and transactions related to general fixed assets and general long-term debt and describe required schedules related to long-term debt.

The focus of Chapters 3 through 7 has been the preparation of fund-basis financial statements. The focus of this chapter is the preparation of the government-wide statements (i.e., Statement of Net Position and Statement of Activities) and required schedules that reconcile the government-wide and fund-basis financial statements. Our approach is consistent with the practice of most governments. That is, we assume the initial recording of transactions is done at the fund level, using the measurement focus and basis of accounting used for each fund's statements (current financial resources focus and modified accrual basis for governmental funds and economic resources focus and accrual basis for all others). At the end of the reporting period, governments adjust governmental fund balances to the economic resources focus and accrual basis required in the government-wide statements. This is accomplished through worksheet entries. Worksheet entries differ from other journal entries, in that they are *not* posted to the general ledger—in effect, they are never "booked."[1]

Illustration 8-1 summarizes this process. The government-wide statements are separated into governmental activities and business-type activities (discretely presented component units are also separately displayed). The governmental-type funds' Balance Sheet and Statement of Revenues, Expenditures, and Changes in Fund Balances serve as inputs to the governmental activities sections of the government-wide statements. However, because the fund-basis statements reflect modified accrual accounting, they must be adjusted to the accrual basis. In contrast, balances from the enterprise funds' Statement of Net Position and Statement of Revenues, Expenses, and Changes in Fund Net Position are entered directly to the business-type activities sections of the government-wide statements. No adjustment is necessary because enterprise funds use the accrual basis.

As Illustration 8-1 suggests, internal service funds are typically reported in the governmental activities sections of the government-wide statements, while fiduciary activities are not included in the government-wide statements at all. Finally, preparation of the government-wide statements requires information on the balances and changes in general capital assets and general long-term debt. As the illustration shows, these amounts are not included in the fund-basis statements but must be recorded in the government's accounting records if they are to be available at the time the government-wide statements are prepared. Entries to record events affecting general capital assets and general long-term debt are illustrated later in the chapter. Like earlier chapters, the Village of Riverside example is extended in this chapter to illustrate the preparation of government-wide statements and certain required schedules.

CONVERSION FROM FUND FINANCIAL RECORDS TO GOVERNMENT-WIDE FINANCIAL STATEMENTS

The conversion worksheet is illustrated within the shaded area of Illustration 8-1. The fund-basis financial statements for the governmental funds are entered directly into the left-hand column of the worksheet. General capital assets, general long-term debt, and internal service funds are added through worksheet journal entries. In addition, worksheet entries eliminate elements of the modified accrual basis fund statements that do not conform to accrual accounting, such as expenditures for capital assets and principal repayments. Expenditures that are not eliminated become

[1] Worksheet entries are commonly used by corporations in the process of consolidating subsidiary companies.

ILLUSTRATION 8-1 **Information Flow to the Government-wide Statements**

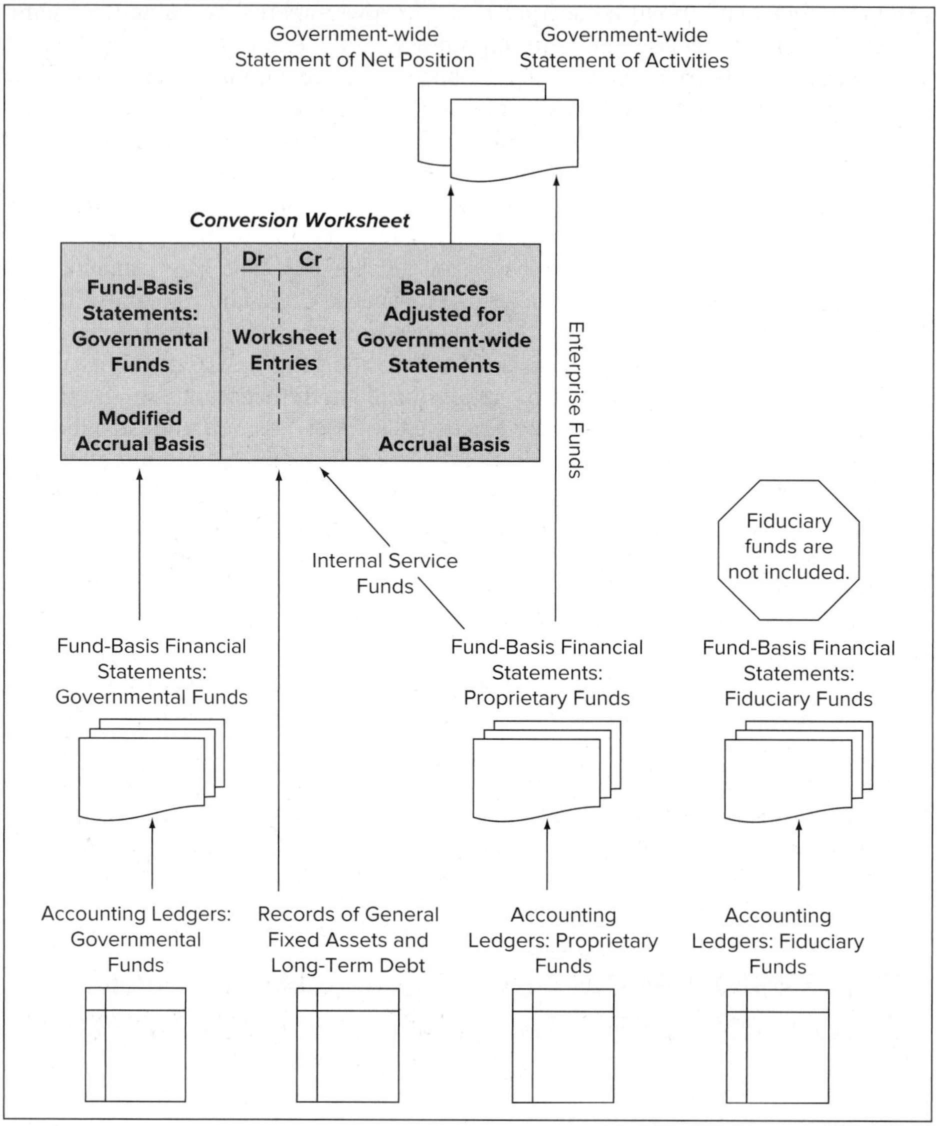

expenses in the right-hand column. Additional entries are necessary to adjust revenues to the accrual basis, record expenses not recognized under the modified accrual basis, and eliminate interfund transfers and balances. The resulting balances appearing in the far right column are entered into the governmental activities sections of the government-wide statements. No entries are necessary to eliminate fiduciary funds; they are simply left out of the worksheet and therefore never appear in the government-wide statements.

A process similar to Illustration 8-1 is followed in the event a government has a discretely presented component unit. Component units are displayed as a separate column in the Statement of Net Position (see Illustration 2-5) and as separate rows in the Statement of Activities (see Illustration 2-6). Many component units use the accrual basis of accounting, and the balances of assets, liabilities, and net position may be entered directly into the component unit column in the Statement of Net Position. Similarly, the revenues and expenses are entered directly into the component unit rows of the Statement of Activities. Other component units use the modified accrual basis in their accounting records and must be converted to the accrual basis for presentation in the government-wide statements. If this is the case, the component unit's information flow is similar to that of governmental funds. Worksheet entries are needed to convert the component unit to the accrual basis and economic resources measurement focus. Component units that are fiduciary in nature are not included in the government-wide statements.

The next section of the text discusses and presents adjustments necessary to convert from fund financial statements to government-wide statements. The fund-basis statements from the Village of Riverside example serve as inputs to this process. These examples are not exhaustive but contain the major changes and include

1. Capital Asset–Related Entries: Recording capital assets, removing expenditures for capital outlays, recording depreciation, and converting sales of capital assets to the accrual basis.
2. Long-Term Debt–Related Entries: Recording long-term liabilities, changing "proceeds of bonds" to increases in debt, changing expenditures for debt service principal to reduction of liabilities, amortizing bond premiums, and adjusting for interest accruals.
3. Adjusting to convert revenue recognition to the accrual basis.
4. Adjusting expenses to the accrual basis.
5. Adding internal service funds to governmental activities.
6. Eliminating interfund activities and balances within governmental activities.

Each of these is discussed and illustrated in turn, using the information in the governmental funds Balance Sheet (Illustration 5-3) and Statement of Revenues, Expenditures, and Changes in Fund Balances (Illustration 5-4) as the starting point.

CAPITAL ASSET–RELATED ENTRIES

GASB requires that general capital assets be included in the government-wide financial statements. General capital assets include fixed assets other than those used by proprietary or fiduciary funds and are usually acquired through General, special revenue, or capital projects funds. Fixed assets acquired through proprietary funds are reported in the Statement of Net Position of those funds. Assume that the Village of Riverside maintains records for general capital assets, including the original cost and accumulated depreciation. Categories include land, buildings, improvements other than buildings (infrastructure), and equipment. The first worksheet entry is needed to record the capital assets and related accumulated depreciation as of the beginning of the year:

	Debits	Credits
1. Land	3,100,000	
Buildings	38,300,000	
Improvements Other Than Buildings	15,400,000	
Equipment	5,600,000	
Accumulated Depreciation—Buildings		15,100,000
Accumulated Depreciation—Improvements Other Than Buildings		6,300,000
Accumulated Depreciation—Equipment		3,700,000
Net Position (beginning of year)		37,300,000

The amount of detail necessary in this journal entry depends on whether a government intends to report individual capital asset balances (e.g., land, buildings, etc.). Assuming the Village of Riverside only reports capital assets in total, the journal entry could be condensed to a debit to Capital Assets of $62,400,000, a credit to Accumulated Depreciation of $25,100,000, and a credit to Net Position of $37,300,000. Because worksheet entries are not posted to the fund general ledger, an entry to record beginning balances will be required each year. Note that the account, Net Position, is credited for the difference. The difference between assets and liabilities in the government-wide statements is called net position.

A second adjustment is required to eliminate the charge to expenditures for capital outlay and to record those expenditures as capital assets. In the Village of Riverside example, it is assumed that the only capital assets acquired this year were reflected in the capital projects fund example in Chapter 5. Note that the amount of expenditures, including interest, closed out in entry 17 of the capital projects fund example in Chapter 5 is $1,963,500.

GASB specifically prohibits interest during construction from being capitalized in the government-wide statements. As a result, the $2,500 in interest is charged to interest expense, and the $1,961,000 is capitalized. The following adjustment is required:

	Debits	Credits
2. Buildings	1,961,000	
Interest Expense	2,500	
Expenditures—Capital Outlay		1,963,500

A third adjustment is necessary to record depreciation expense. Assume that the Village of Riverside uses straight-line depreciation with no salvage value and that buildings have a 40-year life, improvements other than buildings have a 20-year life, and equipment has a 10-year life. Also assume the building capitalized this year was completed late in the year, and that no depreciation is charged. The adjustment would be

3. Depreciation Expense.	2,287,500	
Accumulated Depreciation—Buildings ($38,300,000/40) . . .		957,500
Accumulated Depreciation—Improvements Other Than Buildings ($15,400,000/20).		770,000
Accumulated Depreciation—Equipment ($5,600,000/10) . . .		560,000

If a government sold or disposed of capital assets during the year, an additional entry is required. Entry 28 in the General Fund example in Chapter 4 reflects proceeds in the amount of $300,000 on the sale of land. That amount was properly reported as an other financing source in the Governmental Fund Statement of Revenues, Expenditures, and Changes in Fund Balances (Illustration 5-4). Assume now that the cost of that land was $225,000, which is included in the land amount reported in entry 1 above. It is necessary to convert this to an accrual basis so that the gain on the sale is reflected in the Statement of Activities and land removed from the Statement of Net Position.

4. Special Item—Proceeds from the Sale of Land.	300,000	
Land		225,000
Special Item—Gain on Sale of Land		75,000

Remember that these entries are only worksheet entries used to prepare the government-wide statements and would not be posted to the general ledgers of the governmental funds. Together these four worksheet entries record all items affecting capital assets during the year with the result that ending capital assets appear in the government-wide Statement of Net Position:

Beginning capital assets
plus capital acquisitions
less depreciation
less sales or dispositions of capital assets.

Panel A of Illustration 8-2 demonstrates how the worksheet entries act with the existing modified accrual outcomes to produce accrual basis results. The first column of the illustration displays the journal entry that took place during the year under the modified accrual basis of accounting and the second column displays the related worksheet entry. The final (shaded) column is the net effect of the previous two entries and is the entry that *would have* been made had the government recorded the events using the accrual basis. Note that the entry appearing in the "accrual basis" column is never made, either during the year or at year-end. It is simply the outcome of the previous two entries. This illustration summarizes for capital asset transactions the process we will use throughout this chapter. We begin the process with the results for the year computed using the modified accrual basis, then apply worksheet entries, and end the process with results "as if" we had kept the records on the accrual basis.

ILLUSTRATION 8-2 **Panel A: How Worksheet Entries Produce Accrual Basis Outcomes: Capital Assets**

Entry under Modified Accrual (entry made sometime during the year)		Worksheet Entry for Preparation of Government-wide Statements		Net Effect after Worksheet Entry (same as accrual basis)	
1. Capital Asset Acquisitions					
		Capital Assets – Buildings	Dr	Capital Assets – Buildings	Dr
Expenditures – Capital Outlay	Dr	Expenditures – Capital Outlay	Cr	*account eliminated*	–
Cash	Cr			Cash	Cr
2. Annual Depreciation					
		Depreciation Expense	Dr	Depreciation Expense	Dr
No entry		Accumulated Depreciation	Cr	Accumulated Depreciation	Cr
3. Sale of Capital Assets					
Cash	Dr			Cash	Dr
Proceeds sale of capital asset	Cr	Proceeds sale of capital asset	Dr	*account eliminated*	–
		Capital asset – equipment (net)	Cr	Capital asset – equipment (net)	Cr
		Gain on sale of capital asset	Cr	Gain on sale of capital asset	Cr

ILLUSTRATION 8-2 Panel B: How Worksheet Entries Produce Accrual Basis Outcomes: Long-Term

Entry under Modified Accrual (entry made sometime during the year)		Worksheet Entry for Preparation of Government-wide Statements		Net Effect after Worksheet Entry (same as accrual basis)	
1. Sale of Bonds					
Cash	Dr			Cash	Dr
OFS: Proceeds of bonds	Cr	OFS: Proceeds of bonds	Dr	*account eliminated*	–
OFS: Premium on bonds	Cr	OFS: Premium on bonds	Dr	*account eliminated*	–
		Bonds Payable	Cr	Bonds Payable	Cr
		Premium on Bonds	Cr	Premium on Bonds	Cr
2. Amortization of Bond Premium					
		Premium on Bonds	Dr	Premium on Bonds	Dr
No entry		Interest Expense	Cr	Interest Expense	Cr
3. Principal Payment					
		Bonds Payable	Dr	Bonds Payable	Dr
Expenditure: Bond Principal	Dr	Expenditure: Bond Principal	Cr	*account eliminated*	–
Cash	Cr			Cash	Cr

LONG-TERM DEBT–RELATED ENTRIES

In this section we examine typical worksheet entries related to long-term debt. Once again, we are only concerned about debt arising from governmental fund activities. Proprietary fund debts are already recorded as liabilities. The Village of Riverside had no outstanding bonds, notes, or capital leases at the beginning of the year. However, if there were such liabilities, the beginning of the year balances would be recorded through a worksheet entry that credits the liability and debits Net Position.

	Debits	Credits
Net Position (beginning balance)	$ XXX	
Bonds or Long-Term Notes Payable		$ XXX

Additional entries are necessary to reflect changes in long-term debt that occur during the year and that are recorded differently under the accrual and modified accrual bases of accounting. Under accrual accounting, debt principal is recorded as a liability, interest expense is accrued at year-end, and premiums and discounts are amortized over the life of bonds. In the Village of Riverside example, 10-year serial bonds with a principal amount of $1,200,000 were sold on January 2 for $1,212,000. Annual interest of 8 percent was paid semiannually on June 30 and December 31, and the first principal payment of $120,000 was paid on December 31. The $1,212,000 was recorded as an *other financing source* in the capital projects fund (entries 8a and 8b in Chapter 5). To convert to accrual accounting, the following entry would be required:

5. Other Financing Sources—Proceeds of Bonds	1,200,000	
Other Financing Sources—Premium on Bonds	12,000	
Bonds Payable		1,200,000
Premium on Bonds Payable		12,000

The account Premium on Bonds Payable is an addition to the liability, as would be the case in business accounting. To adjust the principal payment (entry 22b, debt service funds, Chapter 5), the following would be required:

6. Bonds Payable	120,000	
Expenditures—Bond Principal		120,000

Normally, an adjustment would be required to accrue interest at year-end. In the Village of Riverside example, the last interest payment coincides with the final day of the fiscal year, so an accrual is not necessary. If there had been an interval of time between the last interest payment and the end of the fiscal year, the entry to accrue the interest would take the following form:

2020 government-wide worksheet entry:		
Interest Expense	$ XXX	
Accrued Interest Payable		$ XXX

It is important to recognize that accruals such as interest require entries in two years. The interest accrued above for the 2020 fiscal year would have been paid and recorded as an expenditure in 2021 under modified accrual accounting. Therefore, in 2021 we have too much interest and an additional worksheet entry would be required to move the accrued interest expense out of 2021, as follows:

2021 government-wide worksheet entry:		
Net Position (beginning of year)	$ XXX	
Interest Expense		$ XXX

Why is the debit to Net Position rather than to Accrued Interest Payable? Recall that the 2020 entry was a worksheet entry—never booked to the general ledger. Therefore, there is no Accrued Interest Payable to remove in 2021. However, the net position (at the government-wide level) at the beginning of 2021 would have been smaller as a result of the 2020 accrual.

Although interest accruals are not required in the Village of Riverside example, the bond premium must be amortized. Assume, for simplicity, that the straight-line method of amortization is considered not materially different from the effective interest method. As a result, the amortization would be $1,200 ($12,000/10). An adjusting entry to provide for the amortization would be as follows:

7. Premium on Bonds Payable	1,200	
Interest Expense		1,200

The adjusted balance of interest ($96,000 + $2,500 − $1,200) will be reported as "interest expense" in the government-wide Statement of Activity.

Panel B of Illustration 8-2 demonstrates how the worksheet entries act with the existing modified accrual outcomes to produce accrual basis results for long-term debt. Again, the first column of the illustration displays the journal entry that took place during the year under the modified accrual basis of accounting and the second column displays the related worksheet entry. The final (shaded) column is the net effect of the previous two entries and is the entry that *would have been made* had the government recorded transactions affecting long-term debt on the accrual basis. Accounts that exist only under the modified accrual basis, such as *Other Financing Sources,* are eliminated and long-term liability balances are recorded and adjusted.

Again, no entries would be required for debt issued by proprietary funds because those funds already report long-term liabilities and interest expense on the accrual basis.

ADJUSTING TO CONVERT REVENUE RECOGNITION TO THE ACCRUAL BASIS

Chapter 3 introduced the concept of revenue recognition under modified accrual accounting. We observed that revenues are recognized when available and measurable. Revenues are deemed to be *available* if they are collectible within the current fiscal year or soon enough after the year-end that they could be used to settle current period liabilities. A special rule applied to property taxes—the 60-day rule. Under modified accrual, property taxes expected to be collected more than 60 days following year-end are deferred and recognized as revenue in the following year.

Chapter 3 also introduced the four classes of nonexchange transactions and described how they are reported in the modified accrual basis financial statements (Illustration 3-5). The government-wide statements are prepared using accrual accounting. GASB *Statement 33* (§N50.104), *Accounting and Financial Reporting for Nonexchange Transactions,* describes how nonexchange transactions should be reported in the government-wide financial statements under the accrual basis. Whenever revenue is recognized in a different time period under the modified accrual basis than under the accrual basis, worksheet entries will be required.

Illustration 8-3 presents the four classes of nonexchange transactions. Panel A describes and contrasts revenue recognition under the modified accrual and accrual bases. Panel B illustrates the journal entries to record the revenue under the modified accrual basis in the governmental fund-basis financial statements. The final column of panel B illustrates the journal entry to convert the governmental fund-basis financial statements to the accrual basis used in the government-wide statements. Generally, government-mandated and voluntary nonexchange transactions recognize revenue in the same time periods and no worksheet entries are needed. Property, sales, and income taxes deferred under the *available* criteria will require worksheet entries to convert to the accrual basis.

When converting to government-wide statements, governments need to examine all revenue sources to see which should be accrued. Assume, for the Village of Riverside, the only revenue that needs adjustment is property taxes. Chapter 4 reflected property tax revenue of $3,178,800 (see Illustration 4-5). Entry 27 of the General Fund example in Chapter 4 indicated that the Village deferred $40,000 in property tax revenues because that amount was not considered "available" for fiscal year 2020 expenditures. Since the property tax levy is for 2020, the full amount (less uncollectible taxes) should be recognized in the 2020 government-wide statements. Therefore the entry to defer a portion of the 2020 tax levy is reversed:

	Debits	Credits
8a. Deferred Inflows—Property Taxes	40,000	
Revenues—Property Taxes.........................		40,000

Like accruals, deferrals affect two time periods. Because the deferred revenue at December 31, 2019, is recognized in the 2020 fund-basis statements (see entry 3 in Chapter 4) but would have been recognized through a journal entry similar to 8a in last year's government-wide statements, an additional worksheet entry is required. That entry debits property tax revenues and credits net position for the $20,000 recognized as revenue under modified accrual accounting.

8b. Revenues—Property Taxes	20,000	
Net Position (beginning of year)		20,000

Generally speaking, *Net Position* will be the offset to worksheet entries that affect revenues or expenses recognized in a prior year, as well as worksheet entries affecting beginning asset and liability balances (for example, worksheet entries 1 and 9). In this case, property tax revenue of $20,000 was recognized in the previous year's government-wide Statement of Activity. The revenue had the effect of increasing the net position at the end of 2019. However, because worksheet entries are not posted, beginning fund balance computed under the modified accrual basis will not reflect the increase. Entry 8b has the effect of correcting the current year's revenues as well as restating the beginning net position balance. Note that the Net Position account appearing in these worksheet entries is the *beginning* of year net position. End of year net position will only be determined once all revenues and expenses have been adjusted.

Adjusting Expenses to the Accrual Basis

Under modified accrual, most expenditures are recorded when current obligations exist. A major exception is interest on long-term debt, which is recorded when due. As indicated earlier, interest payments on the general obligation long-term debt for the Village of Riverside were paid on the last day of the fiscal year; as a result, no accrual is necessary. Another exception to recording expenditures on the accrual basis arises because expenditures for various long-term accrued obligations (such as compensated absences or pensions) are recognized only to the extent they are payable from currently available resources. Assume the Village of Riverside had memorandum records indicating accumulated compensated absences payable at the beginning of the year totaled $300,000 and that an additional accrual of $25,000 is necessary in 2020. The following worksheet entries record the beginning balance and current year increase in this liability.

9. Net Position (beginning of year)	300,000	
Compensated Absences Payable.....................		300,000
10. Compensated Absences Expense......................	25,000	
Compensated Absences Payable......................		25,000

ILLUSTRATION 8-3 **Panel A: Classes and Timing of Recognition of Revenue from Nonexchange Transactions**

Type	Description and Examples	Modified Accrual Basis (Governmental Fund-Basis Reporting)	Accrual Basis (Government-wide Reporting)
Imposed Nonexchange Revenues	Taxes and other assessments that do not result from an underlying transaction. Examples include property taxes and special assessments imposed on property owners. Also includes fines and forfeits.	Record the receivable (and an allowance for uncollectibles) when an enforceable claim exists. Revenues should be recognized in the period for which the taxes are levied (i.e., budgeted), but are also subject to the 60-day rule. Revenues expected to be collected more than 60 days after year-end are reported as deferred inflows of resources.	Record the receivable (and allowance) when an enforceable claim exists. Revenues should be recognized in the period for which the taxes are levied—not subject to the 60-day rule.
Derived Tax Revenues	These are taxes assessed on exchange transactions conducted by businesses or citizens. Examples include sales, income, and excise taxes.	Record the receivable when the taxpayer's underlying transaction takes place. Revenues should be recognized when available and measurable. Revenues not expected to be collected in time to settle current liabilities are deferred (i.e., available and measurable criteria).	Record the receivable when the underlying transaction takes place. Revenues should be recognized when the taxpayer's underlying transaction takes place, regardless of when it is to be collected.
Government-Mandated Nonexchange Transactions	Grants from higher levels of government (federal or state) given to support a program. Since the program is required, the lower-level government has no choice but to accept. For example, a state may require schools to mainstream certain students and provide funds to carry out this mandate.	Record the receivable and the revenue when all eligibility requirements have been met. Many of these are reimbursement grants. In this case, revenue is recognized only when qualified expenditures have been incurred. Advance receipts are deferred until expenditures are incurred. Revenue recognition is subject to the available and measurable criteria.	The recognition criteria for grants under accrual accounting are generally the same as modified accrual. However, recognition in the government-wide statements does not require revenues to be collected in time to settle current liabilities (i.e., available and measurable criteria do not apply).
Voluntary Nonexchange Transactions	Donations and grants given to support a program. Since the program is not required, the receiving government voluntarily agrees to participate.	The recognition rules are the same as mandated grants.	The recognition rules are the same as mandated grants.

ILLUSTRATION 8-3 **Panel B: Representative Nonexchange Transactions and Example Journal Entries**

Type	Representative Transaction	Modified Accrual Basis (Governmental Fund-Basis Reporting)	Adjustment to Accrual Basis (Government-wide Reporting)
Imposed Nonexchange Revenues	1. Property taxes levied.	1. Taxes Receivable ....Dr Estimated Uncollectible Taxes ....Cr Revenues Control....Cr	1. No adjustment needed for current year levy.
	2. Deferral of portion expected to be collected more than 60 days after year-end.	2. Revenues Control ....Dr Deferred Inflows—Property Taxes....Cr	2. Deferrals resulting from the 60-day rule would be reversed. **Deferred Inflows ....Dr** **Revenues — Property Tax....Cr**
Derived Tax Revenues	1. Income tax withholdings are received.	1. Cash....Dr Revenues Control ....Cr	1. No adjustment needed for collections resulting from taxable income earned in the current year.
	2. Additional income taxes expected to be received after year-end. Part of this will not be received in time to be available to settle current liabilities.	2. Taxes Receivable ....Dr Revenues Control....Cr Deferred Inflows—Income Taxes....Cr	2. Deferrals resulting from applying the "available" criterion would be reversed. **Deferred Inflows ....Dr** **Revenues — Income Taxes ....Cr**
Government-Mandated Nonexchange Transactions & Voluntary Nonexchange Transactions	Reimbursement-type grant: 1. Incur qualified expenditures. 2. Recognize revenue.	1. Expenditures Control....Dr Accounts Payable/Cash....Cr 2. Due from Grantor ....Dr Revenues Control....Cr	Generally no adjustment needed for government-wide reporting.
	Advance funded grant: 1. Receipt of advance funding. 2. Incur qualified expenditures and recognize revenue.	1. Cash ....Dr Deferred Inflows—Grants ....Cr 2a. Expenditures Control....Dr Accounts Payable/Cash ....Cr 2b. Deferred Inflows—Grants....Dr Revenues Control ....Cr	Generally no adjustment needed for government-wide reporting.

A worksheet entry similar to entry 9 would be used to record any long-term liabilities outstanding at the beginning of the year, including bonds, notes, and capital leases payable.

ADDING INTERNAL SERVICE FUNDS TO GOVERNMENTAL ACTIVITIES

Internal service funds are proprietary funds and as such are not included in the governmental fund balances used as the starting point for the government-wide conversion. Most internal service funds serve primarily governmental departments and should therefore be included with the governmental activities in the government-wide statements. However, if an internal service fund predominantly provides goods and services to departments reported in enterprise funds, it should be reported in the business activities column of the government-wide Statement of Net Position.

Four steps are necessary to incorporate internal service funds into the governmental activities category. The first step is to bring in the balance sheet accounts. For the Village of Riverside, these are found in the internal service fund column of the proprietary funds Statement of Net Position (Illustration 6-3). To be consistent with entry 1 in this section, the same detail of the capital assets is posted:

	Debits	Credits
11. Cash	3,500	
Investments	50,000	
Due from Other Funds	55,000	
Inventory of Materials and Supplies	233,500	
Land	80,000	
Buildings	270,000	
Equipment	140,000	
Accumulated Depreciation—Capital Assets		27,500
Accounts Payable		11,000
Advance from Water Utility Fund		190,000
Net Position		603,500

The remaining steps relate to the current period changes in the internal service fund's assets and liabilities. Changes in net position are reflected in the Statement of Revenues, Expenses, and Changes in Fund Net Position, reproduced in Illustration 8-4. It is important to identify the sources of those changes, including exchange transactions with external parties, exchange transactions with other government departments, and interfund transfers.

ILLUSTRATION 8-4 **Sources of Change in Internal Fund Net Position**

VILLAGE OF RIVERSIDE
Internal Service Fund
(Condensed) Statement of Revenues, Expenses, and Changes in Fund Net Position

The change in net position comes from three distinct sources:

Operating revenues	$377,000
Operating expenses	372,500
Operating income	4,500
Nonoperating revenues (expenses)	
Interest revenue	3,000
Income before contributions and transfers	7,500
Transfers in	596,000
Change in net position	603,500
Net position - January 1	-0-
Net position - December 31	$603,500

1. This represents income earned from transactions with other government departments.
2. This represents income earned from external entities.
3. This is an interfund transfer. The General Fund has a corresponding Transfer Out.

Transactions between the government and external parties should be reflected in the government-wide Statement of Activities. In this case the only such transaction is investment income of $3,000. This income is added to the Statement of Activities through the following journal entry:

12. Net Position (beginning of year)	3,000	
Investment Income		3,000

The third step is to eliminate the effect of exchange transactions between the internal service fund and other departments accounted for within the General Fund. The net effect of these transactions (revenues less expenses) is reflected in the $4,500 of operating income. Recall from our discussion in Chapter 6 that if an internal service fund has positive operating income, the expenditures reported in the General Fund overstate the true cost of running the government. To correct for this overstatement of expenditures in the General Fund, the operating income of $4,500 is deducted from the appropriate expense function categories. If the operating income was large, an effort would be made to determine which functions contributed to that profit and deduct the profit on a proportionate basis. In this case the amount is small and the Village chooses to credit Expenditures—General Government:

13. Net Position (beginning of year)	4,500	
Expenditures—General Government		4,500

Finally, an entry is made to incorporate the internal service fund's Transfer In from the General Fund in the amount of $596,000. (This transfer is recorded in entry 22 of the General Fund example in Chapter 4 and entry 1 of the internal service fund example in Chapter 6.) The transfer that is established here will be eliminated in the next section.

	Debit	Credit
14. Net Position (beginning of year)	596,000	
Other Financing Sources—Transfers In		596,000

The previous three entries have all debited Net Position. The purpose here is to establish the beginning balance of the internal service fund's net position. Recall that entry 11 recorded the end-of-year balances of assets, liabilities, and net position. Beginning-of-year net position can be determined by subtracting the change in net position from the end-of-year balance, as follows:

End-of-Year Net Position (Entry 11)	$603,500
Less: Entry 12	(3,000)
Entry 13	(4,500)
Entry 14	(596,000)
Beginning-of-Year Net Position	$ -0-

Because the internal service fund was established this year, the beginning net position balance is zero. Next year these journal entries should combine to reflect a beginning net position balance of $603,500, this year's ending balance.

Eliminating Interfund Activities and Balances within Governmental Activities

The final set of worksheet entries serves to eliminate transactions and balances between governmental funds (including internal service funds). After considering entry 14, the governmental funds report Transfers In of $1,048,500 and Transfers Out of $848,500, comprising the following:

Transfers In—Governmental Funds		Transfers Out—Governmental Funds	
Fire Station Debt Service Fund	$ 204,000	General Fund	$204,000
Fire Station Debt Service Fund	48,500	Fire Station Capital Projects Fund	48,500
Supplies, Internal Service Fund	596,000	General Fund	596,000
Fire Station Capital Projects Fund	200,000		
	$1,048,500		$848,500

Because enterprise funds are reported in the business-type activities column of the government-wide statements, the transfer of $200,000 from the Water Utility

Enterprise Fund (entry 13, Chapter 6) to help finance the construction of a new fire station cannot be eliminated through worksheet entry. Therefore, the smaller of the two amounts (Transfers In or Transfers Out) is eliminated as follows:

	Debits	Credits
15. Other Financing Sources—Transfers In	848,500	
Other Financing Uses—Transfers Out		848,500

This leaves a $200,000 transfer in from the enterprise fund to the Fire Station Capital Projects Fund, which should be reported as a transfer between governmental activities and business-type activities in the government-wide Statement of Activities.

When looking at the governmental funds Balance Sheet (Illustration 5-3), note the liability account Due to Other Funds in the amount of $135,000. This consists of $55,000 due to internal service funds, now incorporated into the governmental funds through entry 11 recording the internal service fund's assets and $80,000 due to the Water Utility Fund, an enterprise fund (see Illustration 6-2 for the detail). The $55,000 must be eliminated; the $80,000 should remain, as it is a liability from governmental activities to business-type activities and will be reported as internal balances in the government-wide Statement of Net Position:

16. Due to Other Funds.	55,000	
Due from Other Funds		55,000

Worksheet to Illustrate the Adjustments

Illustration 8-5 presents a worksheet incorporating the adjustments listed above. The worksheet begins by reproducing the accounts from the governmental funds Balance Sheet (Illustration 5-3) and Statement of Revenues, Expenditures, and Changes in Fund Balances (Illustration 5-4). The worksheet uses a trial balance format with accounts classified as to whether they are debits or credits. Items appearing in parentheses represent credit balances.

Because the balances of revenues and expenditures appear in this worksheet, it represents a preclosing trial balance. Like all preclosing trial balances, residual equity accounts (fund balances or net position) represent beginning balances and (as a starting point) have been grouped into a single Net Position account. The $502,500 entry appearing at the bottom of the first column of numbers is the *beginning* of the year balance and is in agreement with "*Fund Balances—Beginning*" found on the second line from the bottom of the Statement of Revenues, Expenditures, and Changes in Fund Balance from Illustration 5-4. The worksheet entries are then incorporated into the worksheet. The right-hand column balances are measured on

ILLUSTRATION 8-5 Worksheet to Convert to Government-wide Statement

	Governmental Fund Balances	Adjustments & Eliminations				Internal Service Funds				Balances for Government-wide Statements
		ref.	Debits	Credits	ref.	ref.	Debits	Credits	ref.	
DEBITS:										
Cash	728,000					*(11)*	3,500			731,500
Investments	302,000					*(11)*	50,000			352,000
Due from Other Funds						*(11)*	55,000	(55,000)	*(16)*	—
Interest Receivable, net	40,490									40,490
Taxes Receivable, net	528,800									528,800
Due from State Govt.	185,000									185,000
Inventories						*(11)*	233,500			233,500
Capital Assets		*(1)* *(2)*	62,400,000 1,961,000	(225,000)	*(4)*	*(11)*	490,000			64,626,000
Expenditures (expenses) Current										
General Govt.	810,000							(4,500)	*(13)*	805,500
Public Safety	2,139,500									2,139,500
Public Works	1,605,000									1,605,000
Health & Welfare	480,100									480,100
Cemetery	11,000									11,000
Parks and Recreation	527,400									527,400
Contribution to Retirement Funds	423,000									423,000
Miscellaneous	20,300									20,300
Compensated Absences		*(10)*	25,000							25,000
Other Expenditures (expenses)										
Debt Service Principal	120,000			(120,000)	*(6)*					—
Debt Service Interest	96,000	*(2)*	2,500	(1,200)	*(7)*					97,300
Capital Outlay	1,963,500			(1,963,500)	*(2)*					—
Depreciation		*(3)*	2,287,500							2,287,500
										—
Other Financial Uses—Transfers Out	848,500							(848,500)	*(15)*	—
Total Debits	10,828,590									75,118,890

CREDITS:										
Accounts Payable	(185,300)							(11,000)	***(11)***	(196,300)
Due to Other Funds	(135,000)					***(16)***	55,000			(80,000)
Deferred Inflows—Property Taxes	(40,000)	***(8a)***	40,000							—
Bonds Payable		***(6)***	120,000	(1,200,000)	***(5)***					(1,080,000)
Premium on Bonds		***(7)***	1,200	(12,000)	***(5)***					(10,800)
Compensated Absence Payable				(300,000) (25,000)	***(9)*** ***(10)***					(325,000)
Advances from Water Utility Fund								(190,000)	***(11)***	(190,000)
Accumulated Depreciation				(25,100,000) (2,287,500)	***(1)*** ***(3)***			(27,500)	***(11)***	(27,415,000)
Revenues										
Property Taxes	(3,178,800)	***(8b)***	20,000	(40,000)	***(8a)***					(3,198,800)
Motor Fuel Taxes	(650,000)									(650,000)
Sales Taxes	(1,410,000)									(1,410,000)
Interest & Penalties on Taxes	(42,490)									(42,490)
Licenses & Permits	(540,000)									(540,000)
Fines & Forfeits	(430,000)									(430,000)
Investment Income	(20,000)							(3,000)	***(12)***	(23,000)
Miscellaneous	(30,000)									(30,000)
State Grant for Road Repairs	(350,000)									(350,000)
Capital Grant for Fire Station	(600,000)									(600,000)
Capital Contributions—Endowment	(300,000)									(300,000)
Grant for Law Enforcement	(350,000)									(350,000)
Charges for Services	(100,000)									(100,000)
Other Financing Sources										
Proceeds of Bonds	(1,200,000)	***(5)***	1,200,000							—
Premium on Bonds	(12,000)	***(5)***	12,000							—
Transfers In	(452,500)					***(15)***	848,500	(596,000)	***(14)***	(200,000)
Special Items										
Proceeds of Sale of Land	(300,000)	***(4)***	300,000							—
Gain on Sale of Land				(75,000)	***(4)***					(75,000)
Net Position at beginning of year	(502,500)	***(9)***	300,000	(20,000) (37,300,000)	***(8b)*** ***(1)***	***(14)*** ***(12)*** ***(13)***	596,000 3,000 4,500	(603,500)	***(11)***	(37,522,500)
Total Credits	(10,828,590)									(75,118,890)

Note: Amounts in parentheses represent credits.

the economic resources measurement focus and accrual basis of accounting. Items previously labeled as expenditures are now expenses. These account balances are, in effect, a preclosing trial balance for the governmental activities section of the government-wide statements.

To take full advantage of the presentation in this chapter, trace the beginning balances from the governmental funds statements (Illustrations 5-3 and 5–4) to the worksheet. Then, trace the entries discussed previously in this chapter to the worksheet by number. Finally, trace the ending balances in the worksheet to the statements presented in the next section.

GOVERNMENT-WIDE FINANCIAL STATEMENTS

The GASB requires two government-wide financial statements: the Statement of Net Position and the Statement of Activities. These two statements are presented in this section, using the Village of Riverside example presented in Chapters 4 to 7 and continued in the first section of this chapter.

Statement of Net Position

The Statement of Net Position for the Village of Riverside is presented as Illustration 8-6. Assets, liabilities, and net position are separately displayed for governmental activities and business-type activities. In the case of the Village of Riverside, governmental activities include those activities accounted for by the governmental funds (General, special revenue, debt service, capital projects, and permanent) and internal service funds. Business-type activities include activities of enterprise funds. The Village of Riverside has no component units; if it had component units, they would be displayed in a separate column as shown in Illustration 2-5. Previous sections of this chapter reflected how the governmental funds statements were adjusted to prepare this statement.

Assets and liabilities are reported in order of liquidity, or GASB standards permit reporting a classified statement with subtotals for current assets and liabilities. It is also permissible to use a balance sheet format, where Assets = Liabilities + Net Position.

ILLUSTRATION 8-6 **Statement of Net Position**

VILLAGE OF RIVERSIDE
Statement of Net Position
December 31, 2020

	Governmental Activities	Business-type Activities	Total
Assets			
Cash	$ 731,500	$ 124,930	$ 856,430
Investments	352,000	—	352,000
Interest receivable	40,490	—	40,490
Taxes receivable, net	528,800	—	528,800
Accounts receivable	—	74,925	74,925

	Governmental Activities	Business-type Activities	Total
Due from state government	185,000	—	185,000
Due from governmental activities	—	80,000	80,000
Inventories	233,500	31,000	264,500
Restricted cash and cash equivalents	—	110,000	110,000
Long-term advance to governmental activities	—	190,000	190,000
Capital assets, net of depreciation	37,211,000	3,770,465	40,981,465
Total assets	39,282,290	4,381,320	43,663,610
Liabilities			
Accounts payable	196,300	89,600	285,900
Due to business-type activities	80,000	—	80,000
Payroll taxes payable	—	9,000	9,000
Advance from business-type activities	190,000	—	190,000
Revenue bonds payable	—	2,700,000	2,700,000
General obligation bonds payable	1,090,800	—	1,090,800
Compensated absences payable	325,000	—	325,000
Total liabilities	1,882,100	2,798,600	4,680,700
Net position			
Net investment in capital assets	35,930,200	1,070,465	37,000,665
Restricted	612,500	110,000	722,500
Unrestricted	857,490	402,255	1,259,745
Total net position	$37,400,190	$1,582,720	$38,982,910

The net position balances to be reported in the December 31, 2020, Statement of Net Position are calculated as follows:

	Net Investment in Capital Assets	Restricted	Unrestricted	Total
Net investment in capital assets				
Capital assets	$64,626,000			$64,626,000
Less accumulated depreciation	(27,415,000)			(27,415,000)
Less bonds payable + premium	(1,090,800)			(1,090,800)
Less advance from enterprise fund	(190,000)			(190,000)
Restricted:				
Permanent fund principal		$300,000		300,000
Restricted for public works		75,000		75,000
Restricted for road repair		237,500		237,500
Unrestricted (plug)			$857,490	857,490
Total net position	$35,930,200	$612,500	$857,490	$37,400,190

Note that the advance from the enterprise fund ($190,000) was for the purchase of capital assets by the internal service fund and is subtracted in calculating the balance of Net investment in capital assets. Restricted net position includes the balances of the restricted fund balances appearing in the governmental funds Balance Sheet (Illustration 5-3) plus the *nonspendable fund balance,* representing the nonexpendable principal of the permanent fund. Unrestricted net position is a "plug" figure ($37,400,190 − $35,930,200 − $612,500 = $857,490) calculated as the difference between total net position and the balances of the two previously determined net position components. The net position amounts appearing in the business-type activities column correspond with those reported in the enterprise fund Statement of Net Position (Illustration 6-3).

Although interfund receivables and payables were eliminated for funds appearing within the governmental activities column (entry 16), receivables and payables between governmental and business-type funds remain. In particular, Due from Governmental Activities ($80,000) and Long-Term Advance to Governmental Activities ($190,000) appear as assets in the business-type activities column, with liabilities in equal amounts appearing in the governmental activities column. GASB standards also permit offsetting these accounts by displaying them together in rows titled *Internal Balances.* In this case there would be two rows with negative balances in the governmental activities column offset by positive amounts in the business-type activities column as follows:

	Governmental Activities	Business-type Activities	Total
(Asset Section)			
Internal balances—current	(80,000)	80,000	0
Internal balances—long-term	(190,000)	190,000	0

Statement of Activities

Illustration 8-7 reflects the Statement of Activities for the Village of Riverside. The general concept is that program/function expenses are reduced by direct (program) revenues, yielding net expenses. General revenues (i.e., not attributable to a specific program) are subtracted from net expenses in the lower right-hand corner to get the change in net position. Information is available separately for governmental and business-type activities. Information would also be presented for component units if the Village of Riverside had component units.

Expenses for governmental activities are taken from the governmental funds Statement of Revenues, Expenditures, and Changes in Fund Balances (Illustration 5-4) as modified by the worksheet developed in this chapter (Illustration 8-5). The program revenues were identified as follows:

- $350,000 of General Fund intergovernmental revenues were considered a grant for law enforcement.
- $600,000 was received, through capital projects funds, as a grant for the construction of the police station addition.
- $350,000 was received, through a special revenue fund, as a state reimbursement grant for road repairs.
- $300,000 was received as a gift for establishment of a permanent fund for the maintenance of the city cemetery.
- $100,000 in charges for services were assumed to be for charges for city parks and recreation.

These revenues are deducted from related expenses to arrive at net expenses. Although the format of this statement may seem strange, the objective is to allow statement users to determine the "net cost" of each major government function. For example, Parks and Recreation had total expenses of $527,400. However, Parks and Recreation charged for certain services (e.g., rental of picnic shelters) and earned $100,000 of program revenues. The result is that the cost of Parks and Recreation that is supported by tax revenues is $427,400.

All taxes, including motor fuel taxes, are classified as general revenues. These are not subtracted when determining the net expense of a government function; instead, they appear at the bottom of the statement. Transfers, special items, and extraordinary items are to be reported separately. In the case of the Village of Riverside, a transfer is shown in the amount of $200,000 from business-type activities to governmental activities. This represents a transfer from the Water Utility Enterprise Fund to the Fire Station Addition Capital Projects Fund (see entry 2 in the capital projects section of Chapter 5 and entry 13 in the enterprise fund section of Chapter 6). All other transfers were eliminated through the worksheet entries, as those transfers were between funds that are reported within governmental activities.

Required Reconciliation to Government-wide Statements

GASB requires a reconciliation from the fund financial statements to the government-wide financial statements. Normally no reconciliation is required when going from the proprietary fund financial statements to the government-wide statements' business activities columns because enterprise funds use accrual accounting. On the other hand, reconciliations are required from the governmental fund Balance Sheet to the Statement of Net Position and from the governmental fund Statement of Revenues, Expenditures, and Changes in Fund Balances to the Statement of Activities. These reconciliations are required to be presented on the face of the governmental fund financial statements or in separate schedules immediately after the fund financial statements.

Illustration 8-8 reflects a reconciliation between the governmental fund Balance Sheet (Illustration 5-3) and the governmental activities column in the Statement of Net Position (Illustration 8-6) for the Village of Riverside. The elements in this reconciliation can be traced through earlier sections of this chapter.

Illustration 8-9 presents a reconciliation between the changes in fund balances in the governmental fund Statement of Revenues, Expenditures, and Changes in Fund Balances (Illustration 5-4) and the governmental activities change in net position in the Statement of Activities (Illustration 8-7). Again, the elements in the reconciliation are generated in earlier sections of this chapter.

ILLUSTRATION 8-7 Statement of Activities

VILLAGE OF RIVERSIDE
Statement of Activities
For the Year Ended December 31, 2020

		Program Revenues			Net (Expense) Revenue and Changes in Net Position		
Functions/Programs	**Expenses**	**Charges for Services**	**Operating Grants and Contributions**	**Capital Grants and Contributions**	**Governmental Activities**	**Business-type Activities**	**Total**
Governmental activities:							
General government	$ 805,500	—	—	—	$ (805,500)	—	$ (805,500)
Public safety	2,139,500	—	$350,000	$600,000	(1,189,500)	—	(1,189,500)
Public works	1,605,000	—	350,000	—	(1,255,000)	—	(1,255,000)
Health and welfare	480,100	—	—	—	(480,100)	—	(480,100)
Cemetery	11,000	—	—	300,000	289,000	—	289,000
Parks and recreation	527,400	100,000	—	—	(427,400)	—	(427,400)
Contribution to retirement funds	423,000	—	—	—	(423,000)	—	(423,000)
Compensated absences	25,000	—	—	—	(25,000)	—	(25,000)
Depreciation expense	2,287,500	—	—	—	(2,287,500)	—	(2,287,500)
Interest expense	97,300	—	—	—	(97,300)	—	(97,300)
Miscellaneous	20,300	—	—	—	(20,300)	—	(20,300)
Total governmental activities	8,421,600	100,000	700,000	900,000	(6,721,600)	—	(6,721,600)
Business-type activities:							
Water utility	845,900	1,053,100	—	12,500	—	219,700	219,700
Total government	$9,267,500	$1,153,100	$700,000	$912,500	$(6,721,600)	219,700	$(6,501,900)

General revenues:			
Taxes:			
Property taxes	3,198,800	—	3,198,800
Motor fuel taxes	650,000	—	650,000
Sales taxes	1,410,000	—	1,410,000
Interest and penalties on taxes	42,490	—	42,490
Licenses and permits	540,000	—	540,000
Fines and forfeits	430,000	—	430,000
Investment income	23,000	—	23,000
Miscellaneous	30,000	—	30,000
Special item—gain on sale of park land	75,000	—	75,000
Transfers	200,000	(200,000)	—
Total general revenues, special items, and transfers	6,599,290	(200,000)	6,399,290
Change in net position	(122,310)	19,700	(102,610)
Net position—beginning	37,522,500	1,563,020	39,085,520
Net position—ending	$37,400,190	$1,582,720	$38,982,910

ILLUSTRATION 8-8 **Reconciliation of the Balance Sheet of Governmental Funds to the Statement of Net Position**

VILLAGE OF RIVERSIDE Reconciliation of the Balance Sheet of Governmental Funds to the Statement of Net Position December 31, 2020	
Fund balances reported in governmental funds Balance Sheet (Illustration 5-3)	$ 1,423,990
Amounts reported for *governmental activities* in the Statement of Net Position are different because:	
Capital assets used in governmental activities are not financial resources and, therefore, are not reported in the funds.	36,748,500*
Internal service funds are used by management to charge the costs of certain activities (stores and services) to individual funds. The assets and liabilities of internal service funds are included in governmental funds in the Statement of Net Position.	603,500
Deferred revenue for property taxes is reported in the funds but accrued as revenue in the government-wide statements and added to net position.	40,000
Long-term liabilities, including bonds payable, are not due and payable in the current period and, therefore, are not reported in the funds.	(1,415,800)
Net position of governmental activities (Illustration 8-6)	$37,400,190

* This number does not include the capital assets of internal service funds, which are included in the $603,500 that follows.

SUMMARY

In addition to the fund-basis statements, GASB requires government-wide statements that are prepared on the accrual basis using the economic resources measurement focus. The statements separately present information on component units, business-type activities (generally limited to enterprise funds), and governmental activities. Fiduciary activities are not reported in the government-wide statements.

Government-wide information may be taken directly from the fund-basis financial statements of enterprise funds and component units using the accrual basis. However, governmental funds are prepared using the modified accrual basis and current financial resources measurement focus and must be adjusted to meet the requirements for government-wide reporting. Our approach is similar to that used by most governments. Specifically, we use the modified accrual–based governmental fund financial statements as a starting point. These are adjusted for

- Capital asset–related events.
- Long-term debt–related events.

ILLUSTRATION 8-9 **Reconciliation of the Statement of Revenues, Expenditures, and Changes in Fund Balances of Governmental Funds to the Statement of Activities**

VILLAGE OF RIVERSIDE Reconciliation of the Statement of Revenues, Expenditures, and Changes in Fund Balances of Governmental Funds to the Statement of Activities For the Year Ended December 31, 2020	
Net change in fund balances—total governmental funds (Illustration 5-4)	$ 921,490
Amounts reported for *governmental activities* in the Statement of Activities are different because	
Governmental funds report capital outlays as expenditures. However, in the Statement of Activities, the cost of those assets is allocated over their estimated useful lives as depreciation expense. This is the amount by which depreciation exceeded capital outlays in the current period. (See entries 2 and 3.)	(326,500)
In the Statement of Activities, only the *gain* on the sale of land is reported, whereas in the governmental funds, the proceeds from the sale increase financial resources. Thus, the change in net position differs from the change in fund balance by the cost of the land sold. (See entry 4.)	(225,000)
Revenues in the Statement of Activities that do not provide current financial resources are not reported as revenues in the funds. (See entries 8a and 8b.)	20,000
Bond proceeds provide current financial resources to governmental funds, but issuing debt increases long-term liabilities in the Statement of Net Position. Repayment of bond principal is an expenditure in the governmental funds, but the repayment reduces long-term liabilities in the Statement of Net Position. This is the amount by which proceeds exceeded repayments. (See entries 5 and 6.)	(1,080,000)
Some expenses reported in the Statement of Activities do not require the use of current financial resources and therefore are not reported as expenditures in governmental funds. (See entry 10.)	(25,000)
Internal service funds are used by management to charge the costs of certain activities, such as stores and services. The income before transfers of the internal service funds is reported with governmental activities.	7,500
A transfer was made from the General Fund to an internal service fund; that transfer reduced the changes in fund balance of governmental funds but not the change in net position of governmental activities. (See entry 14.)	596,000
Bond premium was reported as another financing source in the governmental funds. The amortization of bond premium was reported as an expense reduction in the Statement of Activities. This is the amount by which the bond premium exceeded the amortization for the period. (See entries 5 and 7.)	(10,800)
Change in net position of governmental activities (Illustration 8-7)	$ (122,310)

- Differences in timing of the recognition of revenue and expenses between accrual and modified accrual accounting.
- Internal service fund activities.
- Interfund activities and balances.

The adjusted amounts are then presented in the governmental activities sections of the government-wide Statement of Activities and Statement of Net Position.

Many of the differences that arise between accrual and modified accrual accounting relate to the capital assets and long-term debt of governmental funds. These are often termed **general capital (or fixed) assets** and **general long-term debt.** Although GASB standards require these capital assets and long-term liabilities to be reported in the government-wide statements, the day-to-day accounting for these items is not prescribed. In the appendix to this chapter, we demonstrate a common method for recording capital asset and long-term debt transactions so that the information is available for preparation of government-wide financial statements. Reporting requirements for capital assets and long-term liabilities are also described.

APPENDIX: ACCOUNTING FOR CAPITAL ASSETS AND LONG-TERM DEBT IN GOVERNMENTAL ACTIVITIES

Accounting for General Capital Assets, Including Infrastructure

Accountants commonly define things in terms of what they are not. Such is the case with *general capital assets.* These are capital assets that are not associated with proprietary or fiduciary activities. They are most commonly acquired by a General or capital project fund. Even though general capital assets are not reported in fund financial statements, it is necessary to maintain fixed asset records to support the reporting that is done in the government-wide statements. Prior to the adoption of GASB *Statement 34,* government accounting principles required the use and reporting of a General Fixed Asset Account Group that reflected capital assets by category (land, buildings, equipment, etc.).

Account groups are used only for capital assets and long-term debt arising from governmental activities. Since proprietary and fiduciary funds use the economic resources measurement focus, capital assets and long-term debt are recorded directly in those funds. Account groups provide a place to record (noncurrent) assets and liabilities that are not otherwise recorded in a governmental fund. Since most accounting systems will not accept an unbalanced journal entry (i.e., debits must equal credits), an offset account was often used termed *Investment in General Fixed Assets.* Entries to record changes in capital asset balances would be reflected as follows:

	Debits	Credits
To record asset acquisitions		
Capital Assets—Buildings	1,961,000	
Investment in General Fixed Assets		1,961,000
To record depreciation		
Investment in General Fixed Assets	2,287,500	
Accumulated Depreciation—Buildings		957,500
Accumulated Depreciation—Improvements		770,000
Accumulated Depreciation—Equipment		560,000
To record asset sales/disposals		
Investment in General Fixed Assets	225,000	
Land		225,000

The Investment in General Fixed Assets account has no significance and does *not* appear in any financial statements.

GASB (§1400.113) provides guidance regarding depreciation. Any of the generally recognized methods might be used, such as straight-line or declining-balance methods. Most governments use the straight-line method. GASB indicates that useful lives for fixed assets may be estimated from (1) general guidelines obtained from professional or industry organizations, (2) information for comparable assets of other governments, or (3) internal information.

GASB requires significant disclosures in the notes to financial statements regarding capital assets. These disclosures should be by major classes of capital assets (land, buildings, improvements other than buildings, equipment, etc.) and separated between capital assets associated with governmental activities and business-type activities. Disclosure must be made of the beginning balances, capital acquisitions, sales and other dispositions, ending balances, and current period depreciation expense. In addition to note disclosures, GASB requires that summary information be presented in the Management's Discussion and Analysis.

Governments are required to include infrastructure assets in the Statement of Net Position and note disclosures. Infrastructure assets have long lives and (unlike equipment) cannot be moved. They also can be used for many years if properly maintained. Examples of infrastructure assets include roads, bridges, tunnels, drainage systems, water and sewer systems, dams, and lighting systems (GASB §1400.103).

Governments are permitted a choice regarding depreciation of infrastructure. Governments can record depreciation in the same manner as for other depreciable fixed assets. This is the method assumed in the Village of Riverside example, where a 20-year life was assumed. Alternatively, governments can use the modified approach.

The Modified Approach for Reporting Infrastructure

Infrastructure assets are characterized by long useful lives, if properly maintained. For example, it is not uncommon to find aqueducts, bridges, and roads constructed by the Roman Empire that are still in use today. Because of the long life of these assets, it may be argued that infrastructure assets have an indefinite life. For this reason, GASB permits governments to choose an alternative to depreciation that expenses costs incurred to extend the life of infrastructure assets.

Governments electing to use the modified approach must meet several conditions. First, the government must have an asset management system that (1) keeps an up-to-date inventory of eligible infrastructure assets; (2) performs condition assessments of those eligible infrastructure assets at least every three years, using a consistent measurement scale; and (3) estimates each year the annual amount to maintain and preserve those assets at the condition level established and disclosed by the government. Second, the government must document that the eligible infrastructure assets are being maintained at a level at or above the condition level established and disclosed by the government.

Two additional RSI schedules are required of governments using the modified approach. These schedules describe (1) the assessed condition of eligible infrastructure assets and (2) the estimated annual amount necessary to maintain and preserve eligible infrastructure assets compared with the amount actually expended for each of the preceding five fiscal periods. An example is provided in Illustration 2-15. Certain note disclosures are also required.

When using the modified approach, expenditures *to extend the life* of infrastructure assets are charged to expense; if governments choose to depreciate infrastructure assets rather than use the modified approach, expenditures to extend the life of infrastructure assets would be capitalized in the government-wide statements. In either case, expenditures to add to or improve infrastructure assets would be capitalized.

For example, assume a government expends the following for infrastructure: $2,000,000 for general repairs (always expensed); $2,500,000 for improvements that extend the life (but not the quality) of existing infrastructure; and $3,000,000 to add to and improve existing infrastructure. If the government chooses to simply depreciate infrastructure, the current year provision would be $2,750,000. The accounting treatment of these costs under the traditional depreciation approach and the modified approach are as follows:

	Added to Capital Assets	Expensed
Depreciation Approach		
General repairs		$2,000,000
Improvements to extend life	$2,500,000	
Additions to existing infrastructure	3,000,000	
Provision for depreciation		2,750,000
Total	$5,500,000	$4,750,000
Modified Approach		
General repairs		$2,000,000
Improvements to extend life		2,500,000
Additions to existing infrastructure	$3,000,000	
Depreciation: *The modified approach does not depreciate infrastructure.*		n/a
Total	$3,000,000	$4,500,000

Collections

Governments are encouraged, but not required, to capitalize collections. To qualify as a **collection,** a donated or purchased item must meet all of the following conditions (GASB §1400.109):

- Held for public exhibition, education, or research in furtherance of public service, rather than for financial gain.
- Protected, kept unencumbered, cared for, and preserved.
- Subject to an organizational policy that requires the proceeds from sales of collection items to be used to acquire new collections or for the direct care of existing collections.

Disclosures are required for collections. Donated collections would be reported as revenues. If capitalized, the offsetting amount would be to *collections,* an asset account; otherwise the offsetting amount would be charged to the proper expense category. Collections are especially important for public colleges and universities and for governmental museums reported as special entities.

Asset Impairment

GASB has also addressed the issue of what governments should do in the event of an unexpected decline in the usable capacity of a capital asset. GASB provides a two-step process for determining whether an asset is impaired.

Step 1: Identify Potential Impairment Events Examples include physical damage through fire or flood, changes in regulation, technological changes, construction stoppage, and discontinued use of a capital asset. However, a decrease in the demand for a particular service does not (in and of itself) indicate impairment.

Step 2: Test for Impairment Impairment is deemed to exist if both of the following factors are present:

1. The decline in the service utility is unexpected (not part of the normal life cycle of an asset).
2. The amount of the decline in service utility is large.

For example, the following might be determined to result in asset impairments:

- A bridge is damaged by an earthquake.
- Congress enacts new water quality standards and it is not economical to modify an existing water treatment plant to meet the new standards.
- A costly piece of diagnostic equipment at a city hospital is no longer used because new technology exists that does a better job.
- An expansion project at the city airport is halted because a major airline stops service to the city.

Capital assets that are determined to be permanently impaired are written down with a resulting expense or loss in the government-wide Statement of Activities and the Statement of Revenues, Expenses, and Changes in Fund Net Position (proprietary funds only). The expense or loss is reported net of any insurance recovery in these accrual basis statements. Insurance proceeds received by modified accrual basis funds are generally classified as Other Financing Sources in the Statement of Revenues, Expenditures, and Changes in Fund Balances. Since the governmental funds do not report capital assets, it is not necessary to record a loss in the fund-basis statements.

ACCOUNTING FOR LONG-TERM DEBT

As is the case for capital assets, long-term liabilities associated with proprietary funds and fiduciary funds are reported with those funds. However, long-term liabilities associated with governmental funds are not reported in the governmental fund financial statements. These long-term liabilities are referred to as **general long-term debt** and are reported in the government-wide statements only. General long-term debt includes debt that is intended to be paid with general governmental resources. Sometimes this is called **general obligation debt (or bonds).** General obligation debt is backed by the **full faith and credit** of the governmental unit, including its taxing power. However, it should be noted that in some cases, general obligation debt will be paid with enterprise fund resources and would properly be reported in the enterprise funds. The term *general long-term debt* represents debt that is to be paid out of general government resources.

Types of General Long-Term Debt

General long-term debt includes the principal of unmatured bonds, the noncurrent portion of capital lease agreements, compensated absences, claims and judgments, pensions (the net pension obligation), OPEB liabilities, special termination benefits, pollution remediation costs, and landfill closure and postclosure care liabilities (when paid out of general government resources).

As is the case with general fixed assets, governments need detailed records of long-term debt. Historically, this has been accomplished through the General Long-Term Debt Account Group. Again, since most accounting systems will not accept an unbalanced journal entry, an offset account is often used, termed *Amount to be Provided.* Entries to record changes in long-term liability balances would be reflected as follows:

	Debits	Credits
To record bond issue		
Amount to Be Provided	1,212,000	
Bonds Payable		1,200,000
Bond Premium		12,000
To record premium amortization		
Bond Premium	1,200	
Amount to Be Provided		1,200
To record payment of principal		
Bonds Payable	120,000	
Amount to Be Provided		120,000

The *Amount to Be Provided* account has no significance and does *not* appear in any financial statements.

Debt Disclosures and Schedules

Governments are required to prepare a number of note disclosures related to long-term debt. Among these are

- **Schedule of Changes in Long-Term Debt.** This schedule lists the long-term debt obligations (including enterprise fund debt) and displays the beginning balance, additions, reductions, and ending balance of each.

- **Schedule of Debt Service Requirements.** This schedule displays the amount of principal and interest due on debt issues by year.
- **Schedule of Legal Debt Margin.** This schedule displays a government's debt margin; that is, how much of the government's legal debt limit has been used. **Debt limit** is the total amount of indebtedness allowed by law and is generally determined as a proportion of the assessed value of property. **Debt margin** is the difference between the amount of debt outstanding and the debt limit. If the debt margin is small, a government may be unable to issue additional debt in periods of financial need.
- **Schedule of Direct and Overlapping Debt.** This schedule reflects the fact that taxpayers often reside simultaneously within multiple jurisdictions. For example, a resident could live in a county and an independent school district with identical geographic boundaries. This schedule displays the total debt burden placed on residents of a government from these multiple sources.

Questions and Exercises

8–1. Using the annual financial report obtained for Exercise 1–1, answer the following questions:

a. Examine the reconciliation between the governmental fund balances and the governmental-type activities net position. This might be on the governmental fund Balance Sheet or in a separate schedule in the basic financial statements. List the major differences. What is the amount shown for capital assets? How much (if any) is due to the incorporation of internal service funds? Was an adjustment made for deferred property taxes or any other revenue? What is the adjustment due to the inclusion of long-term liabilities? What other adjustments are made?

b. Examine the reconciliation between the governmental fund changes in fund balances and the governmental-type activities changes in net position. This might be on the governmental Statement of Revenues, Expenditures, and Changes in Fund Balances or in a separate schedule. List the major differences. How much is due to the difference between depreciation reported on the Statement of Activities and the reported expenditures for capital outlays on the Statement of Revenues, Expenditures, and Changes in Fund Balances? How much is due to differences in reporting expenditures versus expenses for debt service? How much is due to the incorporation of internal service funds? How much (if any) is due to differences in reporting proceeds versus gains on sale of capital assets? How much is due to additional revenue accruals? How much is due to additional expense accruals? What other items are listed?

c. Examine the Statement of Net Position. Attempt to prove the Net Investment in Capital Assets figure from the information in the statement or the notes. List the individual items that are restricted; this might require examination of the notes to the financial statements.

d. Examine the Statement of Activities. List the net expenses (revenues) for governmental activities, business-type activities, and component units. List the change in net position for governmental activities, business-type activities, and component units. Attempt to find from the notes the component units that are discretely presented.

e. Look throughout the annual report for disclosures related to capital assets. This would include the notes to the financial statements, any schedules, and information in the Management's Discussion and Analysis (MD&A). Summarize what is included. What depreciation method is used? Are lives of major classes of capital assets disclosed?

f. Look throughout the annual report for disclosures related to long-term debt. This would include the notes to the financial statements, any schedules in the financial and statistical sections, and the MD&A. Summarize what is included. Are the schedules listed in this chapter included? What is the debt limit and margin? What is the direct debt per capita? The direct and overlapping debt per capita?

8–2. Identify the types of nonexchange revenues that are most likely to result in differences in the timing of recognition between the accrual and modified accrual bases of accounting.

8–3. The government-wide Statement of Net Position separately displays governmental activities and business activities. Why are internal service funds most commonly displayed as governmental activities?

8–4. Answer the following questions with regard to infrastructure:

a. What is infrastructure?

b. What are the two methods that might be used to record infrastructure expense from year to year? How is the accounting different under the two methods?

c. What conditions must exist in order to use the modified approach to record and report infrastructure?

d. What are the disclosure requirements if the modified approach is used?

8–5. Under the reporting model required by GASB, fund statements are required for governmental, proprietary, and fiduciary funds. Government-wide statements include the Statement of Net Position and Statement of Activities. Answer the following questions related to the reporting model:

a. What is the measurement focus and basis of accounting for governmental fund statements; proprietary fund statements; fiduciary fund statements; and government-wide statements?

b. Indicate differences between fund financial statements and government-wide statements with regard to component units; fiduciary funds; and location of internal service funds.

c. Indicate what should be included in the Statement of Net Position categories: Net Investment in Capital Assets; Restricted; and Unrestricted.

8–6. List some of the major adjustments required when converting from fund financial statements to government-wide statements.

8–7. The following information is available for the preparation of the government-wide financial statements for the City of Southern Springs as of April 30, 2020:

Cash and cash equivalents, governmental activities	$ 480,000
Cash and cash equivalents, business-type activities	700,000
Receivables, governmental activities	450,000
Receivables, business-type activities	1,330,000
Inventories, business-type activities	520,000
Capital assets, net, governmental activities	12,500,000
Capital assets, net, business-type activities	7,200,000
Accounts payable, governmental activities	650,000
Accounts payable, business-type activities	559,000
General obligation bonds, governmental activities	7,800,000
Revenue bonds, business-type activities	3,210,000
Long-term liability for compensated absences, governmental activities	359,000

From the preceding information, prepare (in good form) a Statement of Net Position for the City of Southern Springs as of April 30, 2020. Assume that outstanding bonds were issued to acquire capital assets and restricted assets total $554,000 for governmental activities and $200,000 for business-type activities. Include a *Total* column.

8–8. The following information is available for the preparation of the government-wide financial statements for the City of Northern Pines for the year ended June 30, 2020:

Expenses:	
General government	$11,960,000
Public safety	23,900,000
Public works	11,290,000
Health and sanitation	6,010,000
Culture and recreation	4,198,000
Interest on long-term debt, governmental type	721,000
Water and sewer system	10,710,000
Parking system	409,000
Revenues:	
Charges for services, general government	1,510,000
Charges for services, public safety	210,000
Operating grant, public safety	798,000
Charges for services, health and sanitation	2,355,000
Operating grant, health and sanitation	1,210,000
Charges for services, culture and recreation	1,998,000
Charges for services, water and sewer	11,588,000
Charges for services, parking system	388,000

Property taxes	27,112,000
Sales taxes	20,698,000
Investment earnings, business-type	325,000
Special item—gain on sale of unused land, governmental type	1,250,000
Transfer from business-type activities to governmental activities	700,000
Net position, July 1, 2019, governmental activities	5,800,000
Net position, July 1, 2019, business-type activities	4,600,000

From the previous information, prepare, in good form, a Statement of Activities for the City of Northern Pines for the year ended June 30, 2020. Northern Pines has no component units.

8–9. The City of Grinders Switch maintains its books in a manner that facilitates the preparation of fund accounting statements and uses worksheet adjustments to prepare government-wide statements. You are to prepare, in journal form, worksheet adjustments for each of the following situations.

1. General fixed assets as of the beginning of the year, which had not been recorded, were as follows:

Land	$ 7,554,000
Buildings	33,355,000
Improvements Other Than Buildings	14,820,000
Equipment	11,690,000
Accumulated Depreciation, Capital Assets	25,800,000

2. During the year, expenditures for capital outlays amounted to $7,500,000. Of that amount, $4,800,000 was for buildings; the remainder was for improvements other than buildings.
3. The capital outlay expenditures outlined in (2) were completed at the end of the year (and will begin to be depreciated next year). For purposes of financial statement presentation, all capital assets are depreciated using the straight-line method, with no estimated salvage value. Estimated lives are as follows: buildings, 40 years; improvements other than buildings, 20 years; and equipment, 10 years.
4. In the governmental funds Statement of Revenues, Expenditures, and Changes in Fund Balances, the City reported proceeds from the sale of land in the amount of $600,000. The land originally cost $505,000.
5. At the beginning of the year, general obligation bonds were outstanding in the amount of $4,000,000. Unamortized bond premium amounted to $16,000. Note: This entry is not covered in the text, but is similar to entry 9 in the chapter.

6. During the year, debt service expenditures for the year amounted to: interest, $580,000; principal, $412,000. For purposes of government-wide statements, $1,600 of the bond premium should be amortized. No adjustment is necessary for interest accrual.
7. At year-end, additional general obligation bonds were issued in the amount of $6,000,000, at par.

8–10. The City of South Pittsburgh maintains its books so as to prepare fund accounting statements and records worksheet adjustments in order to prepare government-wide statements. You are to prepare, in journal form, worksheet adjustments for each of the following situations:

1. Deferred inflows of resources—property taxes of $51,200 at the end of the previous fiscal year were recognized as property tax revenue in the current year's Statement of Revenues, Expenditures, and Changes in Fund Balance.
2. The City levied property taxes for the current fiscal year in the amount of $10,000,000. When making the entries, it was estimated that 2 percent of the taxes would not be collected. At year-end, $200,000 is thought to be uncollectible, $349,000 would likely be collected during the 60-day period after the end of the fiscal year, and $53,800 would be collected after that time. The City had recognized the maximum of property taxes allowable under modified accrual accounting.
3. In addition to the expenditures recognized under modified accrual accounting, the City computed that $29,000 should be accrued for compensated absences and charged to public safety.
4. The City's actuary estimated that pension expense under the City's public safety employees pension plan is $229,000 for the current year. The City, however, only provided $212,000 to the pension plan during the current year.
5. In the Statement of Revenues, Expenditures, and Changes in Fund Balances, General Fund transfers out included $500,000 to a debt service fund, $200,000 to a special revenue fund, and $850,000 to an enterprise fund.

8–11. The City of Southern Pines maintains its books so as to prepare fund accounting statements and records worksheet adjustments in order to prepare government-wide statements. As such, the City's internal service fund, a motor pool fund, is included in the proprietary funds statements. Prepare necessary adjustments in order to incorporate the internal service fund in the government-wide statements as a part of governmental activities.

1. Balance sheet asset accounts include: Cash, $100,000; Investments, $125,000; Due from the General Fund, $15,000; Inventories, $325,000; and Capital Assets (net), $960,000. Liability accounts include: Accounts Payable, $50,000; Long-Term Advance from Enterprise Fund, $600,000.
2. The only transaction in the internal service fund that is external to the government is interest revenue in the amount of $3,600.

3. Exclusive of the interest revenue, the internal service fund reported net income in the amount of $24,000. An examination of the records indicates that services were provided as follows: one-third to general government, one-third to public safety, and one-third to public works.

8–12. Presented on the following pages are partial financial statements for the City of Shenandoah, including

Fiscal year 2020:
- A. Total Governmental Funds:
  - Balance Sheet
  - Statement of Revenues, Expenditures, and Changes in Fund Balances
- B. Internal Service Fund:
  - Statement of Net Position
  - Statement of Revenues, Expenses, and Changes in Net Position

Fiscal year 2019:
- A. Total Governmental Funds:
  - Balance Sheet
- B. Government-wide—Governmental Activities:
  - Statement of Net Position

CITY OF SHENANDOAH
Balance Sheet
Governmental Funds

	December 31, 2020 Total Governmental Funds	**December 31, 2019 Total Governmental Funds**
Assets		
Cash and cash equivalents	$1,372,900	$1,029,675
Investments	136,450	102,338
Receivables:		
Taxes	97,522	73,142
Interest	28,768	31,325
Due from state government	513,000	384,750
Total assets	2,148,640	1,621,230
Liabilities and deferred inflows		
Accounts payable	46,600	17,950
Due to other funds	10,200	10,400
Deferred inflows: property taxes	78,000	65,000
Total liabilities and deferred inflows	134,800	93,350

(Continued)

Fund balances		
Restricted	259,300	124,248
Committed	1,009,450	807,560
Assigned	438,390	350,712
Unassigned	306,700	245,360
Total fund balances	2,013,840	1,527,880
Total liabilities and fund balances	$2,148,640	$1,621,230

CITY OF SHENANDOAH
Statement of Revenues, Expenditures, and Changes in Fund Balances—Governmental Funds
For the Year Ended December 31, 2020

	Total Governmental Funds
Revenues	
Property taxes	$ 6,469,000
Sales taxes	3,115,000
Interest	32,000
Licenses and permits	800,000
Intergovernmental	1,763,000
Miscellaneous	270,000
Total revenues	12,449,000
Expenditures	
Current	
General government	1,717,300
Public safety	4,974,150
Landfill operations	2,337,400
Cultural and recreational	3,258,700
Capital outlay	2,483,600
Debt service	
Principal	500,000
Interest	445,000
Total expenditures	15,716,150
Revenues over (under) expenditures	
Other financing sources (uses)	(3,267,150)
Proceeds of bonds	4,000,000
Premium on bonds	50,000
Transfers from other funds	145,900
Transfers (to) other funds	(145,900)
	4,050,000

Excess of revenues and other sources over (under) expenditures and other uses	782,850
Fund balance—beginning of year	1,230,990
Fund balance—end of year	$2,013,840

CITY OF SHENANDOAH
Statement of Net Position
Proprietary Funds

	December 31, 2020 Governmental Activities: Internal Service Fund
Current assets	
Cash and cash equivalents	$ 27,000
Receivables:	
Due from General Fund	10,200
Due from Enterprise Fund	11,000
Inventories	25,000
Total current assets	73,200
Noncurrent assets	
Land	25,000
Buildings	44,000
Accumulated depreciation—buildings	(13,200)
Equipment	21,000
Accumulated depreciation—equipment	(12,600)
	64,200
Total assets	$137,400
Liabilities	
Accounts payable	18,400
Total current liabilities	18,400
Noncurrent liabilities	
Advance from Enterprise Fund	10,000
Total noncurrent liabilities	10,000
Total liabilities	28,400
Net position	
Net investment in capital assets	54,200
Unrestricted	54,800
Total net position	$109,000

CITY OF SHENANDOAH
Statement of Revenues, Expenses, and Changes in Fund Net Position Proprietary Funds
For the Year Ended December 31, 2020

	Governmental Activities: Internal Service Fund
Revenues	
Charges for sales and services	$ 370,200
Total revenues	370,200
Operating expenses	
Cost of sales and services	357,600
Administration	10,300
Depreciation	5,300
Total expenditures	373,200
Operating (loss)	(3,000)
Nonoperating income	
Investment income	5,000
	5,000
Change in net position	2,000
Net position—beginning of year	107,000
Net position—end of year	$109,000

CITY OF SHENANDOAH
Statement of Net Position
Government-wide Statements

	December 31, 2019 Governmental Activities
Current assets	
Cash and cash equivalents	$ 1,230,000
Investments	95,500
Receivables (net)	
Taxes receivable	69,500
Due from business activities	23,000
Due from state government	156,000
Total current assets	1,574,000
Noncurrent assets	
Land	7,030,000
Buildings	22,600,000

Accumulated depreciation—buildings	(12,800,000)
Infrastructure	27,500,000
Accumulated depreciation—buildings	(9,000,000)
Equipment	6,370,000
Accumulated depreciation—equipment	(3,100,000)
Total capital assets	38,600,000
Total assets	$40,174,000
Liabilities	
Accrued interest on bonds	180,000
Accounts payable	96,500
Total current liabilities	276,500
Noncurrent liabilities	
General obligation bonds payable	6,000,000
Accrued costs for landfill closure and postclosure care	29,500
Total noncurrent liabilities	6,029,500
Total liabilities	6,306,000
Net position	
Net investment in capital assets	32,600,000
Unrestricted	1,268,000
Total net position	$33,868,000

Additional information:

1. $856,700 of the capital assets purchased in fiscal year 2020 was equipment. All remaining capital acquisitions were for a new building.
2. Depreciation of general fixed assets: buildings $1,100,000, infrastructure $975,000, and equipment $537,500.
3. The City had $6,000,000 of 6 percent general obligation bonds (issued at par) outstanding at December 31, 2019. In addition, the City issued $4,000,000 of 5 percent bonds on January 2, 2020 (sold at a premium). Interest payments on both bond issues are due on January 1 and July 1. Principal payments are made on January 1. Interest and principal payments for the current year include

	6 Percent General Obligation Bonds	5 Percent General Obligation Bonds
Principal Payment—January 1	$500,000	—
Interest Payment—January 1	180,000	—
Interest Payment—July 1	165,000	$100,000

The January interest payments are accrued for purposes of the government-wide statements but not the fund-basis statements. The bond premium is to be amortized in the amount of $2,500 per year.

4. Property taxes expected to be collected more than 60 days after year-end are deferred in the fund-basis statements.
5. At the end of 2020, the accumulated liability for landfill closure and postclosure care costs is estimated to be $36,500. Landfill operations are reported in the General Fund—Public Works.
6. The internal service fund serves several departments of the General Fund, all within the category of "General Government." The internal service fund was created at the end of 2019 and had no capital assets or long-term liabilities at the end of 2019.

Prepare all worksheet journal entries necessary for fiscal year 2020 to convert the governmental fund-basis amounts to the economic resources measurement focus and accrual basis required for the governmental activities sections of the government-wide statements.

Excel-Based Problems

8–13. The fund-basis financial statements of Jefferson County have been completed for the year 2020 and appear in the first tab of the Excel spreadsheet provided with this exercise. The following information is also available:

1. Capital Assets
   - Capital assets purchased in previous years through governmental-type funds totaled $7,950,000 (net of accumulated depreciation) as of January 1.
   - Depreciation on capital assets used in governmental-type activities amounted to $327,000.
   - No capital assets were sold or disposed of and all purchases are properly reflected in the fund-basis statements as capital expenditures.
2. Long-Term Debt
   - There was no outstanding long-term debt associated with governmental-type funds as of January 1.
   - April 1, 6 percent bonds with a face value of $700,000 were issued at a premium. Bond payments are made on October 1 and April 1 of each year. Interest is based on an annual rate of 6 percent, and principal payments are $22,000 each. The first payment (interest and principal) was made on October 1.
   - Amortization of the bond premium for the current year is $1,800.
3. Deferred Inflows of Resources
   - Deferred inflows (comprised solely of property taxes) are expected to be collected more than 60 days after year-end. The balance of deferred taxes at the end of 2019 was $18,700.
4. Transfers
   - Transfers were between governmental-type funds.

5. Internal Service Fund
   - The (motor pool) internal service fund's revenue is predominantly derived from departments classified as governmental-type activities.
   - There were no amounts due to the internal service fund from the General Fund. The outstanding balance of Due to Other Funds was with the enterprise fund and is not capital related.
   - The enterprise fund provided a long-term advance to the internal service fund (not capital related).

   Required:

   Use the Excel template provided to complete the following requirements; a separate tab is provided in Excel for each of these steps.

   a. Prepare the journal entries necessary to convert the governmental fund financial statements to the accrual basis of accounting.

   b. Post the journal entries to the conversion worksheet provided.

   c. Prepare a government-wide Statement of Activities and Statement of Net Position for the year 2020. All of the governmental fund revenues are "general revenues."

This is an involved problem, requiring many steps. Here are some hints.

1. Tab 1 is information to be used in the problem. You do not enter anything here.
2. After you make the journal entries (Tab 2), post these to the worksheet to convert to the accrual basis. This worksheet is set up so that you enter *debits as positive* numbers and *credits as negative.* After you post your entries, look at the numbers below the total credit column to see that debits equal credits. If not, you probably entered a credit as a positive number.
3. Make sure that total debits equal total credits in the last column (balances for government-wide statements).
4. When calculating Restricted Net Position, recall that permanent fund principal is added to restricted fund balances.

8–14. The fund-basis financial statements of the City of Cottonwood have been completed for the year 2020 and appear in the first tab of the Excel spreadsheet provided with this exercise. In addition, the government-wide Statement of Net Position from the previous fiscal year is provided and should be used to determine beginning balances for accounts not appearing in the fund-basis statements. The following information is also available:

1. Capital Assets
   - Capital assets purchased by governmental funds are charged to capital expenditure and do not appear as assets in the fund-basis balance sheet. However, the balance is reflected in the Statement of Net Position in the government-wide financial statements.

- Depreciation on capital assets used in governmental-type activities amounted to $3,070,000 for the year.
- No capital assets were sold or disposed of and all purchases are properly reflected in the fund-basis statements as capital expenditures.

2. Long-Term Debt
   - Proceeds from bonds issued by governmental funds are reflected in other financing sources and do not appear as liabilities in the fund-basis balance sheet. Payments of principal are recognized as expenditures when due. The balance of outstanding bonds balance is reflected in the Statement of Net Position in the government-wide financial statements.
   - Interest is recognized in the fund-basis statements only when payment is due. Interest accrued but not yet payable amounted to $167,000 at December 31, 2020. Interest accrued for purposes of the government-wide statements in 2019 has been paid and is reflected in interest expenditure in 2020.
   - There are no bond discounts or premiums.
3. Deferred Inflows of Resources
   - Deferred inflows are comprised solely of property taxes expected to be collected more than 60 days after year-end. The balance of deferred taxes at the end of 2019 was $192,000 and was recognized as revenue in the fund-basis statements in 2020.
4. The City accounts for its solid waste landfill in the General Fund (public works department). The estimated liability for closure and postclosure care costs as of December 31, 2020, is $2,750,000 and appears only in the government-wide statements.
5. Transfers
   - During the year, the General Fund transferred cash to the courthouse renovation, debt service, and enterprise funds.
6. The City does not operate any internal service funds.
7. When entering amounts in the Statement of Activities, *Charges for Services Revenue* in the governmental funds is attributable to the following functions:

General Government	$1,156,497
Judicial Administration	44,018
Public Safety	275,492
Parks and Recreation	604,359
Community Development	51,611
Total	$2,131,977

Required:

Use the Excel template provided to complete the following requirements; a separate tab is provided in Excel for each of these steps:

a. Prepare the journal entries necessary to convert the governmental fund financial statements to the accrual basis of accounting.

b. Post the journal entries to the conversion worksheet provided.

c. Prepare a government-wide Statement of Activities and Statement of Net Position for the year 2020.

This is an involved problem, requiring many steps. Here are some hints:

1. Tab 1 is information to be used in the problem. You do not enter anything here.
2. After you make the journal entries (Tab 2), post these to the worksheet to convert to the accrual basis. This worksheet is set up so that you enter *debits as positive* numbers and *credits as negative.* After you post your entries, look at the numbers below the total credit column to see that debits equal credits. If not, you probably entered a credit as a positive number.
3. Make sure that total debits equal total credits in the last column (balances for government-wide statements).
4. When calculating Restricted Net Position, recall that permanent fund principal is added to restricted fund balances.

Continuous Problem

The continuous problem is available in Connect through the Additional Student Resources in the eBook or instructor library. Complete the assignments for Chapter 8.

Chapter **Nine**

Advanced Topics for State and Local Governments

Taxpayers should demand that their states honestly assess public pension plans, accurately measure the assets and liabilities, and take steps to provide fair benefits to public employees that limit taxpayers' liability. Elaine Chao, U.S. Secretary of Transportation. Born in Taiwan, she is the first Chinese American to be appointed to a cabinet position. She is married to Senate Majority Leader, Mitch McConnell.

Republicans and Democrats have used accounting gimmicks and competing government analyses to deceive the public into believing that 2 + 2 = 6. If our leaders cannot agree on the numbers, if "facts" are fictional, how can they possibly have a substantive debate on solutions? J.C. Watts, ordained minister and Republican congressman from Oklahoma. The former University of Oklahoma and Canadian Football League quarterback was the first African American to win a statewide office in Oklahoma.

Learning Objectives

- Describe characteristics of special-purpose entities and identify the required financial statements of varying types of entities.
- Understand the purpose of special assessment taxes and identify the appropriate funds for the recording and reporting of special assessment activities.
- Apply accounting principles for lease transactions.
- Apply employer reporting principles for pension and other postemployment benefits.

Many of the early efforts of the Governmental Accounting Standards Board were dedicated to the development of its conceptual framework and the financial reporting model. Governments have now been preparing government-wide (along with fund-basis) statements for 15 years. With these early efforts behind them, the GASB has increasingly turned its attention to providing guidance for individual events, circumstances, or transactions.

In keeping with the title of this textbook, Chapters 2 through 8 emphasized the *essential* events and transactions that most governments encounter. The focus of this chapter is on events and conditions that affect many, but not all, state and local governments. The accounting and reporting requirements described here rely upon the concepts and principles of the earlier chapters.

Most of these topics pertain to governmental as well as businesslike activities and therefore may occur within a variety of funds. Our approach is to examine these topics as they apply to both accrual and modified accrual–based financial statements.

In particular, the following topics are described in detail:

- Reporting by special-purpose entities.
- Special assessment activities.
- Acquisition of capital assets through leases.
- Employer reporting for pensions and other postemployment benefits.

REPORTING BY SPECIAL-PURPOSE ENTITIES

Chapters 2 through 8 provide accounting and financial reporting guidance for *general-purpose* state and local governments. General-purpose local governments include states, counties, cities, towns, and villages. Other governments are called *special-purpose* local governments and include governments such as fire protection districts, park districts, library districts, tollway authorities, and transit authorities. Special-purpose governments are numerous; according to the Census Bureau there are over 12,000 independent school districts and 38,000 special districts in the United States. Special-purpose governments may be stand-alone local governments or may be component units of other governments that are issuing separate reports.

GASB does not give a clear definition of either general-purpose or special-purpose governments. The distinction is not always between types of governments, as one government (say, a township) may be either a general-purpose or special-purpose government for purposes of financial reporting. General-purpose governments commonly provide multiple government services; for example, public safety, transportation, health, and welfare. In contrast, services provided by special-purpose governments are commonly limited to one service or program. For example, government-operated hospitals, public school systems, or public colleges may be considered special-purpose entities for financial reporting purposes.

The issue is whether a special-purpose government must prepare financial statements following the complete model described in Chapters 2 through 8 or whether they can prepare a condensed set of financial statements. The determining factor is whether the special-purpose government is engaged solely in governmental-type activities, business-type activities, or fiduciary-type activities. In addition to the financial statements, all special-purpose governments must present Management's Discussion & Analysis, notes, and Required Supplementary Information (when applicable).

Special-Purpose Governments Engaged in Governmental Activities

A special-purpose local government may be engaged in (1) both governmental activities and business-type activities, (2) more than one governmental activity, or

(3) a single governmental activity. Special-purpose governments that are engaged in both governmental and business-type activities or in more than one governmental activity are required to follow the reporting outlined in Chapters 2 through 8 of this text. That is, the full reporting model is required, including *both* government-wide and fund-basis financial statements.

However, special-purpose governments that are engaged in only one governmental-type activity are permitted to combine the fund and government-wide financial statements. This is commonly done by showing reconciliations between governmental fund accounting policies (modified accrual) and government-wide statements (accrual) on the face of the statements.

Illustration 9-1 presents a (combined) Balance Sheet/Statement of Net Position for the Salem Independent Fire District, a special-purpose entity engaged in a single governmental activity. The first three columns of numbers reflect the fund-basis statements prepared using the current financial resources measurement focus and the modified accrual basis of accounting. An adjustment column is added to convert to the economic resources measurement focus and accrual basis of accounting as required in the government-wide statements.

Illustration 9-2 presents a (combined) Governmental Funds Statement of Revenues, Expenditures, and Changes in Fund Balances/Statement of Activities for the same independent fire district. Again, an adjustment column is added to convert to the economic resources measurement focus and accrual basis of accounting as required in the government-wide statements. As with all activity statements, fund balance or net position is reconciled at the bottom of this statement to the balances appearing in Illustration 9-1. Again, only governments that have a single program should use the formats shown in Illustrations 9-1 and 9-2.

Examine the adjustments column in the two statements. Adjustments have been made for the following items:

1. Interfund receivables/payables in the amount of $23,747 are eliminated.
2. Interfund transfers in the amount of $25,395 are eliminated.
3. Capital expenditures in the amount of $23,589 are reclassified as capital assets.
4. Depreciation expense in the amount of $26,805 is recorded.
5. Beginning of the year capital assets (net of depreciation) in the amount of $241,595 are recorded.
6. Expenditures for payments of principal in the amount of $15,000 are reclassified as a reduction in long-term liabilities.
7. Long-term notes payable of $161,000 are included (beginning balance of $176,000 less expenditures for principal of $15,000).

These adjustments are similar to those prepared in the worksheets in Chapter 8. Additional items can include reversing entries made to defer tax revenues not collectible within 60 days or accruals of interest on long-term debt not recorded in the governmental funds.

ILLUSTRATION 9-1 **Governmental Funds Balance Sheet/Statement of Net Position (Special-Purpose Entity Engaged in a Single Governmental Activity)**

SALEM FIRE PROTECTION DISTRICT Governmental Funds Balance Sheet/Statement of Net Position As of December 31, 2020					
Assets	**General Fund**	**Special Revenue Fund**	**Total**	**Adjustments to Government-wide**	**Statement of Net Position**
Cash and cash equivalents	$140,821	$15,280	$156,101		$156,101
Inventories	5,784	—	5,784		5,784
Receivables (net)	—	—	—		—
Taxes receivable	195,860	—	195,860		195,860
Due from other governments	85,184	6,589	91,773		91,773
Due from other funds	—	23,747	23,747	(23,747)	—
Capital assets	—	—	—	238,379	238,379
Total assets	$427,649	$45,616	$473,265	$214,632	$687,897
Liabilities					
Accounts payable	185,378	43,458	228,836		228,836
Due to other funds	23,747	—	23,747	(23,747)	—
Notes due in more than one year	—	—	—	161,000	161,000
Total liabilities	209,125	43,458	252,583	137,253	389,836
Fund balance					
Nonspendable (inventories)	5,785	—	5,785		
Assigned for other purposes	—	2,158	2,158		
Unassigned	212,739	—	212,739		
Total fund balance	218,524	2,158	220,682		
Total liabilities and fund balance	$427,649	$45,616	$473,265		
Net position					
Net investment in capital assets					77,379
Unrestricted					220,682
Total net position					$298,061

Special-Purpose Governments Engaged Only in Business-type Activities

Special-purpose governments engaged only in business-type activities are not required to prepare government-wide statements. These entities provide only the fund-basis statements required of proprietary funds:

1. Statement of Net Position or Balance Sheet.
2. Statement of Revenues, Expenses, and Changes in Net Position.
3. Statement of Cash Flows.

ILLUSTRATION 9-2 **Governmental Funds Statement of Revenues, Expenditures, and Changes in Fund Balances/Statement of Activities (Special-Purpose Entity Engaged in a Single Governmental Activity)**

SALEM FIRE PROTECTION DISTRICT
Governmental Funds: Statement of Revenues, Expenditures, and Changes in Fund Balances/Statement of Activities
For the Year Ended December 31, 2020

Revenues	**General Fund**	**Special Revenue Fund**	**Total**	**Adjustments to Government-wide**	**Statement of Activities**
Property taxes	$361,830	—	$361,830		$361,830
Charges for services	1,435	—	1,435		1,435
Intergovernmental	23,589	$209,143	232,732		232,732
Miscellaneous	2,549	—	2,549		2,549
Total revenues	389,403	209,143	598,546		598,546
Expenditures/expenses					
Current					
Personnel services	153,250	235,492	388,742		388,742
Supplies	56,735		56,735		56,735
Depreciation				26,805	26,805
Capital outlay	23,589	—	23,589	(23,589)	—
Debt service					
Principal	15,000	—	15,000	(15,000)	—
Interest	18,500	—	18,500		18,500
Total expenditures	267,074	235,492	502,566	(11,784)	490,782
Excess of revenues over (under) expenditures	122,329	(26,349)	95,980		
Other financing sources (uses)					
Transfers from other funds	—	25,395	25,395	(25,395)	—
Transfers to other funds	(25,395)	—	(25,395)	25,395	—
Total	(25,395)	25,395	—		
Excess of revenues and other sources over (under) expenditures and other uses	96,934	(954)	95,980		
Change in net position					107,764
Fund balance/net position—Beginning of year	121,590	3,112	124,702		190,297
Fund balance/net position—End of year	$218,524	$2,158	$220,682		$298,061

All of the requirements for enterprise financial statements described in Chapter 6, such as the format of the Statement of Cash Flows, are required for the separate financial statements for single-purpose governments engaged only in business-type activities. Nearly all government hospitals and public (government-owned) colleges report as single-purpose governments engaged only in business-type activities.

Special-Purpose Governments Engaged Only in Fiduciary-type Activities

Special-purpose governments engaged only in fiduciary activities provide only the fund-basis statements required of fiduciary funds:

1. Statement of Fiduciary Net Position.
2. Statement of Changes in Fiduciary Net Position.

Many states have special-purpose governments that exist solely to manage retirement systems for state and/or local government employees. These are often statewide systems. They prepare separate financial statements as special-purpose governments that are engaged only in fiduciary-type activities.

SPECIAL ASSESSMENTS

A special assessment is a tax levy that is assessed only against certain taxpayers—those taxpayers who are deemed to benefit from the service or project paid for by the proceeds of the special assessment (property tax) levy. The issue is where (which fund?) to account for the activities of a special assessment. Special assessments may be either service types or construction types. Service-type special assessments, such as an assessment on downtown businesses for special garbage removal or police protection, would be accounted for in the appropriate fund, often the General or a special revenue fund.

Construction-type special assessment projects account for longer-term projects that often require debt financing. Identifying the appropriate fund to account for construction-type special assessments depends on the terms of the agreement between the government and the property owners. Special assessments for construction projects may be accounted for in one of two ways.

For example, assume that $500,000 is borrowed to install street lighting and build sidewalks in a newly annexed subdivision. Five-year special assessment bonds were issued to finance the project, which is administered by the city. Since city law requires that the provision of lighting and sidewalks is the responsibility of property owners, a special assessment (property tax) is levied against the property owners in that subdivision for a five-year period. The proceeds of the assessment are used to pay the principal and interest on the debt.

Only rarely is the use of a certain fund type mandated by GASB standards rather than by law or by decision of the governing board of a government. However, GASB standards mandate that a government should account for special assessment activities in a custodial fund if the government has no obligation to assume responsibility for debt payments, even if the property owners default. This is true even though the government may perform the functions of billing property owners for the assessments, collecting installments from the property owners, and making the principal and interest payments.

On the other hand, if the government *is* liable (either primarily or secondarily) for payment of special assessment debt in the event of default by the property owners, the transactions are handled as if it were a governmental project. A capital projects fund should account for the proceeds of the debt and the construction expenditures. The capitalized cost of the project will be recorded in the government-wide statements. The debt should be recorded in the government-wide statements, and the special assessment tax levy and debt service expenditures should be recorded in a debt service fund.

LEASES

Recently, all three standard-setting bodies (FASB, GASB, and FASAB) issued new standards for the reporting of leases. A lease is a contract by which one party (the lessor) conveys the use of property or equipment to another party (the lessee) in return for periodic payments (rent). From the perspective of the lessee, the basic issue involves determining when a noncancelable lease represents a long-term obligation that should be reported as a liability on the Statement of Net Position. GASB standards recognize three types of leases:

1. Short-term lease — This is any lease contract that has a maximum term of 12 months or less from the commencement of the lease.
2. Contract that transfers ownership — This is a lease contract that transfers ownership of the leased asset to the lessee by the end of the lease contract.
3. Other lease — This is any lease contract that does not necessarily transfer ownership and has a lease term longer than 12 months.

Short-term leases are sometimes called **operating leases** and do not result in the recording of liabilities in either proprietary or governmental-type funds. The periodic payments (usually monthly) are simply charged to expense or expenditure in the month due. In contrast, leases with initial terms exceeding 12 months result in the reporting of an intangible (or capital) asset and a liability on statements reporting under the accrual basis of accounting.

GASB requires that the lease obligation be recorded at the present value of the payments using the interest rate implied in the lease (if known) or the lessee's incremental borrowing rate. The lease payments are comprised of two amounts: (1) interest on the outstanding obligation and (2) payment of principal. In addition, an intangible asset is recognized for the present value of payments plus any down payment made at the inception of the lease. The intangible asset is amortized to expense over the shorter of the lease term or the underlying asset's estimated useful life. GASB uses the term *lease asset* to refer the intangible, but the term *right-to-use asset* may also appear in practice.

Illustrative Example Assume a county government signs a four-year lease contract on December 31, 2019, for equipment. The lease is noncancelable and has no provisions for extending the lease term. Further, assume the lease calls for annual payments of $10,000 to be made on December 31 of each year, beginning in 2019 and the lessor's implicit interest rate is 5 percent. Since the first lease payment is made at the inception of the lease, it would have no interest component and is not discounted. The present value of the remaining three payments is $27,240. The second lease payment of $10,000 is to be made on December 31, 2020, and includes interest of $1,362 ($27,240 × 5%) and a payment of principal of $8,638 ($10,000 – $1,362). The lease asset is to be amortized over four years ending December 31, 2023, when the equipment is to be returned to the lessor.

The preceding paragraph provides everything we need to record this lease. However, the process we use depends on whether the equipment is leased by an enterprise activity or a department within the General Fund. The center column of Illustration 9-3 provides the journal entries for 2019 and 2020 assuming the equipment is leased by the county water department, an enterprise fund. The right-hand column assumes it is leased by the public works department of the General Fund.

Because the enterprise fund uses the economic resource measurement focus, the lease asset and lease liability are recorded at the inception of the lease and no government-wide conversion entries are necessary. However, the General Fund records events using the current financial resource measurement focus and does not recognize capital assets or long-term debt. The lease asset and lease liability will not appear in the General Fund Balance Sheet but do appear in the government-wide Statement of Net Position in the same amounts recognized by the enterprise fund. If you sum each year's entries appearing in the two columns, you should see that the leases will be reported in the same manner at the government-wide level.

The example above illustrates lessee reporting for a long-term lease classified as an "other lease." The reporting of leases that transfer ownership is very similar except that a capital asset (rather than an intangible) is recognized and depreciated over the estimated useful life, which may be longer than the lease term. It is less common for governments to be the lessor, but GASB standards for lessors generally mirror those of lessees. The standards also contain guidance for leases containing options to extend or terminate the lease. These options should be considered in determining the initial lease term if it is reasonably certain they will be exercised. Finally, the standards provide guidance for more complex situations, including lease modifications, subleases, and leaseback transactions.

EMPLOYER REPORTING FOR PENSIONS

Pension trust funds are established when a government acts as trustee for a retirement plan. Throughout Chapter 7 we discussed and illustrated "reporting for the plan," which takes place in the fiduciary funds. The other category of pension reporting is termed "employer reporting." It is important to understand that the accounting procedures for pension plans apply only to governments administering

ILLUSTRATION 9-3 Comparative Journal Entries for Equipment Lease

Date	Enterprise Fund 2019			General Fund 2019		
12/31/2019	*Lease Inception*			*Lease Inception*		
	Lease Asset	37,240		Capital Expenditure	37,240	
	Lease Liability		27,240	OFS – Lease Proceeds		27,240
	Cash		10,000	Cash		10,000
12/31/2019	*Government-wide Conversion Entries*			*Government-wide Conversion Entries*		
	(not applicable)			OFS – Lease Proceeds	27,240	
				Lease Liability		27,240
				Lease Asset	37,240	
				Capital Expenditure		37,240
Date	**Enterprise Fund 2020**			**General Fund 2020**		
12/31/2020	*Lease Payment*			*Lease Payment*		
				Debt Service Expenditure:		
	Interest Expense	1,362		Interest	1,362	
	Lease Liability	8,638		Principal	8,638	
	Cash		10,000	Cash		10,000
12/31/2020	*Amortization*			*Amortization*		
	Amortization Expense	9,310		(not applicable)		
	Lease Asset		9,310			
	($37,240/4 years)					
12/31/2020	*Government-wide Conversion Entries*			*Government-wide Conversion Entries*		
	(not applicable)			Net Position	27,240	
				Lease Liability		27,240
				Lease Asset	37,240	
				NetPosition		37,240
				Lease Liability	8,638	
				Debt Service Expenditure:		
				Principal		8,638
				Amortization Expense	9,310	
				Lease Asset		9,310

pensions. Most local governments (cities, counties, school districts) do not administer their own pension plans. State governments establish multigovernment retirement systems and invite or require local governments to participate.

While plan reporting (a fiduciary activity) applies only to governments administering pension plans, employer reporting requirements apply whether a government manages its own plan or participates in a state plan. The central issues of employer reporting are the measurement and presentation of the net pension liability in statements displaying financial position and the related recognition of pension expenditure or expense in statements displaying activity.

Employer reporting depends on the type of plan. Defined contribution plans are simple because the government is merely obligated to contribute a given amount to the employee's retirement savings account. Pension contributions to such plans are reported as an expenditure or expense for the amount required by the terms of the employment agreement. Pension liabilities arise only if the required contribution has not been fully paid by year-end. Typically such pending contributions are paid within a short period following year-end and are reported as liabilities in both governmental and proprietary fund-basis financial statements.

In contrast, defined benefit plans provide benefits based on the employee's salary, years of service, and age, rather than depending directly on individual investment returns. A government's obligation for pension benefits is more difficult to measure and relies on estimates and assumptions about the future. The actuarial present value of projected pension benefits that are attributable to years of service already performed is termed the *total pension liability.*

Governments contribute resources to pension trust funds, which are established for the purpose of accumulating sufficient resources to pay the total pension liability. The *fiduciary net position* of the pension trust fund is the excess of these accumulated resources over benefits currently payable to retired employees. By subtracting the fiduciary net position of the pension fund from the total pension liability, we determine a government's *net pension liability.* The net pension liability is the amount that a government anticipates paying to current employees in the future in excess of the resources currently accumulated for that purpose.

This is an important measure for employer reporting of pensions. Financial statements prepared using the economic resources measurement focus and accrual basis of accounting must report a liability equal to the net pension liability. Proprietary funds report the net pension liability for their employees in the fund-basis Statement of Net Position. However, the governmental funds do not recognize long-term obligations. The General Fund reports a pension liability in the fund-basis statements only to the extent the amount is expected to be paid with current financial resources. This would normally be the case if a required contribution to the pension fund is routinely made in a month or two following each payroll period. Since the net pension liability and related pension expense of governmental funds do not appear in the fund-basis statements of the governmental funds, these amounts must be recorded through worksheet entries similar to those described throughout Chapter 8.

Illustrative Example

Assume that a county government participates in a state retirement system, providing a defined benefit pension plan to certain employees. The pension trust fund associated with this plan appears among the fiduciary funds of the state government, not the county. Nevertheless, the county must report a pension liability and pension expense in statements prepared on the accrual basis.

The county provides payroll and demographic information about each participating employee to the state retirement system. The state administers the plan and with the assistance of trained actuaries computes the required contributions each local government must make to the plan. The county pays the annual required contribution ($300,000 for 2020) to the retirement system which invests the money and pays current retirees. Every year the state retirement system, sends a Schedule of Changes in Net Pension Liability to each local government participating in the pension plan. The schedule for 2020 appears in Illustration 9-4.

Notice that the net pension liability at the end of 2020 of $830,000 is reported at the bottom of this schedule and is the difference between the total pension liability and the plan assets (fiduciary net position). Observe also that benefit payments made to retired employees reduce both the pension liability and plan assets and thereby

ILLUSTRATION 9-4 **Schedule of Changes in Net Pension Liability (this is prepared by the State Retirement System)**

Example County Government
Schedule of Changes in Net Pension Liability
For the Years Ended December 31, 2020 and 2019

	2020	2019
Total pension liability		
Service cost	$ 350,000	$ 240,000
Interest	500,000	490,000
Change in benefit terms	—	—
Changes of assumptions	—	50,000
Benefit payments (including refunds)	(170,000)	(160,000)
Net change in total pension liability	680,000	620,000
Total pension liability—beginning of year	7,000,000	6,380,000
Total pension liability—end of year (a)	$7,680,000	$7,000,000
Plan assets (fiduciary net position)		
Contributions—Employer	$ 300,000	$ 280,000
Net investment earnings	520,000	500,000
Benefit payments (including refunds)	(170,000)	(160,000)
Net increase in fiduciary net position	650,000	620,000
Fiduciary net position—beginning of year	6,200,000	5,580,000
Fiduciary net position—end of year (b)	$6,850,000	$6,200,000
Net pension liability—ending (a) – (b)	$ 830,000	$ 800,000

have no effect on the net pension liability. The 2019 column provides two amounts that represent beginning balances for 2020: (1) the net pension liability $800,000 and (2) $50,000 from a change in pension assumptions (fourth line from the top). This second item will be described later, but is reported as a *Deferred Outflow.*

Every year, three items affect both the net pension liability and pension expense: current-period service cost, interest on the total pension liability, and the *projected* net investment earnings on plan assets. The net earnings on the plan's investments in 2020 is $520,000, the service cost component is $350,000, and interest on the pension liability is $500,000. Pension expense for 2020 is $330,000 ($350,000 + $500,000 – $520,000). The service cost and interest components increase expense and investment returns decrease expense. Service cost is the increase in projected benefits attributable to employees having an additional year of service.

The schedule received from the state provides everything we need to record pension expense for 2020. However, the process we use depends on whether the employees work for an enterprise activity or a department within the General Fund. The center column of Illustration 9-5 provides the journal entries for 2020 assuming the employees work for the water department, an enterprise fund. The right-hand column assumes they work for the public safety department of the General Fund.

Because the enterprise fund uses the economic resource measurement focus, the beginning net pension liability of $800,000 would already appear among the fund liabilities. The two entries recorded in 2020 increase the net pension liability to $830,000 and record pension expense of $330,000.

The General Fund records events using the current financial resource measurement focus and reports no beginning balance for the net pension liability. The annual contribution of $300,000 is recorded as an expenditure at the fund level. The government-wide entries then establish the beginning balance of the net pension liability of $800,000 and record the increase in the net pension liability from the previous year of $30,000. The $30,000 expense recognized in the second government-wide conversion entry is added to the $300,000 expenditure already recorded. The result is that the net pension liability reported in the government-wide statements is $830,000 and the pension expense for the public safety department is $330,000, the same results obtained by the enterprise fund.

Changes in Actuarial Assumptions and Net Pension Liability

Other (nonroutine) events may affect the net pension liability. Among these are changes in demographic and economic assumptions, differences between projected and actual investment returns, and changes in the benefit terms. While all of these are reflected in the net pension liability appearing on the Statement of Net Position, they do not all immediately affect pension expense.

Total pension liability is an estimate that relies on a number of assumptions, including expectations for inflation, future salaries, mortality, and the discount rate used to obtain a present value. These assumptions are reviewed periodically. Occasionally it becomes apparent that one or more assumptions should be changed to more accurately reflect the government's experience. Changes in important assumptions can significantly affect the estimate of total pension liability, which

ILLUSTRATION 9-5 Comparative Journal Entries: Employer Reporting for Pensions

Date	Enterprise Fund 2019			General Fund 2019		
12/31/2019	*Beginning Balance*			*Beginning Balance*		
	Net Pension Liability	$800,000		(not applicable)		
Date	**Enterprise Fund 2020**			**General Fund 2020**		
2020	*Pension Contribution*			*Pension Contribution*		
				Current expenditures:		
	Net Pension Liability	300,000		Public safety	300,000	
	Cash		300,000	Cash		300,000
12/31/2020	*Record annual expense*			*Record annual expense*		
	Pension Expense	330,000		(not applicable)		
	Net Pension Liability		330,000			
	($350,000 + $500,000 – $520,000)					
12/31/2020	*Government-wide Conversion Entries*			*Government-wide Conversion Entries*		
	(not applicable)			Net Position	800,000	
				Net Pension Liability		800,000
				Public Safety Expense	30,000	
				Net Pension Liability		30,000

in turn affects the estimated net pension liability. Changes in the net pension liability resulting from changes in estimates are not immediately recognized in pension expense. Rather, they are deferred and recognized in expense over the average remaining service life of the plan's employees.

From Illustration 9-4, it is apparent that the water department made a change of pension assumptions in 2019 that resulted in an increase in the estimated total pension liability of $50,000. At that time the department would calculate how much longer current employees are likely to continue working before drawing retirement benefits. Assuming that the average remaining service life of water department employees is 10 years, the enterprise fund would make the following entries in 2019 and 2020:

2019—Enterprise Fund	**Debits**	**Credits**
Deferred Outflows of Resources—Pension Related	50,000	
Net Pension Liability		50,000
Pension Expense	5,000	
Deferred Outflows of Resources—Pension Related		5,000

The deferred outflow of resources is presented after assets on the enterprise fund's Statement of Net Position. Over time, the deferred outflow is amortized to pension expense.

2020—Enterprise Fund		
Pension Expense	5,000	
Deferred Outflows of Resources—Pension Related		5,000

If the employees are part of the public works department, the General Fund would make no entries for the change in assumptions. However, the following government-wide conversion entries would be added in 2019 and 2020:

2019—Government-wide conversion entries		
Deferred Outflows of Resources—Pension Related	50,000	
Net Pension Liability		50,000
Public Safety (Pension) Expense	5,000	
Deferred Outflows of Resources—Pension Related		5,000

2020—Government-wide conversion entries		
Deferred Outflows of Resources—Pension Related	45,000	
Net Position		45,000
Public Safety (Pension) Expense	5,000	
Deferred Outflows of Resources—Pension Related		5,000

Notice that the (unamortized) deferred outflow has to be re-established in 2020. This is because the government-wide conversion entries are worksheet entries only and are never actually booked. Deferred outflows of resources are presented after assets on the Statement of Net Position.

Other Items Affecting Net Pension Liability

The estimated net pension liability may also change because of differences between the projected and actual returns on pension plan investments. Similar to changes in actuarial assumptions, changes in the net pension liability resulting from such differences are required to be deferred and recognized in pension expense. In this case the deferred amount is amortized over a five-year period. If the actual returns exceed projected, the government will record a deferred inflow of resources and the amortization will reduce pension expense. If actual returns are less than projected, the government will record a deferred outflow of resources and the amortization will increase pension expense.

Occasionally governments change the terms of the pension plan. For example, the pension benefit might be increased from 2 percent of an employee's salary per year of service to 2.25 percent. Unlike changes in assumption or differences between actual and projected returns, the resulting change in net pension liability is not deferred but recognized in pension expense of the period in which the benefit is changed. Changes that increase pension benefits result in an increase in both pension expense and the net pension liability, whereas changes that decrease pension benefits are recognized through a decrease in both pension expense and the net pension liability.

A Final Note: Pension Discount Rates

The selection of the discount rate to apply to future retirement benefits has two important effects. First, it determines the estimated total pension liability, which in turn determines the net pension liability that appears in Statements of Net Position. Secondly, it determines the interest cost component of annual pension expense. In the past, governments have been justly criticized for selecting high discount rates, which had the effect of understating both pension expense and the reported pension liability.

Under ideal circumstances, governments would fund pension plans according to an actuarially computed formula designed to ensure adequate resources are available to pay pension benefits as they come due. The earnings expected to be provided by pension plan investments reduce the amount of annual contributions necessary to satisfy pension obligations. If pensions are being fully funded, then the appropriate discount rate is the long-term expected rate of return on pension plan investments. However, many governments have significantly underfunded their pension plans with the result that investment earnings are not adequate. In such cases, a discount rate based on the assumption of a fully funded plan is unrealistically high.

GASB standards require governments to use a discount rate equal to the long-term expected rate of return on plan investments if the pension plan's fiduciary net position is projected to be sufficient to pay pension benefits. The projected rate of return must also be realistic—that is, reflective of the actual investment strategy being used. To the extent these conditions are not met, governments are required to use a discount rate based on municipal bond yields. Underfunded plans therefore report net pension liability using a lower discount rate that reflects an average of investment returns and municipal borrowing rates. Irrespective of how discount rates are determined, GASB standards require governments to disclose (in the notes) the net pension liability using a discount rate that is 1 percentage point lower and 1 percentage point higher than the rate used to calculate the net pension liability appearing in the statements. This analysis permits the statement user to evaluate the sensitivity of the net pension liability to the discount rate assumed.

Employer Reporting for Other Postemployment Benefits

Other postemployment benefits (OPEB) are retiree benefits other than pensions and include health care, disability, long-term (i.e., nursing home) care, and life insurance. Like pensions, there are two levels of reporting: reporting for the plan (a fiduciary activity) and employer reporting. Unlike pensions, however, many governments operate on a pay-as-you-go basis, meaning that no assets are set aside for OPEB benefits and there is no trust to report among the fiduciary funds. While a government may not have an OPEB trust, the requirements for employer reporting apply to all governments offering postemployment benefits to their retirees.

GASB standards for OPEB obligations are very similar to that described for pensions. Financial statements prepared using the economic resources measurement focus and accrual basis of accounting must report a liability equal to the net OPEB liability. Like pensions, the net liability is the actuarially computed present value of projected benefit payments less the assets currently available in the plan to meet those obligations. For many governments, there are no assets currently available and the net liability will equal the total projected OPEB liability.

The annual OPEB *expenditure* for governmental-type funds is equal to the amount paid in the current year plus any accruals for amounts to be paid from current financial resources. The amount of OPEB *expense* recognized in financial statements prepared on the accrual basis is closely tied to measurement of the net OPEB liability. Like pensions, OPEB expense includes a service cost component and interest on the present value of the (total) OPEB obligation. The expense is then reduced by the expected return (if any) on plan assets.

SUMMARY

Special-Purpose Entities: Financial reporting by a special-purpose government depends upon whether that entity is engaged in governmental- and business-type activities, multiple governmental activities, a single governmental activity, business-type activities only, or fiduciary activities only. Special-purpose entities that are engaged only in one governmental activity are allowed to combine fund and government-wide statements. Special-purpose governments that are engaged in business-type or fiduciary activities only are permitted to report only fund-basis information. Entities engaged in governmental- and business-type activities or multiple governmental activities must complete both fund-basis and government-wide statements.

Special Assessments: A special assessment is a tax levy that is assessed only against certain taxpayers. The appropriate fund to account for a special assessment tax depends on whether the tax is to provide a service or construction of capital assets. Generally these activities are reported in governmental funds, but if the tax supports debt issued for a capital project and the government bears no liability for that debt, the tax is reported in a custodial fund.

Leases: Governments commonly enter leases as a means to acquire the use of capital assets. A lease is not reported as a liability if the term of the lease is 12 months or less. The (monthly) lease payments are charged to expense or expenditure as they come due. Other leases report the present value of lease payments as liabilities on the Statement of Net Position. The lease asset is recorded and charged to expense over the shorter of the lease term or its economic useful life.

Employer Reporting for Retirement Benefits: Governments commonly provide pensions and other postretirement benefits to their employees. Unfunded obligations and expenses for these future benefits are recognized over the service period of the employees and reported in financial statements prepared on the economic resources measurement focus.

Questions and Exercises

Special-Purpose Entities

9–1. GASB provides guidance for reporting by special-purpose entities. That guidance depends upon whether special-purpose entities are engaged in activities that are governmental-type, business-type only, or fiduciary-type only. Discuss the guidance and list required basic financial statements for

a. Governments engaged in governmental-type activities. Include those that are engaged in governmental- and business-type activities, more than one governmental activity, and only one governmental activity.

b. Governments engaged in business-type activities only.

c. Governments engaged in fiduciary-type activities only.

9–2. Presented below is the Governmental Funds Balance Sheet for the Warrenton Library District, a special-purpose entity engaged in a single governmental activity. Prepare a combined Governmental Funds Balance Sheet/Statement of Net Position in the format presented in Illustration 9-1.

WARRENTON LIBRARY DISTRICT
Governmental Funds Balance Sheet
As of December 31, 2020

Assets	**General Fund**	**Special Revenue Fund**	**Total**
Cash and cash equivalents	$130,000	$12,000	$142,000
Inventories	6,000		6,000
Receivables (net)			
Taxes receivable	90,000		90,000
Due from General Fund		7,500	7,500
Total assets	$226,000	$19,500	$245,500
Liabilities			
Accounts payable	85,000	3,500	88,500
Due to special revenue fund	7,500		7,500
Total liabilities	92,500	3,500	96,000
Fund balance			
Nonspendable (inventories)	6,000		6,000
Restricted for other purposes		16,000	16,000
Unassigned	127,500		127,500
Total fund balance	133,500	16,000	149,500
Total liabilities and fund balance	$226,000	$19,500	$245,500

Additional information:

a. Capital assets (net of accumulated depreciation) amounted to $335,000 at year-end.

b. The liability for long-term compensated absences is estimated to be $85,000 at year-end.

c. Long-term notes payable amounted to $222,000 at year-end.

9–3. Presented below is the Governmental Funds Statement of Revenues, Expenditures, and Changes in Fund Balances for the Trinity Parish Fire District, a special-purpose entity engaged in a single governmental activity. Prepare a combined Governmental Funds Balance Sheet/Statement of Net Position in the format presented in Illustration 9-2.

TRINITY PARISH FIRE DISTRICT
Governmental Funds: Statement of Revenues, Expenditures, and Changes in Fund Balances
For the Year Ended December 31, 2020

Revenues	**General Fund**	**Special Revenue Fund**	**Total**
Property taxes	$320,000	—	$320,000
Intergovernmental	28,000	$19,500	47,500
Miscellaneous	5,000	—	5,000
Total revenues	353,000	19,500	372,500
Expenditures			
Current			
Personnel services	150,000	15,000	165,000
Supplies	25,000	—	25,000
Capital outlay	125,000	—	125,000
Debt service			
Principal	5,000	—	5,000
Interest	8,000	—	8,000
Total expenditures	$313,000	$15,000	$328,000
Excess of revenues over expenditures	40,000	4,500	44,500
Other financing sources (uses):			
Issuance of debt	25,000	—	25,000
Transfers from other funds		5,000	5,000
Transfers (to) other funds	(5,000)	—	(5,000)
	20,000	5,000	25,000
Excess of revenues and other sources over (under) expenditures and other uses	60,000	9,500	69,500
Fund balance—beginning of year	22,000	(8,000)	14,000
Fund balance—end of year	$ 82,000	$ 1,500	$ 83,500

Additional information:

a. Property taxes expected to be collected more than 60 days following year-end are deferred in the fund-basis statements. Deferred taxes totaled $39,000 at the end of 2019 and $36,000 at the end of 2020.

b. The current year provision for depreciation totaled $65,000.

c. Interest on long-term notes payable is paid monthly (no accrual is necessary).

d. Total Net Position on the December 31, 2019, Statement of Net Position totaled $128,000.

Special Assessments

9-4. Residents of a neighborhood financed the installation of sidewalks through a note payable. The note was to be repaid through a special assessment tax on their properties. When is it appropriate to account for special assessment activities in a custodial fund? In which fund should the special assessment tax receipts be reported if they do not meet the criteria for a custodial fund?

9-5. Beachfront property owners of the Town of Eden Beach requested a seawall be constructed to protect their beach. The seawall was financed through a note payable, which was to be repaid from taxes raised through a special assessment on their properties. The Town guarantees the debt and accounts for the special assessment through a debt service fund. Assume the special assessments were levied in 2019, recording a special assessment tax receivable and deferred inflow in the amount of $450,000. One-third of the assessment is to be collected each year and used to pay the interest and principal on the note. Record the following transactions that occurred in 2020:

1. June 30, $150,000 of the assessments became due and currently receivable. (*Hint:* The special assessment tax is recorded as revenue in the debt service fund when it becomes due.)
2. July 31, the $150,000 was collected.
3. September 30, interest of $22,500 and principal of $127,500 were paid.
4. December 31, the books were closed.

Leases

9-6. Assume a government leases equipment to be used in governmental activities under a noncancelable lease with an initial term of three years. Where would the lease and the payments on the lease be reported in the government's financial statements?

9-7. On January 1, 2020, the Mount Rogers city water department leases a truck for five years under a noncancelable lease agreement. The present value (4 percent interest) of the minimum lease payments is $55,560, and the lease calls for five lease payments of $12,000. The first of these takes place on January 1, 2020, and the remaining will take place on December 31st of each year, beginning December 31, 2020. The leased truck has a five-year life.

1. Prepare journal entries for the first year of the lease.
2. How would the lease be reflected in the Statement of Cash Flows prepared for the enterprise fund for the year ended December 31, 2020?

9-8. On July 1, 2019, a five-year agreement is signed between the City of Genoa and the Computer Leasing Corporation for the use of equipment not associated with proprietary funds activity. The minimum lease payment under the lease is $7,500 per year. The first payment is to be made by the General Fund at the inception of the lease. Subsequent payments, beginning July 1, 2020, are also to be made by the General Fund. The present value of the lease payments, including the first payment, is $34,095. The interest rate implicit in the leasè is 5 percent.

1. Assuming the agreement meets the criteria for a capital lease, make the entries required in (1) the capital projects fund and (2) the debt service fund on July 1, 2019, and July 1, 2020.
2. Comment on where the fixed asset and long-term liability associated with this capital lease would be recorded and the impact of the journal entries recorded for *1*.

Pensions and Postemployment Benefits

9-9. With regard to current GASB standards for pension reporting:

1. Distinguish between (1) defined contribution plans and (2) defined benefit plans.
2. Distinguish between defined benefit pension reporting for (1) governmental fund statements and (2) for enterprise fund and government-wide statements.

9-10. Amherst City provides a defined benefit pension plan for employees of the city electric utility, an enterprise fund. Assume that the projected level of earnings on plan investments is $190,000, the service cost component is $260,000, and interest on the pension liability is $170,000 for the year. The City is amortizing a deferred outflow resulting from a change in plan assumptions from a prior year in the amount of $7,000 per year. Prepare journal entries to record annual pension expense for the enterprise fund.

9-11. With regard to current GASB standards for other postemployment benefit reporting:

1. What are other postemployment benefits?
2. What are the reporting requirements of OPEB obligations for financial statements prepared using the economic resources measurement focus?
3. How is the the annual OPEB *expenditure* for governmental-type funds determined?
4. What are the three components of the annual OPEB *expense* that may be expected each year? (Assume this is for financial statements prepared using the economic resources measurement focus.)

Excel-Based Problems

9–12. The fund-basis financial statements of Cherokee Library District (a special-purpose government engaged only in governmental activities) have been completed for the year 2020 and appear in the second and third tabs of the

Excel spreadsheet provided with this exercise. The following information is also available:

a. Capital Assets
- Capital assets purchased in previous years through governmental-type funds totaled $21,050,000 and had accumulated depreciation of $5,770,000.
- Depreciation on capital assets used in governmental-type activities amounted to $434,000 for 2020.
- No capital assets were sold or disposed of in 2020, and all purchases are properly reflected in the fund-basis statements as capital expenditures.

b. Long-Term Debt
- There were $10,500,000 of outstanding long-term notes associated with governmental-type funds as of January 1, 2020. Interest is paid monthly.
- December 31, 2020, notes with a face value of $6,370,000 were issued at par. In addition, principal payments totaled $1,340,000.
- The notes, and any retained percentage on construction contracts, are associated with the purchase of capital assets.

c. Deferred Inflows
- Deferred inflows are comprised solely of property taxes expected to be collected more than 60 days after year-end. The balance of deferred taxes at the end of 2019 was $92,800.

d. Transfers: Transfers were between governmental-type funds.

e. Beginning net position for the government-wide statements totaled $20,247,121 as of January 1, 2020. This amount has already been entered in the Statement of Activities.

Required:

Use the Excel template provided to complete the following requirements. A separate tab is provided for each requirement:

a. Prepare the journal entries necessary to convert the governmental fund financial statements to the accrual basis of accounting.

b. Post the journal entries to the (shaded) Adjustments column to produce a Statement of Activities. You do not have to post amounts debited or credited to "(beginning) net position." These have been reflected in item *e* above.

c. Post the journal entries to the (shaded) Adjustments column to produce a Statement of Net Position. Calculate the appropriate amounts for the Net Position accounts, assuming there are no restricted net position.

Chapter Ten

Accounting for Private Not-for-Profit Organizations

Every dollar makes a difference. And that's true whether it's Warren Buffet's remarkable $31 billion pledge to the Gates Foundation or my late father's $25 check to the NAACP. Michael Bloomberg, three-term mayor of New York City

It is more difficult to give money away intelligently than to earn it in the first place. Andrew Carnegie, founder of Carnegie Steel: between 1901 and 1919 he contributed over $380 million (approximately $5 billion in current dollars) to charities, universities, and foundations.

Learning Objectives

- Describe characteristics of private not-for-profit organizations and the accounting for contributions.
- Apply the accrual basis of accounting in the recording of typical transactions of private not-for-profit organizations.
- Prepare the financial statements for private not-for-profit organizations.

Within the United States, two organizations are authorized to establish GAAP for not-for-profit entities. The Financial Accounting Standards Board (FASB) has standard-setting authority over **private organizations,** including businesses and private not-for-profit organizations. The Governmental Accounting Standards Board (GASB) has standard-setting authority over state and local governments, including governmentally related not-for-profit organizations such as hospitals and universities. This chapter describes the accounting and reporting of private (non-governmental) not-for-profit organizations.

A distinguishing characteristic of the organizations described in this chapter is that they are not owned or controlled by a government. Like governments, these organizations do not have an identifiable individual or group of individuals who hold an enforceable residual claim to the net assets of the organization. The activities of private not-for-profits are commonly financed through membership dues or voluntary contributions. Although these organizations may have creditors, the financial statements are intended primarily for use by either constituents (such as members) or present and potential donors.

Private not-for-profits must follow all applicable FASB standards in recording transactions.[1] FASB standards regarding contingencies, leases, pensions, foreign exchange, and compensated absences all apply to not-for-profits engaged in those types of transactions. In addition, the FASB issues some standards that apply *only* to not-for-profit organizations. Examples include accounting for contributions, donor-imposed restrictions, mergers and acquisitions, and gifts that are to be directed to another beneficiary.

Like the GASB, the FASB publishes a **codification** of its accounting standards. FASB's *Codification* includes statements, interpretations, and technical bulletins issued by the board. The first seven areas of the codification cover general principles, financial statements, and the elements of the financial statements (assets, liabilities, expenses, etc.). The eighth summarizes professional standards for individual industries. Within the industry segment, Section 958 provides reporting standards specific to not-for-profit organizations.

The FASB's direct involvement in standard setting for private not-for-profits substantively began in 1993 with the issuance of two standards: the first dealing with accounting for contributions and the second with the content and form of the financial statements. Prior to this, the financial reporting practices of not-for-profits had been established primarily through audit and accounting guides issued by the American Institute of Certified Public Accountants (AICPA). Under the old AICPA guides, universities, museums, and religious organizations reported by fund types while hospitals and trade associations focused on the consolidated entity. The 1993 standard (Statement No. 117) established uniformity among these varying not-for-profit organizations. Although revised in 2016, the not-for-profit reporting model continues to focus on the organization as a whole and provides a uniform reporting format across varying industries in the nonprofit sector.

ORGANIZATIONS COVERED IN THIS CHAPTER

Voluntary health and welfare organizations are what most commonly come to mind when people consider not-for-profit organizations. Typically, these organizations generate some revenues through user charges but receive most of their support from donors who do not receive direct benefits in return. For example, a community mental health center may charge patients a fee based on their ability to pay, receive allocations from a United Way drive, be awarded federal and state grants, and obtain donations of cash, services, and materials. Other examples of voluntary health and welfare organizations include the American Heart Association and the American

[1] Not all FASB statements are applicable to private not-for-profit organizations (e.g., earnings per share would not be applicable since not-for-profits don't issue stock).

Cancer Society, Meals on Wheels, senior citizen centers, Girl and Boy Scouts, and Big Brothers/Big Sisters. **Other not-for-profit organizations** include cemetery associations, civic organizations, fraternal organizations, labor unions, libraries, museums, other cultural institutions, performing arts organizations, political parties, private schools, professional and trade associations, social and country clubs, research and scientific organizations, and religious organizations.

Private not-for-profit colleges and universities are covered in Chapter 11 and health care organizations in Chapter 12. Not-for-profit entities that operate essentially as commercial businesses for the direct economic benefit of members or stockholders (such as employee benefit and pension plans, mutual insurance companies, mutual banks, trusts, and farm cooperatives) are not covered in this text.

OVERVIEW OF NOT-FOR-PROFIT ACCOUNTING

Financial Reporting

Financial Statements The required financial statements include

1. Statement of Financial Position,
2. Statement of Activities,
3. Statement of Cash Flows, and
4. Additional disclosures, including Notes to the Financial Statements and a Schedule of Functional Expenses.

Private not-for-profits report both current and long-term assets and liabilities and measure revenues and expenses using the accrual basis of accounting. The financial statements of these organizations do not report by fund, and the excess of assets over liabilities is termed net assets, not fund balance.

Statement of Financial Position

The **Statement of Financial Position** reports assets, liabilities, and net assets (residual equity). Assets and liabilities are reported in order of liquidity, or a classified statement may be prepared. Net assets must be broken down into two classes: *Net Assets without Donor Restrictions* and *Net Assets with Donor Restrictions.*

Statement of Activities

The **Statement of Activities** reports revenues, expenses, gains, losses, and reclassifications (between classes of net assets). Expenses, including depreciation, are measured on the accrual basis. Revenues, gains, losses, and reclassifications are separately displayed for the two classes of net assets. However, all expenses are reported as decreases in *Net Assets without Donor Restrictions* and must be identified as program or supporting. Program activities relate to the mission of the organization (medical research, youth welfare, health services, education, etc.) and vary across organizations. Supporting activities include management and general, fundraising, and membership development. The excess of revenues over expenses is called *Change in Net Assets,* not net income.

Statement of Cash Flows

The **Statement of Cash Flows** uses the standard FASB categories (operating, investing, and financing). Either the indirect or the direct method may be used. The indirect method reconciles the *change in net assets* to the net cash used or provided by operating activities. Unlike business organizations, not-for-profits choosing the direct method are not required to prepare a reconciliation of changes in net assets and cash flows from operations. Restricted contributions or restricted investment proceeds that will be used for long-term purposes (endowments or capital assets) are reported as financing activities.

Additional Disclosures

Many of the note disclosures required for business entities also are required for not-for-profits. In some cases, not-for-profits are required to disclose information not typically presented in business financial statements. FASB requires all not-for-profits to provide information on expenses by both functional and natural categories. Functional categories include fund-raising, management and general, as well as individual programs that the organization has undertaken. In contrast, natural categories include salaries and benefits, supplies, professional fees, depreciation and interest, among other operating costs and expenses. This information is typically presented as a matrix with functional categories as columns and natural categories as rows. The detail of expenses may be provided on the face of the Statement of Activities, in the notes to the financial statements, or through a separate schedule such as the Schedule (or Statement) of Functional Expenses.

Additional nonprofit specific requirements include: (1) information useful in assessing liquidity and a description of how the organization manages its liquid assets to meet general expenditures over the next year; (2) detailed information regarding the nature of donor-imposed restrictions; (3) the amount of unconditional promises (i.e., pledges) receivable due in less than one year, one to five years, and more than five years from the balance sheet date; (4) the amount of the allowance for uncollectible pledges receivable; (5) the total of conditional amounts pledged; and (6) methods used to allocate costs among program and supporting activities

Net Asset Classifications The FASB requires residual equity to be displayed within two classes of net assets: *Net Assets without Donor Restrictions* and *Net Assets with Donor Restrictions.* **Net Assets with Donor Restrictions** include unexpended resources that are to be used for a particular purpose, such as to support an identified program or to acquire fixed assets. Additionally resources may be restricted to a future time period or may be required to be invested and remain in endowment indefinitely. Sometimes not-for-profits permanently invest excess resources by a resolution of the governing board. These *quasi-endowments* are classified among net assets without donor restrictions since future governing boards have the ability to undo the designation.

Net Assets without Donor Restrictions include board-designated amounts and all other resources, such as unrestricted contributions, revenues from providing services, and unrestricted income from investments. Resources are presumed to be without donor restrictions unless there is evidence of donor-imposed restrictions. Donor-imposed restrictions are commonly satisfied at some point in the future either through the passage of time or as a result of the organization using the resources according to the donor's wishes. In such cases, the amount is reclassified as "net assets released from restriction" and added to Net Assets without Donor Restrictions. Reclassifications appear as offsetting amounts on the face of the *Statement of Activities.*

Issues Involving Reporting of Assets

Property and Equipment

Fixed assets, including those purchased with donated funds, are reported among net assets without donor restrictions. Property and equipment, other than land and museum collections, are depreciated. Collections, such as artwork in a museum, may or may not be recorded. To be classified as collections, the items must be held for public display and preserved. In the event of sale, the proceeds must be reinvested in other collections or used to support the direct care of existing collections. If not recorded, note disclosures are required.

Investments

FASB (§ 958-320) requires investments in equity securities with determinable fair values and investments in debt securities be carried at fair value. Income from these investments is recorded as increases in net assets with or without restrictions, depending upon the presence or absence of donor restrictions or legal requirements. Unrealized gains and losses and realized gains and losses on investments are reported together in the Statement of Activities (with or without donor restrictions depending on the presence or absence of donor instructions or legal requirements).

FASB (§ 958-815) requires investments in derivative instruments be recorded as either assets or liabilities and be measured at fair value. Additionally, Statement of Position 94–3, *Reporting of Related Entities by Not-for-Profit Organizations,* requires consolidation of entities controlled through majority stock ownership or if there is an economic interest or control and the not-for-profit appoints a majority of the related entity's governing board. Similar to commercial businesses, fair value reporting does not apply to investments that are accounted for under the equity method or investments in consolidated subsidiaries. Additionally, some investments (interest in trusts, real estate ventures, and closely held companies and partnerships) are not covered by not-for-profit standards. In such cases, not-for-profits would follow the reporting rules in effect for commercial businesses with similar investments.

ACCOUNTING FOR CONTRIBUTIONS

In general, not-for-profit organizations record and measure transactions and events in the same manner as commercial businesses. Both accrue interest, report long-term assets and liabilities, and expense depreciation. Not-for-profits, however, differ from commercial enterprises in two important ways: (1) not-for-profit organizations receive considerable amounts of resources in the form of contributions (including grants and donations of cash or other assets), and (2) resource providers frequently impose restrictions on the use of these resources.

FASB addressed the recognition of revenue in 2014 through Accounting Standards Update, *Revenue from Contracts with Customers* (§ 606). Generally speaking, commercial businesses recognize revenue when it is earned. For most transactions, this occurs at the time goods or services are provided to a customer with the expectation of payment. A full explanation of the provisions of this standard are beyond the scope of this book. However, two points are worth mentioning with respect to the revenue standard and private not-for-profit organizations.

1. Contribution revenue is explicitly excluded from the scope of § 606. As we shall see, FASB has separate standards to address when to recognize contribution revenue.
2. Not-for-profit organizations, however, are subject to guidance provided by § 606 for revenue derived from exchange transactions (providing goods or services in exchange for resources). For example, patient service revenue in a private not-for-profit hospital is an exchange transaction.

FASB first addressed reporting of contributions in 1993. FASB (§ 958-25-2) requires contributions, including unconditional promises to give (i.e., pledges), to be recorded as revenues when the promise is made. Contributions may also take the form of cancellation of a liability, rather than a receipt of assets. For example, a business may choose to forgive a note receivable it holds from a not-for-profit organization, releasing the organization from its obligation to pay interest and principal.

In 2018, FASB issued a standard intended to clarify the recognition of contributions. Illustration 10-1 provides a visual representation of the decision process in determining how to report revenues by a private not-for-profit organization.

Exchange Transactions: The first step in recording revenue is to determine whether the transaction is an exchange transaction (i.e., reciprocal in nature) or a contribution (nonreciprocal). Reciprocal exchanges are reported following § 606 guidance for contracts with customers. These are in substance purchases of goods or services. A transaction is deemed to be reciprocal if the resource provider receives commensurate value in return. Commensurate value is judged from the perspective of the resource provider and indicates that the individual or organization receives something of value in return for the assets. Payment by a software company to a not-for-profit trade association for advertising space in a newsletter is an exchange transaction because the software company receives services in return. Similarly, payment by a pharmaceutical company to a private university to perform clinical trials of a new drug is also an exchange transaction. In practice, it is generally clear when a not-for-profit organization has fulfilled its obligation to provide goods or services under a reciprocal exchange and revenue should be recognized.

FASB standards clearly state that the resource provider must receive a direct benefit. In many cases, donors receive an indirect benefit in the belief and personal satisfaction that their contributions have made the world or community a better place. This is an indirect benefit and is not deemed to be of commensurate value.

ILLUSTRATION 10-1 Reporting of Revenues

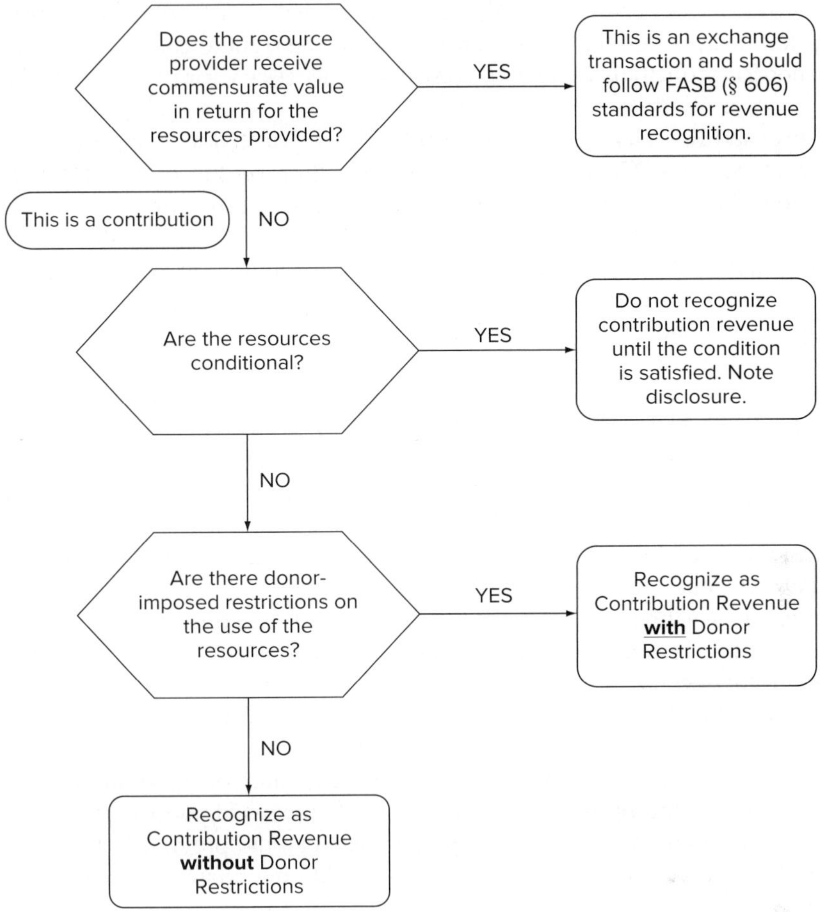

Donor-Imposed Conditions: Nonreciprocal transactions are contributions but the reporting of these transactions depends on the existence of donor-imposed conditions and restrictions. Conditional promises to give are not recognized as revenues until the conditions are met. For example, a donor may pledge a gift of $10,000 to a not-for-profit provided a matching $10,000 can be raised from other donors. If the organization fails to raise the additional amount, the potential donor is not bound by the promise. In the case of matching gifts, the $10,000 would not be recognized as revenue at the time of the offer but the not-for-profit would recognize the pledge as contribution revenue when the matching $10,000 is raised.

FASB identifies two requirements for a donor-imposed condition to exist. First, there must be a performance barrier that must be overcome. A barrier is a stipulation that the recipient must meet in order to be entitled to the assets. Second, there must exist a right of return or a right of release of the donor from its obligation.

A right of return exists if the not-for-profit has received the contribution but must return the funds if the donor-imposed stipulation is not met. A right of release exists if the donor has not yet paid the not-for-profit and has the right to cancel the agreement if the not-for-profit fails to meet the conditions necessary for payment to take place.

Donor-Imposed Restrictions: It is important to distinguish donor-imposed conditions from restrictions. Conditions require some action on the part of the not-for-profit before the contribution is recognized as revenue. Restrictions are created by the donor when the donor imposes purpose or time restrictions on the use of the donated resources. Donors may restrict their contributions to particular purpose such as cancer research, acquiring capital assets, or permanent endowment. Additionally, donors may restrict their contributions to future time periods.

All revenues should be identified as *with* or *without* donor restrictions. Since contributions are recognized at the time a pledge is received, revenue recognition often precedes the collection of cash. Some payments may be partially exchange transactions and partially contributions. If significant, the two parts should be measured and reported separately. For example, a not-for-profit orchestra might sell annual memberships for $500 that include a season ticket valued at $200. In this case, the season ticket is considered an exchange transaction and $300 is recognized as contribution revenue.

It is important to estimate the expected time period of the collection of pledged contributions for two reasons. First, there may be an implied time restriction. That is, a donation to be received in a future period may not be expected to be available to support current operations. Therefore, there is an implied time restriction and the contribution would be recorded as "with donor restrictions." Second, FASB requires multiyear pledges to be recorded at the present value of the future collections. As time passes, the present value of the pledge receivable will increase. At the end of each accounting period the difference between the previously recorded revenue and the new present value is recorded as additional contribution revenue, not interest.

In the case of contributions restricted for purpose or capital asset acquisition, a presumption is made that subsequent disbursements are made first from restricted resources and any additional disbursements are made from unrestricted resources. Contributions are to be recorded at fair market value at the date of receipt. Pledges or promises to contribute in the future are recorded as receivables. The contribution revenue is recorded at the time of the pledge, net of an allowance for estimated uncollectible amounts.

Revenue from Grants: FASB's 2018 standard on reporting of contributions was issued largely to clarify the reporting of grants. In the past many not-for-profit organizations reported government grants as exchange transactions. Two features of the 2018 standard result in most government grants now being reported as *conditional contributions*. First, the standard specifically states that benefits received by the general public (e.g., scientific knowledge) are not equivalent to commensurate value received by the resource provider and therefore most government grants are not exchange transactions. Second, the standard establishes two characteristics of conditional contributions. Government grants typically have both a performance barrier and a right of return.

Typically government grants are cost-reimbursement arrangements and require compliance with guidelines such as those provided by the U.S. Office of Management and Budget (OMB). Performance barriers exist because a grant recipient has limited discretion in the way the grant proceeds may be spent and specific reporting requirements. In addition, the granting agency has a right of return for funds transferred to a not-for-profit that are not spent in accordance with OMB cost principles. The result is that contribution revenue on these grants is conditional and recognized only as the conditions are satisfied. That means contribution revenue is not recognized at the time the grant is awarded, but as the not-for-profit incurs allowable expenses. If grant proceeds are received in advance, the not-for-profit organization would record deferred revenue.

Memberships: It is sometimes difficult to determine whether membership dues are a nonreciprocal gift (i.e., contribution) or an exchange of goods and services. Assume an organization with a June 30 year-end collects annual dues in January. At fiscal year-end, six months remain on these memberships. How these amounts are recorded depends on whether the memberships are deemed to be contributions or exchange transactions.

Assume that the organization is a public radio station, there are no gifts exchanged at the time of membership, and membership provides little direct benefit (e.g., simply receiving a monthly schedule of programming). Since the benefits of public radio are not restricted to members, the dues have the characteristic of a contribution and would be recorded as follows:

		Debits	Credits
Jan. 1	Cash	5,000	
	Contribution Revenue—without Donor Restrictions		5,000

Assume instead that the organization is a YMCA and that members have access to a gym, pool, and other facilities that nonmembers do not enjoy. In this case the dues have the characteristic of an exchange transaction. Payments received in advance of exchange transactions are recorded as deferred revenue, a liability, rather than as a revenue and would be recorded as follows:

		Debits	Credits
Jan. 1	Cash	5,000	
	Deferred Revenues		5,000
June 30	Deferred Revenues	2,500	
	Membership Revenue—without Donor Restrictions		2,500

Contributed Services: Surveys suggest that more than 60 million U.S. adults volunteer with a not-for-profit annually, contributing more than 8 billion hours. Many such organizations have no paid staff and rely entirely on unpaid volunteers. Since the contributed services are vital to operations, it raises a question whether not-for-profit organizations should report contributed services in the financial report.

Contributed services are recognized as revenue only under specific circumstances; if the service (1) creates or enhances nonfinancial assets or (2) requires specialized skills, is provided by someone possessing those skills, and typically would be purchased if not provided by donation. The journal entry to record donated services would debit a fixed asset if the service created or enhanced a nonfinancial asset (e.g., carpenter) or an expense if the service required specialized skills and would have been purchased if not donated (e.g., lawyer). In both cases the credit would be to Contribution Revenue—without Donor Restrictions (donated services) and the amount would be the fair value of the services contributed. The requirements for recognizing donated services apply even if the service is donated by personnel of an affiliated organization (FASB § 958-605).

Intentions to Give: Assume a parishioner informs her church that she has named the church in her will and provides a written copy of the will to the church. At what point should the church record this as a contribution? FASB standards explain that an intention to give is not the same thing as an unconditional promise to give. Therefore, the church would make no entry to record a contribution until the individual dies and the probate court declares the estate distribution valid.

Transfers to a Not-for-Profit That Holds Contributions for Others: It is common for a not-for-profit organization to accept cash or other assets that are intended to be redirected to other organizations or individuals. For example, an individual transfers cash to a seminary and instructs the seminary to grant a scholarship to a specified student. Under most circumstances, the recipient organization (i.e., the seminary) records the asset. The central issue is whether the recipient organization should record a liability or contribution revenue as the other half of the journal entry.

FASB (§ 958-605-35) provides guidance on how the original donor, intermediary recipient organization, and final beneficiary should record the transaction. Generally, if the not-for-profit organization agrees to transfer the assets to a specified beneficiary, the organization is deemed to be merely an agent; therefore, a liability, rather than contribution revenue, is recorded. If the not-for-profit organization has the ability to redirect the assets to another beneficiary, or if the organization and beneficiary are financially interrelated, the transfer is recorded as a contribution.

Third-Party Payors: Transfers of assets to a not-for-profit that are part of an existing exchange transaction with an identified customer are not contribution revenue. For example, payments made by Medicare or Medicaid to a health care organization for services provided to an eligible patient are not contribution revenue. Instead these payments are treated as collection of receivables which were created (as an exchange transaction) at the time the service was provided to the patient. Other examples include tuition assistance programs, such as Pell Grants, in which government entities make payments on behalf of eligible students to a private not-for-profit college.

ILLUSTRATIVE TRANSACTIONS AND FINANCIAL STATEMENTS

This section demonstrates the accounting practices described on the preceding pages. As with all organizations, the fiscal year begins with a trial balance, displaying the asset, liability, and residual equity balances at the end of the preceding year. The Performing Arts Organization reported $49,992 of Net Assets with Donor Restrictions at the end of the previous year. Although not required by FASB standards, the organization keeps separate accounts for each donor-restricted category and reports this additional detail in its Statement of Financial Position.

Beginning Trial Balance

Assume the organization maintains an endowment. Endowment principal of $42,000 is to be maintained permanently invested and income from this endowment is unrestricted. The remaining $7,992 in donor restricted net assets is for the following:

PERFORMING ARTS ORGANIZATION
Trial Balance
July 1, 2019

	Debits	Credits
Cash	$ 1,128	
Accounts receivable	240	
Interest receivable	744	
Contributions receivable	996	
Supplies inventories	264	
Investments: Undesignated	4,344	
Investments: Endowment	42,000	
Land	6,000	
Buildings	14,400	
Accumulated depreciation: Buildings		$ 4,800
Equipment	15,000	
Accumulated depreciation: Equipment		3,600
Accounts payable		64
Grants payable		360
Notes payable		2,400
Deferred revenue		2,400
Long-term debt		9,600
Net assets—without donor restrictions		11,900
Net assets—with donor restrictions:		
Restricted for professional education		3,480
Restricted for future time periods		4,272
Restricted for musical instrument purchase		240
Restricted for endowment		42,000
Totals	$85,116	$85,116

(1) $3,480 restricted for continuing professional education; (2) $4,272 restricted for future time periods; and (3) $240 restricted for purchases of musical instruments.

Also assume the Performing Arts Organization reports expenses by function and has four programs (performance, ballet school, neighborhood productions, and grants). Management and General, Fund-Raising, and Membership Development are supporting services.

Transactions

During the fiscal year ended June 30, 2020, unrestricted cash receipts included $240 accounts receivable at the beginning of the year (for tuition), $2,640 in contributions, $1,440 in single ticket admission charges, $600 in tuition, $480 in concessions, and $960 in interest revenue. Note that revenue accounts are identified as *with* or *without* donor restrictions. It is not necessary to label asset and liability accounts in this manner.

	Debits	Credits
1. Cash	6,360	
Accounts Receivable		240
Contribution Revenue—without Donor Restrictions		2,640
Admission Revenue—without Donor Restrictions		1,440
Tuition Revenue—without Donor Restrictions		600
Concession Revenue—without Donor Restrictions		480
Interest Revenue—without Donor Restrictions		960

A receivable of $360 was accrued for tuition related to the current fiscal year:

	Debits	Credits
2. Accounts Receivable	360	
Tuition Revenue—without Donor Restrictions		360

The deferred revenue liability at the end of the previous year represented the unexpired portion of season tickets. The related performances were completed in the current fiscal year:

	Debits	Credits
3. Deferred Revenue	2,400	
Admission Revenue—without Donor Restrictions		2,400

Season tickets totaling $6,240 were sold in the current year. In addition, 60 memberships were sold at $200 each. Members receive a season ticket ($80 value), but no other direct benefit.

	Debits	Credits
4. Cash	6,240	
Deferred Revenue		6,240
5. Cash	12,000	
Deferred Revenue		4,800
Contribution Revenue—without Donor Restrictions		7,200

Notice that part of the membership ($120) is deemed to be a contribution and recognized as revenue immediately. The other part ($80) is deemed to be an exchange transaction and deferred until earned. Half of the performances were completed by year-end [($6,240 + $4,800)/2 = $5,520]:

	Debits	Credits
6. Deferred Revenue	5,520	
Admission Revenue—without Donor Restrictions		5,520

Interest received on the endowment investments amounted to $2,280. This included $744 accrued at the end of the previous year. Accrued interest at the end of the current year was $240. By agreement with donors, endowment income is not restricted.

	Debits	Credits
7a. Cash	2,280	
Interest Receivable		744
Interest Income—without Donor Restrictions		1,536
7b. Interest Receivable	240	
Interest Income—without Donor Restrictions		240

Note: Commonly, endowments are established for the purpose of supporting a specific activity. In those cases, income earned on the endowment would be credited to *Interest Revenue—with Donor Restrictions.* In some instances the trust agreement governing endowment resources may specify that the principal must grow by a certain percentage or by the excess of earnings over a specified annual draw. In such cases, the income that is required to remain in the endowment would be credited to *Interest Revenue—with Donor Restrictions* even if the remainder of the investment income was not restricted.

Pledges are received for the following: $1,080 for current unrestricted purposes, $2,280 to support specific programs, and a promise to provide $600 in each of the next five years to support an educational program in those years (the present value of five payments discounted at 6 percent is $2,527). Assume the five-year pledge was made on January 1, 2020. Entry 8b records contribution revenue for the increase in present value from January 1 to June 30 ($2,527 × 6% × 6/12 = $76):

Account	Debit	Credit
8a. Contributions Receivable	5,887	
Contribution Revenue—with Donor Restrictions		4,807
Contribution Revenue—without Donor Restrictions		1,080
8b. Contributions Receivable	76	
Contribution Revenue—with Donor Restrictions		76

Cash of $996 pledged in the prior year for unrestricted use in the current year was received. No additional contribution revenue is recorded upon collection of the pledge.

Account	Debit	Credit
9. Cash	996	
Contributions Receivable		996

Cash of $3,360 was received on the pledges recorded in journal entry 8a, including the $1,080 for current unrestricted purposes:

Account	Debit	Credit
10. Cash	3,360	
Contributions Receivable		3,360

Continuing professional education (CPE) expenses for instructors were incurred and paid as follows: $1,920 performance assistance, $600 ballet school, and $960 neighborhood productions. These were supported by donor restricted gifts received in the previous year (see Net Assets—with Donor Restrictions from the trial balance).

Account	Debit	Credit
11a. Performance Expense—CPE	1,920	
Ballet School Expense—CPE	600	
Neighborhood Productions Expenses—CPE	960	
Cash		3,480
11b. Reclassification from net assets with donor restrictions—for satisfaction of program restrictions	3,480	
Reclassification to net assets without donor restrictions—for satisfaction of program restrictions		3,480

Note: The organization has now expended the donor-restricted funds of $3,480 according to the terms of the contribution. At this point, the purpose-related restriction is satisfied and the organization must make an entry reclassifying the net assets from "with donor restrictions" to "without donor restrictions." In this case the increase in net assets without donor restrictions will be offset by program expenses.

It is not uncommon for not-for-profits to receive noncash donations. In such cases, the assets are recorded at their fair values on the date of the contribution. A new harp with a fair value of $22,500 was donated to the organization:

		Debit	Credit
12.	Equipment (musical instruments)	22,500	
	Contribution Revenue—without Donor Restrictions		22,500

The $240 received in a prior year for musical instrument acquisitions, together with an additional $90, was used to acquire percussion instruments:

		Debit	Credit
13a.	Equipment (musical instruments)	330	
	Cash		330
13b.	Reclassification from net assets with donor restrictions—for satisfaction of program restrictions	240	
	Reclassification to net assets without donor restrictions—for satisfaction of capital assets restrictions		240

Note the amount of the reclassification is limited to the amount of the restricted contribution, even though the cost of the equipment exceeds that amount.

At the beginning of this year, Net Assets with Donor Restrictions included $4,272 restricted for future time periods. Of this total, $2,100 collected in the prior year plus the $996 received in entry 9 relates to the current year. The time restriction has now expired and these assets are released from restriction.

		Debit	Credit
14.	Reclassification from net assets with donor restrictions—for expiration of time restrictions	3,096	
	Reclassification to net assets without donor restrictions—for expiration of time restrictions		3,096

A gift of securities with a fair market value of $12,000 is received for the endowment. The principal of the gift is to be maintained indefinitely with interest to be used for unrestricted purposes:

		Debit	Credit
15.	Investments—Endowment	12,000	
	Contribution Revenue—with Donor Restrictions		12,000

FASB standards (§ 958-320) require that investments in equity securities with readily determinable values and all debt investments be reported at fair market value. The resulting gains or losses are recorded as increases or decreases in net assets without donor restrictions, unless unrealized gains or losses are explicitly restricted by donor or by law. It was determined the endowment investments had a fair value of $2,100 in excess of recorded amounts:

16. Investments—Endowment	2,100	
Investment Income—without Donor Restrictions—net gains on endowment investments		2,100

Salaries were paid in the following amounts: $2,400 performance, $4,800 ballet school, $600 neighborhood productions, $4,200 management and general, $500 fund-raising, and $700 membership development. Note the account titles for expenses identify both the function (e.g., performance) and object (salaries). This is done to facilitate preparation of functional expense disclosures (Illustration 10-6).

17. Performance Expense—Salaries	2,400	
Ballet School Expense—Salaries	4,800	
Neighborhood Productions Expense—Salaries	600	
Management and General Expense—Salaries	4,200	
Fund-Raising Expense—Salaries	500	
Membership Development Expense—Salaries	700	
Cash		13,200

During the year, depreciation is recorded as follows: $720 buildings and $3,330 equipment. Depreciation on dedicated equipment is assigned to the specific function, while the remaining depreciation is allocated on the basis of relative square footage of the building. Depreciation was allocated to functional categories in the following amounts: $1,610 performance, $840 ballet school, $60 neighborhood productions, $720 management and general, $520 fund-raising, and $300 membership development.

18. Performance Expense—Depreciation	1,610	
Ballet School Expense—Depreciation	840	
Neighborhood Productions Expense—Depreciation	60	
Management and General Expense—Depreciation	720	
Fund-Raising Expense—Depreciation	520	
Membership Development Expense—Depreciation	300	
Accumulated Depreciation—Buildings		720
Accumulated Depreciation—Equipment		3,330

Grants are periodically awarded to assist local schools in fostering performing arts programs. In the current year $960 of grants were awarded. A total of $1,200, including the $360 beginning grants payable, was paid during the year.

	Debit	Credit
19a. Performing Arts Expense—Grants	960	
Grants Payable		960
19b. Grants Payable	1,200	
Cash		1,200

Supplies were purchased on account in the amount of $2,280. A total of $2,316, including $64 of beginning accounts payable, was paid during the year.

	Debit	Credit
20a. Supplies	2,280	
Accounts Payable		2,280
20b. Accounts Payable	2,316	
Cash		2,316

Supplies were used for the following activities: $720 performance, $600 ballet school, $120 neighborhood productions, $564 management and general, $240 fund-raising, and $120 membership development.

	Debit	Credit
21. Performance Expense—Supplies	720	
Ballet School Expense—Supplies	600	
Neighborhood Productions Expense—Supplies	120	
Management and General Expense—Supplies	564	
Fund-Raising Expense—Supplies	240	
Membership Development Expense—Supplies	120	
Supplies		2,364

Interest expense in the amount of $720 was paid during the year, along with $500 of the principal of the notes payable and $400 of the long-term debt. Interest expense was allocated to functional categories in the following amounts: $256 performance, $180 ballet school, $20 neighborhood productions, $200 management and general, $32 fund-raising, and $32 membership development.

22. Performance Expense—Interest	256	
Ballet School Expense—Interest	180	
Neighborhood Productions Expense—Interest	20	
Management and General Expense—Interest	200	
Fund-Raising Expense—Interest	32	
Membership Development Expense—Interest	32	
Notes Payable	500	
Long-Term Debt	400	
Cash		1,620

Journal entries 1 through 22 are posted to general ledger accounts appearing in Illustration 10-2. In the interest of saving space, Net Assets with Donor Restrictions are reflected in a single account. In practice, many not-for-profits would use separate accounts for each source of donor-restricted net assets. Similarly, revenues are summarized in the general ledger in just two accounts (with or without donor restrictions), but would commonly be posted in greater detail, as follows:

Revenues without Donor Restrictions			**Revenues with Donor Restrictions**		
Revenue Source	**Amount**	**Reference**	**Revenue Source**	**Amount**	**Reference**
Contribution Revenue	$ 2,640	1	Contribution Revenue	$ 4,807	8a
	7,200	5		76	8b
	1,080	8a		12,000	15
	22,500	12		16,833	
	33,420				
Admission Revenue	1,440	1			
	2,400	3			
	5,520	6			
	9,360				
Concession Revenue	480	1			
Interest Revenue	960	1			
	1,536	7a			
	240	7b			
	2,736				
Investment Gains	2,100	16			
Tuition Revenue	600	1			
	360	2			
	960				
Total	$49,056		**Total**	$16,883	

ILLUSTRATION 10-2 Journal Entries Posted to General Ledger Accounts

General Ledger

CASH

	Debit	Credit	
bb	1,128		
1	6,360	3,480	11a
4	6,240	330	13a
5	12,000	13,200	17
7a	2,280	1,200	19b
9	996	2,316	20b
10	3,360	1,620	22
	10,218		

ACCOUNTS RECEIVABLE

	Debit	Credit	
bb	240		
2	360	240	1
	360		

INTEREST RECEIVABLE

	Debit	Credit	
bb	744		
7b	240	774	7a
	240		

CONTRIBUTIONS RECEIVABLE

	Debit	Credit	
bb	996		
8a	5,887	996	9
8b	76	3,360	10
	2,603		

SUPPLIES

	Debit	Credit	
bb	264		
20a	2,280	2,364	21
	180		

INVESTMENTS: UNDESIGNATED

	Debit	Credit	
bb	4,344		
	4,344		

ENDOWMENT INVESTMENTS

	Debit	Credit	
bb	42,000		
15	12,000		
16	2,100		
	56,100		

PROPERTY, PLANT, AND EQUIPMENT

	Debit	Credit	
bb	35,400		
12	22,500		
13a	330		
	58,230		

ACCUMULATED DEPRECIATION

	Debit	Credit	
		8,400	bb
		4,050	18
		12,450	

ACCOUNTS PAYABLE

	Debit	Credit	
		64	bb
20b	2,316	2,280	20a
		28	

GRANTS PAYABLE

	Debit	Credit	
		360	bb
19b	1,200	960	19a
		120	

DEFERRED REVENUE

	Debit	Credit	
		2,400	bb
3	2,400	6,240	4
6	5,520	4,800	5
		5,520	

NOTES PAYABLE

	Debit	Credit	
		2,400	bb
22	500		
		1,900	

LONG-TERM DEBT

	Debit	Credit	
		9,600	bb
22	400		
		9,200	

NET ASSETS WITHOUT DONOR RESTRICTIONS

	Debit	Credit	
		11,900	bb
		11,900	

NET ASSETS WITH DONOR RESTRICTIONS

	Debit	Credit	
		49,992	bb
		7,992	

RECLASSIFICATION FROM NET ASSETS WITH DONOR RESTRICTIONS

	Debit	Credit	
11b	3,480		
13b	240		
14	3,096		
	6,816		

UNRESTRICTED REVENUES

	Debit	Credit	
		6,120	1
		360	2
		2,400	3
		7,200	5
		5,520	6
		1,776	7a,7b
		1,080	8a
		22,500	12
		2,100	16
		49,056	

RECLASSIFICATION TO NET ASSETS WITHOUT DONOR RESTRICTIONS

	Debit	Credit	
		3,480	11b
		240	13b
		3,096	14
		6,816	

REVENUES WITH DONOR RESTRICTIONS

	Debit	Credit	
		4,807	8a
		76	8b
		12,000	15
		16,883	

PROGRAM EXPENSE PERFORMANCES

	Debit	Credit	
11a	1,920		
17	2,400		
18	1,610		
21	720		
22	256		
	6,906		

PROGRAM EXPENSE BALLET SCHOOL

	Debit	Credit	
11a	600		
17	4,800		
18	840		
21	600		
22	180		
	7,020		

PROGRAM EXPENSE NEIGHBORHOOD PRODUCTIONS

	Debit	Credit	
11a	960		
17	600		
18	60		
21	120		
22	20		
	1,760		

PROGRAM EXPENSE PERFORMING ARTS GRANT

	Debit	Credit	
19a	960		
	960		

SUPPORTING EXPENSE MGMT & GENERAL

	Debit	Credit	
17	4,200		
18	720		
21	564		
22	200		
	5,684		

SUPPORTING EXPENSE FUND-RAISING

	Debit	Credit	
17	500		
18	520		
21	240		
22	32		
	1,292		

SUPPORTING EXPENSE MEMBERSHIP DEVELOP

	Debit	Credit	
17	700		
18	300		
21	120		
22	32		
	1,152		

Closing entries for the two categories of net assets are as follows:

Closing Entry—Revenues without Donor Restrictions	Debits	Credits
23. Contribution Revenue	33,420	
Admission Revenue	9,360	
Concession Revenue	480	
Interest Income	2,736	
Investment Income (gains)	2,100	
Tuition Revenue	960	
Reclassification to net assets without donor restrictions—for satisfaction of time restrictions	3,096	
Reclassification to net assets without donor restrictions—for satisfaction of capital assets restrictions	240	
Reclassification to net assets without donor restrictions—for expiration of program restrictions	3,480	
Performance Expense		6,906
Ballet School Expense		7,020
Neighborhood Productions Expense		1,760
Performing Arts Grants Expense		960
Management and General Expense		5,684
Fund-Raising Expense		1,292
Membership Development Expense		1,152
Net Assets without Donor Restrictions		31,098
Closing Entry—Revenues with Donor Restrictions		
24. Contribution Revenue with Program Restrictions	4,883	
Contribution Revenue with Endowment Restriction	12,000	
Reclassification from net assets with donor restrictions—for satisfaction of time restrictions		3,096
Reclassification from net assets with donor restrictions—for satisfaction of capital assets restrictions		240
Reclassification from net assets with donor restrictions—for expiration of program restrictions		3,480
Net Assets with Donor Restrictions		10,067

The following table summarizes activity within the varying types of donor-imposed restrictions for the year. Note revenues are identified as with donor restrictions or without donor restrictions. All expenses appear in the financial statements as without donor restrictions, and entries 11b, 13b, and 14 have been made in response to net assets being released from restrictions due to the expiration of time restrictions or the satisfaction of program restrictions.

	Nature of Donor-Imposed Restrictions				
	Purpose	Capital Assets	Time	Endowment	Total
Donor-restricted contributions	(8) $4,883			(15) 12,000	$16,883
Less: Satisfaction of restrictions	(11b) (3,480)	(13b) (240)	(14) (3,096)		(6,816)
Change in donor-restricted net assets	1,403	(240)	(3,096)	12,000	10,067
Plus: Beginning balances	3,480	240	4,272	42,000	49,992
Ending donor-restricted net assets	$4,883	0	1,176	54,000	$60,059

Financial Statements

FASB requires three basic statements for nonprofit organizations: (1) Statement of Activities, (2) Statement of Financial Position, and (3) Statement of Cash Flows. Additionally, nonprofits are required to present information on expenses by both functional and natural categories. The detail of expenses may be provided on the face of the Statement of Activities, in the notes to the financial statements, or through a separate statement. Performing Arts Organization elects to present this information in a Statement of Functional Expenses.

Statement of Activities FASB provides flexibility in this statement and illustrates a variety of formats. Requirements are to provide totals for revenues, expenses, gains, losses, the amounts of assets released from restrictions, and the change in net assets for each of the two classes (with and without donor restrictions). Generally, revenues and expenses are reported gross, and gains and losses may be reported net. Expenses must be reported by functional classifications, with particular emphasis on distinguishing program from supporting services.

Illustration 10-3 presents a Statement of Activities for the Performing Arts Organization. Note all expenses appear in the without donor restrictions category and the net assets released from restrictions (i.e., the effects of entries 11b, 13b, and 14) appear at the bottom of the revenue section as decreases in net assets with donor restrictions. By definition, amounts reported as reclassifications between with and without donor restrictions must offset.

Statement of Financial Position Illustration 10-4 presents the Statement of Financial Position for the Performing Arts Organization. Again, alternative formats are permitted. In place of an equity section, the statement presents separate totals for net assets with and without donor restrictions. Although not required to be presented on the face of the Statement of Financial Position, the Performing Arts Organization presents a breakdown of net assets with donor restrictions

ILLUSTRATION 10-3 Statement of Activities

PERFORMING ARTS ORGANIZATION
Statement of Activities
For the Year Ended June 30, 2020

	Net Assets without Donor Restrictions	Net Assets with Donor Restrictions	Total
Revenues			
Contributions	$33,420	$16,883	$ 50,303
Admissions	9,360		9,360
Concessions	480		480
Interest income	2,736		2,736
Net gains on endowment investments	2,100		2,100
Tuition	960		960
Net assets released from restriction:			
Expiration of time restrictions	3,096	(3,096)	—
Satisfaction of capital asset restrictions	240	(240)	—
Satisfaction of program restrictions	3,480	(3,480)	—
Total revenues and other support	55,872	10,067	65,939
Expenses			
Performances	6,906		6,906
Ballet school	7,020		7,020
Neighborhood productions	1,760		1,760
Performing arts grants	960		960
Total program expenses	16,646		16,646
Management and general	5,684		5,684
Fund-raising	1,292		1,292
Membership development	1,152		1,152
Total supporting expenses	8,128		8,128
Total expenses	24,774	—	24,774
Change in net assets	31,098	10,067	41,165
Net assets—beginning of year	11,900	49,992	61,892
Net assets—end of year	$42,998	$60,059	$103,057

by category of restriction. Additionally, some organizations present additional details of net assets without donor restrictions, such as net assets internally designated for some purpose or net assets invested in property, plant, and equipment net of related debt.

Statement of Cash Flows The third required statement is the Statement of Cash Flows. Either the direct or indirect method may be used. Illustration 10-5 presents the indirect method in which *cash flows from operating activities* are reconciled to *change in net assets* from the Statement of Activity. Generally, classification of cash flows follows the format for business entities (operating, investing, and financing activities). However, Statement 117 requires donor-restricted cash that must be used for long-term purposes be classified as cash flows from financing activities.

ILLUSTRATION 10-4 **Statement of Financial Position**

PERFORMING ARTS ORGANIZATION
Statement of Financial Position
As of June 30, 2020 and 2019

	2020	2019
Assets		
Cash	$ 10,218	$ 1,128
Contributions receivable	2,603	996
Accounts receivable	360	240
Interest receivable	240	744
Investments—undesignated	4.344	4,344
Supplies inventory	180	264
Total current assets	17,945	7,716
Land, building, and equipment (net of accumulated depreciation of $12,450 in 2020, $8,400 in 2019)	45,780	27,000
Long-term investments in endowment	56,100	42,000
Total assets	$119,825	$76,716
Liabilities		
Accounts payable	$28	$64
Grants payable	120	360
Deferred revenues	5,520	2,400
Notes payable	1,900	2,400
Total current liabilities	7,568	5,224
Long-term debt	9,200	9,600
Total liabilities	16,768	14,824
Net Assets		
Without donor restrictions	42,998	11,900
With donor restrictions:		
Purpose restrictions	4,883	3,480
Time restrictions	1,176	4,272
Capital asset restrictions		240
Endowment	54,000	42,000
Total net assets	103,057	61,892
Total liabilities and net assets	$119,825	$76,716

Noncash investing and financing activities must also be disclosed, typically at the bottom of the statement.

Statement of Functional Expenses Beginning in 2020, all not-for-profits are required to disclose detailed information about expenses. FASB provides flexibility, permitting disclosure on the Statement of Activities, within the notes to the financial statements, or by providing a separate statement. Illustration 10-6 presents a Statement of Functional Expenses for the Performing Arts Organization. Note the total expenses of $24,774 reported in the bottom right-hand corner agrees with the total expenses

ILLUSTRATION 10-5 **Statement of Cash Flows**

PERFORMING ARTS ORGANIZATION Statement of Cash Flows For the Year Ended June 30, 2020		
CASH FLOWS FROM OPERATING ACTIVITIES		
Change in net assets	$41,165	
Depreciation expense	4,050	
Noncash contributions	(34,500)	
Gains on fair value of endowment investments	(2,100)	
Increase in accounts receivable	(120)	
Decrease in interest receivable	504	
Increase in contributions receivable (net)	(1,607)	
Decrease in supplies	84	
Decrease in accounts payable	(36)	
Decrease in grants payable	(240)	
Increase in deferred revenues	3,120	
Net cash provided (used) by operating activities		$10,320
CASH FLOWS FROM INVESTING ACTIVITIES		
Purchase of equipment	(330)	
Net cash provided (used) from investing activities		
CASH FLOWS FROM FINANCING ACTIVITIES		(330)
Payment of note principal	(500)	
Payment of long-term debt principal	(400)	
Net cash provided (used) by financing activities		
Increase in cash		(900)
Cash and cash equivalents beginning of year		9,090
Cash and cash equivalents end of year		1,128
Noncash investing and financing activities:		$10,218
Gift of investments	$12,000	
Gift of equipment (musical instruments)	22,500	
Supplemental disclosure of cash flow information:		
Cash paid during the year for interest	$ 720	

reported in the Statement of Activities (Illustration 10-3). Similarly, each of the column totals agree with the amounts reported in the Statement of Activities.

PERFORMANCE EVALUATION

The not-for-profit organizations described in this chapter apply accrual accounting concepts and measure revenues and expenses in much the same manner as business enterprises. In the Statement of Activities, change in net assets is computationally equivalent to net income reported on the financial statements of business enterprises (i.e., revenues–expenses). However, change in net assets is not as effective a performance measure for not-for-profits as net income is for businesses. This is not surprising since not-for-profit organizations are established for purposes other than generating net income.

ILLUSTRATION 10-6 Statement of Functional Expenses

PERFORMING ARTS ORGANIZATION
Statement of Functional Expenses
For the Year Ended June 30, 2020

	Program Services					Supporting Services				
	Performance	Ballet School	Neighborhood Productions	Performing Arts Grants	Total	Management & General	Fund-Raising	Member-ship	Total	Total Expenses
Salaries	$2,400	$4,800	$ 600		$ 7,800	$4,200	$ 500	$ 700	$5,400	$13,200
Continuing education	1,920	600	960		3,480					3,480
Supplies	720	600	120		1,440	564	240	120	924	2,364
Grants				$960	960					960
Interest	256	180	20		456	200	32	32	264	720
Depreciation	1,610	840	60		2,510	720	520	300	1,540	4,050
Total expenses	$6,906	$7,020	$1,760	$960	$16,646	$5,684	$1,292	$1,152	$8,128	$24,774

It is commonly perceived that not-for-profit organizations should not generate surpluses. However, there are a number of reasons why a not-for-profit organization would need to generate a surplus (positive change in net assets). These include

- Establishing working capital.
- Expanding or replacing physical facilities.
- Retiring debt.
- Continuing a program beyond the period that initial funding is provided.

If these needs are satisfied, a not-for-profit organization may also find it desirable to draw upon earlier surpluses and operate at a deficit for a period of time. For these reasons, a positive change in net assets is not inherently either a good or a bad condition.

Program Service Ratio: The financial measure of greatest interest in evaluating not-for-profit organizations is the ratio of program service expenses to total expenses (commonly called the *program expense ratio*). The ratio is readily calculated from the financial statements. For example, Illustration 10-6 reports program expenses totaling $16,646 and total expenses of $24,774 for a ratio of approximately 67 percent. The ratio is a measure of the efficiency of a not-for-profit organization in utilizing resources to fulfill its mission, rather than for fund-raising and administration. The ratio is commonly reported in rankings of charitable organizations. For example, *Money* magazine does an annual ranking of charitable organizations. The Better Business Bureau recommends a minimum ratio of 60 percent.

Because of the importance of this ratio, care is taken in the allocation of costs between program and supporting expense categories. Not-for-profits frequently require employees to keep detailed records of their time for purposes of allocating salary and benefit costs. Additionally, depreciation is commonly allocated on the basis of square feet dedicated to program versus administrative functions.

The American Institute of CPAs issued Statement of Position 98–02, which establishes guidance for allocation of costs that involve fund-raising. Examples of the activities covered by the statement are mass mailings, annual dinners, and TV or radio commercials. The statement indicates that it is appropriate to allocate costs from fund-raising to a program function when the activity meets three conditions:

1. *Purpose:* The purpose of the joint activity includes accomplishing program functions. (Merely asking the audience to make contributions is not an activity that fulfills the organization's mission.)
2. *Audience:* The audience is selected based on characteristics other than ability or likelihood to make contributions.
3. *Content:* The activity calls for specific action by the recipient that will help accomplish the organization's mission.

If any of the conditions are not met, all costs of the joint activity should be reported as fund-raising expenses.

Liquidity Management: Donors and creditors are particularly interested in information related to a not-for-profit's ability to sustain operations, even in the event of unexpected expenditures or revenue shortfalls. FASB standards require not-for-profit organizations to provide both qualitative and quantitative disclosures related to liquidity management. Qualitative information includes a description of how the organization manages its cash, investments, and other liquid assets to meet general expenditures over the next year. Quantitative measures include the amount of financial resources available to meet the cash needs for general expenditures over the next year and the effect (if any) of limits imposed by grantors, donors, laws, contractual arrangements, or the governing board on the availability of financial resources.

The disclosures related to liquidity assist creditors, donors, and other users in assessing the near-term availability of (and requirements for) cash. Without these disclosures resources may appear to be available for short-term cash needs, but in fact are not available to the organization because of donor-imposed limitations on the use of the resources. For example, cash or pledges restricted for capital additions may appear as current financial assets but are in fact not available for other purposes. Additionally, resources invested as quasi-endowments may appear to be unavailable for near-term cash needs but could be liquidated by action of the governing board if cash needs arose. An example note disclosure for a hypothetical not-for-profit foundation appears in Illustration 10-7.

ILLUSTRATION 10-7 Liquidity Management Disclosures

Liquidity management: ABC Foundation's financial assets available within one year of the balance sheet date for general expenditures are as follows:

Cash and cash equivalents	$ 47,000
Investments for current use	65,000
Contributions receivable (current) less pledges designated by the donor for capital additions of $45,000	100,000
Total	$212,000

The current contributions receivable of $145,000 consist of $45,000 restricted by the donor for capital additions. The remaining $100,000 of contributions receivable are subject to an implied time restriction, but are expected to be collected within one year. The Foundation has a goal to maintain cash and short-term investment balances on hand to meet 60 days of ordinary business expenses (exclusive of depreciation) which are on average $104,000. The Foundation has a policy to structure its financial assets to be available as its general expenditures, liabilities, and other obligations come due. As part of its liquidity management, the Foundation invests excess cash in certificates of deposit and short-term treasury instruments.

The Foundation's endowment investments consist of donor-restricted endowments and a quasi-endowment of $1,000,000. Income from donor-restricted endowments is restricted and not available for general expenditures. Although the Foundation does not intend to spend from its quasi-endowment other than investment income appropriated for general expenditures, amounts from the quasi-endowment could be made available if necessary. Additionally, the Foundation has committed lines of credit totaling $100,000, which can be drawn upon in the event of an unforeseen liquidity need.

MERGERS AND ACQUISITIONS

The AICPA Audit and Accounting Guide, Not-for-Profit Organizations, requires consolidation of entities in which a not-for-profit organization has a controlling financial interest. Control may be determined by a majority ownership interest or by holding a majority voting interest in the governing board of an entity in which the not-for-profit has an economic interest through contractual or affiliation agreements. This is similar to practices followed in the public sector with component unit reporting.

Similar to commercial businesses, not-for-profit organizations occasionally merge or acquire a controlling interest in other organizations. This may be done voluntarily to leverage the comparative advantages of two organizations. For example, the American Federation of Labor and Congress of Industrial Organizations merged to form the AFL-CIO, becoming the most influential federation of labor unions in the United States. Alternatively, mergers can be forced upon organizations. Some years ago, the Girl Scouts of America required the merger of many of its independently incorporated councils, reducing the number of chartered councils to approximately one-third of the original number.

FASB requires all mergers and acquisitions among commercial enterprises to be accounted for as purchase transactions. In contrast, FASB Statement 164, Not-for-Profit Entities: Mergers and Acquisitions (FASB § 958-805), permits two different accounting treatments for combinations by not-for-profit organizations. The central issue is whether the combination is a merger or an acquisition.

Mergers A *merger* is a transaction in which the governing bodies of two or more not-for-profit entities relinquish control of those entities to create a new not-for-profit entity. To qualify as a new entity, the combined entity must have a newly formed governing body. Although commonly there will be a new legal entity, that is not a requirement. The resulting not-for-profit entity will account for the merger using the **carryover method.** Under the carryover method

- The new entity recognizes the assets and liabilities of the separate merging entities in the amounts (and classifications) reported in the financial statements of the merging entities.
- No internally developed intangible assets (such as goodwill) are recognized.
- The entity resulting from the merger is a new reporting entity, with no activity before the date of the merger.

The essential element of the carryover method is the entity does not recognize either additional assets (intangibles) or changes in the fair value of recognized assets and liabilities. The two merging organizations' asset and liability book balances are "carried over" to the new reporting entity.

Acquisitions Combinations not meeting the definition of a merger are reported as acquisitions. In an *acquisition*, a not-for-profit may acquire control of either business enterprises or other not-for-profit organizations. Under the *acquisition method*

- The not-for-profit entity recognizes the identifiable assets acquired and liabilities assumed at their fair values at the date of acquisition. Noncontrolling interest (if any) is reported at fair value at the acquisition date and is adjusted in subsequent periods in a manner similar to business organizations.

- Goodwill can be reported.
- The financial statements of the acquirer report the acquisition as activity of the period in which it occurs. Contribution revenue is recognized if the acquired entity is donated (i.e., no purchase price) or if the price paid is less than the fair value of the net assets acquired.

The essential element of the acquisition method is that the entity records the acquired assets and liabilities at their fair values, not at the acquired entity's book values. In this manner, the acquisition method is similar to purchase accounting. However, in many cases the treatment of goodwill is substantially different from that of business enterprises.

FASB Statement 164 recognizes there are varying types of not-for-profit organizations. Some derive revenues principally from contributions (or earnings of investments from previously contributed resources). Other not-for-profit organizations (such as hospitals) receive most of their revenues from the sale of goods and services. This distinction determines how the not-for-profit reports goodwill resulting from an acquisition.

Not-for-profit entities that derive their revenues from businesslike activities are required to measure and report goodwill as an asset in a similar manner as businesses. However, entities that derive revenues primarily from contributions are to charge (i.e., expense) the goodwill at the date of acquisition. In making this distinction, the FASB recognizes goodwill can be useful in evaluating the activities of entities engaged in business activities, but is of limited usefulness to donors in deciding whether to contribute resources to a not-for-profit entity. Since donated acquisitions commonly result in the not-for-profit entity reporting contribution revenue, the charge for goodwill has the effect of reducing what might otherwise be a large reported increase in the Statement of Activities.

SUMMARY

Not-for-profit organizations in the private sector are required to follow FASB standards. The FASB requires three statements: (1) Statement of Financial Position, (2) Statement of Activities, and (3) Statement of Cash Flows. Specific disclosures are required for not-for-profits, including information on liquidity and detailed presentation of expenses by both functional and natural categories.

Accrual accounting is required, and most expenses (including depreciation) are recognized in the same manner as commercial businesses. Residual equity accounts are called "net assets" and are classified as (1) *Net Assets without Donor Restrictions* or (2) *Net Assets* with *Donor Restrictions.* Contributions are recorded as revenue in the appropriate net asset classification upon receipt of an unconditional promise. This means unconditional pledges, even multiyear pledges, are recorded as revenue when pledged. Expenses are classified as program or supporting services and deducted from net assets without donor restrictions. As donor-restricted resources are released from restrictions, reclassification entries are made.

Questions and Exercises

10–1. Obtain a copy of the annual report of a private not-for-profit organization. Answer the following questions from the report (if obtaining a report online, use the site search or the "about us" button to locate the annual report). For examples, try the following:

The American Accounting Association	www.aaahq.org
American Red Cross	www.redcross.org
Habitat for Humanity	www.habitat.org
American Diabetes Association	www.diabetes.org
Save the Children	www.savethechildren.org

a. What financial statements are presented?

b. How are the contribution revenues recognized?

c. Does the organization have net assets with donor restrictions? What is the nature of the restrictions?

d. Compute the ratio of program expenses to total expenses.

10–2. Consider FASB standards for reporting by private not-for-profit organizations and answer the following:

a. What are the financial reports required of all not-for-profits? What additional disclosures are required?

b. List the two classes of net assets.

c. Outline the accounting required for property and equipment, including those classified as collections.

d. Outline accounting and reporting for investments.

10–3. Consider FASB's 2018 guidelines for accounting for contributions and answer the following:

a. Identify the characteristics of exchange transactions and describe when revenue should be recognized.

b. Identify the characteristics of donor-imposed conditions and describe when revenue should be recognized.

c. Identify the characteristics of donor-imposed restrictions and describe when revenue should be recognized.

10–4. Consider FASB standards for accounting for contributions and answer the following:

a. Outline revenue recognition criteria for resources restricted for (1) time and (2) purpose.

b. Outline the requirements for recognizing contributed services as revenue.

c. Outline accounting for multiyear pledges.

10–5. Consider FASB standards for reporting revenues from government grants received by a not-for-profit organizations. Answer the following questions:

a. What features of government grants indicate they are conditional contributions?

b. When should revenue be recognized under a cost-reimbursement grant?

10–6. Consider FASB standards for mergers and acquisitions by not-for-profit organizations. Answer the following questions:

a. What is the difference between a merger and an acquisition?

b. What is the principal difference in the accounting treatment of assets and liabilities under mergers and acquisitions?

c. Under what circumstances will a not-for-profit organization record goodwill?

10–7. For the following transactions and events, indicate what effect each will have on the two classes of net assets using this format. Put an X in the appropriate column. If the net assets are unaffected, leave the column blank.

	Net Assets without Donor Restrictions		Net Assets with Donor Restrictions	
	Increase	**Decrease**	**Increase**	**Decrease**
Ex1			X	
Ex2	X			X

Ex1: Received a pledge from a donor to provide $1,000 a year to support summer educational programs to be held each July for five years.

Ex2: A time restriction on cash received in a prior year expired in the current period.

1. The governing board approved a capital fund-raising campaign in support of a new building. The capital campaign brought in pledges of $150,000.
2. In addition to outside pledges, the board set aside $100,000 of unrestricted resources for the new building.
3. Cash collections on the pledges described in (1) totaled $97,000 in the current year.
4. $25,000 was expended from the capital campaign on architects' fees.
5. Operating revenues (admission fees and gift shop sales) amounted to $80,000.
6. Salaries, utilities, and operating supplies totaled $76,000.
7. Depreciation on plant and equipment amounted to $25,000.
8. Volunteers staffing the gift shop contributed 500 hours. The services did not require specialized skills but are estimated at a value of $8.50 per hour.
9. Securities valued at $100,000 are received for permanent endowment. The terms of the endowment require income earned on the endowment to be used to sponsor visiting speakers.
10. Interest and dividends received on the endowment totaled $2,000.
11. An individual makes a pledge on December 31, promising to donate $100,000 on the condition that the not-for-profit organization can raise matching pledges before July of the next year

10–8. Presented below is a partially completed Statement of Activities for a homeless shelter. Complete the Statement of Activities by filling in any missing amounts. (Include zero amounts.)

CENTERVILLE AREA HOMELESS SHELTER
Statement of Activities
For the Year Ended December 31, 2020

	Net Assets without Donor Restrictions	Net Assets with Donor Restrictions	Total
Revenues			
Contribution revenues			$1,560,810
Net assets released from restriction		(22,000)	0
Total Revenues			1,560,810
Expenses			
Temporary shelter program			1,012,600
Self-sufficiency program			353,000
Fund-raising			7,000
Administration			78,900
Total Expenses			1,451,500
Increase in net assets	85,000	24,310	109,310
Net assets January 1	18,000	13,850	31,850
Net assets December 31	$103,000	$ 38,160	$ 141,160

10–9. Youth Empowerment, a private not-for-profit organization with a fiscal year ending on June 30, was awarded a cost-reimbursement grant from the U.S. Department of Labor to provide job training to at-risk youth, such as young offenders and youth living in high-poverty areas.

Part A. Prepare journal entries for the following events:

1. On May 1, 2020, Youth Empowerment is awarded a Department of Labor grant in the amount of $400,000. The grant is to cover the period June 1, 2020, to May 31, 2021.
2. During June 2020, Youth Empowerment expends $80,000 providing training activities as described in the grant award. A monthly invoice is sent to the Department of Labor.

Part B. Assume instead that the grant is paid when awarded. Prepare journal entries for the following events:

1. On May 1, 2020, Youth Empowerment is awarded a Department of Labor grant in the amount of $400,000. The grant is to cover the period June 1, 2020, to May 31, 2021, and Youth Empowerment receives the full amount of the grant proceeds.
2. During June 2020, Youth Empowerment expended $80,000 providing training activities as described in the grant award.

10–10. On October 1, 2020, the Voluntary Action Agency (which has a December 31 fiscal year-end) received a cash contribution of $450,000 restricted to the purchase of buses to be used in transporting senior citizens as part of the organization's "Active Seniors Program." On January 2, 2021, buses were purchased with the $450,000 cash. The buses are expected to be used for five years and have no salvage value at the end of that time. Record the journal entries on October 1, 2020, January 2, 2021, and December 31, 2021, for the receipt of cash, the purchase of buses, and one year's depreciation.

10–11. On January 1, 2020, a foundation made a pledge to pay $15,000 per year at the end of each of the next five years to the Cancer Research Center, a non-profit voluntary health and welfare organization, as a salary supplement for a well-known researcher. On December 31, 2020, the first payment of $15,000 was received and paid to the researcher.

1. On the books of the Cancer Research Center, record the pledge on January, assuming the appropriate discount rate is 5 percent on an annual basis. The appropriate present value annuity factor is 4.33.
2. Record the increase in the present value as of December 31.
3. Record the receipt of the first $15,000 on December 31 and the payment to the researcher.

10–12. The Evangelical Private School follows FASB standards of accounting and reporting. Record journal entries for the following transactions during the year ended June 30, 2020.

1. Cash contributions were received as follows: (a) $968,000 for any purpose desired by the school; (b) $300,000 designated by donors for salary supplements for school faculty; (c) $417,000 designated by donors to be used during the next fiscal year in any manner desired by the school; (d) $550,000 designated by donors for the construction of a new auditorium; and (e) $400,000 designated by donors to be invested permanently, with the income to be used as desired by the school. The school's policy is to record all restricted gifts as with donor restrictions and then reclassify when the restriction is lifted.
2. The school expended $400,000 of the $968,000 mentioned in 1(a) for school furniture.
3. The school expended the $280,000 for salary supplements as directed by the donor in 1(b).
4. The $417,000 in 1(c) was retained for use next year, as directed by the donor.
5. $780,000 was expended for the construction of the new auditorium.
6. The $400,000 mentioned in 1(e) was invested permanently, as directed by the donor, and in the year ended June 30, 2020, the school received interest of $19,000, none of which was expended.

10–13. The Ombudsman Foundation is a private not-for-profit organization providing training in dispute resolution and conflict management. The Foundation had the following preclosing trial balance at December 31, 2020, the end of its fiscal year:

Account:	Debits	Credits
Accounts payable		$ 23,500
Accounts receivable (net)	$ 45,000	
Accrued interest receivable	15,500	
Accumulated depreciation		3,250,500
Cash	109,000	
Contributed services		35,000
Contributions—no restrictions		2,300,000
Contributions—purpose restrictions		780,000
Contributions—endowment		2,650,000
Current pledges receivable	75,000	
Education program expenses	1,555,000	
Fund-raising expenses	116,000	
Investment revenue—purpose restrictions		86,000
Training seminars expenses	4,456,000	
Land, buildings, and equipment	5,500,000	
Long-term investments	2,690,000	
Management and general expenses	365,000	
Net assets without donor restrictions		448,000
Net assets with donor restrictions		1,909,000
Net gains on endowments—no restrictions		17,500
Noncurrent pledges receivable	365,000	
Program service revenue—no restrictions		5,592,000
Postemployment benefits payable (long-term)		188,000
Reclassification—Satisfaction of program restrictions	250,000	
Reclassification—Satisfaction of time restrictions	205,000	
Reclassification—Satisfaction of program restrictions		250,000
Reclassification—Satisfaction of time restrictions		205,000
Research program expenses	1,206,000	
Short-term investments	750,000	
Supplies inventory	32,000	
Totals	$17,734,500	$17,734,500

a. Prepare closing entries for the year-end, using separate entries for each net asset classification.

b. Prepare a Statement of Activities for the year ended December 31, 2020.

c. Prepare a Statement of Financial Position as of December 31, 2020. (Use a classified approach, providing separate totals for current and noncurrent items.)

10–14. The Blair Museum Association, a nonprofit organization, had the following transactions for the year ended December 31, 2020.

1. Cash contributions to the Association for the year included (a) unrestricted, $950,000; (b) restricted by donors for traveling displays, $250,000; (c) restricted by the donor for endowment purposes, $1,400,000; and (d) restricted by the donor for museum security equipment, $470,000.
2. Additional unrestricted cash receipts included (a) admission charges, $365,000; (b) interest income, $210,000; and (c) tuition for museum school, $70,000.
3. Donors made pledges in 2020 in a pledge drive specifically for funds to be used in 2021. The amount was $400,000.
4. A multiyear pledge was made at the end of the year by a private foundation. The foundation pledged $50,000 per year for the next five years (at the end of each year). The present value (rounded) of those future payments is $211,000, using a 6 percent discount rate.
5. Expenses associated with the traveling display program amounted to $230,000 and were paid in cash before year-end.
6. The Museum collected pledges receivable from the previous year of $135,000. Although not restricted in purpose, the revenue (last year) had been classified as time restricted because collection was not scheduled until 2020.
7. The Museum purchased security equipment for $475,000 (cash).
8. In addition to the amount expended in transaction 5, expenses (paid in cash) amounted to (a) museum displays, $1,300,000; (b) museum school, $85,000; (c) management and general, $350,000; (d) fundraising, $250,000; and (e) membership development, $145,000.
9. Depreciation on museum fixed assets amounted to: (a) $40,000 for museum displays, (b) $7,000 for museum school, (c) $12,000 for management and general, (d) $4,000 for fund-raising, and (e) $4,000 for membership development.

Required:

a. Prepare journal entries to record these transactions, including closing entries. Prepare a Statement of Activities for the Blair Museum Association for the year ended December 31, 2020. Use the format in the text. The beginning net asset balances were $412,000 without donor restrictions; $150,000 with donor-imposed time restrictions; and $3,500,000 in an endowment created by donors.

b. The Museum School program expenses are substantially larger than its revenues. Do you recommend that the program be discontinued?

Excel-Based Problems

10–15. Jefferson Animal Rescue is a private not-for-profit clinic and shelter for abandoned domesticated animals, chiefly dogs and cats. At the end of 2019, the organization had the following account balances:

Account:	Debits	Credits
Pledges receivable	$ 3,800	
Cash	24,700	
Land, buildings, and equipment	41,000	
Supplies inventory	4,000	
Accounts payable		$ 5,000
Accrued wages payable		500
Accumulated depreciation		19,300
Note payable to bank		25,000
Net assets with donor restrictions—KDAC program		2,500
Net assets with donor restrictions—capital assets		7,200
Net assets without donor restrictions		14,000
Total	$73,500	$73,500

The following took place during 2020:

1. Additional supplies were purchased on account in the amount of $16,050.
2. Unconditional (and unrestricted) pledges of support were received totaling $95,000. In light of a declining economy, 4 percent is expected to be uncollectible. The remainder is expected to be collected in the current year.
3. Supplies used for animal care amounted to $17,200.
4. Payments made on accounts payable amounted to $17,100.
5. Cash collected from pledges totaled $90,500.
6. Salaries were paid in the amount of $47,500. Included in this amount is the accrued wages payable at the end of 2019. (The portion of wages expense attributable to administrative expense is $15,000 and fund-raising expense is $2,000. The remainder is for animal care.)
7. Jefferson Animal Rescue entered an agreement with KDAC, Channel 8 News, to find more homes for shelter pets. This special adoption program highlights a shelter animal in need of a home on the evening news the first Thursday of each month. The program was initially funded by a restricted gift. During 2020, Jefferson Animal Rescue paid $1,800 ($150 per month) for the production of the monthly videos. In December 2020, the original donor unconditionally pledged to support the project for an additional 24 months by promising to pay $3,600 in January 2021 (all of this is expected to be collectible).

8. The shelter's building was partially financed by a bank note with an annual interest rate of 6 percent. Interest totaling $1,250 was paid during 2020. Interest is displayed as Administrative Expense in the Statement of Activities.
9. Animal medical equipment was purchased during the year in the amount of $5,200. Funding came from a special capital campaign conducted in 2019.
10. Depreciation for the year amounted to $6,000. (The portion of depreciation expense attributable to administrative is $2,000, and the remainder is related to animal care.)
11. Unpaid wages relating to the final week of the year totaled $715 (all animal care).

Using the information above and the Excel template provided:

a. Prepare journal entries and post entries to the T-accounts.

b. Prepare closing entries.

c. Prepare a Statement of Activities, Statement of Financial Position, and Statement of Cash Flows for the year ending December 31, 2020.

10–16. The Association of Women in Government established an Educational Foundation to raise money to support scholarship and other education initiatives. The Educational Foundation is a private not-for-profit. Members of the Association of Women in Government periodically make donations to the Educational Foundation. With the exception of the gift described below, these are unrestricted.

In December 2019, a donor established a permanent endowment with an initial payment of $120,000 and a pledge to provide $10,000 per year for three years, beginning in December 2020. At the time, the pledge was recorded at the present value ($27,232), discounted at 5 percent. Earnings of the endowment (interest and investment gains) are derived from investment in AAA-rated corporate bonds and are restricted for the payment of scholarships. At the end of 2019, the organization had the following account balances:

Account:	**Debits**	**Credits**
Cash	$ 22,900	
Interest receivable	700	
Investment in bonds	120,000	
Pledges receivable	27,232	
Supplies inventory	400	
Scholarships payable		$ 5,000
Net assets with donor restrictions—endowment		147,232
Net assets with donor restrictions—scholarships		2,600
Net assets without donor restrictions		16,400
Totals	$171,232	$171,232

The following took place during 2020:

1. The Educational Foundation has no employees. Administrative costs are limited to supplies, postage, and photocopying. Postage and photo copying expenses (paid in cash) totaled \$1,980 for the year. The Foundation purchased supplies of \$1,900 on account and made payments of \$1,700. Unused supplies at year-end totaled \$510.
2. Unrestricted donations received totaled \$9,600.
3. Interest received on the bonds totaled \$6,800, which included amounts receivable at the end of 2019. Accrued interest receivable at December 31, 2020, totaled \$600.
4. The fair value of the bonds at year-end was determined to be \$123,400. Income, including increases in the value of endowment investments, may be used for scholarships in the year earned.
5. The donor who established the permanent endowment made the scheduled payment of \$10,000 at the end of 2020. (*Hint:* First record the increase in the present value of the pledge and then record the receipt of the \$10,000.)
6. New scholarships were awarded in the amount of \$17,000. Payments of scholarships (including those amounts accrued at the end of the previous year) totaled \$19,500 during the year. Consistent with FASB standards, scholarships are assumed to be awarded first from resources provided from restricted revenues. (*Hint:* Add beginning net assets for scholarships to endowment earnings to determine the amount to reclassify from donor restricted net assets.)

Using the information above and the Excel template provided

a. Prepare journal entries and post entries to the T-accounts.

b. Prepare closing entries.

c. Prepare a Statement of Activities, Statement of Financial Position, and Statement of Cash Flows for the year ending December 31, 2020.

Chapter Eleven

College and University Accounting

Education is "the guardian genius of our democracy." Nothing really means more to our future, not our military defenses, not our missiles or our bombers, not our production economy, not even our democratic system of government. For all of these are worthless if we lack the brain power to support and sustain them. Lyndon Johnson, 36th president. In 1965 Johnson signed the Higher Education Act that created Pell Grants and a national student loan program.

Students often approached me about state-paid tuition while I was out campaigning. After I explain to them that if the state pays their tuition now, they will pay higher taxes to pay other people's tuition for the rest of their lives, most of them ended up agreeing with me. Jesse "The Body" Ventura, former professional wrestler and 38th governor of Minnesota. He was the first and only member of the Reform Party to win a major government office.

Learning Objectives

- Apply the accrual basis of accounting in the recording of typical transactions for public and private not-for-profit colleges and universities
- Prepare the financial statements for public and private not-for-profit colleges and universities
- Identify the various types of split-interest agreements and describe accounting practices for each.

Miami University in Oxford, Ohio, and the University of Miami in Coral Gables, Florida, share many things in common beyond a similarity in name. Students from both live in residence halls, attend classes, and study in the libraries. Faculty conduct research and publish in their fields, and alumni attend football games and proudly display diplomas on their office walls. However, the two universities differ in an important way that not only affects their operations but also has accounting implications.

Miami University is a public university, created by a land grant (passed by Congress and signed by then President George Washington) and operated within and by the state of Ohio. In contrast, the University of Miami was created when a private citizen donated 160 acres of land and $5 million for the creation of a university in Coral Gables. The University of Miami operates as a private not-for-profit and is governed by a board of trustees.

Every state in the United States has at least one public university. Many well-known state universities came about as a result of an 1862 act granting federal lands to states that agreed to create universities specifically offering education in agricultural and mechanical studies. Other public universities were originally chartered by state legislatures as "normal schools." Normal schools were established to train high school graduates as teachers. One purpose of these schools was to promote teaching "norms" (or standards), from which they derived their name.

About one in five U.S. college students attend private colleges and universities. Many are associated with religious organizations (e.g., University of Notre Dame, Liberty University) and are necessarily private. Others are nonsectarian, such as New York University, the University of Chicago, and Tuskegee University.

The distinguishing characteristic of public colleges is they receive substantial funding from their state government in the form of state appropriations. Private colleges do not receive state subsidies and must support themselves through tuition, donations, and other income. This is why the tuition of private colleges is generally higher than public. Additionally, state officials are reluctant to subsidize out-of-state students. Since their families did not contribute to the state's tax resources, these students are charged higher tuition than in-state students. In contrast, there is no reason for private colleges to make a distinction between in-state and out-of-state students. Some of the funding advantage of public education is disappearing. In recent years, budget pressures have caused state legislatures to curtail per-student appropriations to state colleges. Like private colleges, public colleges are increasingly dependent on tuition, donations, and other sources of income.

OVERVIEW OF COLLEGE AND UNIVERSITY ACCOUNTING

Public colleges and universities follow accounting standards established by the GASB while private colleges (like other not-for-profits) follow standards established by the FASB. At one time, this distinction made a significant difference because public colleges used multiple funds, similar to general purpose governments. Now most public colleges and universities report as special purpose governments engaged in business-type activities. They may appear as discretely presented component units of the state government. Their financial reports closely follow those of enterprise funds, measuring events using the accrual basis of accounting and the economic resources measurement focus. The result is that both public and private institutions measure and report most transactions in a similar manner.

There is a third type of higher education institution, for-profit colleges (sometimes called proprietary schools). The University of Phoenix, DeVry University, and Institute of Culinary Education are among the largest with multiple campuses across the U.S. These investor-owned colleges follow FASB standards for commercial organizations. In keeping with the purpose of this textbook, proprietary schools are only briefly mentioned. This chapter demonstrates the accounting and reporting for public and private not-for-profit colleges and universities. The emphasis will be on recording transactions unique to higher education and providing a comparison between the two types of institutions.

Financial Statements

Illustration 11-1 summarizes the authoritative standards-setting board and required financial statements for the three types of colleges and universities. The most apparent difference in the financial statements between the varying institutional forms appears in the equity section of the balance sheet. The varying equity account titles are also summarized in the illustration.

Among the more obvious differences in the financial report is the absence of a required MD&A for private institutions. In 2014 the FASB considered and dropped a research project to require not-for-profits to include a management discussion and analysis. Nevertheless, many such organizations choose to voluntarily include this in their financial statements.

Revenue and Expense Classification

In addition to standards issued by GASB and FASB, further reporting guidance is provided by the **National Association of College and University Business Officers (NACUBO),** an industry group composed of university financial vice presidents, comptrollers, and other finance officers. Both public and private sector institutions follow guidelines issued by NACUBO. The association publishes its recommendations in the *Financial Accounting and Reporting Manual for Higher Education.*

The manual does not supersede GASB or FASB standards but provides guidance on issues not specifically addressed by either board. For example, colleges often issue tuition discounts and other forms of financial aid, such as scholarships. The issue is whether these are expenses or reductions of revenue. NACUBO advises that scholarships (including athletic scholarships) that do not require service to the college or university are to be treated as reductions in revenue. This is normally accomplished through contra-revenue accounts. On the other hand, fees waived by the institution in return for services provided by work-study and graduate student assistantships are shown as expenses, and tuition and fee revenue is reported at the gross amount.

GASB's enterprise fund standards and FASB's not-for-profit standards are written for broad categories of entities, not just higher education. Accordingly, considerable latitude is permitted in the presentation of financial statement elements. To promote greater comparability across institutions of higher education, NACUBO

ILLUSTRATION 11-1 **College and University Reporting—Institutional Forms**

Type of Entity	Authoritative Standards	Components of Financial Report	"Residual Equity" Section of Statement of Net Position (GASB) or Statement of Financial Position (FASB)
Public Colleges and Universities*	GASB	MD&A Statement of Net Position Statement of Revenues, Expenses, and Changes in Fund Net Position Statement of Cash Flows Notes to the Financial Statements RSI Other Than MD&A	Net Investment in Capital Assets Restricted Net Position Unrestricted Net Position
Private, Not-for-Profit Colleges and Universities	FASB	Statement of Financial Position/Balance Sheet Statement of Activities Statement of Cash Flows Notes to the Financial Statements	Net Assets without Donor Restrictions Net Assets <u>with</u> Donor Restrictions
Investor-Owned Colleges and Universities—"Proprietary Schools"	FASB	Statement of Financial Position/Balance Sheet Income Statement Statement of Changes in Owners' Equity Statement of Cash Flows Notes to the Financial Statements	Paid-in Capital Retained Earnings

*Typically these are special-purpose entities engaged in business-type activities.

provides recommendations on the format of financial statements. For example, NACUBO recommends the following functional categories for expenses:

- Educational and General, with subcategories for instruction, research, public service, academic support, student services, institutional support, and fellowships.
  - Academic support includes expenses incurred to facilitate instruction, research, and public service (e.g., libraries, computer labs).
  - Institutional support includes expenses associated with central management, planning, and administration.
- Auxiliary Enterprises (e.g., residence halls, dining services, and bookstores).
- Hospitals.
- Independent Operations (generally limited to funded research and development centers).

This presentation may be done on the face of the financial statements or in the notes. NACUBO also has recommendations on the classification of revenues. Revenue items are reported as operating or nonoperating, per Illustration 11-2:

ILLUSTRATION 11-2 **Classification of Revenues**

Operating Revenues	Nonoperating Revenues
Tuition and Fees	Investment Income
Grants and Contracts:	Gifts
– Federal	State Appropriations (public)
– State	Pell Grant Revenue (public)
Auxiliary Enterprises	Time-Restricted Contributions (private)
	Net Assets Released from Restriction (private)

As the illustration indicates, there is considerable agreement between public and private institutions in the reporting of operating revenues. Differences exist, however, in what appears as nonoperating revenues. Public institutions commonly receive state appropriations and private do not, so this is not so much a difference in accounting as a difference in the nature of funding sources. In contrast, the other differences reflect differences in how GASB and FASB treat similar items.

The federal Pell Grant program assists students from lower income families who are attending college. The college first applies the grant money toward a student's tuition and fees. If any funds remain, they are applied to room and board, books, and other expenses. Public institutions treat Pell receipts as nonexchange revenue (GASB *Codification* Sec. N50.104) upon receipt of the funds. Private institutions treat these as resources held for the student in an agency relationship (i.e., offsetting asset and liability).

FASB standards recognize contributions with donor restrictions upon receipt of an unconditional pledge. Since all expenses are reported in the *without donor restrictions* category under FASB guidelines, a reclassification between the two net asset categories is necessary once qualifying expenditures have been made. Such reclassifications do not exist for public institutions.

GASB also differs in the treatment of contributions restricted to future periods (**time requirements**). Time restrictions are viewed as an eligibility requirement (GASB *Codification* Sec. N50.117), and time-restricted contributions are not recognized as revenue until the time period has commenced. Since funds cannot be expended until received, many pledges of support entail "implied time restrictions." Consequently, public universities generally do not recognize pledged donations until received, even if there is no restriction on the use of the funds. For similar reasons, pledges for endowments are not recognized as revenue by public institutions until received.

Finally, GASB has no provision for recognizing contributed services. Although not typically a significant source of support in higher education, contributed services meeting the criteria for recognition under FASB standards would be recognized as revenue by private institutions.

ILLUSTRATIVE CASE—COMPARISON OF PUBLIC AND PRIVATE COLLEGES

This section provides comparative examples of accounting for representative transactions for a pair of small colleges. Mountain State College of Design is a public college for fine arts. St. Charles Seminary is a private not-for-profit college preparing graduates for careers in ministry. Both colleges have fiscal years that run from July 1 to June 30 and began the 2019/2020 academic year with the following asset and liability balances:

Beginning Asset and Liability Balances
July 1, 2019

	Debits	Credits
Cash	$ 100,000	
Student accounts receivable	25,000	
Receivables: other	–	
Investments—endowment	800,000	
Restricted cash	400,000	
Capital assets	1,250,000	
Accumulated depreciation		$550,000
Accounts payable and accrued liabilities		17,000
Deferred revenues		12,000
(Capital) bonds payable		400,000

Both colleges have endowment investments of $800,000 and $400,000 of restricted cash designated by a donor for a new library. The outstanding bonds were issued in the past to construct a dormitory. Since the College of Design is a public institution and the Seminary is private, the two colleges differ in their residual equity accounts. The June 30, 2019, balances for these accounts are

Beginning Residual Equity Balances July 1, 2019	
Mountain State College of Design: A Public Institution	
Net investment in capital assets	$ 300,000
Restricted net position	1,200,000
Unrestricted net position	96,000
St. Charles Seminary: A Private Institution	
Net assets with donor restrictions—permanent endowment	$800,000
Net assets with donor restrictions—capital acquisitions	400,000
Net assets without donor restrictions	396,000

Above and throughout the remainder of this illustrative case, items relating to the public College of Design will appear in shaded regions of the illustrations and those related to the private not-for-profit Seminary will appear in unshaded regions. Journal entries for the two colleges for the 2019/2020 academic year are illustrated in the following section.

Although not required by FASB standards, the Seminary chooses to separately display net assets restricted for permanent endowment and capital additions. In most cases, separate accounts will be maintained for each source of donor restricted funds.

Illustrative Case—Journal Entries

The College of Design received its state appropriations of $4,500,000 and undesignated gifts of support of $80,000.

Public Institutions	Debits	Credits
1. Cash	4,580,000	
Nonoperating Revenue—State Appropriations		4,500,000
Nonoperating Revenue—Gifts		80,000

Students were billed for tuition and fees of $3,500,000 and room and board of $2,100,000. A total of $3,900,000 was received on student accounts throughout the year.

Public Institutions	Debits	Credits
2. Student Accounts Receivable	5,600,000	
Operating Revenue—Tuition and Fees		3,500,000
Operating Revenue—Auxiliary Enterprises		2,100,000
Cash	3,900,000	
Student Accounts Receivable		3,900,000

Throughout the remainder of this illustration, we will present identical transactions and demonstrate concurrently the necessary journal entries for both the College of Design and the Seminary. However, this would not be appropriate for these first two events since private institutions typically do not receive state appropriations but must rely upon other sources of funds, including higher tuition and donor support.

Assume the Seminary received $580,000 of undesignated gifts of support.

Private Institutions	Debits	Credits
1. Cash	580,000	
Nonoperating Revenue—Contributions without Donor Restrictions		580,000

Students were billed for tuition and fees of $7,500,000 and room and board of $2,100,000. A total of $7,900,000 was received on student accounts throughout the year.

Private Institutions	Debits	Credits
2. Student Accounts Receivable	9,600,000	
Operating Revenue—Tuition and Fees		7,500,000
Operating Revenue—Auxiliary Enterprises		2,100,000
Cash	7,900,000	
Student Accounts Receivable		7,900,000

Summer school terms run from June 1 to July 15. The deferred revenue appearing on the beginning of the year trial balance represents the portion (one-third) of summer school tuition (an exchange transaction) received in the previous academic year, which relates to classes held in the current year. The following entry reverses the deferral so the revenue may now be recognized in the current year.

Public Institutions	Debits	Credits
3. Deferred Revenues	12,000	
Operating Revenue—Tuition and Fees		12,000
Private Institutions		
Deferred Revenues	12,000	
Operating Revenue—Tuition and Fees		12,000

Students in both public and private colleges are eligible for financial assistance through Pell Grants. Assume the colleges received $1,350,000 of Pell Grants during the academic year. These amounts were immediately applied to student accounts receivable for amounts due for tuition and fees.

Tuition assistance is an area of difference for public and private institutions. Public institutions treat Pell Grant receipts as a nonexchange revenue (GASB *Codification* Sec. N50.104) upon meeting eligibility requirements. Eligibility is assumed to have occurred when a student qualifies for the grant and the institution receives the cash. However, if some adjustment is not made, the college will have recorded revenue twice, once when they billed the student and again upon receipt of the grant. This is addressed at the time the grant is applied to individual students' accounts. *Student financial aid* is a contra-revenue account and is deducted from *student tuition and fee revenue* on the face of the Statement of Revenues, Expenses, and Changes in Fund Net Position. The result of the two entries is $1,350,000 of revenue is moved from the operating portion of this statement to the nonoperating.

In contrast, private institutions treat Pell Grants as resources held for the student in an agency relationship. As such, the college records an offsetting asset (cash) and liability (*due to student accounts*) when the grant is received. The liability is then reduced when the grant is applied to students' accounts (or paid to the student).

Public Institutions	Debits	Credits
4. Cash	1,350,000	
Nonoperating Revenue—Pell Grants		1,350,000
Student Financial Aid (operating contra-revenue)	1,350,000	
Student Accounts Receivable		1,350,000
Private Institutions		
Cash	1,350,000	
Due to Student Accounts (liability)		1,350,000
Due to Student Accounts (liability)	1,350,000	
Student Accounts Receivable		1,350,000

Students are awarded academic scholarships of $270,000 that are applied to their accounts. Additionally, several students are hired by the college to do clerical work in the college's administrative function (institutional support). As part of their compensation for working, tuition in the amount of $50,000 is waived. Under NACUBO guidelines, scholarships that do not require service to the college or university are to be treated as reductions in revenue. This is normally accomplished through contra-revenue accounts. On the other hand, tuition and fees waived by the institution in return for services provided by work-study and student assistants are shown as expenses.

Public Institutions	Debits	Credits
5. Institutional Support Expense	50,000	
Student Financial Aid (operating contra-revenue)	270,000	
Student Accounts Receivable		320,000
Private Institutions		
Institutional Support Expense	50,000	
Student Financial Aid (operating contra-revenue)	270,000	
Student Accounts Receivable		320,000

Expenses totaling $9,675,000 for salaries, supplies, utilities, and other items to be paid in cash are approved for payment through accounts payable. A total of $9,640,000 of outstanding accounts payable were paid by year-end. Although both GASB and FASB permit classification by natural category, the functional categories appearing below are recommended by NACUBO (amounts are assumed).

Public Institutions	Debits	Credits
6. Instruction Expense	3,900,000	
Research Expense	1,500,000	
Student Services Expense	1,400,000	
Academic Support Expense	1,200,000	
Auxiliary Enterprise Expense	875,000	
Institutional Support Expense	800,000	
Accounts Payable and Accrued Liabilities		9,675,000
Accounts Payable and Accrued Liabilities	9,640,000	
Cash		9,640,000
Private Institutions		
Instruction Expense	3,900,000	
Research Expense	1,500,000	
Student Services Expense	1,400,000	
Academic Support Expense	1,200,000	
Auxiliary Enterprise Expense	875,000	
Institutional Support Expense	800,000	
Accounts Payable and Accrued Liabilities		9,675,000
Accounts Payable and Accrued Liabilities	9,640,000	
Cash		9,640,000

Depreciation expense of $310,000 is recorded on buildings and equipment. The expense is allocated to functional areas on the basis of actual equipment in use and square footage for buildings (amounts assumed).

Public Institutions	Debits	Credits
7. Instruction Expense	80,000	
Research Expense	40,000	
Student Services Expense	20,000	
Academic Support Expense	30,000	
Auxiliary Enterprise Expense	75,000	
Institutional Support Expense	65,000	
Accumulated Depreciation		310,000
Private Institutions		
Instruction Expense	80,000	
Research Expense	40,000	
Student Services Expense	20,000	
Academic Support Expense	30,000	
Auxiliary Enterprise Expense	75,000	
Institutional Support Expense	65,000	
Accumulated Depreciation		310,000

Included in the expenses recorded in the previous transactions are $450,000 incurred under federal and state government grants. Bills were sent to the granting agencies and $412,000 was received by the end of the year.

Under both GASB and FASB standards, reimbursement-type grants are recorded as revenue when qualifying expenses have been incurred. In the case of GASB, eligibility requirements are deemed to have been met only after expenses have been incurred. Similarly under FASB standards, the grant is considered conditional and not recognized as revenue until the condition is satisfied through qualifying expenses.

Public Institutions	Debits	Credits
8. Receivable from Federal and State Governments	450,000	
Operating Revenue—Federal and State Grants		450,000
Cash	412,000	
Receivable from Federal and State Governments		412,000
Private Institutions		
Receivable from Federal and State Governments	450,000	
Operating Revenue—Federal and State Grants		450,000
Cash	412,000	
Receivable from Federal and State Governments		412,000

During the year, $200,000 of cash and pledges for an additional $800,000 were received as a result of fundraising campaigns to enhance the college's endowment. By the terms of the agreement, such contributions are to be invested and remain permanently in the endowment. The $200,000 was immediately used to purchase additional investments.

GASB standards do not recognize pledges to permanent endowments as revenue until received. The reason is that eligibility requirements (particularly the requirement that the funds be permanently invested) cannot be met until the funds have been received. In contrast, FASB standards require the recognition of unconditional pledges of support as revenue when the pledge is received.

Public Institutions	Debits	Credits
9. Restricted Cash	200,000	
Other Revenues—Additions to Permanent Endowment		200,000
Endowment Investments	200,000	
Restricted Cash		200,000
Private Institutions		
Restricted Cash	200,000	
Pledges Receivable	800,000	
Contribution Revenue—with Donor Restrictions (Permanent endowment)		1,000,000
Endowment Investments	200,000	
Restricted Cash		200,000

The bonds outstanding at July 1, 2019, call for annual payments of principal of $50,000. This was paid along with interest for the year of $20,000. Public colleges commonly report interest as a nonoperating expense. FASB standards, however, require all expenses to be reported as without donor restrictions and within the functional expense categories. Since the loan was used to build a dormitory, interest is reported as part of auxiliary enterprise expenses.

Public Institutions	Debits	Credits
10. Bonds Payable	50,000	
Nonoperating—Interest Expense	20,000	
Cash		70,000
Private Institutions		
Bonds Payable	50,000	
Auxiliary Enterprise Expense	20,000	
Cash		70,000

The $400,000 restricted cash balance at the beginning of the year was donated for a new library. During the year, an additional $425,000 donation was received. These funds, together with an additional $375,000 of unrestricted cash, were used to purchase land and a building adjacent to the campus that could be remodeled into the library.

Note that the private institution has an additional journal entry. Because the donated funds are restricted for purchase of land and buildings, FASB standards require that they be reported as *with* donor restrictions. When the college uses the funds as designated, the resources are released from restriction.

Public Institutions	Debits	Credits
11. Restricted Cash	425,000	
Other Revenue—Capital Grants and Gifts		425,000
Capital Assets	1,200,000	
Restricted Cash		825,000
Cash		375,000
Private Institutions		
Restricted Cash	425,000	
Contribution Revenue—with Donor Restrictions (Capital additions)		425,000
Land, Buildings, and Equipment	1,200,000	
Restricted Cash		825,000
Cash		375,000
Reclassification from Net Assets with Donor Restrictions—for satisfaction of capital asset restrictions	825,000	
Reclassification to Net Assets without Donor Restrictions—for satisfaction of capital asset restrictions		825,000

By terms of the endowment agreement, interest and dividends received on the investments are available for unrestricted purposes. Gains or losses from changes in the fair value of the investments, however, are not distributed but remain in the endowment. During the year, $32,000 of interest and dividends were received on endowment investments. At year-end, the fair value of the investments had increased by $2,000.

Public Institutions	**Debits**	**Credits**
12. Cash	32,000	
Nonoperating—Investment Income		32,000
Endowment Investments	2,000	
Nonoperating—Additions to Permanent Endowment		2,000
Private Institutions		
Cash	32,000	
Investment Income—without Donor Restrictions		32,000
Endowment Investments	2,000	
Investment Income—with Donor Restrictions (Permanent endowment)		2,000

Included in the tuition and fees recorded earlier (Item 2) are amounts for the summer school term that runs from June 1 to July 15, 2020. Each year, a portion of the amount received as summer school tuition is deferred to the next academic year. The amount to be deferred is determined to be $15,000.

Public Institutions	**Debits**	**Credits**
13. Operating Revenue—Tuition and Fees	15,000	
Deferred Revenues		15,000
Private Institutions		
Operating Revenue—Tuition and Fees	15,000	
Deferred Revenues		15,000

The bonds call for annual principal payments of $50,000. The amount due in the following year is reclassified as a current liability.

Public Institutions	**Debits**	**Credits**
14. Bonds Payable (long-term)	50,000	
Bonds Payable (current)		50,000
Private Institutions		
Bonds Payable (long-term)	50,000	
Bonds Payable (current)		50,000

Illustrative Case—Closing Entries

Closing entries are prepared at the end of the year. Revenues and expenses of public institutions are closed to *net position.*

Public Institutions	Debits	Credits
Operating Revenue—Tuition and Fees	3,497,000	
Operating Revenue—Auxiliary Enterprises	2,100,000	
Operating Revenue—Federal and State Grants	450,000	
Nonoperating Revenue—State Appropriations	4,500,000	
Nonoperating Revenue—Gifts	80,000	
Nonoperating Revenue—Pell Grants	1,350,000	
Nonoperating—Additions to Permanent Endowment	202,000	
Nonoperating—Capital Grants and Gifts	425,000	
Nonoperating—Investment Income	32,000	
Student Financial Aid (contra-revenue)		1,620,000
Instruction Expense		3,980,000
Research Expense		1,540,000
Student Services Expense		1,420,000
Academic Support Expense		1,230,000
Auxiliary Enterprise Expense		950,000
Institutional Support Expense		915,000
Nonoperating—Interest Expense		20,000
Net Position		961,000

Following this entry, the balance of Net Position is $2,557,000 ($1,596,000 beginning balance + $961,000) and is comprised of the following:

	Net Investment in Capital Assets	Restricted Net Assets	Unrestricted	Total
Capital Assets	$2,450,000			$2,450,000
Accumulated Depreciation	(860,000)			(860,000)
Bonds Payable	(350,000)			(350,000)
Restricted Cash		—		
Endowment Investments		1,002,000		1,002,000
Plug			315,000	315,000
	$1,240,000	1,002,000	315,000	2,557,000

Revenues and expenses of private institutions are closed to *net assets.* Typically separate closing entries are prepared for both of the net asset categories. Expenses are always reported as without restrictions. It is assumed here that all operating revenues are unrestricted. Finally, recall that reclassifications of net assets released from restriction must also be included in both the with and without donor restrictions closing entries.

Private Institutions—Net Assets without Donor Restrictions	Debits	Credits
Operating Revenue—Tuition and Fees	7,497,000	
Operating Revenue—Auxiliary Enterprises	2,100,000	
Operating Revenue—Federal and State Grants	450,000	
Nonoperating Revenue—without Donor Restrictions Contributions	580,000	
Nonoperating—Investment Income	32,000	
Reclassification to Net Assets without Donor Restrictions	825,000	
Student Financial Aid (contra-revenue)		270,000
Instruction Expense		3,980,000
Research Expense		1,540,000
Student Services Expense		1,420,000
Academic Support Expense		1,230,000
Auxiliary Enterprise Expense		970,000
Institutional Support Expense		915,000
Net Assets without Donor Restrictions		1,159,000

Private Institutions—Net Assets with Donor Restrictions	Debits	Credits
Restricted for Capital Additions		
Contribution Revenue—with Donor Restrictions (Capital additions)	425,000	
Net Assets with Donor Restrictions—Capital Additions	400,000	
Reclassification from Net Assets with Donor Restrictions		825,000
Restricted for Permanent Endowment		
Contribution Revenue—with Donor Restrictions—Permanent Endowment	1,000,000	
Investment Income—with Donor Restrictions—Permanent Endowment	2,000	
Net Assets with Donor Restrictions—Permanent Endowment		1,002,000

Illustrative Case—Financial Statements

Illustration 11-3 presents the Statement of Revenues, Expenses, and Changes in Fund Net Position for the College of Design and Illustration 11-4 presents the Statement of Activity for the Seminary. Generally speaking, public and private colleges record transactions and events similarly and differences between these two statements are mainly differences of presentation. For example, the issue of whether interest is shown separately or allocated to a functional activity.

However, this is not always the case. Notice the change in net position reported by the College of Design is $961,000 while the change in net assets reported by the Seminary is $1,761,000. This difference is attributable to inconsistencies in revenue recognition criteria between the two sets of accounting standards. In this case the $800,000 difference is caused by the fact that FASB standards require the recording of unconditional pledges of support (Item #9) while GASB standards do

ILLUSTRATION 11-3 **Public Institution Activity Statement**

MOUNTAIN STATE COLLEGE OF DESIGN Statement of Revenues, Expenses, and Changes in Fund Net Position For the year ended June 30, 2020	
Operating revenues:	
Student tuition and fees	$ 3,497,000
Less student financial aid	(1,620,000)
Net student tuition and fees	1,877,000
Federal and state grants	450,000
Auxiliary enterprises	2,100,000
Total operating revenues	4,427,000
Operating expenses:	
Instruction	3,980,000
Research	1,540,000
Student services	1,420,000
Academic support	1,230,000
Institutional support	915,000
Auxiliary enterprises	950,000
Total operating expenses	10,035,000
Operating income (loss)	(5,608,000)
Nonoperating revenues (expenses):	
State appropriations	4,500,000
Pell Grants	1,350,000
Gifts	80,000
Investment income	32,000
Interest on capital related debt	(20,000)
Net nonoperating revenues	5,942,000
Income before other revenues	334,000
Other revenues:	
Capital grants and gifts	425,000
Additions to permanent endowments	202,000
Increase in net position	961,000
Net position:	
Net position—beginning of year	1,596,000
Net position—end of year	$2,557,000

not permit the recording of time-restricted revenues. Recall GASB's time period eligibility requirement had not been satisfied with respect to pledges for the permanent endowment.

Note also the difference in operating income between the two statements. The College of Design reports an operating loss of $5,608,000 while the Seminary reports a much smaller loss of $278,000. This difference is not related to pledges

ILLUSTRATION 11-4 Private Institution Activity Statement

ST. CHARLES SEMINARY
Statement of Activity
For the year ended June 30, 2020

	Net Assets without Donor Restrictions	Net Assets with Donor Restrictions: Capital Additions	Net Assets with Donor Restrictions: Permanent Endowment	Total
Operating revenues:				
Student tuition and fees	$ 7,497,000			$ 7,497,000
Less student financial aid	(270,000)			(270,000)
Net student tuition and fees	7,227,000			7,227,000
Federal and state grants	450,000			450,000
Auxiliary enterprises	2,100,000			2,100,000
Total operating revenues	9,777,000			9,777,000
Expenses:				
Program expenses:				
Instruction	3,980,000			3,980,000
Research	1,540,000			1,540,000
Student services	1,420,000			1,420,000
Academic support	1,230,000			1,230,000
Auxiliary enterprises	970,000			970,000
Supporting expenses:				
Institutional support	915,000			915,000
Total expenses	10,055,000			10,055,000
Operating income (loss)	(278,000)			(278,000)
Nonoperating revenues:				
Contributions	580,000	425,000	1,000,000	2,005,000
Investment income	32,000		2,000	34,000
Net assets released from restriction	825,000	(825,000)		—
Change in net assets from nonoperating activities	1,437,000	(400,000)	1,002,000	2,039,000
Total change in net assets	1,159,000	(400,000)	1,002,000	1,761,000
Net assets—beginning of year	396,000	400,000	800,000	1,596,000
Net assets—end of year	$ 1,555,000	—	1,802,000	$ 3,357,000

and revenue recognition. Rather it is largely attributable to the requirement that state appropriations be reported as nonoperating revenue by public institutions. Further, public institutions report Pell Grants as nonoperating revenues with an offsetting reduction in operating (tuition and fees) revenues. These requirements are controversial among public colleges, almost all of which report large operating losses, even though they may be profitable overall.

Illustrations 11-5 and 11-6 present the balance sheets for the two colleges. The $800,000 pledge receivable recognized by the Seminary explains the difference in total assets between the two statements. There are fewer differences in presentation

ILLUSTRATION 11-5 **Public Institution Balance Sheet**

MOUNTAIN STATE COLLEGE OF DESIGN Statement of Net Position June 30, 2020	
Assets:	
Current assets:	
Cash	$ 289,000
Student accounts receivable	55,000
Receivable from federal and state governments	38,000
Total current assets	382,000
Noncurrent assets:	
Endowment investments	1,002,000
Capital assets, net of accumulated depreciation	1,590,000
Total noncurrent assets	2,592,000
Total assets	$2,974,000
Liabilities:	
Current liabilities:	
Accounts payable and accrued liabilities	52,000
Deferred revenue	15,000
Bonds payable—current portion	50,000
Total current liabilities	117,000
Noncurrent liabilities:	
Bonds payable	300,000
Total noncurrent liabilities	300,000
Net Position:	
Net investment in capital assets	1,240,000
Restricted	1,002,000
Unrestricted	315,000
Total net position	$2,557,000

between these two statements than was the case with the activity statements. Except for the residual equity account titles and balances, these two statements are very similar in appearance.

Illustrations 11-7 and 11-8 present the statements of cash flows for the two colleges. GASB requires the direct method and the College of Design statement is presented in that format. FASB permits a choice and the Seminary, like most organizations, chose the indirect method. Further observe that the GASB format statement has four sections instead of three and differences exist in the definition of each section. The result is that individual cash flows appear in different sections of the Statement of Cash Flows depending upon whether the college is following GASB or FASB guidelines (see, for example, purchases of fixed assets in the examples presented).

Note also in Illustration 11-7 that state appropriations and Pell Grants are reported as noncapital-related financing activities, interest expense is reported among financing activities, and investment income is reported as an investing activity.

ILLUSTRATION 11-6 **Private Institution Balance Sheet**

ST. CHARLES SEMINARY Statement of Financial Position June 30, 2020	
Assets:	
Current Assets:	
Cash	$ 289,000
Student Accounts Receivable	55,000
Receivable from Federal and State Governments	38,000
Pledges Receivable	800,000
Total Current Assets	1,182,000
Noncurrent Assets:	
Endowment Investments	1,002,000
Land, Buildings and Equipment, Net of Accumulated Depreciation	1,590,000
Total Noncurrent Assets	2,592,000
Total Assets	$3,774,000
Liabilities:	
Current Liabilities:	
Accounts Payable and Accrued Liabilities	$ 52,000
Deferred Revenue	15,000
Bonds Payable—Current Portion	50,000
Total Current Liabilities	117,000
Noncurrent Liabilities:	
Bonds Payable	300,000
Total Noncurrent Liabilities	300,000
Total Liabilities	417,000
Net Assets:	
Net Assets with Donor Restrictions	
Permanent Endowment	1,802,000
Capital Additions	—
Net Assets without Donor Restrictions	1,555,000
Total Net Assets	$3,357,000

SPLIT-INTEREST AGREEMENTS

Both public and private colleges encourage donors to consider giving to the institution in their estate planning. This may include creating a trust agreement. When these trusts provide that the college share resources with another beneficiary, they are termed **split-interest agreements.** There are two basic types of agreements. The first is a "lead trust" in which the charity receives income during the life of the trust (commonly the life of the donor). When the donor dies and the trust terminates, the resources of the trust go to the heirs. The other type is a "remainder trust" in which the roles are reversed and the college receives the resources upon termination of the trust.

ILLUSTRATION 11-7 Public Institution Statement of Cash Flows

MOUNTAIN STATE COLLEGE OF DESIGN Statement of Cash Flows For the year ended June 30, 2020	
Cash Flows from Operating Activities	
Cash Received from Students	$ 3,900,000
Cash Received from Federal and State Grants	412,000
Cash Paid for Operating Expenses	(9,640,000)
Net Cash Provided (Used) by Operating Activities	(5,328,000)
Cash Flows from Noncapital Financing Activities	
Cash Received from State Appropriations	4,500,000
Cash Received from Noncapital Grants—Student Financial Aid	1,350,000
Contributions other than for endowments	80,000
Net Cash Provided by Noncapital Financing Activities	5,930,000
Cash Flows from Capital Related Financing Activities	
Acquisition of Capital Assets	(1,200,000)
Principal Paid on Long-term Debt	(50,000)
Interest Paid on Long-term Debt	(20,000)
Cash Received—Capital Gifts	425,000
Net Cash Provided from Capital and Related Financing Activities	(845,000)
Cash Flows from Investing Activities	
Purchase of endowment investments	(200,000)
Cash Received for Endowments	200,000
Cash Received—Investment Income	32,000
Net Cash Provided from Investing Activities	32,000
Increase in Cash	(211,000)
Cash and Restricted Cash—Beginning of Year	500,000
Cash and Restricted Cash—End of Year	$ 289,000
Reconciliation of Operating Income (Loss) to Net Cash Provided by Operating Activities	
Operating Income (Loss)	$(5,608,000)
Depreciation Expense	310,000
Increase in Student Accounts Receivable	(30,000)
Increase in Receivable from Governments	(38,000)
Increase in Accounts Payable and Accrued Liabilities	35,000
Increase in Deferred Revenues	3,000
Net Cash Provided (Used) by Operating Activities	$(5,328,000)

ILLUSTRATION 11-8 **Private Institution Statement of Cash Flows**

ST. CHARLES SEMINARY Statement of Cash Flows For the year ended June 30, 2020	
Cash Flows from Operating Activities	
Change in Net Assets	$1,761,000
Depreciation Expense	310,000
Unrealized Gain on Investments	(2,000)
Increase in Student Accounts Receivable	(30,000)
Increase in Receivable from Governments	(38,000)
Increase in Pledges Receivable	(800,000)
Increase in Accounts Payable and Accrued Liabilities	35,000
Increase in Deferred Revenues	3,000
Contributions Restricted to Purchase of Fixed Assets	(425,000)
Contributions to Permanent Endowments	(200,000)
Net Cash Provided by Operating Activities	614,000
Cash Flows from Financing Activities	
Contributions Restricted to Purchase of Fixed Assets	425,000
Contributions to Permanent Endowments	200,000
Payment of Principal on Long-Term Debt	(50,000)
Net Cash Provided by Financing Activities	575,000
Cash Flows from Investing Activities	
Purchase of Endowment Investments	(200,000)
Purchases of Land, Building, and Equipment	(1,200,000)
Net Cash Used for Investing Activities	(1,400,000)
Increase in Cash	(211,000)
Cash and Restricted Cash—Beginning of Year	500,000
Cash and Restricted Cash—End of Year	$ 289,000

The AICPA's *Not-for-Profit Guide* provides guidance for the reporting of split-interest agreements by private sector not-for-profits. Recently the GASB issued guidance for governmental entities with split-interest agreements. Once again, the two sets of standards differ in the timing of the recognition of revenue. Split-interest agreements are categorized into five types: (1) charitable lead trusts, (2) perpetual trusts held by third parties, (3) charitable remainder trusts, (4) charitable gift annuities, and (5) pooled (life) income funds. Each of these is discussed in the following paragraphs.

A **charitable lead trust** is an arrangement whereby a donor establishes a trust in which a portion of the trust is distributed to a nonprofit organization for a certain term, after which the remaining resources are paid to a beneficiary. For example, a college receives cash from a donor under an irrevocable charitable lead trust agreement. Under the terms of the trust, the college invests the assets and receives a specified dollar amount each year for its use until the donor dies and the trust ceases to exist. Upon the death of the donor, the remaining assets in the trust revert to the donor's estate for distribution according to the donor's will.

When the trust is created and is irrevocable, the college records the assets of the trust at fair value. The college then determines the present value of the anticipated receipts that will be retained by the college. The difference between the trust assets and the present value of anticipated receipts is recognized as a liability (to the estate). The difference in the accounting between private and public sector colleges is in the recognition of revenue. Private sector colleges recognize (immediately) the present value of anticipated future receipts as contribution revenue. In contrast, public colleges record this present value as a deferred inflow and recognize income as it becomes available each year.

A **perpetual trust held by a third party** is not exactly a split-interest agreement but is accounted for in a similar fashion. Assume a person establishes a permanent trust at a bank with the income to go to a college in perpetuity. If the college is a private not-for-profit, the fair value of the assets contributed is recorded as an asset and as contribution revenue in the *with* donor restrictions net asset class. If the college is a public institution, the resources are recorded as an asset at fair value and a deferred inflow is recorded. In both cases, income received each year is recorded as revenue (unrestricted or restricted according to the terms of the trust agreement).

A **charitable remainder trust** is a trust established by a donor to ensure that a specified dollar amount or a specified percentage of the trust's fair market value is paid to a beneficiary, such as a surviving spouse or children. At the end of the term of the trust the college receives the trust assets. For example, a donor establishes a charitable remainder trust, with a college serving as trustee. Under the terms of the trust, the donor's spouse is to receive an annual distribution equal in value to 6 percent of the fair market value of the trust's assets each year until the spouse dies. At that time, the trust principal is paid to the college for unrestricted or restricted purposes or as an endowment.

The college should recognize the assets held in trust at fair values when received. Additionally, a liability to the donor's spouse should be recorded at the present value of the future payments to be distributed over the spouse's expected life. The difference between the asset and liability is recognized as contribution revenue if the college is a private not-for-profit and as a deferred inflow if the college is a public institution. In the case of the public college, the deferred inflow is recognized as revenue at the termination of the trust (i.e., the death of the surviving spouse).

A **charitable gift annuity** is the same as a charitable remainder trust except no formal trust agreement exists; normally a contract is signed. The accounting is the same as for a charitable remainder trust.

A **pooled (life) income fund** represents a situation in which the assets of several life income agreements are pooled together. A life income fund represents a situation in which the income is paid to a donor or a beneficiary during his or her lifetime. For example, a donor contributes assets to a college's pooled (life) income fund. The donor is assigned a specific number of units in the pool based on the proportion of the fair value of his contributions to the total fair value of fund. Until the donor's death, the donor receives the income earned on the donor's assigned units.

Upon the donor's death, the value of the resources represented by his assigned units reverts to the college.

In a pooled (life) income fund, the assets are recorded and entered into the pool based on the fair value. For private colleges, revenue is recognized immediately as the present value of the expected assets, which will revert to the college upon the death of the donor. The contribution would be classified among net assets *with* donor restrictions because of the implied time restriction. The difference between the fair value of the assets received and the revenue is recorded as deferred revenue, representing the amount of the discount for future interest. GASB standards do not specifically address pool income funds but the board indicated that may be done in a future implementation guide.

SUMMARY

Accounting for college and universities is complicated by the fact that there are three distinct types of entities, each of which follow different accounting standards. Private colleges (like other not-for-profits) follow standards established by the FASB, including those specifically for not-for-profit entities. Public colleges and universities follow accounting standards established by the GASB and commonly report as special purpose governments engaged in business-type activities. Their financial reports closely follow those of enterprise funds. Finally, investor-owned colleges follow FASB standards for commercial organizations.

Additional guidance is provided by the National Association of College and University Business Officers. The association publishes its recommendations in the *Financial Accounting and Reporting Manual for Higher Education.* The manual provides guidance on issues not specifically addressed by either board. For example, NACUBO advises that scholarships that do not require service to the college or university are to be treated as reductions in revenue while fees waived by the institution in return for services are reported as expenses.

Like other private not-for-profits, private colleges and universities report using accrual accounting. Similarly, public colleges and universities measure events using the accrual basis of accounting and the economic resources measurement focus. The result is both public and private institutions measure and report most transactions in a similar manner. Exceptions exist, especially in the area of time-restricted pledges of support. Private institutions recognize unconditional pledges of support as revenue, while public institutions delay revenue recognition until receipt of the funds.

Similar differences exist in the reporting of split-interest agreements. These are agreements that provide that the college share resources of a trust with another beneficiary. As with time-restricted pledges, private sector colleges and universities recognize revenue immediately upon execution of the trust. Public sector standards typically require deferral of revenues until the trust is terminated.

Questions and Exercises

11–1. Obtain the annual reports for a private not-for-profit and public college or university and answer the following questions:

a. Examine the two activity statements (revenues and expenses). What are the titles of these statements? Do they display income from operations? What items are reported as nonoperating? Which has financial aid grants as part of nonoperating revenue? Which entity has state appropriations?

b. Examine the two balance sheets. Are the statements in classified format? What are the titles of these statements? Examine the residual equity accounts and list the net position/net asset categories of each.

c. Examine the statements of cash flow. What are the major sections of each? What method is used for each to present cash flows from operating activities (direct or indirect)? Where are additions to plant and equipment reported for each? Where is cash received from investments reported?

11–2. For each of the following, identify (1) which accounting standards–setting body has primary authority, (2) the required financial statements, and (3) the account titles used in the equity section of the balance sheet or equivalent statement.

a. Public (government-owned) colleges and universities.

b. Private not-for-profit colleges and universities.

c. Investor-owned proprietary schools.

11–3. What is the role of the National Association of College and University Business Officers in providing guidance in the reporting of colleges and universities?

11–4. Distinguish between the accounting treatment of time-restricted pledges by private and public sector colleges and universities.

11–5. Define and outline the accounting required for each of the following types of agreements:

a. Charitable lead trusts.

b. Charitable remainder trusts.

c. Perpetual trust held by a third party.

11–6. The New City College reported deferred revenues of $335,000 as of July 1, 2019, the first day of its fiscal year. Record the following transactions related to student tuition and fees and related scholarship allowances for New City College for the year ended June 30, 2020.

1. The deferred revenues related to unearned revenues for the summer session, which ended in August.
2. During the fiscal year ended June 30, 2020, student tuition and fees were assessed in the amount of $12,000,000. Of that amount $9,650,000 was collected in cash. Also of that amount, $422,000 pertained to that portion of the summer session that took place after June 30, 2020.

3. Student scholarships, for which no services were required, amounted to $780,000. These scholarships were applied to student tuition bills at the beginning of each semester.
4. Student scholarships and fellowships for which services were required (graduate research assistantships) amounted to $872,000. These were applied to student tuition bills at the beginning of each semester.
5. The college incurred $200,000 of qualified expenditures under a cost-reimbursement grant from the Department of Agriculture.
6. By year-end, $160,000 had been received by the Department of Agriculture on the grant.

11–7. Eastern University had the following transactions at the beginning of its academic year:

1. Student tuition and fees were billed in the amount of $8,100,000. Of that amount $5,500,000 was collected in cash.
2. Pell Grants in the amount of $2,250,000 were received by the university.
3. The Pell Grants were applied to student accounts.
4. Student scholarships, for which no services were required, amounted to $450,000. These were applied to student tuition bills at the beginning of each semester.

Required:

Prepare journal entries to record the above transactions assuming:

a. Eastern University is a public university.

b. Eastern University is a private university.

11–8. Southeastern College began the year with endowment investments of $1,200,000 and $700,000 of restricted cash designated by a donor for capital additions.

1. During the year, an additional $950,000 donation was received for capital additions. These funds together with those contributed in the prior year were used to purchase 150 acres of land adjacent to the university.
2. An alum contributed $200,000 to the permanent endowment and pledged to provide an additional $400,000 early next year. The cash was immediately invested.
3. By terms of the endowment agreement, interest and dividends received on the investments are restricted for scholarships. Gains or losses from changes in the fair value of the investments, however, are not distributed but remain in the endowment. During the year, $48,000 of interest and dividend were received on endowment investments.
4. At year-end, the fair value of the investments had increased by $8,500.

Required:

Prepare journal entries to record the above transactions assuming:

a. Southeastern College is a public university.

b. Southeastern College is a private university.

Excel-Based Problems

11–9. The Great Lakes Maritime Institute is a public institution preparing cadets for careers in commercial shipping and includes instruction in piloting, navigation, maritime law, and other fields.

1. The Institute began the year with the following account balances:

Beginning Balances
July 1, 2019

	Debits	Credits
Cash	125,000	
Student Accounts Receivable	40,000	
Investments—Endowment	500,000	
Restricted Cash	250,000	
Capital Assets	1,100,000	
Accumulated Depreciation		350,000
Accounts Payable and Accrued Liabilities		4,000
Deferred Revenues		7,000
Net Investment in Capital Assets		650,000
Restricted Net Position		750,000
Unrestricted Net Position		254,000

2. The Institute received a state appropriation of $75,000 and unrestricted gifts of $10,000.
3. The deferred revenue appearing on the beginning of the year trial balance represents the portion of summer school tuition received in the previous academic year, which relates to classes held in the current year.
4. Students were billed for tuition and fees of $500,000 and room and board of $190,000. A total of $350,000 was received on student accounts throughout the year.
5. The Institute received $103,000 of Pell Grants during the academic year. These amounts were immediately applied to student accounts for amounts due for tuition and fees.
6. Students are awarded academic scholarships of $150,000, which are applied to their accounts. Additionally, several other students are hired by the Institute to work in the Institute's dining hall (auxiliary enterprise). As part of their compensation for working, tuition in the amount of $25,000 is waived.
7. The $250,000 restricted cash balance at the beginning of the year was donated for a new training ship. During the year, an additional $250,000 donation was received.
8. The Institute signed a long-term note payable for $200,000. These funds, together with the restricted cash, were used to buy the training ship. The training ship's expenses are classified as instruction.
9. During the year, $100,000 of cash and pledges for an additional $200,000 were received as a result of fund-raising campaigns to enhance the

Institute's endowment. By the terms of the agreement, such contributions are to remain permanently in the endowment. The $100,000 was immediately used to purchase additional investments.

10. By terms of the endowment agreement, interest and dividends received on the investments are restricted for need-based scholarships. Gains or losses from changes in the fair value of the investments, however, are not distributed but remain in the endowment. During the year, $18,000 of interest and dividend were received on endowment investments. At year-end, the fair value of the investments had increased by $4,000.
11. Expenses totaling $685,000 for salaries, supplies, utilities, and other items to be paid in cash are approved for payment through accounts payable. A total of $580,000 of outstanding accounts payable were paid by year-end. Although both GASB and FASB permit classification by natural category, the functional categories appearing below are recommended by NACUBO (amounts are assumed):

Instruction expense	300,000
Research expense	100,000
Auxiliary enterprise expense	160,000
Institutional support expense	125,000

12. Included in the expenses recorded in the previous transactions are $132,000 incurred under federal and state government grants. Bills were sent to the granting agencies and $106,500 was received by the end of the year.

Adjusting entries:

13. The note payable was dated April 1, 2020. Interest is paid annually on March 31. The Institute accrued three months of interest at 6 percent.
14. Each year, a portion of the amount received as summer school tuition is deferred to the next academic year. The amount to be deferred is determined to be $9,100.
15. Depreciation expense of $165,000 is recorded on buildings and equipment. The expense is allocated to functional areas on the basis of actual equipment in use and square footage for buildings (amounts assumed).

Instruction expense	75,000
Research expense	30,000
Auxiliary enterprise expense	35,000
Institutional support expense	25,000

Required:

a. Prepare journal entries recording the events above for the year ending December 31, 2020.

b. Post the journal entries to T-accounts.

c. Prepare closing entries.

d. Prepare a Statement of Revenues, Expenses, and Changes in Fund Net Position.

e. Prepare a Statement of Net Position.

f. Prepare a Statement of Cash Flows

11–10. This exercise uses the same fact setting as 11-9 except Items 1 and 2 are changed to be consistent with a private institution.

The Great Lakes Maritime Institute is a private not-for-profit institution preparing cadets for careers in commercial shipping and includes instruction in piloting, navigation, maritime law, and other fields.

1. The Institute began the year with the following account balances:

Beginning Balances July 1, 2019		
	Debits	**Credits**
Cash	125,000	
Student accounts receivable	40,000	
Investments—endowment	500,000	
Restricted cash	250,000	
Capital assets	1,100,000	
Accumulated depreciation		350,000
Accounts payable and accrued liabilities		4,000
Deferred revenues		7,000
Net assets with donor restrictions—permanent endowment		500,000
Net assets with donor restrictions—capital acquisitions		250,000
Net assets without donor restrictions		904,000

2. The Institute received an unrestricted operating grant of $75,000 from the Maritime Shipping Association, a trade association for commercial shipping firms. Additionally, the Institute received unrestricted gifts of $10,000

Items 3–15, same as Exercise 11-9.

Required:

a. Prepare journal entries recording the events above for the year ending December 31, 2020.

b. Post the journal entries to T-accounts.

c. Prepare closing entries.

d. Prepare a Statement of Activity—present net assets without donor restrictions in a single column.

e. Prepare a Statement of Financial Position.

f. Prepare a Statement of Cash Flows

Chapter Twelve

Accounting for Hospitals and Other Health Care Providers

A lifetime in medicine taught me that the best health care decisions are made between patient and doctor. As decision-making moves further away from patients and providers, the medical outcomes become less effective. Dr. Ben Carson, Secretary of Housing and Urban Development and retired neurosurgeon

We are the only major country on earth that doesn't guarantee health care to all people as a right and yet we end up spending much more than they do, so I do believe that we have to move toward a Medicare for all, single-payer system. Bernie Sanders, Senator from Vermont

Learning Objectives

- Describe the reporting requirements of varying types of health care organizations.
- Apply the accrual basis of accounting in the recording of typical transactions of a not-for-profit health care organization.
- Prepare the financial statements for a not-for-profit health care organization.

According to the World Health Organization, the United States spends more on health care ($9,400 per capita) than any other nation.[1] At the same time, the quality of care lags behind many industrialized nations. As indicated by the two quotes above, a major national debate continues over how health care should be provided and paid for. The interests of patients, physicians, health care entities, insurance companies, and regulators are often in conflict and there is no agreement among political leaders on the solution.

[1] World Bank, https://data.worldbank.org/indicator/SH.XPD.CHEX.PC.CD

In the United States 60 percent of hospitals are organized as private not-for-profits. Of the remainder, roughly half are owned by governments and half by private investors. Like colleges and universities, each group of health care providers follows a different set of accounting standards. Private not-for-profit health care organizations follow FASB standards, including those specifically applicable to not-for-profits. If a health care organization is owned or controlled by a government, it is typically considered a special-purpose entity engaged only in business-type activities (GASB *Codification* § Ho5) and would use proprietary fund accounting. Other health care organizations are privately owned and operated to provide a return to investors. For example, Hospital Corporation of America (HCA) owns or operates hundreds of hospitals in the United States and internationally and its stock is traded on the New York Stock Exchange. HCA and other private for-profit health care organizations follow FASB standards *excluding* those written specifically for not-for-profits.

While the three types of health care organizations follow different sets of generally accepted accounting standards, the differences lie mainly in presentation. All three types of organizations measure assets and liabilities similarly, recognize revenue and expenses under the accrual basis, and present comparable performance (i.e., income) measures. Helping to assure comparability across health care organizations with varying ownership structures, the *AICPA Audit and Accounting Guide: Health Care Organizations* applies equally to private not-for-profit, governmentally owned, and investor-owned health care organizations.[2]

This chapter concentrates on reporting by private not-for-profit health care organizations, the most numerous of the three types. However, unique features of governmental health care reporting are also described in a separate section. Health care organizations include the following:

- Clinics, medical group practices, individual practice associations, individual practitioners, emergency care facilities, laboratories, surgery centers, and other ambulatory care organizations.
- Continuing care retirement communities.
- Health maintenance organizations (HMOs) and similar prepaid health care plans.
- Home health agencies.
- Hospitals.
- Nursing homes that provide skilled, intermediate, and less intensive levels of health care.
- Drug and alcohol and other rehabilitation facilities.

Payments to these health care organizations come from many sources, including Medicare, Medicaid, commercial insurance companies, nonprofit insurance companies, state and local assistance programs, and directly from patients.

The *Health Care Guide* makes a distinction between health care organizations and voluntary health and welfare organizations, a distinction that is sometimes

[2] American Institute of Certified Public Accountants, AICPA Audit and Accounting Guide: Health Care Organizations (New York: AICPA, 2018).

difficult in practice. The organizations just listed are legally nonprofit but raise essentially all revenues from services provided to patients or clients. These health care organizations are subject to the *Health Care Guide*. The *Health Care Guide* calls these organizations Not-for-Profit Business-Oriented Organizations. If similar organizations raise a significant amount or nearly all their resources from voluntary contributions or grants, then they are subject to the guidance in the *Not-for-Profit Guide* as illustrated in Chapter 10 of this text. The *Health Care Guide* calls these organizations Not-for-Profit Nonbusiness-Oriented Organizations.

ACCOUNTING AND REPORTING REQUIREMENTS OF THE *HEALTH CARE GUIDE*

The AICPA *Health Care Guide* provides certain additional accounting and reporting requirements beyond those required by FASB and GASB standards. As both the FASB and the GASB approved the *Health Care Guide,* its requirements constitute Category B GAAP and must be followed by all health care organizations.

Illustration 12-1 summarizes the reporting requirements for the three types of health care organizations. While governmental health care organizations follow GASB standards, they typically report as special-purpose entities engaged only in business-type activities. Because they are engaged in business-type activities, governmental health care organizations use the accrual basis and economic resources measurement focus. The result is that public and private sector health care organizations measure transactions and events similarly.

The three types of health care organizations use different residual equity accounts, reflecting the varying ownership categories. Other differences exist in the format and title of the financial statements. For example, private sector organizations use the three-category FASB format for the Statement of Cash Flows, while public sector organizations use the four-category GASB format.

Financial Statements

The Balance Sheet (or Statement of Net Assets/Position) must separately display current assets from noncurrent and current liabilities from noncurrent. Activities (revenues, expenses, and reclassifications) are commonly divided between two financial statements, a Statement of Operations and a Statement of Changes in Net Assets. The **Statement of Operations** reflects changes among unrestricted (without donor restrictions) net assets and must include a **performance indicator** (commonly called operating income or loss) that reports results from continuing operations. Therefore, it is important to distinguish operating revenues and expenses from nonoperating. The Audit and Accounting Guide identifies the following items that should ***not*** be included in the determination of operating income:

- Receipt of donor-restricted contributions.
- Transfers among affiliated organizations.
- Transactions with the owners, other than in exchange for services.

ILLUSTRATION 12-1 **Health Care Organization Reporting—Ownership Forms**

Type of Entity	Authoritative Standards	Accrual Basis of Accounting	Components of Financial Report	Equity Section of Balance Sheet/Statement of Net Assets
Not-for-Profit Business-Oriented Organizations	FASB	✓	Balance Sheet/Statement of Financial Position Statement of Operations Statement of Changes in Net Assets Statement of Cash Flows Notes to the Financial Statements	Net Assets without Donor Restrictions Net Assets with Donor Restrictions
Investor-Owned Health Care Enterprises	FASB	✓	Balance Sheet/Statement of Financial Position Statement of Operations Statement of Changes in Equity Statement of Cash Flows Notes to the Financial Statements	Paid-in Capital Retained Earnings
Governmental Health Care Organizations*	GASB	✓	Management Discussion & Analysis Statement of Net Position Statement of Revenues, Expenses, and Changes in Fund Net Position Statement of Cash Flows Notes to the Financial Statements RSI Other Than MD&A	Net Investment in Capital Assets Restricted Net Position Unrestricted Net Position

*Typically these are special-purpose entities engaged in business-type activities.

- Items identified by FASB standards as elements of other comprehensive income (such as foreign currency translation adjustments).
- Items requiring separate display (such as discontinued operations).
- Unrealized gains and losses on investments other than those classified as trading securities.

Patient Service Revenue

In Chapter 10 we described two recent efforts by the FASB to clarify the reporting of revenues. A 2018 standard (codification §958) provides guidance on reporting of contributions while a 2014 standard (§606) deals with recognition of exchange revenue. Not-for-profit entities that derive most of their revenue from contributions (such as those illustrated in Chapter 10) are mainly affected by the 2018 standard. In contrast, health care organizations derive most of their revenues from services provided to customers. Because the health care environment has unique characteristics, private health care entities must carefully consider the requirements of the 2014 standard (§606) in determining the amount of revenue to recognize from patient services.

Revenue from Contracts with Customers (§606) The revenue recognition standard defines a five-step model for revenue recognition:

1. Identify the contract with the customer.
2. Identify the performance obligations in the contract.
3. Determine the transaction price.
4. Allocate the transaction price to the performance obligations.
5. Recognize revenue when (or as) the entity satisfies a performance obligation.

A performance obligation is a good or service promised to a customer as part of a sales contract. For example, a business may package the sale of a service agreement with the sale of equipment. These two parts could represent separate performance obligations, with the result that revenue from each part is recognized in different accounting periods. For businesses that sell bundled products and services, the steps dealing with performance obligations (2, 4, and 5) present the biggest reporting issues. However, for health care organizations, steps 1 and 3 are the more challenging and require significant judgment.

Step 1 indicates that a contract must exist for revenue to be recognized. A contract exits when a willing buyer and seller agree to exchange services for payment. In most health care organizations a patient is required to sign a patient responsibility form prior to receiving service and this serves as the basis for identifying the contract. In other instances it is not so clear whether a contract exists. Patients in need of immediate medical treatment could arrive at an emergency room and be unconscious or otherwise lack the capacity to enter a binding contract. Further, the emergency room may be required by law or the entity's own policies to provide service without regard to whether the patient is insured or has the ability to pay. In the case of trauma care, the health care organization may have to delay recording revenue until it can be determined whether the patient has the ability to pay or should be classified as charity care.

Charity care is the term used in the health care industry to describe a situation in which services are provided to a patient without the expectation of receiving payment. FASB characterizes charity care patients as those with a demonstrated inability to pay at the time of treatment. For a contract to exist, there must be an expectation of (some) payment. The result is there is no contract in a charity care situation and no revenue is recognized. Although the costs of providing charity care (supplies, wages) are included in expense, charity care does not result in bad debt expense.

The third step in revenue recognition (determine the transaction price) also presents challenges for health care organizations. The amount of revenue recognized at the time of service should not exceed the amount the health care organization actually expects to receive in payment. Determining the amount of expected cash receipts is complicated by the existence of discounts, explicit contractual adjustments, and implicit price concessions. Prompt pay discounts (e.g., customers receive a 2 percent discount if their bill is paid within 10 days) are treated as contra-revenues in the same manner as "cash discounts" by commercial businesses. Contra-revenues are accounts with debit balances that are reductions in the revenue reported in the financial statements.

Far more common than discounts are price concessions. Health care entities commonly agree to accept payment on behalf of patients from third-party payors such as insurance companies or government programs (e.g., Medicare and Medicaid). Typically these third parties do not pay the standard rate (i.e., list price) for services provided to patients. The difference between the standard rate and the reimbursement rate is termed **contractual adjustment** (or explicit price concession). Patient service revenues are reported net of these contractual adjustments.

For example, assume that a patient with hospital charges of $25,000 is covered by a commercial insurance policy that includes a $1,000 deductible (patient's responsibility). By contractual agreement between the hospital and the insurance company, an explicit price concession reduces the total bill (and the reported revenue) by $14,000. So at this point $10,000 is collected from the insurer and $1,000 is the patient's responsibility. In the past, the hospital would have recorded net patient service revenue of ($25,000 – $14,000) $11,000. The hospital would then begin collection efforts from the patient for the remaining $1,000. If the hospital was unable to collect the full $1,000 from the patient, the uncollected portion would be reported as bad debts (also a contra-revenue).

However, under the 2014 standard (§606), the hospital is now required to consider implicit price concessions and deduct these from revenue at the time of service. **Implicit price concessions** exist when an entity has a customary business practice of accepting less than their stated charges for medical treatment. Implicit price concession may be estimated based on historical collection experience from similar patients. In determining historical collection experience, the hospital may group patients into categories such as uninsured self-pay, high deductible insured, or elective versus non-elective procedures, and calculate expected collections based on group averages.

Assume that the hospital's experience with patients similar to the example above indicates that it can expect to collect $700 of the $1,000 deductible billed to the patient, resulting in an expected implicit price concession of $300. The hospital would report the following net patient service revenue:

Charges for services	$ 25,000
Less contractual adjustments	(14,000)
Less implicit price concessions	(300)
Net patient service revenue	$ 10,700

It should be noted that just because a health care entity has a customary practice of receiving less than the full amount of a patient receivable, it does not follow that the entity will not attempt to collect the full amount due. Implicit price concessions are estimates based on patient averages. These averages assume that the entity has taken all reasonable steps to collect patient accounts. Like other accounting estimates, changes in the estimated transaction price is recorded in the current period by adjusting one of the components of net patient service revenue (either contractual adjustments or implicit price concessions).

In addition to price concessions, health care entities may also report bad debts. The difference is that price concessions are reductions in revenue while bad debts are an expense. After the initial recording of revenue, patient receivables are subject to impairment evaluations. Bad debts result from specific events that indicate a patient no longer has the ability or intent to pay. For example, if the hospital learned that the patient lost his job and is filing for bankruptcy, a $700 impairment loss (the $1,000 patient receivable, less the $300 implicit price concession) should be reported as an expense.

The following summarizes the reporting of net patient service revenues as follows:

Gross charges for services	$700,000
Less: Charges associated with charity patients	(50,000)
Gross patient service revenue	650,000
Less deductions from revenue:	
Contractual adjustments	(100,000)
Provision for implicit price concessions	(40,000)
Net patient service revenue	$510,000

Items in the shaded area above would typically not appear in the Statement of Operations. Bad debt expense would be reported with expenses.

Other Revenues While patient service revenue is the largest category of operating revenues for most health care entities, other common sources include charges for parking, gift shops, cafeterias, and tuition. Unrestricted gifts and bequests and investment income for current unrestricted purposes may be reported as either operating or nonoperating revenue, depending on the policy of the entity. Additionally, premium revenue arising from capitation agreements is classified as operating revenue. Under a capitation contract, an HMO or managed care organization pays a fixed amount of money each month to a health care organization to serve its members. The health care organization receives a single flat fee regardless of how many visits a patient schedules in a particular month.

Classifications

- Expenses may be reported by either natural classifications (salaries, supplies, etc.) or functional classifications (professional care of patients, general services, etc.). Private sector not-for-profit health care entities must disclose expenses by functional classifications (program and supporting) in the notes, if not provided in the Statement of Operations.
- *Assets Limited as to Use* is an unrestricted (i.e., without donor restrictions) balance sheet category used in health care reporting to show limitations on the use of assets due to bond covenant restrictions or governing board intentions for future use of these assets. This category is especially important for private sector, not-for-profit health care entities as the "with donor restrictions" category is limited to restrictions placed by contributors.

ILLUSTRATIVE TRANSACTIONS

Entries for typical transactions for a hypothetical not-for-profit business-oriented hospital are listed next. The entries are directly traceable to the financial statements that follow (Illustrations 12-2 through 12-5).

Beginning Trial Balance

Assume the beginning trial balance for the Nonprofit Hospital, as of January 1, 2020, is as follows:

Cash	$ 2,450,000	
Patient Accounts Receivable	14,100,000	
Allowance for Contractual Adjustments (3rd-party payors)		$ 1,500,000
Allowance for Implicit Price Concessions		800,000
Supplies	400,000	
Investments—Assets Limited as to Use	1,500,000	
Investments—Restricted for Capital Acquisition	12,900,000	
Investments—Undesignated	4,200,000	
Property, Plant, and Equipment	27,550,000	
Accumulated Depreciation—Property, Plant, and Equipment		15,800,000
Accounts Payable		800,000
Accrued Expenses		900,000
Long-Term Debt—Current Installments		1,000,000
Long-Term Debt—Noncurrent		10,800,000
Net Assets without Donor Restrictions—Board Designated		1,500,000
Net Assets without Donor Restrictions—Undesignated		13,100,000
Net Assets with Donor Restrictions		16,900,000
Totals	$63,100,000	$63,100,000

Assume the $16,900,000 of donor-restricted net assets are restricted as follows:

- program, $4,000,000
- capital improvements, $12,900,000.

Although less common than among colleges and universities, hospitals may also maintain permanent endowments. If this were the case, those resources would also be included among Net Assets with Donor Restrictions.

The account caption *Assets Limited as to Use* is commonly used by hospitals to indicate board (rather than donor) restrictions on the use of particular assets. In the present case assume the hospital launched a fund-raising campaign to finance a new outpatient building annex. The hospital's governing board designated $1,500,000 of investments for this purpose. This is identified in the trial balance in two places: *Investments—Assets Limited as to Use* among the asset section and *Net Assets without Donor Restrictions—Board Designated* within the residual equity section. Since the board, rather than an outside donor, designated these resources, they are classified as without donor restrictions.

Illustrative Transactions—Operating Activities

During the year, gross patient service revenue (at standard billing rates) amounted to $92,656,000. Contractual adjustments to third-party payors, such as insurance companies, Medicare, and Medicaid, are estimated to be $12,000,000. In addition, implicit price concessions to individuals are estimated to be $1,300,000. Finally, an additional $9,000,000 of services were provided to uninsured individuals with a demonstrated inability to pay at the time of treatment.

1a. Patient Accounts Receivable	92,656,000	
Operating Revenues—Unrestricted—Gross Patient Service Revenue		92,656,000
1b. Contractual Adjustments	12,000,000	
Allowance for Contractual Adjustments		12,000,000
1c. Provision for Implicit Price Concessions	1,300,000	
Allowance for Implicit Price Concessions		1,300,000

Services provided to patients without an ability to pay are charity care and are not reported as patient service revenue. *Contractual Adjustments* and *Provision for Implicit Price Concessions* are contra-revenues and are deducted from Gross Patient Service Revenue in the Statement of Operations. *Allowance for Contractual Adjustments* and *Allowance for Implicit Price Concessions* are valuation accounts and are deducted from Patient Accounts Receivable.

Cash of $64,100,000 was received from insurance companies and government programs for patient services totaling $74,200,000. Contractual adjustments of $10,100,000 were applied to patient accounts. Additionally, cash of $19,550,000 was received directly from patients after applying price concessions of $1,700,000.

		Debit	Credit
2a.	Cash	64,100,000	
	Allowance for Contractual Adjustments	10,100,000	
	Patient Accounts Receivable		74,200,000
2b.	Cash	19,550,000	
	Allowance for Implicit Price Concessions	1,700,000	
	Patient Accounts Receivable		21,250,000

Capitation agreements are plans that allow an HMO or other organization to pay the hospital a fixed amount of money (i.e., a premium) for each of its members. Generally capitation payments are received at the beginning of each month and obligate the health care organization to render covered services during the month. Capitation revenue is earned as a result of agreeing to provide services to the qualified beneficiaries. During the year, premium revenue from capitation agreements amounted to $12,000,000, all of which was received in cash.

Other operating revenues were also received in cash in the amount of $5,460,000; these included revenues from the gift shop, parking lot, cafeteria operations, and tuition from nursing students:

		Debit	Credit
3.	Cash	17,460,000	
	Operating Revenues—without Donor Restrictions—Premium Revenue		12,000,000
	Operating Revenues—without Donor Restrictions—Other Revenue		5,460,000

Supplies were purchased in the amount of $500,000 (on account). $1,300,000 of accounts payable and $900,000 of accrued expenses were paid:

		Debit	Credit
4a.	Supplies	500,000	
	Accounts Payable		500,000
4b.	Accounts Payable	1,300,000	
	Accrued Expenses	900,000	
	Cash		2,200,000

The following information relates to operating expenses for the year:

- Depreciation for the year was $4,800,000.
- Supplies used amounted to $400,000.
- Salaries and benefits amounted to $88,006,000, of which $87,006,000 was paid during the year and $1,000,000 was accrued.
- Utilities totaled $10,800,000, of which $9,900,000 was paid and $900,000 remained in accounts payable at year-end.

5a. Operating Expenses—Depreciation	4,800,000	
Accumulated Depreciation—Property, Plant, and Equipment		4,800,000
5b. Operating Expenses—Supplies	400,000	
Supplies		400,000
5c. Operating Expenses—Salaries and Benefits	88,006,000	
Cash		87,006,000
Accrued Expenses		1,000,000
5d. Operating Expenses—Utilities	10,800,000	
Cash		9,900,000
Accounts Payable		900,000

Included in the amounts above is $3,500,000 of expended resources received in the previous year that were restricted by the donor for program purposes.

6. Reclassification from Net Assets with Donor Restrictions—Satisfaction of Program Restrictions	3,500,000	
Reclassification to Net Assets without Donor Restrictions—Satisfaction of Program Restrictions		3,500,000

Interest on long-term debt is paid on the last day of each month. A total of $600,000 was paid. Interest is classified as an operating expense in the Statement of Operations.

7. Operating Expense—Interest	600,000	
Cash		600,000

Principal on long-term debt was paid in the amount of $1,000,000; an additional $1,000,000 was classified as current.

8a. Long-Term Debt—Current Installment	1,000,000	
Cash		1,000,000
8b. Long-Term Debt—Noncurrent	1,000,000	
Long-Term Debt—Current Installment		1,000,000

Illustrative Transactions—Nonoperating Activities

Contribution Revenue: Imaging equipment was acquired at a cost of $5,200,000 and paid in full. Of that amount, $1,200,000 was from resources restricted by a donor for this purpose.

9a. Property, Plant, and Equipment	5,200,000	
Cash		5,200,000
9b. Reclassification from Net Assets with Donor Restrictions—Satisfaction of Capital Acquisition Restrictions	1,200,000	
Reclassification to Net Assets without Donor Restrictions—Satisfaction of Capital Acquisition Restrictions		1,200,000

Unrestricted gifts and bequests in the amount of $1,856,000 were received in cash.

10. Cash	1,856,000	
Nonoperating Income—without Donor Restrictions—Gifts and Bequests		1,856,000

Cash contributions were received totaling $6,500,000. Of this amount, $5,100,000 was restricted by the donors for capital acquisition and $1,400,000 was restricted for specific programs.

11. Cash	6,500,000	
Nonoperating revenues—Contributions with Donor Restrictions (Capital Acquisition)		5,100,000
Nonoperating revenues—Contributions with Donor Restrictions (Program Restrictions)		1,400,000

Income on Investments: Assume the hospital initiated a capital campaign in the previous year intended to raise money for an outpatient care annex to its existing building. At that time, the governing board designated $1,500,000 of undesignated investments for that purpose. This money is being invested by a trustee and any income from those investments is also designated for the addition to the building. Assume contributions from the capital campaign are forwarded to the trustee and invested until needed (i.e., when construction begins). By agreement with the donors, any income from those investments is restricted for the project. The hospital therefore has three pools of investments: Designated by the Board, Restricted by Donors, and Undesignated.

Investment income received from undesignated investments amounted to $244,000.

12. Cash	244,000	
Nonoperating Income—Investment Income on Undesignated Investments		244,000

Investment income received from *Investments—Assets Limited as to Use* amounted to $120,000, which is designated by the hospital's board for future capital improvements:

13. Cash—Assets Limited as to Use	120,000	
Nonoperating Income—Investment Income Limited by Board Actions for Capital Improvements		120,000

A total of $5,220,000 in investments was purchased during the year. This included the $120,000 designated by the board for capital improvements (above) and $5,100,000 previously collected from donors for the new outpatient building annex.

	Debits	Credits
14a. Investments—Assets Limited as to Use	120,000	
Cash—Assets Limited as to Use		120,000
14b. Investments—Restricted for Capital Acquisitions	5,100,000	
Cash		5,100,000

Investment income received from the donor-restricted investments amounted to $400,000.

	Debits	Credits
15. Cash	400,000	
Investment Income—with Donor Restrictions (Capital Acquisition)		400,000

Certain investments held for the outpatient building annex campaign were sold for $4,100,000. These investments had a carrying value of $4,000,000.

	Debits	Credits
16. Cash	4,100,000	
Investments—Restricted for Capital Acquisitions		4,000,000
Net Realized and Unrealized Gains on Investments—with Donor Restrictions (Capital Acquisition)		100,000

The $4,100,000 realized above was reinvested in new securities.

	Debits	Credits
17. Investments—Restricted for Capital Acquisitions	4,100,000	
Cash		4,100,000

At year-end, the market value of *Investments—Restricted for Capital Acquisitions* had increased in value by $150,000. The market value of all other investments equaled their book values at year-end.

	Debits	Credits
18. Investments—Restricted for Capital Acquisitions	150,000	
Net Realized and Unrealized Gains on Investments—with Donor Restrictions (Capital Acquisition)		150,000

Illustrative Transactions—Closing Activities

Journal entries 1 through 18 are posted to general ledger accounts appearing in Illustration 12-2. In the interest of saving space, various revenues and expenses are summarized in a few accounts but would be posted in greater detail in an actual general ledger.

ILLUSTRATION 12-2 General Ledger

General Ledger

CASH

	Debit	Credit	
bb	2,450,000		
2a	64,100,000	2,200,000	4b
2b	19,550,000	87,006,000	5c
3	17,460,000	9,900,000	5d
10	1,856,000	600,000	7
11	6,500,000	1,000,000	8a
12	240,000	5,200,000	9a
15	400,000	5,100,000	14b
16	4,100,000	4,100,000	17
	1,554,000		

PATIENT ACCOUNTS RECEIVABLE

	Debit	Credit	
bb	14,100,000		
1a	92,656,000	74,200,000	2a
		21,250,000	2
	11,306,000		

ALLOWANCE FOR CONTRACTUAL ADJUSTMENTS

	Debit	Credit	
		1,500,000	bb
2a	10,100,000	12,000,000	1b
		3,400,000	

ALLOWANCE FOR IMPLICIT PRICE ADJUSTMENTS

	Debit	Credit	
		800,000	bb
2b	1,700,000	1,300,000	1c
		400,000	

SUPPLIES

	Debit	Credit	
bb	400,000		
4a	500,000	400,000	5b
	500,000		

CASH–ASSETS LIMITED AS TO USE

	Debit	Credit	
bb	-		
13	120,000	120,000	14a
	-		

INVESTMENTS—ASSETS LIMITED AS TO USE

	Debit	Credit	
bb	1,500,000		
14a	120,000		
	1,620,000		

INVESTMENTS—RESTRICTED FOR CAPITAL ACQUISITIONS

	Debit	Credit	
bb	12,900,000		
14b	5,100,000	4,000,000	16
17	4,100,000		
18	150,000		
	18,250,000		

INVESTMENTS-UNDESIGNATED

	Debit	Credit	
bb	4,200,000		
	4,200,000		

PROPERTY, PLANT, AND EQUIPMENT

	Debit	Credit	
bb	27,550,000		
9a	5,200,000		
	32,750,000		

ACCUMULATED DEPRECIATION

	Debit	Credit	
		15,800,000	bb
		4,800,000	5a
		20,600,000	

ACCOUNTS PAYABLE

	Debit	Credit	
		800,000	bb
4b	1,300,000	500,000	4a
		900,000	5d
		900,000	

ACCRUED EXPENSES

	Debit	Credit	
		900,000	bb
4b	900,000	1,000,000	5c
		1,000,000	

CURRENT PORTION LONG-TERM DEBT

	Debit	Credit	
		1,000,000	bb
8a	1,000,000	1,000,000	8b
		1,000,000	

ILLUSTRATION 12-2 General Ledger (*continued*)

NONCURRENT LONG-TERM DEBT

	Debit	Credit	
		10,800,000	bb
8b	1,000,000		
		9,800,000	

NET ASSETS WITHOUT DONOR RESTRICTIONS

	Debit	Credit	
		13,100,000	bb
		13,100,000	

NET ASSETS WITH DONOR RESTRICTIONS—PROGRAM

	Debit	Credit	
		4,000,000	bb
		4,000,000	

NET ASSETS WITH DONOR RESTRICTIONS—CAPITAL ASSETS

	Debit	Credit	
		12,900,000	bb
		12,900,000	

NETS ASSETS—BOARD DESIGNATED (CAPITAL ASSETS)

	Debit	Credit	
		1,500,000	bb
		1,500,000	

UNRESTRICTED OPERATING REVENUES

	Debit	Credit		
		92,656,000	1a	-Patient service (gross)
		12,000,000	3	-Premium revenue
		5,460,000	3	-Other revenues
		110,116,000		

UNRESTRICTED NONOPERATING REVENUES

	Debit	Credit		
		1,856,000	10	-Gifts & bequests
		244,000	12	-Investment income—undesignated
		120,000	13	-Investment income—limited to capital improvement
		2,220,000		

REVENUES WITH DONOR RESTRICTIONS

	Debit	Credit		
		5,100,000	11	-Contributions (capital)
		1,400,000	11	-Contributions (program)
		400,000	15	-Investment income (capital)
		100,000	16	-Net gains on investments (capital)
		150,000	18	-Net gains on investments (capital)
		7,150,000		

CONTRACTUAL ADJUSTMENTS

	Debit	Credit
lb	12,000,0000	
	12,000,0000	

OPERATING EXPENSES

		Debit	Credit
Depreciation-	5a	4,800,000	
Supplies-	5b	400,000	
Salaries & benefits-	5c	88,006,000	
Utilities	5d	10,800,000	
Interest	7	600,000	
		104,606,000	

RECLASSIFICATION TO NET ASSETS WITHOUT DONOR RESTRICTIONS

	Debit	Credit		Satisfaction of:
		3,500,000	6	-Program Restrictions-
		1,200,000	9b	-Plant Acquisitions-
		4,700,000		

RECLASSIFICATION FROM NET ASSETS WITH DONOR RESTRICTIONS

	Debit	Credit
6	3,500,000	
9b	1,200,000	
	4,700,000	

PROVISION FOR IMPLICIT PRICE CONCESSIONS

	Debit	Credit
1c	1,300,000	
	1,300,000	

Separate closing entries are made for each of the net asset categories reported on the Statement of Financial Position.

Closing Entries for Net Assets without Donor Restrictions

	Debit	Credit
19. Operating Revenues—without Donor Restrictions—Gross Patient Service Revenue	92,656,000	
Operating Revenues—without Donor Restrictions—Premium Revenue	12,000,000	
Operating Revenues—without Donor Restrictions—Other Revenue	5,460,000	
Nonoperating Income—without Donor Restrictions—Gifts and Bequests	1,856,000	
Nonoperating Income—Investment Income on Undesignated Investments	244,000	
Reclassification to Net Assets without Donor Restrictions—Satisfaction of Program Restrictions	3,500,000	
Reclassification to Net Assets without Donor Restrictions—Satisfaction of Capital Acquisition Restrictions	1,200,000	
Net Assets without Donor Restrictions—Undesignated	990,000	
Contractual Adjustments		12,000,000
Provision for Implicit Price Concessions		1,300,000
Operating Expense—Depreciation		4,800,000
Operating Expense—Supplies		400,000
Operating Expense—Salaries and Benefits		88,006,000
Operating Expense—Utilities		10,800,000
Operating Expense—Interest		600,000
Board Designated		
20. Nonoperating Income—Investment Income Limited by Board Actions for Capital Improvements	120,000	
Net Assets without Donor Restrictions—Board Designated		120,000

Closing entries are then made for Net Assets with Donor Restrictions.

Closing Entries for Net Assets with Donor Restrictions

	Debit	Credit
Program Restrictions:		
21. Nonoperating Revenues—Contributions with Donor Restrictions (Program Restrictions)	1,400,000	
Net Assets with Donor Restrictions—Program Restrictions	2,100,000	
Reclassification from Net Assets with Donor Restrictions—Satisfaction of Program Restrictions		3,500,000
Capital Acquisitions:		
22. Nonoperating Revenues—Contributions with Donor Restrictions (Capital Acquisition)	5,100,000	
Investment Income—with Donor Restrictions (Capital Acquisition)	400,000	
Net Realized and Unrealized Gains on Investments—with Donor Restrictions (Capital Acquisition)	250,000	
Reclassification from Net Assets with Donor Restrictions—Satisfaction of Capital Acquisition Restrictions		1,200,000
Net Assets with Donor Restrictions—Capital Acquisition Restrictions		4,550,000

The effect of closing entries is summarized as follows:

	Net Assets without Donor Restrictions		Net Assets with Donor Restrictions	
	Undesignated	Board Designated	Program Restrictions	Capital Acquisition
January 1, 2020	13,100,000	1,500,000	4,000,000	12,900,000
Closing Entry	(990,000)	120,000	(2,100,000)	4,550,000
December 31, 2020	12,110,000	1,620,000	1,900,000	17,450,000

ILLUSTRATIVE STATEMENTS FOR PRIVATE SECTOR NOT-FOR-PROFIT HEALTH CARE ENTITIES

Financial statements required for private sector not-for-profit hospitals include the Statement of Operations, Statement of Changes in Net Assets, Statement of Financial Position, and a Statement of Cash Flows. Illustrative statements for the Nonprofit Hospital are shown as Illustrations 12-3 through 12-6.

Statement of Operations As the FASB permits considerable flexibility for the (not-for-profit) Statement of Activities, the Health Care Guide has prescribed a Statement of Operations and a Statement of Changes in Net Assets for health care entities. Illustration 12-3 reflects a Statement of Operations that meets the requirements of FASB not-for-profit reporting and the AICPA Health Care Guide. Since expenses are reported by natural classifications (salaries, depreciation, etc.) the hospital must further disclose expenses by the functional classifications of program and supporting in the notes. At a minimum this would include health services, administration, and fund-raising.

The Net Patient Service Revenue of $79,356,000 is computed by subtracting the Provision for Implicit Price Concessions and Contractual Adjustments from Patient Service Revenue ($92,656,000 – 1,300,000 – 12,000,000).

Statement of Changes in Net Assets The Statement of Changes in Net Assets shown in Illustration 12-4 fulfills the FASB requirement to show the changes in net assets by net asset class and in total. It is acceptable to present a single statement, combining the Statement of Operations and Statement of Changes in Net Assets.

Statement of Financial Position Illustration 12-5 presents a Statement of Financial Position, or Balance Sheet. Because the hospital is a private not-for-profit, the residual equity accounts are net assets *with* or without donor restrictions. In this case, additional details are provided within each of these categories.

Statement of Cash Flows Illustration 12-6 presents a Statement of Cash Flows for the Nonprofit Hospital using the indirect method. The direct method

ILLUSTRATION 12-3 Statement of Operations

NONPROFIT HOSPITAL Statement of Operations for the year ended December 31, 2020	
Revenues without Donor Restrictions:	
Patient Service Revenues—Net of Contractual Adjustments with Third-Party Payors and the Provision for Implicit Price Concessions	$ 79,356,000
Premium Revenue (capitation agreements)	12,000,000
Other Operating Revenues	5,460,000
Total Revenues	96,816,000
Net Assets Released from Restrictions (used for operations):	
Satisfaction of Program Restrictions	3,500,000
Total Operating Revenues	100,316,000
Operating Expenses:	
Salaries and Benefits	88,006,000
Supplies	400,000
Utilities	10,800,000
Depreciation	4,800,000
Interest	600,000
Total Operating Expenses	104,606,000
Operating Loss	(4,290,000)
Other Income:	
Unrestricted Gifts and Bequests	1,856,000
Investment Income (undesignated)	244,000
Investment Income on Assets Limited as to Use	120,000
Total Other Income	2,220,000
Excess (Deficiency) of Revenues over Expenses	(2,070,000)
Net Assets Released from Restrictions:	
Satisfaction of Property, Plant, and Equipment Restrictions	1,200,000
Decrease in Net Assets without Donor Restrictions	$ (870,000)

ILLUSTRATION 12-4 Statement of Changes in Net Assets

NONPROFIT HOSPITAL Statement of Changes in Net Assets for the year ended December 31, 2020	
Net Assets without Donor Restrictions:	
Excess (Deficiency) of Revenues over Expenses	$ (2,070,000)
Net Assets Released from Restrictions:	
Satisfaction of Property, Plant, and Equipment Restrictions	1,200,000
Decrease in Net Assets without Donor Restrictions	(870,000)
Net Assets with Donor Restrictions	
Contribution Revenue	6,500,000
Net Realized and Unrealized Gains on Investments	250,000
Other Investment Income	400,000
Net Assets Released from Restrictions	(4,700,000)
Increase (Decrease) in Net Assets with Donor Restrictions	2,450,000
Increase in Net Assets	1,580,000
Net Assets, beginning of year	31,500,000
Net Assets, end of year	$33,080,000

ILLUSTRATION 12-5 Statement of Financial Position

NONPROFIT HOSPITAL
Statements of Financial Position
as of December 31, 2020 and 2019

ASSETS	2020	2019
Current Assets		
Cash and Cash Equivalents	$ 1,554,000	$ 2,450,000
Patient Accounts Receivable (Net of Allowances for Contractual Adjustments and Implicit Price Concessions)	7,506,000	11,800,000
Supplies Inventories	500,000	400,000
Total Current Assets	9,560,000	14,650,000
Noncurrent Assets		
Investments Limited as to Use	1,620,000	1,500,000
Investments—Restricted for Capital Acquisitions	18,250,000	12,900,000
Investments—Undesignated	4,200,000	4,200,000
Property, Plant, and Equipment	32,750,000	27,550,000
Less: Accumulated Depreciation	(20,600,000)	(15,800,000)
Total Assets	$ 45,780,000	$45,000,000
LIABILITIES AND NET ASSETS		
Current Liabilities		
Accounts Payable	$ 900,000	800,000
Accrued Expenses	1,000,000	900,000
Long-Term Debt: Current Installment	1,000,000	1,000,000
Total Current Liabilities	2,900,000	2,700,000
Long-Term Liabilities	9,800,000	10,800,000
Total Liabilities	12,700,000	13,500,000
Net Assets without Donor Restrictions:		
Board Designated	1,620,000	1,500,000
Undesignated	12,110,000	13,100,000
Total Net Assets without Donor Restrictions	13,730,000	14,600,000
Net Assets with Donor Restrictions:		
Restricted for Program Purposes	1,900,000	4,000,000
Restricted for Capital Asset Acquisition	17,450,000	12,900,000
Total Net Assets	33,080,000	31,500,000
Total Liabilities and Net Assets	$ 45,780,000	45,000,000

is also acceptable (see Illustration 11-7) for private not-for-profit organizations and is required for governmental health care organizations (see Illustration 6-5).

FINANCIAL REPORTING FOR GOVERNMENTAL AND COMMERCIAL HEALTH CARE ENTITIES

Because health care organizations may be private sector or governmental, it is important to identify the appropriate set of standards that govern financial reporting

ILLUSTRATION 12-6 **Statement of Cash Flows**

NONPROFIT HOSPITAL Statement of Cash Flows for the year ended December 31, 2020	
Cash Flows from Operating Activities:	
Change in Net Assets	$ 1,580,000
Adjustments to Reconcile Change in Net Assets to Net Cash Provided by Operating Activities:	
Depreciation	4,800,000
Decrease in Patient Receivable (Net of Allowances for Contractual Adjustments and Implicit Price Concessions)	4,294,000
Increase in Supplies	(100,000)
Increase in Accounts Payable	100,000
Increase in Accrued Expenses	100,000
Gains on Long-Term Investments	(250,000)
Contributions Restricted to Investment in Property, Plant, and Equipment	(5,100,000)
Investment Income Restricted to Investment in Capital Assets	(400,000)
Cash Flows from Operating Activities	5,024,000
Cash Flows from Investing Activities:	
Acquisition of Property, Plant, and Equipment	(5,200,000)
Purchase of Investments	(9,320,000)
Sale of Investments	4,100,000
Cash Flows from Investing Activities	(10,420,000)
Cash Flows from Financing Activities:	
Proceeds from Contributions Restricted for:	
Investment in Capital Assets	5,100,000
Investment Income Restricted to Investment in Capital Assets	400,000
Payments on Long-Term Debt	(1,000,000)
Cash Flows from Financing Activities	4,500,000
Net Increase (Decrease) in Cash and Cash Equivalents	(896,000)
Cash and Cash Equivalents, beginning of year	2,450,000
Cash and Cash Equivalents, end of year	$ 1,554,000
Supplemental Disclosure of Cash Flow Information:	
- Cash Paid for Interest	$ 600,000

for each type. Health care entities that are investor-owned, for-profit enterprises are subject to the FASB (category A GAAP) and the AICPA Health Care Guide (category B GAAP). However, FASB pronouncements specific to not-for-profit organizations do not apply to these business organizations. Accrual accounting applies in the same manner as it would for other commercial enterprises. Equity accounts consist of paid-in capital and retained earnings and either the direct or indirect method of presenting operating cash flows is permitted.

Most governmental health care entities report as special-purpose entities engaged only in business-type activities. Like enterprise funds, these organizations prepare a Statement of Net Position; a Statement of Revenues, Expenses, and Changes in Fund Net Position; and a Statement of Cash Flows. The Statement of Revenues, Expenses, and Changes in Fund Net Position may be separated into two statements, as shown for private health care entities; however, the reporting framework does not encourage such a presentation.

Governmental health care entities reported as enterprise funds of a state or local government use accrual accounting. The statements are similar to those presented in Chapter 6 (Illustrations 6-3, 6-4, and 6-5) with modifications as required by the AICPA Health Care Guide. The **Statement of Net Position** is similar to that presented in Illustration 6-3. It is permissible to use a balance sheet format, where assets equal liabilities plus net position. Net position (residual equity) is categorized as (1) net investment in capital assets, (2) restricted, and (3) unrestricted.

The **Statement of Revenues, Expenses, and Changes in Fund Net Position** is similar to Illustration 6-4. Both GASB and the AICPA require presentation of a performance indicator, such as *income from operations*. In addition, the requirement of the AICPA to place certain items below the performance indicator (such as receipt of restricted contributions) applies. The **Statement of Cash Flows** follows GASB standards, as reflected in Illustration 6-5. The direct method must be used, and four categories of cash flows must be presented. A reconciliation is made between operating income and the cash flows from operating activities.

SUMMARY: ACCOUNTING FOR HEALTH CARE ORGANIZATIONS

Health care entities may be private, not-for-profit, governmental, or commercial (for-profit). Private, not-for-profit, and commercial health care entities have Category A GAAP established by the Financial Accounting Standards Board. State and local governmental health care entities follow principles established by GASB. All, however, are subject to the AICPA Health Care Guide, which is accepted by both FASB and GASB as being Category B GAAP.

This chapter concentrates on accounting and financial reporting required for private not-for-profit health care entities, as these are the most numerous. General FASB requirements regarding financial reporting, including the use of net asset classes, are supplemented by requirements of the Health Care Guide. The financial statements reported as Illustrations 12-3 through 12-6 meet the requirements of both the FASB and the AICPA.

Transactions unique to this industry include charity care, contractual adjustments, implicit price concessions, and capitation premiums. Charity care is not recorded as revenue. Patient Service Revenue is reported net of contractual adjustments and the provision for implicit price concessions. A distinguishing feature of health care organizations is that they report two activity statements. The **Statement of Operations** reports changes in unrestricted (i.e., without donor restrictions) net assets and must include a **performance indicator** (commonly called operating income or loss) that reports results from continuing operations. Within this statement, health care entities must distinguish between operating and nonoperating revenues. The **Statement of Changes in Net Assets** fulfills the FASB requirement to show the changes in net assets by net asset class and in total.

Questions and Exercises

12–1. Describe the accounting treatment by hospitals and health care organizations for each of the following:

a. Charity care

b. Implicit price concessions

c. Contractual adjustments

12–2. Describe the reporting of Board Designated resources.

12–3. For each of the following items, indicate where it would appear in the Statement of Operations for a private not-for-profit hospital:

a. The premium from a capitation agreement, whereby a hospital agrees to provide services to members of an HMO for a prearranged fixed amount.

b. Contractual adjustments for Medicare and Medicaid.

c. Customary charges for charity care.

d. Depreciation expense.

e. Interest expense.

f. Provision for implicit price concessions.

g. Unrestricted investment income.

h. Purchases of equipment.

i. Bad debts.

12–4. Briefly describe the following items related to financial reporting by (*a*) private not-for-profit health care entities; (*b*) government-owned health care entities; and (*c*) commercial health care entities:

(1) Source of Category A and B GAAP.

(2) Residual equity account titles.

(3) Required financial statements.

12–5. With regard to accounting for private not-for-profit health care entities, do the following:

a. Outline the accounting required, under FASB guidance, for a(n)

(1) Endowment gift received in cash.

(2) Pledge received in one year, unrestricted as to purpose but restricted for use in the following year.

(3) Pledge received in one year, restricted as to purpose other than acquisition of fixed assets, which is fulfilled in the following year.

b. List those items required to be reported "outside" the performance indicator in the Statement of Operations.

12–6. During 2020, the following transactions were recorded by the Port Hudson Community Hospital, a private sector not-for-profit institution:

1. Gross charges for patient services, all charged to Patient Accounts Receivable, amounted to $1,800,000. Estimated contractual adjustments with third-party payors amounted to $465,000 and the hospital estimated implicit price concessions would total 10,000.
2. Charity services, not included in transaction 1, would amount to $66,000, had billings been made at gross amounts.
3. Other revenues, received in cash, were parking lot, $20,000; cafeteria, $35,000; gift shop, $5,000.
4. Cash gifts restricted by the donor for programs amounted to $26,000 for the year. During the year, $50,000 was expended for technician salaries supporting the program identified by the donor (Debit Operating Expense—Salaries and Benefits).
5. Mortgage bond payments amounted to $50,000 for principal and $28,000 for interest. Assume unrestricted resources are used.
6. During the year, the hospital received, in cash, unrestricted contributions of $42,000 and unrestricted income of $35,000 from endowment investments. (It is the hospital's practice to treat unrestricted gifts as nonoperating income.)

7. New equipment, costing $152,000, was acquired, using donor-restricted cash that was on hand at the beginning of the year.
8. An old piece of lab equipment that originally cost $50,000 and that had an undepreciated cost of $10,000 was sold for $7,000 cash.
9. At the end of 2020, pledges (restricted as to purpose) were received in the amount of $120,000. These are intended to be received and expended in 2021.
10. Cash contributions were received from donors restricted for plant acquisition, $170,000.
11. Bills were received for the following items: utilities $139,000 and insurance $80,000. These will be paid in January of 2021.
12. Depreciation of plant and equipment amounted to $180,000.
13. Cash payments on accounts payable amounted to $168,000. Another $800,000 was expended on wages and benefits.
14. Cash collections of patient accounts receivable amounted to $1,180,000. These were in settlement of patient accounts totaling $1,587,000. Contractual adjustments associated with these totaled $400,000 and price concessions totaled $7,000.
15. Closing entries were prepared.

Required:

a. Record the transactions in the general journal of the Port Hudson Community Hospital.
b. Prepare, in good form, a Statement of Operations for the Port Hudson Community Hospital for the year ended December 31, 2020.
c. Prepare, in good form, a Statement of Changes in Net Assets for the Port Hudson Community Hospital for the year ended December 31, 2020. Assume beginning net assets are $7,000,000.

12–7. Record the following transactions on the books of Hope Hospital, which follows FASB (not-for-profit) and AICPA standards. The year is 2020.

1. Hope received $15,000 in cash from pledges made in the previous year that were unrestricted as to purpose but intended to be received and expended in 2020.
2. Hope received $31,000 in pledges that indicated the money would be received in 2021. The donors imposed no restrictions other than it could be used for any purpose desired by the board.
3. Hope expended $40,000 for nursing training, using $33,000 of donor-restricted resources received in 2019 for that purpose.
4. On June 15, 2020, Hope was awarded a $50,000 grant for cancer research by the U.S. Department of Agriculture. During 2020, Hope had qualified expenses under the grant totaling $35,000. This is cost reimbursement, grant.
5. Hope received $270,000 in cash. The board decided to invest the funds for future plant expansion.

12–8. St. Joseph's Hospital began operations in December 2019 and had patient service revenues totaling $1,000,000 (based on customary rates) for the month. Of this, $120,000 is billed to patients, representing their insurance deductibles and copayments. The balance is billed to third-party payors, including insurance companies and government health care agencies. St. Joseph's estimates that 20 percent of these third-party payor charges will be deducted by contractual adjustment. The hospital's fiscal year ends on December 31.

Required:

1. Prepare the journal entries for December 2019. Assume 15 percent of the amounts billed to patients will be reduced through implicit price adjustments.
2. Prepare the journal entries for 2020 assuming the following:
   a. $98,000 is collected from the patients during the year and $9,500 of price adjustments are granted to individuals.
   b. Actual contractual adjustments total $181,000. The remaining receivable from third-party payors is collected.
3. The actual contractual adjustments differed from the amount initially estimated by the hospital. Briefly describe the type of accounting change this represents and the appropriate accounting treatment.

Excel-Based Problems

12–9. As of January 1, 2020, the trial balance for Haven Hospital was as follows (these have been entered into the Excel template provided):

	Debits	Credits
Cash	$ 830,000	
Patient Accounts Receivable	3,250,000	
Allowance for Implicit Price Concessions		$ 650,000
Allowance for Contractual Adjustments		353,000
Pledges Receivable	2,480,000	
Supplies	130,000	
Investments—Assets Limited as to Use	1,700,000	
Investments—Undesignated	10,100,000	
Property, Plant, and Equipment	7,500,000	
Accumulated Depreciation—Property, Plant, and Equipment		4,600,000
Accounts Payable		600,000
Long-Term Debt—Current Installment		200,000
Long-Term Debt—Noncurrent		3,100,000
Net Assets without Donor Restrictions—Board Designated		1,700,000
Net Assets without Donor Restrictions—Undesignated		1,644,000
Net Assets with Donor Restrictions—Program Restrictions		13,143,000
Totals	$25,990,000	$25,990,000

During the fiscal year ended December 31, 2020, the following transactions occurred:

1. Patient service revenue amounted to $19,990,000, all recorded on account. Contractual adjustments were recorded in the amount of $3,200,000. Implicit price concessions are estimated to be $620,000.
2. Other revenue (cafeteria, parking lot, etc.) amounted to $2,850,000, all received in cash.
3. Cash was received on patient accounts in the amount of $17,600,000. Contractual adjustments of $3,250,000 and implicit price reductions of $430,000 were applied to customer accounts.
4. Unrestricted gifts and bequests were received in cash in the amount of $328,000. Unrestricted income on investments of endowment funds amounted to $400,000. (It is the hospital's practice to treat unrestricted gifts as nonoperating revenue.)
5. Investment income on board-designated funds, which is limited by board policy to provide renewals and replacements, amounted to $87,000 and was received in cash. Do not increase board-designated net assets at this stage but close out the revenue account to board-designated net assets in entry 19.
6. Investment income, restricted for donor-specified purposes, was received in cash in the amount of $250,000. Investment income, required by donor agreement to be added to endowment balances, was received in cash in the amount of $90,000.
7. Cash contributions were received in the following amounts: $2,001,000 for current restricted purposes; $2,450,000 for future plant expansion; and $1,050,000 required by the donor to be invested permanently in an endowment.
8. Pledges receivable in the amount of $2,100,000 were received in cash. These pledges were on hand at the beginning of the year (reflected in net assets with donor restrictions, for time) and were unrestricted as to purpose. In addition, pledges for endowment purposes were collected in the amount of $450,000.
9. $1,550,000 in restricted net assets was expended, as the donors stipulated. Debit Operating Expense—Salaries and Benefits, $1,400,000; and Operating Expense—Supplies, $150,000. (Assume the supplies were purchased with cash and used in the same year.)
10. A total of $1,850,000 in donor-restricted net assets was expended for equipment, as provided for by the donor. The policy of Haven Hospital is to record all property, plant, and equipment as unrestricted.

11. In addition, $600,000 was received in pledges for program-restricted purposes.
12. Supplies were purchased in the amount of $683,000, on account.
13. Operating expenses (in addition to those already recorded in entries 1 and 9) for the year included: depreciation of $600,000; supplies used of $677,000; and salaries and benefits of $20,985,000 (paid in cash). In addition the following expenses were recorded through Accounts Payable: utilities of $515,000 and insurance of $320,000.
14. Accounts payable were paid in the amount of $1,759,000.
15. Current installments of long-term debt were paid in the amount of $200,000. The portion to be paid next year is $300,000. Interest was paid in the amount of $181,000 and is reported as an operating expense.
16. Investments, carried at a basis of $4,000,000, were sold for $4,050,000. The $50,000 gain is considered to be donor restricted (purpose).
17. Cash in the amount of $6,800,000 was invested. Of that amount, $87,000 was from Cash—Assets Limited as to Use and is designated by the board for renewals and replacements (see entry 5).
18. A reading of the financial press indicated investments increased in market value by $800,000. Of that amount, $250,000 was in investments designated by the board for renewals and replacements, $350,000 is required by donors to be added to endowment balances, and the remainder is unrestricted.
19. Closing entries were prepared.

Required:

a. Using the Excel template provided, prepare journal entries for each of the previous transactions.

b. Prepare a Statement of Operations for Haven Hospital for the year ended December 31, 2020.

c. Prepare a Statement of Changes in Net Assets for Haven Hospital for the year ended December 31, 2020.

d. Prepare a Statement of Financial Position for Haven Hospital as of December 31, 2020.

e. Prepare a Statement of Cash Flows for Haven Hospital for the year ended December 31, 2020, using the indirect method.

12–10. Presented below are account balances for Monterey Hospital. In addition, cash transactions for the year ended December 31, 2020, are summarized in the T-account.

	BALANCE SHEET ACCOUNTS	
	December 31, 2019	**December 31, 2020**
Debits		
Cash	1,000,000	$2,895,700
Patient Accounts Receivable (net)	1,210,000	592,800
Third-Party Accounts Receivable (net)	1,190,000	1,383,200
Contributions Receivable	10,000	12,500
Supplies	—	—
Investments—Endowment	1,500,000	1,620,000
Property, Plant, and Equipment	4,875,000	5,182,000
Credits		
Accumulated Depreciation	2,107,000	2,567,000
Accounts Payable (supplies)	37,500	46,200
Long-Term Debt	2,282,000	2,782,000
Net Assets or Net Position—December 31, 2019	5,358,500	
Net Assets or Net Position—December 31, 2020		6,291,000

ACTIVITY ACCOUNTS	
Debits	
Contractual Adjustments	1,100,000
Provision for Implicit Price Concessions	33,500
Operating Expenses—Depreciation	460,000
Operating Expenses—Salaries	6,900,000
Operating Expenses—Supplies	2,200,000
Reclassification from Net Assets with Donor Restrictions (time restrictions)	19,600
Net Losses on Investments—Permanent Endowment	10,000
Credits	
Patient Service Revenue—(patient portion) Unrestricted	3,156,000
Patient Service Revenue—(insurer portion) Unrestricted	7,364,000
Income on Endowments—Unrestricted	25,000
Reclassification to Unrestricted Net Assets	19,600
Contribution Revenue—without Donor Restrictions	36,000
Contribution Revenue—with Donor Restrictions (endowment)	130,000
Contribution Revenue—with Donor Restrictions (Restricted for Future Years)	25,000
Other Information:	
Sales of Property and Equipment	none
Purchases of Property and Equipment	307,000
Issuance of Long-Term Debt	600,000
Excess Credits over Debits—Activity Accounts	32,500
Beginning Net Assets or Net Position	5,358,500
Ending Net Assets or Net Position 2015	5,391,000

CASH (2020)

	Debit	Credit	
Beginning balance 1/1	1,000,000		
Collections from patients	3,739,700	6,900,000	Salaries
Collections from third parties	6,070,800	2,191,300	Operating expenses
Contributions to Endowment	130,000		
Other Contributions	58,500	307,000	Equipment purchases
Investment Income	25,000	100,000	Payment principal LT Debt
Proceeds—LT debt	600,000	130,000	Purchase Endowment Investments
Ending balance 12/31	1,995,700		

The hospital issued $600,000 of long-term debt during the year and purchased $307,000 of equipment. No fixed assets were sold.

Required:

Using the information above and the Excel template provided, prepare

a. A Statement of Operations and a Statement of Changes in Net Assets for the year ended December 31, 2020, assuming Monterey Hospital is a private not-for-profit.

b. Statements of Cash Flow assuming

1. Monterey Hospital is a private not-for-profit.
2. Monterey Hospital is a government-owned hospital.

Chapter Thirteen

Auditing, Tax-Exempt Organizations, and Evaluating Performance

The Foundation announced its intent to dissolve and is seeking approval to distribute its remaining funds to highly qualified and important Section 501(c)(3) charities. Donald J. Trump Foundation 2016 Form 990, publicly available tax return. The foundation's activities came under scrutiny for ethical violations, including improper campaign contributions. In December 2018, the foundation agreed to shut down under court supervision

This is an unprecedented fraud against the City and our people. Any misuse of taxpayer money is antithetical to our values and commitment to our government. We must, and will, ensure that we enact measures to protect our City from future crimes to every extent possible. Bill Bogaard, mayor of Pasadena, California, in response to an audit finding that a city employee submitted $6.4 million in fraudulent invoices

Learning Objectives

- Describe the unique characteristics of audits of governmental and not-for-profit entities.
- Describe the major requirements of the Single Audit Act.
- Describe the reporting requirements of tax-exempt organizations.
- Identify when a not-for-profit organization is subject to the unrelated business income tax and describe how the tax is determined.
- Identify financial ratios commonly used to evaluate governmental and not-for-profit entities and describe how they are calculated and interpreted.
- Identify the elements of service efforts and accomplishments reporting and explain why governments and not-for-profits report nonfinancial performance measures.

Chapters 2 through 12 present accounting and financial reporting requirements of state and local governments and not-for-profit organizations. This chapter describes (1) the unique aspects of auditing governments and not-for-profit organizations, (2) the taxation and tax filing requirements of not-for-profit organizations, and (3) the use of financial and nonfinancial measures to evaluate the performance and financial position of government and not-for-profit organizations.

GOVERNMENTAL AUDITING

Auditing of governmental and not-for-profit entities has much in common with auditing of business enterprises, including making judgments about internal controls, selectively testing transactions, assessing the fairness of financial statements, and issuing audit reports. However, governmental auditing, like governmental accounting, follows a unique set of professional guidelines established by a separate governing organization.

Governmental units and many not-for-profit organizations are subject to *Government Auditing Standards* in addition to the *Statements on Auditing Standards* issued by the American Institute of Certified Public Accountants (AICPA). *Government Auditing Standards* are issued by the U.S. Government Accountability Office (GAO) and apply to audits conducted to satisfy the requirements of the Single Audit Act as well as other governmental audits. In common terminology, the standards issued by the AICPA are known as **GAAS (Generally Accepted Auditing Standards),** and the standards issued by the GAO are known as GAGAS (Generally Accepted Government Auditing Standards).

Government Auditing Standards (GAS), published in a document commonly known as the *Yellow Book,* incorporate the AICPA standards and provide extensions that are necessary due to the unique nature of public entities. These extensions, for example, require auditor knowledge of government accounting and auditing, public availability of audit reports, written evaluations of internal controls, and distribution of the reports and availability of working papers to federal and state funding authorities. The standards also emphasize the heightened importance of government audits in a democratic society: "in audits performed in accordance with GAGAS, auditors may find it appropriate to use lower materiality levels as compared with the materiality levels used in non-GAGAS audits because of the public accountability of government entities and entities receiving government funding, various legal and regulatory requirements, and the visibility and sensitivity of government programs" (paragraph 4.47). Additional guidance for audits of state and local governments is found in the *AICPA Audit and Accounting Guide: State and Local Governments* (2018) and the *AICPA Audit Guide: Government Auditing Standards and Single Audits* (2018).

Types of Governmental Audits *Government Auditing Standards* identify four categories of professional engagements: financial audits, attestation engagements, performance audits, and nonaudit services. These are described in Illustration 13-1. Nonaudit services are not covered by *Government Auditing Standards* and differ from the other types of engagements in that the auditors are providing information to a requesting party without providing verification or evaluation of the information. These engagements may result in a report but not an opinion on the information.

ILLUSTRATION 13-1 Types of Governmental Audits and Attestation Engagements

1. **Financial Audits** provide an opinion about whether an entity's financial statements are presented fairly in all material respects in conformity with applicable accounting standards.
2. **Attestation Engagements** involve a report of an examination, review, or agreed-upon procedures on a subject matter or an assertion about a subject matter that is the responsibility of another party.
3. **Performance Audits** provide objective analysis to improve program performance and operations, reduce costs, facilitate decision making, and contribute to public accountability.
4. **Nonaudit Services** consist of gathering, providing, or explaining information requested by decision makers or providing advice or assistance to management.

Source: Comptroller General of the United States, Government Auditing Standards (Washington, DC: U.S. Government Accountability Office, 2018).

Financial audits must comply with the AICPA's generally accepted auditing standards for fieldwork and reporting as well as *Government Auditing Standards.* Governmental standards prescribe additional fieldwork and reporting requirements beyond those provided by the AICPA. For example, auditors are specifically required to test compliance with laws and regulations and internal control over financial reporting. With regard to communications, governmental auditors should communicate not only with officials of the audited organization, but also with parties that have oversight responsibility for the audited organization such as legislative members or staff.

Attestation engagements encompass a wide range of activities. These include reporting on an entity's (1) system of internal control, (2) compliance with laws and regulations, (3) prospective financial information, and (4) costs under contracts. Similar to financial audits, attestation engagements must comply with both the AICPA's attestation standards and *Government Auditing Standards.*

Performance audits encompass a variety of objectives and may be more analogous to the functions normally performed by internal auditors in the private sector, except that the results are made public. Generally they are undertaken to assess program effectiveness and results; economy and efficiency; internal controls as they relate to program management and reporting; and compliance with legal requirements and other program matters. Effectiveness audits measure the extent to which a program is achieving its goals, while economy and efficiency audits are concerned with whether an organization is acquiring, protecting, and using its resources in the most productive manner to achieve program objectives.

For example, an auditor performing an economy and efficiency audit of a Head Start program might observe purchasing procedures and evaluate transportation routes, classroom sizes, and general office procedures. An auditor performing an effectiveness audit would look to the original legislation to determine explicit or implicit objectives, develop criteria to determine whether the objectives were being met, and evaluate the relative benefit of alternative approaches. The audit team will often include specialists outside of accounting who are better prepared to assess program effectiveness. Performance audits are not intended to be done on an annual basis but are expected to be performed periodically as a means of holding government accountable for carrying out its legislative mandates.

The Yellow Book is revised periodically. The most recent version is available from the GAO's website (www.GAO.gov). The standards describe five ethical concepts underlying effective auditing:

1. *Public interest* focuses auditors' attention on serving the citizenry and honoring the public trust.
2. *Integrity* requires auditors to conduct their work with an attitude that is objective, fact-based, and nonpartisan.
3. *Objectivity* includes independence in fact and appearance and being free of conflicts of interest.
4. *Proper use of government information, resources, and position* precludes auditors from using sensitive or classified information or resources for personal gain.
5. *Professional behavior* includes auditors conducting their services in accordance with technical and professional standards.

Opinion Units In any audit engagement, the auditor must determine a level of materiality. This determination is then used to plan, perform, and evaluate the results of audit procedures. Because of the various levels of reporting by governments (government-wide, fund-type, and individual fund), it may not be clear which level was most appropriate for determining materiality.

Government auditing standards require a separate (quantitative) materiality evaluation for each opinion unit. Each of the following is considered an opinion unit:

- Governmental activities (government-wide statements).
- Business-type activities (government-wide statements).
- Each major fund (both governmental and enterprise).
- The aggregate of all discretely presented component units.
- The aggregate of all remaining fund information.

The first two categories relate to information contained in the government-wide financial statements, and the remaining three relate to information contained in the fund-basis financial statements. The final category includes nonmajor governmental and enterprise funds, internal service funds, and fiduciary funds.

One effect of reporting on opinion units is that some opinion units may receive unmodified or clean opinions, while others receive modified opinions. For example, failure to report infrastructure assets could result in an adverse opinion regarding the governmental activities reported in the government-wide statements and an **unmodified opinion** for the business-type, major fund, aggregate component unit, and aggregate of all remaining fund information. Audit reports are discussed in the next section.

Audit Reports Reporting requirements are a combination of requirements of the *Government Auditing Standards* and the single audit requirements (described in the next section). A reporting package is due to a designated federal repository nine months after the end of the fiscal year. Part of the reporting is done by the auditor and part by the audited organization. The auditor is required to prepare up to five reports:

1. A report containing an opinion on the financial statements.
2. A report discussing the evaluation and testing of internal control and compliance with laws and regulations.
3. A report discussing significant deficiencies in internal controls.
4. A report describing instances of fraud, illegal acts, or other material noncompliance.
5. A report containing the views of responsible officials of the audited organization regarding any reported significant deficiencies.

Unlike private sector audits, the auditor is required to report directly to appropriate officials, such as funding agencies or legislative bodies, as well as to the organization's board or audit committee. Additionally, the auditor must report the existence of any privileged or confidential information not contained in the audit reports.

Guidelines for conducting and reporting on financial audits of state and local governments as well as sample audit reports are contained in the AICPA *Audit and Accounting Guide: State and Local Governments.* The AICPA has developed standard wording for auditor's reports to make clear the responsibility the auditor is accepting. If the financial statements are prepared in conformity with generally accepted accounting principles, the auditor expresses an "unmodified," or clean, opinion. Because of the unique reporting by governments, the language of the auditor's report is different from those prepared for commercial businesses. For example, the report refers to the various reporting levels (government activities, business activities, and major funds), which is not required of audit reports of business entities.

As we have seen in earlier chapters, the basic financial statements should be accompanied by required supplementary information (RSI), such as management's discussion and analysis and budgetary comparison schedules. Unless the auditor is engaged to render an opinion on the RSI, auditors are required to perform only limited procedures to make sure the information is not misleading.

Additionally, other information may be presented in a CAFR, such as the letter of transmittal, statistical section, and combining statements for nonmajor funds. Unless auditors are engaged to render an opinion on this supplemental information, professional standards require the auditor only to read this *nonrequired* supplemental information and consider whether the information or the manner of its presentation is materially inconsistent with the financial statements. If the auditor believes this information or the RSI is misleading, the auditor should include an explanatory paragraph in the auditor's report to explain the situation.

In addition to issuing the unmodified opinion, independent auditors also issue qualified opinions and adverse opinions. In some circumstances the auditor may disclaim an opinion. Three conditions require a departure from an unmodified report: (1) the scope of the audit has been restricted, (2) the financial statements have not been prepared in accordance with generally accepted accounting principles, and

(3) the auditor is not independent. The appropriate opinion depends on the type and severity of the condition:

- ***Qualified opinion*** A qualified opinion may result from either a limitation on the scope of the audit or failure to follow generally accepted accounting principles (conditions 1 or 2). The opinion states that, except for the effects of the matter(s) to which the qualification relates, the financial statements are fairly presented.
- ***Adverse opinion*** An adverse opinion is used when the auditor believes that the financial statements are so materially misstated or misleading that they do not present fairly the financial position and results of operations (and cash flows, if applicable) in accordance with generally accepted accounting principles (condition 2).
- ***Disclaimer of opinion*** A disclaimer of opinion is appropriate if the auditor is not satisfied that the financial statements are fairly presented because of a severe scope limitation (condition 1). A disclaimer is also appropriate if the auditor is not independent, as defined by the *Code of Professional Conduct* (condition 3). In a disclaimer, the auditor states that no opinion is being expressed.

The Single Audit Act and Amendments

History Federal financial assistance is an important source of financing operating and capital expenditures of state and local governments and not-for-profit organizations. In the past, federal grants-in-aid and federal contracts were subject to accounting, reporting, and auditing requirements that varied depending on which agency of the federal government administered the grant program or contract. Efforts were made during the 1960s and 1970s to standardize requirements but met with only moderate success.

The Single Audit Act of 1984 was enacted to provide uniform requirements for audits of state and local organizations receiving federal financial assistance. Following the legislation, the Office of Management and Budget (OMB) issued Circular A-133 providing requirements for federal agencies in administering grants for nongovernmental not-for-profit organizations, even though those organizations were not covered under the 1984 act. Congress enacted the Single Audit Act Amendments of 1996 that extended the 1984 law to include federal assistance to nongovernmental not-for-profit organizations.

Purpose The main objective of the single audit process is to create a mechanism whereby those auditors conducting the regular financial audits of state and local governments and not-for-profit organizations can provide assurance to the federal government that federal funds are expended in accordance with grant agreements and with financial management and other standards promulgated by the federal government. This is more efficient than having grant-by-grant audits supervised by each agency that provides funds.

Governments and not-for-profit organizations that expend $50 million in federal awards are assigned **cognizant agencies** (normally the federal agencies that provide the most funding). Organizations receiving smaller amounts are expected to use **oversight agencies** (again, the agencies providing the most funding). Cognizant agencies are required to monitor the audit process and resolve findings and questioned costs. Oversight agencies may do the same, at their option. Audits are conducted according to the requirements of the Single Audit Act, as amended, OMB Circular A-133, and a *Compliance Supplement* issued by OMB that includes OMB-approved special requirements for many of the grants.

AICPA Statement of Position 98-3 and OMB Circular A-133 provide guidance for the auditor in implementing the single audit requirement. First, a determination must be made as to whether a client is subject to the Single Audit Act. Entities that expend $750,000 or more in federal awards in a fiscal year have either a single audit (when several grantors are involved) or a program-specific audit (usually when only one grantor is involved).

Major Programs A major program is a program selected for audit under the single audit approach. The auditor is required to express an opinion on compliance for major programs, which generally must add up to 50 percent of the federal funds expended by the government being audited (i.e., auditee). This is reduced to 25 percent if the auditee is determined by the auditor to be a **low-risk auditee.** A low-risk auditee is one that for the past two years has met certain criteria such as unmodified opinions, no material weakness in internal controls, and no material noncompliance on major programs.

Major programs are determined on a risk-based approach. First, the programs are classified into Type A and Type B programs. Type A programs are the larger programs. The minimum threshold for Type A programs begins at $750,000 of federal awards but is adjusted upward based on a percentage of federal funds expended. Type A programs are considered major programs unless they are determined to be low risk. In order for this to happen, a Type A program must have been audited during the past two years as a major program and have had no major audit findings. Type B programs are included as major programs only if the auditor determines that they are high risk. A risk assessment must be made of Type B programs that exceed 25 percent of the Type A threshold.

For example, assume that a city goverment that is not determined to be low risk has five programs, two Type A and three Type B, as follows:

Type A

Housing and Urban Development, $750,000, audited last year with no major control problems or compliance findings

Environmental Protection Agency, $800,000, not audited during the past two years

Type B

Department of Education, $400,000
Department of Energy, $310,000
Department of Agriculture, $90,000

The total amount of grant expenditures is $2,350,000, so at least $1,175,000 (50 percent) must be audited as major programs. The Environmental Protection Agency grant must be audited, as it does not meet the criteria of low risk, not having been audited in the past two years. Then the auditor must choose grants adding up to $375,000.

The other Type A program could be audited, or the auditor could select Type B programs, based on a risk assessment. If any of them are deemed high risk, they would be selected for audit. If not, the auditor could choose either the Department of Education ($400,000) or the programs from the Departments of Energy and Agriculture, which also add up to $400,000.

If the auditee were considered low risk, then only 25 percent of the grant expenditures would be required as major programs; if risk assessments showed that the Departments of Education and Energy were low risk, then the EPA grant could be the only grant audited as a major program. The auditor is not required to perform a risk assessment on the Department of Agriculture grant because it does not exceed 25 percent of the $750,000 threshold applied to Type A grants.

The Sarbanes-Oxley Act

The Sarbanes-Oxley Act was signed into law in 2002 in response to accounting scandals in the business sector. The act is intended to improve corporate governance and limit the services accounting firms may provide to their audit clients. While the act applies only to corporations filing with the Securities and Exchange Commission, it has changed the way public accounting firms relate to all their clients, including governmental and not-for-profit organizations. The act has also influenced governing boards, and many not-for-profit boards have begun to model themselves on corporate governance "best practices" initiated by the Sarbanes-Oxley Act. Several of the provisions of the act already existed in governmental auditing standards. In particular, auditors are to report deficiencies in the design or operation of internal controls. Additionally, GAO standards for independence prohibit auditors from performing many nonaudit services.

As a result of heightened public awareness for the importance of accountability and independence, other provisions of the Sarbanes-Oxley Act are being voluntarily adopted by not-for-profit organizations. These include

- Establishing audit committees composed of nonmanagement board members and assigning the committee responsibility for the appointment, compensation, and oversight of the auditor.
- Requiring the chief executive and chief financial officers to publicly attest to the accuracy and completeness of the financial report and the adequacy of the system of internal controls.
- Requiring audit partner rotation and a concurring partner review of the reports.
- Having all nonaudit services performed by the auditors approved by the audit committee.
- Establishing a code of conduct for the organization and a mechanism for whistle-blowing by employees.

Additional pressure to adopt these practices has come from funding foundations that have announced that Sarbanes-Oxley compliance will be a factor in the awarding of grants.

Summary Like governmental accounting, governmental auditing follows a unique set of professional guidelines. *Government Auditing Standards* are established by the U.S. Government Accountability Office. These standards differ from those governing audits of private businesses. In particular, governmental standards require auditors to evaluate and report on the system of internal controls and compliance with laws and regulations. Governmental auditors are required to report to funding agencies or oversight bodies in addition to the management of the organization under audit.

Frequently state and local governments and not-for-profit organizations receive funding under a variety of federal programs. Many of these organizations are subject to the requirements of the Single Audit Act and its amendments. Auditors of these organizations must be familiar with governmental auditing standards as well as specific requirements under the act for determining major programs subject to audit.

TAX-EXEMPT ORGANIZATIONS

Accountants working for, auditing, or providing consulting services to not-for-profit organizations must be aware of certain tax issues related to those organizations. Generally, not-for-profit organizations are exempt from federal income taxes. However, it is possible for them to engage in activities that result in **Unrelated Business Income Tax (UBIT).** This section of the chapter discusses the provisions in the tax code that provide exemption for certain types of not-for-profit organizations, discusses and illustrates the tax form that is used for many of these organizations (**Form 990**), and concludes by examining the unrelated business income sections of the tax code that may cause an exempt organization to pay taxes or even lose its exempt status.

Tax Code Section 501 provides that nonprofit organizations organized for charitable purposes may be exempt from federal income taxes. These include civic leagues, trade and professional associations, social clubs and country clubs, fraternal societies, and veterans organizations. In order to qualify as tax exempt, the entity must have a limited purpose, must not have the authority to engage in activities other than exempt purposes, and must not be engaged in political activities. Because state laws govern sales taxes, 501(c)(3) status may not exempt the organization from sales taxes.

The most common form of tax-exempt organization are **501(c)(3) entities.** A 501(c)(3) organization is a "corporation and any community chest, fund, or foundation organized and operated exclusively for religious, charitable, scientific, testing for public safety, literary or educational purposes, or to foster national or international amateur sports competition (so long as none of its activities involve the providing of athletic facilities or equipment) or for the prevention of cruelty to children or animals. The organization also agrees that no part of the net earnings inures to the benefit of any individual or shareholder and the organization agrees to refrain from participating in political campaigns or lobbying for legislation."[1] To apply for tax-exempt status, an organization should file IRS Form 1023, *Application for Recognition of*

[1] U.S. Internal Revenue Code Section 501(c)(3).

Exemption Under Section 501(c)(3) of the Internal Revenue Code. Certain special rules apply to private foundations, as distinguished from **public charities.**

A public charity is defined as (1) a church, school, hospital, governmental unit, or publicly supported charity; (2) an organization that receives more than one-third of its support from a combination of contributions, membership fees, and gross receipts from exempt activities and no more than one-third of its support from a combination of investment income and net unrelated business income after taxes; (3) an organization operated exclusively for the benefit of organizations already described; or (4) an organization founded and operated exclusively for public safety. The remainder of this section will concentrate on public charities.

Applying for Tax-Exempt Status

Organizations that receive substantial support from outside contributors find it particularly important to have Section 501(c)(3) status. Contributions made to such organizations are deductible when computing income taxes as well as estate taxes. For this reason, many donors require proof of Section 501(c)(3) status before making contributions. The ability to deduct donations reduces the net cost of contributions to the donor but places some restrictions on the activities of the tax-exempt organization and imposes reporting requirements. For example, exempt organizations are prohibited from supporting political candidates or campaigning to influence legislation. Reporting requirements are described in the next section of this chapter.

To qualify for tax-exempt status, the organization must

1. Have an Employer's Identification Number (IRS Form ss-4).
2. Be organized as a corporation, trust, or association.
3. Complete IRS Form 1023, *Application for Recognition of Exemption.*
4. Receive notice from the IRS that the organization has been determined to be tax exempt.

Form 1023 requires the organization to provide information regarding its purpose and activities and provide up to four years of financial information or budgets. Copies of the organizing documents (articles of incorporation or association, bylaws, or trust agreement) must accompany the application. Again state law determines what an organization must do to incorporate. Many times it is easier for the organization to prepare articles of association, but these articles must include specific language regarding the purpose of the organization, the distribution of any earnings, and the disposition of assets in the event the organization is dissolved.

Federal Filing Requirements

Not-for-profit 501(c)(3) organizations must file an information return with the IRS annually. Several variations of this return are available, depending on the size of the organization:

- Form 990: Titled "Return of Organization Exempt from Income Tax," this return provides the public with financial information and is also used by the IRS to monitor the activities of tax-exempt organizations.

- Form 990-EZ: Shorter than Form 990, this is available for tax-exempt not-for-profits with annual gross receipts under \$200,000 and total assets of less than \$500,000.
- Form 990-N: This "electronic postcard" is available for tax-exempt not-for-profits with annual gross receipts of \$50,000 or less. Filed electronically, this is the simplest of the forms and requires only eight pieces of information.

1. Taxpayer Identification Number.
2. Tax year.
3. Legal name and mailing address.
4. Any other names the organization uses.
5. Name and address of a principal officer.
6. Website address if the organization has one.
7. Confirmation that the organization's annual gross receipts are \$50,000 or less.
8. An indication whether or not the organization is going out of business.

Churches and related associations of churches are exempt from these filing requirements.

Form 990 provides both financial and nonfinancial information. The first section of this form is reproduced in Illustration 13-2. The purpose of Form 990 is to promote tax compliance by ensuring that tax-exempt entities remain within their exempt purpose and to provide the IRS and the public with a transparent and comprehensive view of the organization.

Major sections of Form 990 include

- **Statement of Program Accomplishments** This section requires the organization to report its mission and services. The organization is required to provide specific measures of its service accomplishments.
- **Governance, Management, and Disclosures** In this section the organization describes its governing body, business relationships, management structure, and key policies including fund-raising, compensation, code of ethics, whistle-blowing, document retention, and whether the organization receives a financial audit.
- **Compensation Schedules** Schedules are provided for the compensation of officers, directors, trustees, and highest-paid employees and independent contractors.
- **Financial Information** These include a Statement of Revenues, Statement of Functional Expenses, and Balance Sheet.

The financial information required by Form 990 is very similar to that required under FASB standards for private not-for-profits except that a cash flow statement and notes are not required. A Statement of Functional Expenses is required, with particular emphasis on the distinction between program, management, and fund-raising expenses. The form also requires the organization to state whether it was audited and whether it is subject to the requirements of the Single Audit Act.

ILLUSTRATION 13-2 Part 1 of Form 990

Form **990**

Department of the Treasury
Internal Revenue Service

Return of Organization Exempt From Income Tax

Under section 501(c), 527, or 4947(a)(1) of the Internal Revenue Code (except private foundations)

▶ **Do not enter social security numbers on this form as it may be made public.**

▶ **Go to *www.irs.gov/Form990* for instructions and the latest information.**

OMB No. 1545-0047

2018

Open to Public Inspection

A For the 2018 calendar year, or tax year beginning , 2018, and ending , 20

B Check if applicable:	C Name of organization		D Employer identification number
☐ Address change	Doing business as		
☐ Name change	Number and street (or P.O. box if mail is not delivered to street address)	Room/suite	E Telephone number
☐ Initial return			
☐ Final return/terminated	City or town, state or province, country, and ZIP or foreign postal code		
☐ Amended return			G Gross receipts $
☐ Application pending	F Name and address of principal officer:		H(a) Is this a group return for subordinates? ☐ Yes ☐ No
			H(b) Are all subordinates included? ☐ Yes ☐ No If "No," attach a list. (see instructions)

I Tax-exempt status: ☐ 501(c)(3) ☐ 501(c) ( ) ◀ (insert no.) ☐ 4947(a)(1) or ☐ 527

J **Website:** ▶   **H(c)** Group exemption number ▶

K Form of organization: ☐ Corporation ☐ Trust ☐ Association ☐ Other ▶   **L** Year of formation: **M** State of legal domicile:

Part I Summary

				Prior Year	Current Year
Activities & Governance	1	Briefly describe the organization's mission or most significant activities:			
	2	Check this box ▶☐ if the organization discontinued its operations or disposed of more than 25% of its net assets.			
	3	Number of voting members of the governing body (Part VI, line 1a)	3		
	4	Number of independent voting members of the governing body (Part VI, line 1b)	4		
	5	Total number of individuals employed in calendar year 2018 (Part V, line 2a)	5		
	6	Total number of volunteers (estimate if necessary)	6		
	7a	Total unrelated business revenue from Part VIII, column (C), line 12	7a		
	b	Net unrelated business taxable income from Form 990-T, line 38	7b		
Revenue	8	Contributions and grants (Part VIII, line 1h)			
	9	Program service revenue (Part VIII, line 2g)			
	10	Investment income (Part VIII, column (A), lines 3, 4, and 7d)			
	11	Other revenue (Part VIII, column (A), lines 5, 6d, 8c, 9c, 10c, and 11e)			
	12	Total revenue—add lines 8 through 11 (must equal Part VIII, column (A), line 12)			
Expenses	13	Grants and similar amounts paid (Part IX, column (A), lines 1–3)			
	14	Benefits paid to or for members (Part IX, column (A), line 4)			
	15	Salaries, other compensation, employee benefits (Part IX, column (A), lines 5–10)			
	16a	Professional fundraising fees (Part IX, column (A), line 11e)			
	b	Total fundraising expenses (Part IX, column (D), line 25) ▶			
	17	Other expenses (Part IX, column (A), lines 11a–11d, 11f–24e)			
	18	Total expenses. Add lines 13–17 (must equal Part IX, column (A), line 25)			
	19	Revenue less expenses. Subtract line 18 from line 12			
				Beginning of Current Year	**End of Year**
Net Assets or Fund Balances	20	Total assets (Part X, line 16)			
	21	Total liabilities (Part X, line 26)			
	22	Net assets or fund balances. Subtract line 21 from line 20			

The Taxpayer Bill of Rights (1996) called for an increase in public disclosures of tax-exempt organizations. Exempt organizations are required to provide copies, upon request, of the three most recent annual Form 990s. Many organizations choose to satisfy the requirement to provide copies by placing their documents on their Web page or on that of another entity as part of a database of similar documents.

In addition to having federal filing requirements, an organization has a number of state filing requirements. Many require a copy of Form 990, and others supplement this form with additional requirements. It should be noted that not-for-profit organizations are normally corporations created under the laws of individual states; as such, they are subject to state laws and regulations as well as those of the federal government.

Unrelated Business Income Tax (UBIT)

A tax-exempt organization is required to pay tax at the 21% corporate rate on income generated from any trade or business activities unrelated to the entity's tax-exempt purposes. The purpose of this requirement is to eliminate advantages that tax-exempt organizations have over profit-making organizations. For example, a college bookstore, when selling certain items to nonstudents, would be competing with private business engaged in the same activities.

This provision has created some controversy. Many activities could be judged by some to be related to the tax-exempt purposes of a not-for-profit and by others as unrelated. As a result, a body of case law has evolved, and certain specific situations have been addressed by legislation.

The existence of one or more of the following conditions will exempt income-producing activities from UBIT: (1) the business is not regularly carried on; (2) volunteers perform most of the labor; (3) the not-for-profit sells donated merchandise; and (4) it is operated for the convenience of employees, patients, students, and so on. Additional exceptions have been provided in legislation. Among others, these include (1) royalties, dividends, interest, and annuities (except from controlled corporations); (2) income of a college or university or hospital from research performed for a person or governmental unit; (3) income from qualified public entertainment activities in connection with a fair or exposition; (4) income from labor, agricultural, and horticultural organizations and business trade associations from qualified convention or trade show activities; and (5) income from the rental or exchange of membership lists.

Assume a halfway house for individuals released from prison operates a workshop and sells goods assembled by the clients. It is likely that the revenue produced by those sales would be related to the tax-exempt purpose, as the clients would be engaged in a meaningful activity. On the other hand, instead assume the halfway house operates a business across town, selling manufactured goods that are produced by regular employees, with the sole intent of raising money for the organization. It is likely that this would be perceived as unrelated to the tax-exempt purpose and, therefore, subject to the UBIT.

When computing the unrelated business income tax, not-for-profit organizations are allowed to deduct ordinary and necessary business expenses directly connected with their trade or business (as would any other business), a $1,000 special deduction, charitable contributions, and many of the other deductions available to business organizations.

IRS Oversight

The Internal Revenue Service (IRS) has oversight responsibilities for tax-exempt entities. Several of the areas of concern are cost allocations, excess executive compensation, and organizations operating outside their tax-exempt purpose. The program expense ratio, described in Chapter 10, is commonly used to evaluate not-for-profit organizations and is favorably affected when costs are allocated from fund-raising to program expenses. The IRS is concerned that financial information reported in Form 990 is accurate and may be relied upon by donors. The issue of cost allocations arose when the IRS observed that many tax-exempt organizations reported contribution revenue but reported zero fund-raising expenses.

Another area of concern is executive compensation. If the IRS deems wages and benefits to be in excess of reasonable amounts, the IRS may impose intermediate sanctions on the individual receiving the benefits and the organization managers who approved it. Benefits are defined broadly and include salaries, deferred compensation, insurance, loans, and medical benefits. The term "intermediate sanctions" refers to penalties imposed by the IRS when individuals associated with a tax-exempt organization receive excess benefits. Prior to the existence of intermediate sanctions, the only sanction available to the IRS was revoking the organization's tax-exempt status, an effective death sentence for many tax-exempt organizations.

In the event compensation is found to be unreasonable, the executive is required to pay back the excess benefit to the tax-exempt organization. In addition, there is a tax penalty of 25 percent of the excess benefit on the individual receiving the compensation and a penalty of 10 percent on the individuals responsible for approving it. If the executive receiving the excess benefits fails to repay the amount in a timely manner, an additional tax equal to 200 percent may be imposed.

Summary and Some Conclusions Related to Exempt Entities

A major portion of the practice of CPAs and a major concern of not-for-profit organizations is the obtaining and preservation of tax-exempt status and the avoidance or minimization of unrelated business income tax. During the initial organizing of a nonprofit, care must be taken to define and limit its purpose to tax-exempt activities. Decisions related to fund-raising activities must be monitored to determine the impact of tax law. Some not-for-profit organizations create separate, related organizations that may not be tax exempt to ensure that the primary organization does not lose its tax-exempt status. While the taxation of tax-exempt entities may seem to be a contradiction in terms, not-for-profit organizations must be prepared to file the necessary forms and meet the regulations of the federal and state governments.

EVALUATING PERFORMANCE

Our attention to this point in the text has been on the preparation of financial statements by state and local governments and a variety of not-for-profit organizations. Now we will focus on the use of financial and nonfinancial information in evaluating the performance and financial position of not-for-profit organizations and governments. When organizations vary greatly in size, it is difficult to evaluate their relative performance based on gross amounts reported in the financial statements. To facilitate comparisons, many users of financial statements calculate ratios. We describe commonly used ratios in the following sections.

Analysis of Not-for-Profit Organization Financial Statements

The most commonly used measure of not-for-profit efficiency is the **program expense ratio.** This is calculated as program service expenses divided by total expenses and provides an indication of the extent to which a not-for-profit is dedicating its resources to programs as opposed to administration, fund-raising, and membership development. The program expense ratio may be calculated from the

Statement of Activities or from information reported in Form 990. For example, the program expense ratio for the Performing Arts Organization in Illustration 10-3 is 67 percent, calculated as ($6,906 + $7,020 + $1,760 + $960)/$24,774. Alternative measures of efficiency decompose the expenses into program, administration, and fund-raising, each expressed as a percentage of total expenses. The Better Business Bureau recommends a program expense ratio of not less than 65 percent and maintains a website with financial information for a variety of charities (www.give.org).

Fund-raising efficiency is another measure of performance that expresses how much an organization spends in raising a dollar of donations. The fund-raising efficiency ratio is calculated as fund-raising expense divided by contribution revenues. Generally membership development is combined with fund-raising expenses. The fund-raising efficiency ratio for the Performing Arts Organization in Illustration 10-3 is < $.05, calculated as ($1,292 + $1,152)/$50,303. The interpretation is that the organization spends less than five cents to raise a dollar of contributions.

Days cash on hand measures the number of days of expenses that could be paid from existing cash and cash equivalents. It is calculated as (cash + cash equivalents) / [(total expenses − depreciation) ÷ 365]. Cash equivalents are short-term, highly liquid investments that are both readily convertible to known amounts of cash, and so near their maturity that they present minimal risk of changes in value because of changes in interest rates. Depreciation is removed from total expenses (denominator) since it does not require cash outlay. Liquidity is increasingly a concern of not-for-profit organizations and this ratio is one such measure, with higher values indicating stronger liquidity. The days cash on hand ratio for the Performing Arts Organization in Illustrations 10-4 and 10-6 is 180 days, calculated as ($10,218 + $0) / [($24,774 − $4,050) ÷ 365]. It is common for not-for-profit organizations to have a policy of maintaining 60 to 90 days of cash on hand.

Working capital: Another liquidity ratio begins by calculating working capital, (cash + receivables + short-term investments − current payables). This amount is then reduced by any donor-imposed (purpose) restricted net assets since these resources are not available to meet unrestricted operating needs. Working capital for the Performing Arts Organization in Illustration 10-4 is $10,450, calculated as ($10,218 + $2,603 + $360 + $240 + 4,344) − ($28 + $120 + $1900) − ($5,267). Endowment investments are not included and the note payable is assumed to be due within 12 months.

This ratio may also be expressed in days by dividing it by average daily (cash) expenses in the same manner as the days cash on hand ratio (above): ($10,450) / [($24,774 − $4,050) ÷ 365] = 184 days. Recall that not-for-profit organizations are required to disclose their policy with regard to maintaining liquidity (for example, Illustration 10-7). Expressed in this manner, the ratio provides a measure to be compared to the organization's liquidity policy.

Analysis of State and Local Government Financial Statements

Financial statements are intended to provide information useful in making decisions. In the commercial sector, creditors and investors use financial information to make lending and investment decisions. Donors compare the financial statements of not-for-profits to determine where to contribute money. Similarly, state and local government financial statements are intended to be useful for decision making. However, the information needs of users of governmental reports are more varied than those of private sector organizations. There are at least three distinct groups of users of government financial information: (1) citizens/voters, (2) investors and creditors, and (3) legislative and oversight officials.

Citizens use financial information to monitor the actions of elected officials and to determine where to buy a home or locate a business. Voters use information about government performance in selecting their elected officials and to determine whether to support bond issues or tax referenda. Before lending money or purchasing bonds, creditors and investors use financial information to evaluate the creditworthiness of governments. State governments use financial information to evaluate compliance with the conditions of grants issued to local governments. As we have seen, the federal government requires audited financial statements of state and local governments receiving federal funds.

Part of the reason that government financial reports are so complex is that these different user groups have different information needs. GASB addressed the varying information needs by designing comprehensive financial reports that provide both fund-basis and government-wide statements and by requiring supplemental information. However, this complexity also makes it more difficult to locate and use financial information. In some cases, financial statement users obtain their information directly from government financial reports. In other cases, they rely on intermediaries, which act as a conduit for information. Newspapers, as well as television and radio news programs, report financial information about governments and reach audiences that have never examined financial statements or budget documents. Interest groups and political parties also collect and distribute financial information, although their reporting may be selective and self-serving.

The most established information intermediaries exist in the public finance marketplace. Often described as the municipal bond market, participants include issuers, underwriters, financial advisors, and rating agencies, all of whom serve as information intermediaries. Debt-rating services, such as Moody's and Standard & Poor's, assist investors by rating bonds and other forms of debt. Rating agencies examine a host of financial, economic, and demographic factors and condense the information into a single measure that reflects the overall creditworthiness of a government bond. Moody's, for example, rates bonds (highest to lowest) as Aaa, Aa, A, Baa, Ba, B, Caa, Ca, and C. Governments are keenly interested in their bond rating, since lower ratings translate into higher borrowing costs.

Ratio Analysis To assist citizens in understanding government financial reports, GASB issued a series of user guides. *What You Should Know about Your Local Government's Finances: A Guide to Financial Statements* (2017) is a plain-language explanation of local government financial reports. Illustrative financial statements are provided with annotated boxes explaining the meaning of key items. Similar guides are available for school districts (2018) and business-type activities (2018). In addition, GASB publishes a more detailed *Analyst's Guide to Government*

Financial Statements (2018). The analyst's guide provides a discussion of common financial ratios useful in evaluating governments.

Financial ratios are used to convert information to a more understandable form. The most straightforward form of ratio analysis is common size analysis. In common size analysis, all items on a financial statement are scaled, typically by the largest amount appearing on that statement. Specifically, items on balance sheets are divided by total assets, and items appearing on operating statements are commonly divided by total revenues. For example, capital assets for the Village of Riverside represent nearly 94 percent of the Village's total assets. This ratio was calculated from the primary government column of the government-wide Statement of Net Position (Illustration 8-6). Alternatively, common size analysis may be performed on individual funds. For example, 52 percent of the Village of Riverside's General Fund revenues are derived from property taxes (Illustration 5-4).

Simply calculating ratios is not sufficient to provide insight. Ratios must be compared to something to be useful in making evaluations and judgments. This year's financial ratios are compared to previous years' to identify trends. Even more useful is comparing ratios among various governments. For example, by comparing the Village of Riverside's ratios to those of other villages in the region, we may be able to determine whether the Village's financial condition is strong or weak relative to its peers. Since all governments follow the same set of generally accepted accounting principles, comparisons among governments are valid.

In contrast to accounting principles, there is no generally accepted set of financial ratios, and sometimes there is disagreement on how to compute a given ratio. GASB's *Analyst's Guide to Government Financial Statements* identifies four categories of financial ratios and provides examples within each category. The four categories represent measures intended to assess different characteristics of a government and include financial position, liquidity, solvency, and ability to pay. Illustration 13-3 identifies example ratios from among each of these four categories, provides the formula for computing the ratio, and applies this formula to the financial statements of the Village of Riverside. The interpretation column explains what the ratio is intended to reveal and whether larger or smaller values are preferred. For purposes of illustration, assume the Village has a population of 10,000 and assessed value of property of $100 million.

Ratios may be computed from the government-wide statements using only the governmental activities column, business-type activities column, or in total (using the primary government column). Alternatively, ratios may be computed separately for governmental-type funds or even for the individual fund. Clearly some ratios require information from particular statements. For example, leverage measures necessarily come from the government-wide statements since long-term liabilities do not appear in the governmental-type funds. Debt service coverage can only be directly measured from proprietary fund statements since cash flow statements are not prepared for governmental funds or at the government-wide level. The choice of ratios to compute and the level of reporting (government-wide or fund-basis) is determined by the purpose of the analysis. However, comparisons are valid only if the ratios and computations are consistent across fiscal years and across governments.

ILLUSTRATION 13-3 Financial Ratios for State and Local Governments

Ratio	Source: Formula	Village of Riverside	Interpretation
Financial Position:			
Financial Position: Governmental Activities	Government-wide statements (governmental activities) $\frac{\textit{Unrestricted Net Position:}}{\textit{Total Expenses: Governmental Activities}}$	$\frac{\$\ 857{,}490}{\$\ 8{,}421{,}600} = 10\%$	This is a measure of the availability of resources to meet expenses. Larger values indicate stronger financial condition.
Financial Position: General Fund	General Fund fund-basis statements $\frac{\textit{Unassigned Fund Balance}}{\textit{Total Expenditures + Other Financing Uses}}$	$\frac{\$\ 615{,}990}{\$\ 5{,}030{,}300 + 800{,}000} = 11\%$	This is a more conservative measure of the availability of resources to meet expenses since it excludes resources that are committed to restrictive funds. Larger values indicate stronger financial condition.
Liquidity			
Quick Ratio	Government-wide statements (governmental activities) $\frac{\textit{Cash + Current Investments}}{\textit{Current Liabilities}}$	$\frac{\$\ 731{,}500 + 352{,}000}{\$\ 196{,}300 + 80{,}000 + 190{,}000} = 2.32$	A measure of the government's ability to finance short-term obligations. Higher values indicate greater liquidity.
Solvency			
Leverage—debt to total assets	Government-wide statements (primary government) $\frac{\textit{Total Liabilities – Deferred Outflows}}{\textit{Total Assets – Deferred Inflows}}$	$\frac{\$\ 4{,}680{,}700}{\$\ 43{,}663{,}410} = 0.11$	A measure of the proportion of a government's assets that are financed with debt. Small values indicate greater solvency.
Coverage ratio—debt service coverage	Enterprise fund Statement of Cash Flows $\frac{\textit{Cash Flows from Operations}}{\textit{Interest Paid + Payments of Principal}}$	$\frac{\$\ 465{,}800}{\$\ 189{,}000 + 0} = 2.5$ times	Indicates the availability of cash generated to meet current obligations on outstanding debt. Higher values indicate greater solvency.
Debt service to total expenditures	Governmental fund-basis statements $\frac{\textit{Principal and Interest Expenditure}}{\textit{Total Expenditures: General and Debt Service Fund}}$	$\frac{\$\ 120{,}000 + 96{,}000}{\$\ 5{,}030{,}300 + 216{,}000} = 4\%$	A measure of the degree to which governmental expenditures are committed to debt service. Low values indicate greater flexibility and ability to manage additional debt.
Ability to Pay			
Debt per capita	Government-wide statements (primary government) $\frac{\textit{Total Liabilities}}{\textit{Population}}$	$\frac{\$\ 4{,}680{,}700}{10{,}000} = \$468$	A measure of the government's ability to service debt or incur additional debt. Low values indicate greater flexibility and ability to manage additional debt.
Debt to assessed value of property	Government-wide statements (primary government) $\frac{\textit{Total Liabilities}}{\textit{Assessed Value of Property}}$	$\frac{\$\ 4{,}680{,}700}{\$\ 100{,}000{,}000} = 4.68\%$	A measure of the government's ability to service debt or incur additional debt. Low values indicate greater flexibility and ability to manage additional debt.

Service Efforts and Accomplishments Reporting

Governmental financial statements, notes, and required supplementary information meet many of the needs of citizens, creditors, and oversight authorities. Similarly, the financial statements of private not-for-profits are useful to donors, government regulators, and creditors. However, neither governmental nor not-for-profit financial statements are particularly effective in measuring organizational effectiveness. The fundamental problem is that government and not-for-profit effectiveness cannot be expressed solely in financial terms. Effectiveness in nonbusiness organizations must be measured in terms of the quality of the service provided or the extent to which an organization fulfills its mission. For this reason, many governments and not-for-profits report nonfinancial information in addition to their financial statements. The framework for combining financial and nonfinancial information to more effectively communicate organizational effectiveness is termed **service efforts and accomplishments (SEA)** reporting.

GASB Concepts Statement 2, *Service Efforts and Accomplishments Reporting,* was issued in 1994. In addition, GASB issued a series of research reports related to colleges and universities, economic development programs, elementary and secondary education, fire department programs, hospitals, mass transit, police department programs, public assistance programs, public health, road maintenance, sanitation collection and disposal, water and wastewater treatment, and other activities. Research reports are not GAAP and at this time GASB has issued no standards for SEA reporting and it is therefore voluntary.

SEA Measures Service efforts are measures of costs and other resources dedicated to a program or service. For example, consider the service of police protection. Direct costs include salaries and benefits for police officers who are directly engaged in crime prevention, detection, and apprehension of offenders. To the extent that the costs are separately identifiable, vehicle and equipment costs are directly allocated. Indirect costs of the police department may also be allocated from general government expenditures. Inputs may also include nonfinancial measures such as number of personnel and hours expended.

Service accomplishments include outputs and outcomes. According to the GASB, output measures are the quantity of a service provided or the quantity of a service that meets a certain quality requirement. Examples of output measures for a police department include number of responses, number of arrests, and the hours of patrol. Output measures should be distinguished from measures of outcome. Outcomes measure the extent to which results are achieved or needs are met at least partially due to the services provided. Examples of outcome measures are the number of violent crimes committed, the value of property lost due to crime, and response time. Efficiency measures relate costs and other inputs to output measures, such as the number of responses per dollar spent or per police officer. Cost-outcome measures relate inputs to outcomes, such as the value of property lost to crime per dollar spent.

A variety of measures should be presented. Those measures should be reported consistently, in a timely manner, and in a way that is easily understood. Comparisons with prior periods and with other governments are also useful. Explanatory variables, such as socioeconomic data, should be included to help readers understand that not all the results are controllable.

Some cautions are in order regarding SEA reporting. Until standards are developed and commonly reported and used, there is a risk that governments will present only that information that is favorable. Audit opinions are not associated with this information. Challenges exist in the measurement and allocations of costs, not to mention the measurement of outputs and outcomes. Even with the problems, however, SEA reporting is viewed by many as essential for measuring the performance of a government or an activity of a government. SEA measures are now a part of the budget process of many governments. Standardization and public reporting would make the SEA measures more useful.

Example of SEA Reporting: School Report Cards States require school systems or individual schools to publish annual "school report cards." These reports are an example of service efforts and accomplishments reporting for an important and highly visible government service, public schools. The content is frequently dictated by the state government and varies by state. However, most of these reports contain the following types of information:

Service Inputs:	Tax revenues, state appropriations, and federal grants. Number of teachers, administrators, and support personnel. Education level (certificate levels) of teachers and administrators. Demographics of student population (income, race, language).
Service Outputs:	Enrollment. Gifted or alternative programs. Degrees conferred.
Service Outcomes:	Standardized test scores. Dropout rates. Competency tests and high school graduation tests. Accreditation results.

Questions and Exercises

13–1. Using the annual financial report obtained for Exercise 1–1, answer the following questions:

a. Examine the auditor's report. Is the auditor identified as an independent CPA firm? A state audit agency? Other? Is the wording of the auditor's report the same as illustrated in this chapter? Does the scope paragraph indicate exactly what is covered by the auditor's opinion? If the auditor is expressing an opinion only on the basic financial statements, what responsibility is taken for the combining and individual fund statements? Is the opinion unmodified? If not, what are the qualifications?

b. Does the annual financial report contain a single audit section? If not, does the report refer to the existence of a single audit report? If so, does the report include a Schedule of Federal (and State) Financial Assistance? Are all of the reports illustrated in this chapter included? Can you identify the major programs, if any?

13–2. Go to the Better Business Bureau's Wise Giving Alliance website (http://www.give.org). Select a charity, and open the financial tab. Be sure to select a charity that provides financial information.

a. State the name of the organization and its mission.

b. What are the two largest programs in terms of expenses?

c. What are the two largest sources of funds?

d. Calculate the program expense ratio.

e. Calculate the fund-raising efficiency ratio.

13–3. Using the annual financial report obtained for Exercise 1–1, answer the following questions:

a. Report the following ratios, using the formulas appearing in Illustration 13-3 as a guide:

(1) Financial Position (government-wide, governmental activities)

(2) Financial Position (General Fund)

(3) Quick Ratio (government-wide, governmental activities)

(4) Leverage (government-wide, primary government)

(5) Debt Service Coverage (enterprise funds)

(6) Debt Service to Total Expenditures (governmental fund-basis)

(7) Debt per Capita (government-wide, primary government)*

(8) Debt to Assessed Value of Property (government-wide, primary government)*

b. Write a memorandum, based on the ratios you calculated in part (*a*) of this problem, giving a recommendation as to whether to purchase (1) general obligation or (2) revenue bonds of your governmental unit.

13–4. Use the Internet to locate your state's site for reporting school district "School Report Cards." Select a school district or individual school and answer the following:

a. What measures of service inputs are presented on the report card?

b. What measures of service outputs are presented on the report card?

c. What measures of service outcomes are presented on the report card?

d. What information is presented to provide comparisons between the school selected and other schools in the state?

13–5. Presented below are the computed amounts of ratios for the Village of Riverside example appearing in the chapter.

(1) Financial Position (government-wide, governmental activities)	10%
(2) Financial Position (General Fund)	11%
(3) Quick Ratio (government-wide, governmental activities)	2.32

* Population and property values are disclosed in the statistical section of the CAFR.

(4) Leverage (government-wide, primary government)	0.11
(5) Debt Service Coverage (enterprise funds)	2.5 times
(6) Debt Service to Total Expenditures (governmental fund-basis)	4%
(7) Debt per Capita (government-wide, primary government)	$468
(8) Debt to Assessed Value of Property (government-wide, primary government)	4.68%

a. Using the financial statements provided in Illustrations 2-5 through 2-11, compute ratios for the City of Salem. Assume the population of Salem is 52,000 and the fair value of property totals $970 million.

b. For each ratio, indicate which of the two governments has a stronger financial position.

13–6. Presented below are financial statements (except cash flows) for two not-for-profit organizations.

Statement of Activities	**ABC Not-for-Profit**		**XYZ Not-for-Profit**	
	Unrestricted	**Donor-Restricted**	**Unrestricted**	**Donor-Restricted**
Revenues				
Program service revenue	$5,595,000		$2,250,000	
Contribution revenues	3,327,500	$ 750,000	3,200,000	
Grant revenue		96,000		$1,025,000
Net gains on endowment investments	17,500			
Net assets released from restriction				
Satisfaction of program restrictions	450,000	(450,000)	377,000	(377,000)
Total revenues	9,390,000	396,000	5,827,000	648,000
Expenses				
Education program expenses	5,621,000		1,559,000	
Research program expense	1,256,000		2,256,000	
Total program service expenses	6,877,000		3,815,000	
Fund-raising	456,000		356,000	
Administration	650,000		1,229,000	
Total supporting service expenses	1,106,000		1,585,000	
Total expenses	7,983,000		5,400,000	
Increase in net assets	1,407,000	396,000	427,000	648,000
Net assets January 1	4,208,000	759,000	1,037,500	320,000
Net assets December 31	$5,615,000	$1,155,000	$1,464,500	$ 968,000

STATEMENT OF NET ASSETS	ABC Not-for-Profit	XYZ Not-for-Profit
Current assets		
Cash	$ 205,000	$ 356,000
Short-term cash equivalents	265,000	99,000
Supplies inventories	32,000	150,000
Receivables	439,500	188,500
Total current assets	941,500	793,500
Noncurrent assets		
Noncurrent pledges receivable	265,000	
Endowment investments	2,590,000	
Land, buildings, and equipment (net)	3,175,000	1,768,000
Total noncurrent assets	6,030,000	1,768,000
Total assets	$6,971,500	$2,561,500
Current liabilities		
Accounts payable	$ 23,000	$ 129,000
Total current liabilities	23,000	129,000
Noncurrent liabilities		
Notes payable	178,500	
Total noncurrent liabilities	178,500	
Total liabilities	201,500	129,000
Net Assets		
Unrestricted	4,025,000	2,364,500
Donor restricted for purpose	155,000	68,000
Donor restricted for endowment	2,590,000	0
Total net assets	6,770,000	2,432,500
Total liabilities and net assets	$6,971,500	$2,561,500

a. Calculate the following ratios (assume depreciation expense is $750,000 for both organizations and is allocated among program and supporting expenses):

- Program expense.
- Fund-raising efficiency.
- Days cash on hand.
- Working capital (expressed in days).

b. For each ratio, explain which of the two organizations has the stronger ratio.

13–7. With regard to the Government Auditing Standards

a. Differentiate among the different types of professional engagements.

b. Assume you are auditing a city that has a summer youth employment program. List some factors you might investigate in terms of (1) financial statement audits and (2) performance audits.

13–8. You have been assigned the task of writing the audit report for the City of X. The scope includes the basic financial statements, although the report is attached to a complete Comprehensive Annual Financial Report. Differentiate among opinions that are unmodified, qualified, adverse, and disclaimed. Give examples of situations that might cause you to (1) qualify an opinion, (2) issue an adverse opinion, and (3) disclaim an opinion.

13–9. With respect to the Single Audit Act of 1984 and amendment of 1996 relating to state and local governments and not-for-profit organizations:

a. Distinguish between major and nonmajor programs.

b. List the criteria used to determine whether an entity is subject to the Single Audit Act.

c. List the audit reports that should be included in a single audit report.

13–10. A local government has five federal grants. Expenditures amounted to $3,000,000 during the year, as follows:

Type A	
HUD grant, new and never audited	$900,000
HHS grant, audited last year, no major findings	750,000
Type B	
EPA grant	600,000
Summer Youth Employment grant	675,000
Dept. of Agriculture grant	75,000

Describe how you, as an auditor, would determine major programs for audit, assuming (*a*) the local government is not a low-risk auditee, and (*b*) the local government is a low-risk auditee.

13–11. With regard to tax-exempt organizations:

a. Define a 501(c)(3) organization.

b. Define a public charity.

13–12. With regard to filing requirements for 501(c)(3) organizations: List the three types of Form 990 and indicate the size of the tax-exempt organization to use for each.

13–13. With regard to unrelated business income tax (UBIT), answer the following questions:

a. Which four conditions will automatically exempt entities from UBIT?

b. What are some exceptions to UBIT provided by legislation?

c. How is UBIT computed? What deductions are allowed?

13–14. You and a few friends have decided to establish a not-for-profit organization in your community to help provide shelter and food to the homeless and transients. Outline the steps you would take to obtain tax-exempt status, avoid paying unrelated business income tax, and so on. Consider the creation of a related entity, a foundation, as a part of your planning.

13–15. With regard to service efforts and accomplishments reporting, define the following terms:

a. Service efforts
b. Service accomplishments
c. Inputs
d. Outputs
e. Outcomes
f. Efficiency measures
g. Cost-outcome measures

13–16. What is the role of a bond-rating agency?

13–17. Describe the purpose of ratio analysis. What is common size analysis?

13–18. Identify the three categories of users of governmental financial statements and describe the information needs of each.

Continuous Problem

The continuous problem is available in Connect through the Additional Student Resources in the eBook or instructor library. Complete the assignment for Chapter 13.

Chapter **Fourteen**

Financial Reporting by the Federal Government

Only one thing can save this country, and that's to get a handle on this deficit and debt issue. Mitch McConnell, senior senator from Kentucky and Senate Majority Leader

The unjustified swelling of the budgetary deficit and the accumulation of public debts are just as destructive as adventurous stock speculation. Vladimir Putin, president of Russia (2000–2008 and 2012 to present)

Learning Objectives

- Describe the reporting requirements of federal agencies[1] and the U.S. government.
- Understand the purpose and composition of the required financial statements of federal government units.
- Prepare journal entries for typical transactions of a federal government unit, applying budgetary and proprietary accounting practices.

We the People of the United States, in Order to form a more perfect Union, establish Justice, ensure domestic Tranquility, provide for the common defense, promote the general Welfare, and secure the Blessings of Liberty to ourselves and our Posterity, do ordain and establish this Constitution for the United States of America. (Preamble to the United States Constitution)

The federal government of the United States, as it is known today, did not come into existence on July 4, 1776, but was created by the Constitutional Convention of 1787. The Convention's initial goal was to modify the existing Articles of Confederation to curtail growing divisiveness among the state governments. With George Washington presiding, the convention delegates (notably James Madison and Alexander Hamilton) took on a more ambitious agenda and created the

[1] The term *agency* is used throughout this chapter to represent subunits of the federal government and includes departments, commissions, services, and other distinct organizational units.

Constitution. The Constitutional Convention concluded with a speech by Benjamin Franklin, and the Constitution was sent to the state legislatures for ratification.

It was not clear that the Constitution would be accepted by the states. Patrick Henry, Samuel Adams, and other important patriots in the American Revolution argued against ratification. In reply, Madison, Hamilton, and John Jay wrote the *Federalist Papers,* which argued for a strong central government and are used to this day to interpret the Constitution. By June 1788, nine states (the number necessary for ratification) had accepted the Constitution. The key components of the Constitution are a two-house legislature, executive branch, and judiciary with a system of interrelated checks and balances across the three branches. The Constitution also establishes the role of financial reporting by the federal government:

> *No money shall be drawn from the Treasury, but in consequence of appropriations made by law; and* ***a regular statement and account of the receipts and expenditures of all public money shall be published from time to time.*** (Article 1: Section 9)

FEDERAL GOVERNMENT ACCOUNTING STANDARDS

It took more than 200 years for the federal government to truly begin to fulfill this constitutional requirement to publish meaningful and comprehensive financial reports. The Chief Financial Officers Act of 1990 was passed with the purpose of improving the federal government's financial management. The act created the Office of Federal Financial Management within the **Office of Management and Budget (OMB)** to carry out financial management directives. The act also created the position of chief financial officer within federal departments and agencies and charged those officials with issuing audited financial statements.

The Office of Management and Budget, together with the **Government Accountability Office (GAO)** and the **Department of the Treasury,** are the primary organizations charged with financial management of the federal government. The OMB and Treasury are within the executive branch of government, whereas GAO is an agency in the legislative branch. The Treasury maintains a government-wide system of accounts and prepares the federal government's consolidated financial statements. GAO assists Congress in oversight of the executive branch, establishes governmental auditing standards, and audits the financial statements of some federal agencies and the consolidated statements of the federal government.

To implement the reporting requirements of the 1990 Chief Financial Officers Act, the secretary of the Treasury, director of the OMB, and comptroller general (GAO) established the **Federal Accounting Standards Advisory Board (FASAB).** The purpose of the FASAB is to develop and issue federal accounting standards. The Board comprises ten members: two from the executive branch, two from the legislative, and six who are not employees of the federal government. The Board is considered "advisory" in that the standards must be approved by the three founding organizations (Treasury, OMB, and GAO). The standards (called *Statements of Federal Financial Accounting Standards*) are recognized as the highest level of authoritative standard in the AICPA's Code of Professional Conduct for federal government entities.

Like the FASB and GASB, the FASAB has developed a conceptual framework to guide the Board in the development of new standards. The Concepts Statements are not authoritative, but they identify user needs, the objectives of the financial reports, and definitions of the reporting entity and the elements of the financial statements. The FASAB's elements of the financial statements (presented in Illustration 14-1) are similar to those of the GASB.

FINANCIAL REPORTING BY FEDERAL AGENCIES

The annual financial report of an agency or other organization following federal government reporting standards includes the following:

- Management's Discussion and Analysis: This includes a discussion of the organization's mission and performance goals as well as the most recent year's financial information.

ILLUSTRATION 14-1 Comparison FASAB and GASB Financial Statement Elements

Federal Government	State and Local Governments[2]
An *asset* is a resource that embodies economic benefits or services that the federal government controls.	*Assets* are resources with present service capacity that the government presently controls.
A *liability* is a present obligation of the federal government to provide assets or services to another entity at a determinable date, when a specified event occurs, or on demand.	*Liabilities* are present obligations to sacrifice resources that the government has little or no discretion to avoid.
Net position or its equivalent, net assets, is the arithmetic difference between the total assets and total liabilities.	*Net position* is the residual of all other elements presented in a statement of financial position.
A *revenue* is an inflow of or other increase in assets, a decrease in liabilities, or a combination of both that results in an increase in the government's net position.	An *inflow of resources* is an acquisition of net assets by the government that is applicable to the reporting period.
An *expense* is an outflow of or other decrease in assets, an increase in liabilities, or a combination of both that results in a decrease in the government's net position.	An *outflow of resources* is a consumption of net assets by the government that is applicable to the reporting period.

[2] Statement of Federal Financial Accounting Concepts 5: *Definitions of Elements and Basic Recognition Criteria for Accrual-Basis Financial Statements,* Federal Accounting Standards Advisory Board, 2007; and Concepts Statement No. 2: *Elements of Financial Statements,* Governmental Accounting Standards Board, 2007.

- Audit report: This will include an opinion on the financial statements, as well as reports on internal controls and compliance with laws and regulations.
- Basic financial statements and notes, including
  1. Balance Sheet.
  2. Statement of Net Cost.
  3. Statement of Changes in Net Position.
  4. Statement of Budgetary Resources.
  5. Statement of Custodial Activity (if applicable).
  6. Statement of Social Insurance (if applicable).
- Required supplemental information: this may include a statement of stewardship assets.

The first five financial statements listed above are examined in the following sections. A statement of social insurance is required for federal agencies administering social insurance programs such as Social Security and Medicare. The statement projects income and benefit payments so that users of the statements can evaluate the long-term viability of the programs.

Balance Sheet

The Balance Sheet of the U.S. Securities and Exchange Commission is presented in Illustration 14-2.[3] Assets and liabilities are measured on the accrual basis and separated into intragovernmental (between federal government entities) and other. The difference between assets and liabilities is *net position* and is composed of *unexpended appropriations* and the *cumulative result of operations.* Unexpended appropriations are amounts provided by Congress that are not yet expended or committed (obligated). The cumulative result of operations is the difference between the sum of appropriations and revenues over expenses (cumulative over the life of the agency).

Statement of Net Cost

The Statement of Net Cost of the U.S. Securities and Exchange Commission (SEC) is presented in Illustration 14-3. This statement displays the cost (measured on the accrual basis) of the federal agency by program. Similar to the government-wide Statement of Activities for state and local governments, program revenues are subtracted to determine the net cost of government services. Many federal agencies will have no earned revenues. In the case of the SEC, the commission charges corporations and investment companies when they register securities for sale. Since this is a Statement of Net *Cost* and the SEC has revenues in excess of cost, the bottom line appears as a negative. Typically the bottom line will be a net cost (positive), rather than income.

[3] For presentation purposes, only one year of information is presented. However, two years of information are required on all statements. Additionally, some information has been condensed for presentation purposes.

ILLUSTRATION 14-2 Balance Sheet

U.S. SECURITIES AND EXCHANGE COMMISSION
Balance Sheet
As of September 30, 2018
Dollars in thousands

Assets	
Intragovernmental:	
Fund Balance with Treasury	$ 7,822,331
Investments, Net	2,121,254
Accounts Receivable	0
Advances and Prepayments	5,814
Total Intragovernmental	9,949,399
Cash	2,233
Accounts Receivable, Net	319,787
Advances and Prepayments	0
Property and Equipment, Net	120,459
Total Assets	$10,391,878
Liabilities	
Intragovernmental:	
Accounts Payable	2,751
Employee Benefits	7,300
Unfunded FECA and Unemployment Liability	834
Custodial Liability, Net	65,486
Liability for Non-entity Assets	2,554
Total Intragovernmental	78,925
Accounts Payable	166,938
Actuarial FECA Liability	4,511
Accrued Payroll and Benefits	35,859
Accrued Leave	77,870
Registrant Deposits	40,079
Liability for Disgorgement and Penalties	2,259,278
Contingent Liabilities	63,968
Other Accrued Liabilities	10,556
Total Liabilities	2,737,984
Net Position	
Unexpended Appropriations	145,406
Cumulative Results of Operations	
—Funds from Dedicated Collections	7,508,488
Total Net Position	7,653,894
Total Liabilities and Net Position	$10,391,888

Most agencies do not have cash balances but deposit/draw cash with the U.S. Treasury. (Fund Balance with Treasury)

Assets (including long-term assets) are measured on the accrual basis. (Property and Equipment, Net)

Intragovernmental balances are receivables or payables between federal government entities.

Amounts (penalties) collected from securities law violators are deposited with Treasury and paid as restitution to the harmed investors. This represents the amount due to those investors. (Liability for Disgorgement and Penalties)

ILLUSTRATION 14-3 Statement of Net Cost

U.S. SECURITIES AND EXCHANGE COMMISSION Statement of Net Cost For the Year Ended September 30, 2018 Dollars in thousands	
PROGRAM COSTS	
Enforcement	$ 578,452
Compliance Inspections	411,696
Corporate Finance	164,548
Trading and Markets	95,366
Investment Management	66,339
Economic and Risk Analysis	76,336
General Counsel	53,192
Other Program Offices	85,269
Agency Direction & Administrative Support	256,655
Inspector General	17,788
Total Program Costs	1,805,641
Less: Earned Revenue Not Attributed to Programs	2,302,601
Net (Income) Cost from Operations	$(496,960)

Costs are measured on the accrual basis.

These are the fees the SEC charges companies to register and sell securities.

Statement of Changes in Net Position

The Statement of Changes in Net Position of the U.S. Securities and Exchange Commission is presented in Illustration 14-4. This statement begins with the beginning balance in the equity account, *net position,* and identifies all financing sources used to support its operations. The statement articulates with *net position* appearing on the Balance Sheet. For most government agencies, the primary source of resources is appropriations resulting from congressional legislation and signed by the president. Other sources can include dedicated taxes, donations, and transfers.

Statement of Budgetary Resources

The Statement of Budgetary Resources is presented in Illustration 14-5. Unlike the previous statements, it follows the budgetary (not accrual) basis of accounting. The budgetary basis of accounting is prescribed by OMB, not FASAB. Budgetary accounting practices are described later in this chapter.

The statement provides information on how budgetary resources were obtained and the status (e.g., expended, obligated, etc.) of those resources at year-end. The first part of the statement indicates the source of resources to the agency. The SEC receives most of its resources from fees charged to public companies whereas many federal agencies rely almost entirely on appropriations from Congress. The second part of the statement indicates the status of those resources within the budgetary (spending) process. Note that these two parts sum to the same amount.

ILLUSTRATION 14-4 Statement of Changes in Net Position

U.S. SECURITIES AND EXCHANGE COMMISSION
Statement of Changes in Net Position
For the Year Ended September 30, 2018
Dollars in thousands

CUMULATIVE RESULTS OF OPERATIONS	**Consolidated**	
Beginning Balance	$7,328,904	
Budgetary Financing Sources:		
Appropriations Used	0	← **For many agencies, appropriations will be the largest source of resources.**
Nonexchange Revenue	183,623	
Other Financing Sources:		
Imputed Financing	47,162	
Transferred to the General Fund	(548,161)	
Total Financing Sources	(317,376)	
Net Income from Operations	496,960	← **This agrees with the Statement of Net Cost.**
Net Change	179,584)	
Cumulative Results of Operations	7,508,488	
UNEXPENDED APPROPRIATIONS		
Beginning Balance	0	
Budgetary Financing Sources:		
Appropriations Received	145,406	
Appropriations Used	0	
Total Unexpended Appropriations	145,406	
Net Position, End of Period	$7,653,894	← **This agrees with the Balance Sheet (net position section).**

ILLUSTRATION 14-5 Statement of Budgetary Resources

U.S. SECURITIES AND EXCHANGE COMMISSION
Statement of Budgetary Resources
For the Year Ended September 30, 2018
Dollars in thousands

BUDGETARY RESOURCES	
Unobligated Balance from Prior Year	$ 211,753
Appropriations	394,079
Spending Authority from Offsetting Collections	1,752,538
Total Budgetary Resources	$2,358,370
STATUS OF BUDGETARY RESOURCES	
New Obligations and Upward Adjustments	$1,856,004
Apportioned Unexpired Accounts	382,575
Exempt from Apportionment	15,291
Unapportioned, Unexpired Accounts	104,500
Total Budgetary Resources	$2,358,370

ILLUSTRATION 14-6 Statement of Custodial Activity

U.S. SECURITIES AND EXCHANGE COMMISSION
Statement of Custodial Activity
For the Year Ended September 30, 2018
Dollars in thousands

REVENUE ACTIVITY	
Sources of Cash Collections:	
Disgorgement and Penalties	$ 845,862
Other	2,620
Net Collections	848,482
Accrual Adjustments	(108,409)
Total Custodial Revenue	740,073
DISPOSITION OF COLLECTIONS	
Amounts Transferred to Dept. of Treasury	848,482
Amounts Yet to Be Transferred	(108,409)
Total Disposition of Collections	740,073
NET CUSTODIAL ACTIVITY	$ —

This is analogous to a custodial fund.

The collections are remitted to the Treasury.

Statement of Custodial Activity

The Statement of Custodial Activity for the U.S. Securities and Exchange Commission is presented in Illustration 14-6. This statement is required only if the government agency collects nonexchange funds to be turned over to the Treasury. Because the collecting entity cannot use the funds, the activities are analogous to those of a custodial fund of a state or local government. In addition to the SEC, the U.S. Customs and Border Protection and the Internal Revenue Service perform custodial functions and include this statement within their annual reports.

CONSOLIDATED FINANCIAL REPORT OF THE U.S. GOVERNMENT

The annual report of the U.S. Government is prepared by the Department of the Treasury and audited by the Government Accountability Office. Similar to state and local governments, the annual financial report contains Management's Discussion and Analysis, financial statements, unaudited Supplemental and Stewardship Information, and the auditor's (i.e., GAO's) report. The GAO report contains an audit opinion as well as reports on internal controls and compliance with laws and regulations. The financial statements include

1. Balance Sheet.
2. Statement of Net Cost.
3. Statement of Operations and Changes in Net Position.

4. Reconciliation of Net Operating Cost and Unified Budget Deficit.
5. Statement of Changes in Cash Balance from Budget and Other Activities.
6. Statement of Long-Term Fiscal Projections.
7. Statement of Social Insurance.
8. Statement of Changes in Social Insurance.
9. Notes to the financial statements.

The first five of these are known as the accrual-based consolidated financial statements. The *Statement of Net Cost* and *Balance Sheet* have been previously described. The *Statement of Operations and Changes in Net Position* presents the results of the federal government's operations, measured on the accrual basis. The format of the statement is similar to the operating statements of state and local governments. It begins with revenues, deducts costs, and adds (subtracts) intragovernmental transfers. It is then reconciled to net position on the Balance Sheet.

The *Reconciliation of Net Operating Cost and Budget Deficit* reconciles the net operating result (revenue or cost) from the Statement of Operations and Changes in Net Position with the cash-based federal budget. As such, it is similar to the reconciliation of the Statement of Activities to the governmental funds Statement of Revenues, Expenditures, and Changes in Fund Balance required by state and local governments. The *Statement of Changes in Cash Balance from Budget and Other Activities* shows the relationship between the cash-based budget deficit and the change in the federal government's operating cash balance. The interrelationships among these five statements are depicted in Illustration 14-7.[4]

The *Statement of Social Insurance* and *Statement of Changes in Social Insurance* report the relationship between the estimated receipts and expenditures of social insurance programs. These are almost entirely Social Security and Medicare and are based on 75-year projections of benefits to be provided to citizens participating in these programs. The *Statement of Long-Term Fiscal Projections* displays the present value of 75-year projections by major category of receipts (taxes) and non-interest spending (Social Security, Medicare, defense, etc.).

The Department of Treasury publishes the *Consolidated Financial Statements of the U.S. Government* (https://fiscal.treasury.gov/reports-statements/financial-report/current-report.html). The report is lengthy, but Treasury also provides an executive summary, titled *Nation by the Numbers: A Snapshot of the Government's Financial Position and Condition.* This is better suited for users interested in a highly summarized depiction of the national government's finances (https://fiscal.treasury.gov/reports-statements/financial-report/nation-by-the-numbers.html). To assist citizens in understanding the annual report, GAO publishes a plain language guide titled *Understanding the Financial Report of the United States Government* (https://www.gao.gov/assets/700/690105.pdf).

[4] U.S. Government Accountability Office, *Understanding the Financial Report of the United States Government,* February 2018 (GAO-18-239SP), p. 42.

ILLUSTRATION 14-7 Accrual-Based Consolidated Financial Statements of the U.S. Government

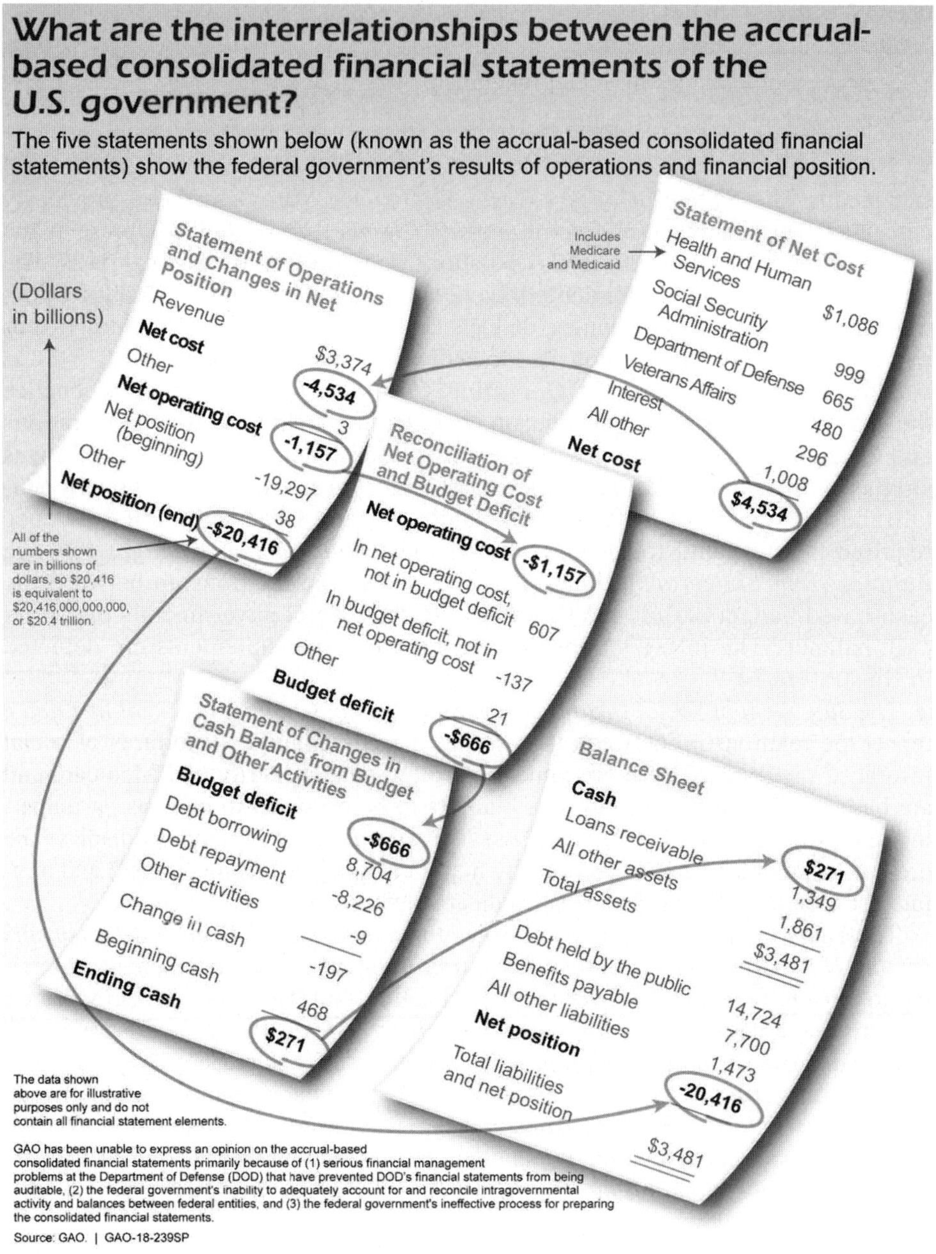

BUDGETARY AND PROPRIETARY ACCOUNTING

The accounting systems of federal agencies must serve both the external financial reporting needs mandated by the Chief Financial Officers Act and the necessity of having internal budgetary controls over the spending of public resources. This is accomplished through the maintenance of two self-balancing sets of accounts, termed *budgetary* and *proprietary accounts.*

Budgetary Accounts

The purpose of **budgetary accounts** is to provide a record by which federal expenditures can be traced back to the budgetary authority granted by Congress through appropriations. The budgetary authority process is depicted in Illustration 14-8,

ILLUSTRATION 14-8 Federal Government Budgetary Authority Process

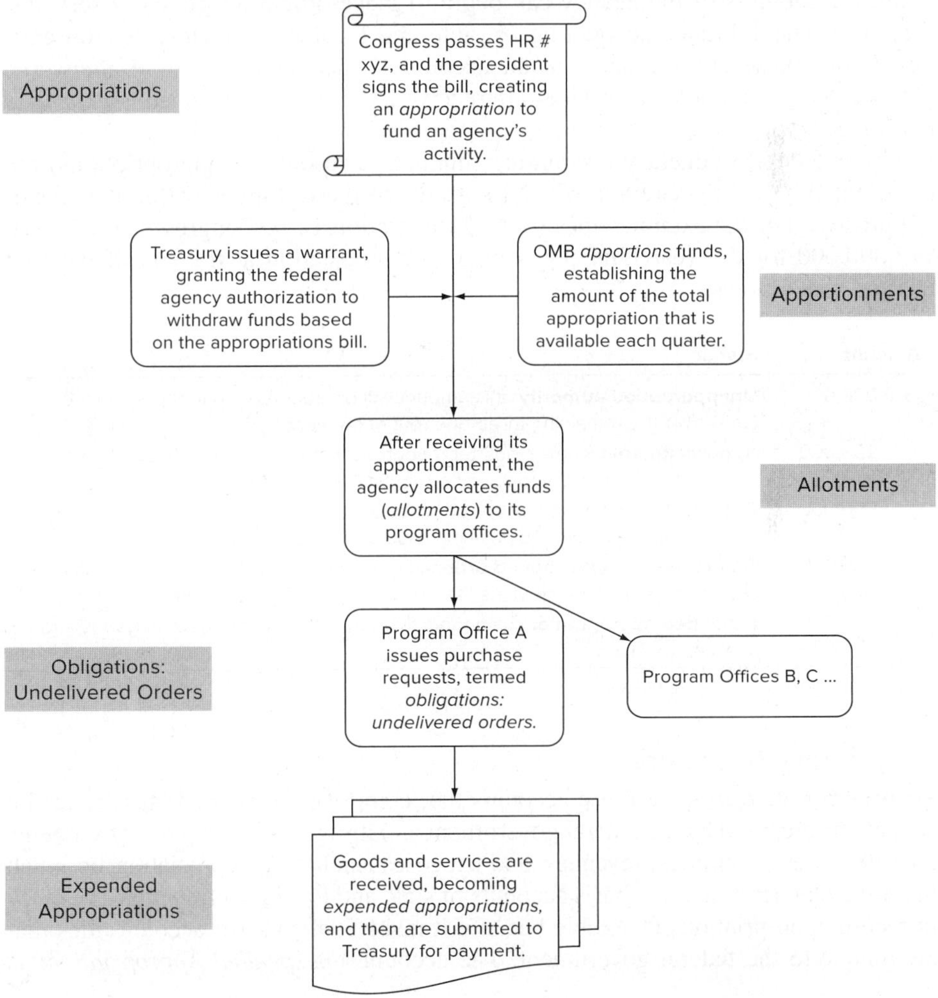

and representative journal entries are presented in Illustration 14-9. Journal entries are recorded at each step in the budgetary authority process so that the budgetary accounts always reflect the status of those resources in the spending cycle.

The process begins with Congress passing an *appropriation,* a spending bill that is signed by the president. The Department of the Treasury then issues a warrant verifying the appropriation and establishment of a line of credit for the agency that will be disbursing the funds. The federal agency records its entire appropriation when it receives the warrant from the Treasury. The OMB issues an *apportionment,* which is an allocation of the total appropriation to specific time periods (frequently three-month periods). The purpose of apportionment is to prevent the federal agency from spending the appropriation too rapidly and having to request a supplemental appropriation later in the year.

The federal agency then has authority to divide the funds among its offices or programs in accordance with the spending bill. These are called *allotments.* At this point, the subunits of the agency can begin to place orders for goods or services. Similar to encumbrance accounting by state and local governments, federal entities record these commitments in an account termed *Obligations—Undelivered Orders.* When the goods or services are received, the status is changed to *expended appropriations.*

Under federal budgetary accounting, budgetary resources (appropriations) are represented by debits. Credits reflect the status of the resources within the spending process. For the example appearing in Illustration 14-9, Congress appropriated $12,000,000 for the year. The status of that appropriation at the end of the first quarter is as follows:

Amount	Status
$ 9,000,000	**Unapportioned authority:** this amount will be apportioned to the agency by OMB over the remaining three quarters of the year.
500,000	**Apportionments:** current quarter resources that have not yet been allotted by the head of the agency to specific subunits of the agency.
600,000	**Allotments:** resources that are currently available to agency offices but have not yet been committed by placing orders for goods or services.
1,000,000	**Obligations for undelivered orders:** commitments for outstanding purchase orders for goods and services that have not yet been received.
900,000	**Expended appropriations:** amounts that have been expended on goods and services received.
$12,000,000	Total appropriation

Proprietary Accounts

Proprietary accounts are those accounts that comprise the accrual basis financial statements prepared by the federal government and its agencies. Proprietary accounts measure assets, liabilities, revenues, and expenses (including depreciation) in much the same manner as accrual basis accounts of state and local governments. The entry to record appropriations is notable because it involves the use of account titles that are unique to the federal government. The account *Unexpended Appropriations* is

ILLUSTRATION 14-9 Comparative Journal Entries

TYPICAL JOURNAL ENTRIES: FEDERAL AGENCY
COMPARISON OF BUDGETARY AND PROPRIETARY ACCOUNTING

Event Description	Budgetary Accounting			Proprietary Accounting		
		Debits	Credits		Debits	Credits
Appropriations: Treasury notifies the agency that Congress passed legislation (signed by the president) granting budgetary authority to fund its activities.	Appropriations Realized	12,000,000		Fund Balance with Treasury	12,000,000	
	Unapportioned Authority		12,000,000	Unexpended Appropriations		12,000,000
Apportionment: OMB apportions ¼ of the appropriated amount, which may now be expended for first-quarter activities.	Unapportioned Authority	3,000,000		No journal entry required		
	Apportionments		3,000,000			
Allotment: The head of the agency allots a portion of the apportionment to the heads of subunits within the agency. The subunits may now expend resources.	Apportionments	2,500,000		No journal entry required		
	Allotments		2,500,000			
Obligations (commitments): A unit of the agency places orders for goods and services related to its activities.	Allotments	1,900,000		No journal entry required		
	Obligations—Undelivered Orders		1,900,000			
Expenditure: Some of the items ordered above (equipment of $100,000 and services of $800,000) are received and approved for payment.	Obligations—Undelivered Orders	900,000		Equipment	100,000	
				Operating (program) Expense	800,000	
	Expended Appropriations		900,000	Accounts Payable		900,000
				Accounts Payable	900,000	
				Fund Balance with Treasury		900,000

credited at the time of an appropriation. This represents a source of funds to the federal agency and is similar to a *transfer in* account in a state or local government fund. Federal agencies do not typically maintain cash balances. Instead, the ability to draw cash from the Treasury is recognized as an asset at the time of an appropriation with the account *Fund Balance with Treasury*. Payments made by the Treasury on behalf of the agency are reflected with a credit to this account. Illustrative transactions, journal entries, and financial statements are presented in the appendix to this chapter.

SUMMARY

Article 1 of the U.S. Constitution requires that the federal government publish financial reports. The Federal Accounting Standards Advisory Board (FASAB) establishes the accounting and reporting standards for the U.S. government overall and for federal agencies and departments. The AICPA's Code of Professional Conduct recognizes FASAB standards as the highest level of authoritative standard for federal government agencies. Like the FASB and GASB, the FASAB issues concepts statements to guide the Board in the development of new standards.

Federal agency financial reports contain a Management's Discussion and Analysis, an audit report, financial statements and notes, and required supplemental and stewardship information. The primary accrual basis financial statements include a Balance Sheet, Statement of Net Cost, and Statement of Changes in Net Position. The Statement of Budgetary Resources is prepared using the budgetary basis and provides information on the status of budgetary resources. In some cases, a Statement of Custodial Activity or Statement of Social Insurance may also be required. Because federal entities have both budgetary and financial reporting requirements, a dual-track accounting system is employed using budgetary and proprietary accounts.

APPENDIX: ILLUSTRATIVE EXAMPLE

The U.S. Office of Government Ethics is an executive branch federal agency dedicated to preventing and resolving conflicts of interest by employees of the federal government. For illustrative purposes, assume the agency began the fiscal year with the following balances:

U.S. OFFICE OF GOVERNMENT ETHICS
Trial Balance
October 1, 2019

	Debits	Credits
Fund Balance with Treasury	$ 150,000	
Supplies	35,000	
Equipment	1,200,000	
Accumulated Depreciation		$ 380,000
Accounts Payable		26,000
Cumulative Results of Operations		979,000
	$1,385,000	$1,385,000

Assume: (1) Congress passed a spending bill providing $8,000,000 to fund the agency's operations for the year. Entries are required in both the budgetary and proprietary accounts.

	Debits	Credits
1a. *Budgetary Accounts*		
Appropriations Realized	8,000,000	
Unapportioned Authority		8,000,000
1b. *Proprietary Accounts*		
Fund Balance with Treasury	8,000,000	
Unexpended Appropriations		8,000,000

(2) The Office of Management and Budget approves quarterly apportionments. Entries are made each quarter.

2. *Budgetary Accounts*		
1st quarter:		
Unapportioned Authority	2,000,000	
Apportionments		2,000,000
Total for other quarters (made throughout the year):		
Unapportioned Authority	6,000,000	
Apportionments		6,000,000

(3) During the year the agency allotted the entire apportionment to its two departments.

3. *Budgetary Accounts*		
Apportionments	8,000,000	
Allotments—(Department A)		3,000,000
Allotments—(Department B)		5,000,000

(4) During the year the agency approved purchase orders and contracts in the following amounts:

Purpose	Total	Dept. A	Dept. B
Salaries and benefits	$1,200,000	$ 500,000	$ 700,000
Supplies	800,000	500,000	300,000
Contracted services	1,500,000	1,500,000	—
Grants	3,000,000	—	3,000,000
Equipment	1,500,000	500,000	1,000,000
Total	$8,000,000	$3,000,000	$5,000,000

4. *Budgetary Accounts*		
Allotments—(Department A)	3,000,000	
Allotments—(Department B)	5,000,000	
Obligations—Undelivered Orders—(Department A)		3,000,000
Obligations—Undelivered Orders—(Department B)		5,000,000

(5) All items were received. The beginning accounts payable of $26,000 and $7,890,000 of the current year obligations were processed and paid before year-end.

5a. *Budgetary Accounts*		
Obligations—Undelivered Orders—(Department A)	3,000,000	
Obligations—Undelivered Orders—(Department B)	5,000,000	
Expended Appropriations—(Department A)		3,000,000
Expended Appropriations—(Department B)		5,000,000
5b. *Proprietary Accounts*		
Supplies	800,000	
Equipment	1,500,000	
Operating Expenses—(Department A)	2,000,000	
Operating Expenses—(Department B)	3,700,000	
Accounts Payable		8,000,000
Accounts Payable	7,916,000	
Fund Balance with Treasury		7,916,000

(6) Ending supplies totaled $25,000 (a decrease of $10,000 from the balance at the beginning of the year). Assume the beginning and ending supplies inventories all relate to Department A. The entry to record supplies expense is

6. *Proprietary Accounts*		
Operating Expenses—(Department A)	510,000	
Operating Expenses—(Department B)	300,000	
Supplies		810,000

(7) The entry to record depreciation on the agency's fixed assets is

7. *Proprietary Accounts*		
Operating Expenses—(Department A)	70,000	
Operating Expenses—(Department B)	200,000	
Accumulated Depreciation		270,000

In this example, the agency expended its full appropriation. Typically budgetary authority that is not obligated by year-end would be returned to Treasury. The entry

ILLUSTRATION 14-10 **Statement of Net Cost**

U.S. OFFICE OF GOVERNMENT ETHICS Statement of Net Cost For the Year Ended September 30, 2020	
Costs by Strategic Goal	
Conflicts of Interest Resolution	$2,580,000
Federal Employee Education	4,200,000
Total Gross Costs	6,780,000
Less Earned Revenues	—
Net Cost from Operations	$6,780,000

ILLUSTRATION 14-11 **Statement of Changes in Net Position**

U.S. OFFICE OF GOVERNMENT ETHICS Statement of Changes in Net Position For the Year Ended September 30, 2020	Cumulative Results of Operations	Unexpended Appropriations
Beginning Balance	$ 979,000	—
Appropriations Received		$ 8,000,000
Appropriations Used	8,000,000	(8,000,000)
Other Financing Sources	—	—
Total Financing Sources	8,979,000	—
Net Cost of Operations	6,780,000	—
Ending Balance	$2,199,000	—

to record this would credit the budgetary account *Appropriations Withdrawn.* The corresponding proprietary entry would reverse entry (lb) to the extent of the unused appropriation.

The Statement of Net Cost is presented in Illustration 14-10. Assume the agency has two strategic goals, corresponding to the two departments. This statement is prepared on the accrual basis using expense information appearing in the proprietary journal entries 5, 6, and 7.

The Statement of Changes in Net Position is also prepared on the accrual basis and reconciles the beginning balance of net position to the end of year balance. This statement appears in Illustration 14-11. Note that *Net Cost of Operations* agrees with the bottom line of the Statement of Net Cost. Illustration 14-11 uses a columnar format, in contrast to that used by the SEC in Illustration 14-4.

The agency's Balance Sheet appears in Illustration 14-12. Note that the balances appearing under *Net Position* agree with the bottom line of the Statement of Changes in Net Position. Assets and liabilities are displayed within the categories of *Intragovernmental* (between government agencies) or *Governmental.*

ILLUSTRATION 14-12 **Balance Sheet**

U.S. OFFICE OF GOVERNMENT ETHICS Balance Sheet As of September 30, 2020	
Assets	
Intragovernmental:	
Fund Balance with Treasury	$ 234,000
Governmental:	
Supplies	25,000
Equipment (Net of Accumulated Depreciation)	2,050,000
Total Assets	$2,309,000
Liabilities	
Governmental:	
Accounts Payable	110,000
Net Position	
Unexpended Appropriations	0
Cumulative Results of Operations	2,199,000
Total Liabilities and Net Position	$2,309,000

Questions and Exercises

14–1. What are the required financial statements of a federal agency?

14–2. What are the required financial statements of the U.S. government?

14–3. What bodies are responsible for establishing accounting standards for the federal government and its agencies?

14–4. The 2017 financial statements of the U.S. government are available at https://fiscal.treasury.gov/reports-statements/financial-report/current-report.html Use these to answer the following questions:

a. Statement of Net Cost

(1) What are the three largest government units based on net cost? (identify $ amount)

(2) Which government department operates at the largest net profit? (identify $ amount)

b. Statement of Operations and Changes in Net Position

(3) What are the two largest sources of outside revenue to the federal government? (identify $ amount)

(4) Which item on this statement articulates (agrees) with the Statement of Net Cost? (identify $ amount)

c. Balance Sheet

(5) What are the two largest liabilities reported on a Balance Sheet? (identify $ amount)

(6) Which item on this statement articulates with the Statement of Operations and Changes in Net Position? (identify $ amount)

14–5. The 2018 financial statements of the Internal Revenue Service are available at https://www.gao.gov/products/GAO-19-150

Use these to answer the following questions:

a. Statement of Net Cost

(1) What are the IRS's two largest programs based on net cost? (identify $ amount)

b. Statement of Changes in Net Position

(2) What is the largest source of financing for the activities of the IRS? (identify $ amount)

c. Statement of Custodial Activity

(3) What activity is reported in this statement (i.e., what is the IRS doing)?

14–6. Assume a federal agency has the following events:

1. Receives a warrant from the Treasury notifying the agency of appropriations of $3,600,000.
2. OMB apportions one-fourth of the appropriation for the first quarter of the year.
3. The director of the agency allots $875,000 to program units.
4. Program units place orders of $600,000.
5. Supplies ($120,000) and services ($420,000) are received during the first quarter. Supplies of $100,000 were used in the quarter. Accounts payable were paid in full.

Required:

Prepare any necessary journal entries to reflect the events described above. Identify whether the entry is a budgetary or proprietary type.

14–7. Using the information from Exercise 14–6, prepare a schedule showing the status of the appropriation at the end of the first quarter.

14–8. The Mosquito Abatement Commission is a newly organized federal agency with three primary programs: coordinating state government abatement functions, conducting research on mosquito abatement, and promoting abatement through public education. The following information is available at the end of the first quarter (December 31, 2020):

	Government Coordination	Research	Public Education	Total
Apportionments from OMB				$5,000,000
Allotments—first quarter	$2,500,000	$1,500,000	$1,000,000	5,000,000
Salaries paid	1,600,000	500,000	720,000	2,820,000
Accrued salaries payable	18,000	30,000	25,000	73,000
Supplies ordered and received	156,000	357,000	136,000	649,000
Supplies used	107,000	355,000	120,000	582,000
Depreciation	35,000	77,000	8,000	120,000
Equipment purchases	850,000	500,000	37,000	1,387,000
Program revenue: Charges for service			225,000	225,000

Required:

Prepare a Statement of Net Cost for the quarter ended December 31.

14–9. Assume the Federal Interstate Commission began the fiscal year with the following account balances:

FEDERAL INTERSTATE COMMISSION
Trial Balance
October 1, 2020

	Debits	Credits
Fund Balance with Treasury	$ 730,000	
Supplies	105,000	
Equipment	1,350,000	
Accumulated Depreciation		$ 480,000
Accounts Payable		126,000
Wages Payable		79,000
Cumulative Results of Operations		1,500,000
	$2,185,000	$2,185,000

1. Congress passed a spending bill providing $16,000,000 to fund the agency's operations for the year.
2. During the first quarter the commission processed the following items for payment (all items were paid by Treasury in the first quarter).

Beginning balances	
Accounts payable	$ 126,000
Wages payable	79,000
Salaries and benefits	495,000
Supplies	500,000
Contracted services	1,000,000
Grants	900,000
Equipment	500,000
Total	$3,600,000

3. Unpaid wages at the end of the quarter totaled $35,000.
4. In addition to the items paid in item 2, the commission received supplies of $12,000 and contracted services of $70,000 that are to be processed for payment in January.
5. Unused supplies on hand totaled $214,000 at December 31.
6. Depreciation for the quarter is $60,000.

Required:

a. Prepare journal entries in the proprietary accounts for the events described above.

b. Prepare a Statement of Changes in Net Position for the quarter ended December 31. (Assume the amount of appropriations used is $3,909,000 and use the format appearing in Illustration 14-11.)

c. Prepare a Balance Sheet as of December 31.

Governmental and Not-for-Profit Accounting Terminology

501(c)(3) entities Not-for-profit organizations that receive tax-exempt status through Section 501(c)(3) of the Internal Revenue Code.

A

accounting entity Where an entity is established for the purpose of accounting for a certain activity or activities. See *fiscal entity.*

activity Specific and distinguishable line of work performed by one or more organizational components of a governmental unit for the purpose of accomplishing a function for which the governmental unit is responsible. For example, "Food Inspection" is an activity performed in the discharge of the "Health" function. See also *Functional classification.*

additions GASB term for fiduciary fund financial reporting, in place of the term *revenues.* Additions are reported on the accrual basis.

advance refunding A bond refunding (q.v.) in which the proceeds are placed in an escrow account pending the call date or the maturity date of the existing debt. In this case, the debt is said to be *defeased* (q.v.) for accounting purposes.

agent multiple-employer defined benefit pension plan Statewide pension plan in which separate account balances are maintained for each participating employer, which are expected to fund any deficits. Contrast with *cost-sharing multiple-employer defined benefit pension plan.*

annuity Series of equal money payments made at equal intervals during a designated period of time. In governmental accounting, the most frequent annuities are accumulations of debt service funds for term bonds and payments to retired employees or their beneficiaries under public employee retirement systems.

appropriation Authorization granted by a legislative body to incur liabilities for purposes specified in the appropriation act (q.v.).

asset retirement obligations Laws, regulations, or contractual terms may require governments to retire certain assets at the end of their useful lives. For example, governments may be responsible for the costs of decommissioning nuclear power plants or sewage treatment facilities. GASB requires that financial statements prepared on the economic resource measurement focus (enterprise funds and government-wide statements) reflect estimates of these liabilities on the Statement of Net Position.

assigned fund balance A classification of fund balance reported in governmental-type funds to indicate net resources of the fund that the government intends for a specific purpose. Assigned resources differ from committed in that constraints imposed on assigned resources are more easily modified or removed. For governmental funds other than the General Fund, this is the category for all (positive) residual fund balances.

attestation agreements Under Government Auditing Standards (q.v.), concerns examining, reviewing, or performing agreed-upon procedures on a subject matter or an assertion about a subject matter and reporting on the results.

available One of two conditions (along with measurable) that must be met before a revenue can be recognized under modified accrual accounting. The amount must be available in time to pay expenditures related to the current period.

B

basic financial statements The primary financial statements required by GASB for state and local governments to comply with GAAP. The nature of the government (general-purpose, special-purpose) and of the governmental activities (governmental-type, business-type, and fiduciary-type) determine which statements are basic.

basis of accounting Rule (or rules) used to determine the point in time when assets, liabilities, revenues, and expenses (expenditures) should be measured and recorded as such in the accounts of an entity. Different funds might use the modified accrual or accrual basis of accounting.

blending, blended presentation One method of reporting the financial data of a component unit. Under this method, the component unit data are combined with the appropriate fund types of the primary government and reported in the same columns as the data from the primary government. See *discrete presentation.*

budgetary accounts (federal) Accounts that provide a record by which federal expenditures can be traced back to the budgetary authority granted by Congress through appropriations, as distinguished from proprietary accounts (q.v.). They include appropriations, apportionments, allotments, and obligations.

budgetary accounts (state and local) Accounts that reflect budgetary operations and conditions, such as Estimated Revenues, Appropriations, and Encumbrances. Other examples include Estimated Other Financing Sources (Uses), Budgetary Fund Balance, and Budgetary Fund Balance Reserve for Encumbrances. Budgetary accounts do not appear in the general purpose financial statements.

budgetary fund balance Budgetary account for state and local governmental funds that reflects the difference between estimated revenues and estimated other financing sources over appropriations and estimated other financing uses. Closed at the end of the year.

budgetary fund balance reserve for encumbrances Budgetary account for state and local governmental funds that reflects the amount offsetting Encumbrances (q.v.), or purchase orders or contracts issued during the current year.

C

capital and related financing activities Cash flow statement category required by GASB. Includes proceeds from bond issues, payment of debt, acquisition of fixed assets, and payment of interest on capital-related debt.

capital projects fund Fund created to account for financial resources restricted, committed, or assigned for the construction or acquisition of fixed assets by a governmental unit except those financed by proprietary or fiduciary funds.

carryover method A method of accounting for mergers among not-for-profit organizations in which the two merging organizations' asset and liability book balances are "carried over" to the new reporting entity.

character classification Grouping of expenditures on the basis of the fiscal periods they are presumed to benefit. The three groupings are (1) current expenditures, presumed to benefit the current fiscal period; (2) debt service, presumed to benefit prior fiscal periods primarily but also present and future periods; and (3) capital outlay, presumed to benefit the current and future fiscal periods.

charitable gift annuity Split-interest agreement that exists when no formal trust agreement is signed but that otherwise is similar to a charitable remainder trust (q.v.) in which a specified amount or percentage of the fair value of assets is paid to a beneficiary during the term of the agreement; at the end of the agreement, the trust assets go to the not-for-profit organization.

charitable lead trust Split-interest (q.v.) agreement in which an organization receives a fixed amount (charitable lead annuity trust) or a percentage of the fair value of the trust (charitable lead unitrust) for a certain term. At the end of the term, the remaining trust assets are paid to the donor or other beneficiary.

charitable remainder trust Split-interest (q.v.) agreement in which a fixed dollar amount (charitable remainder annuity trust) or a specified percentage of the trust's fair market value (charitable remainder unitrust) is paid to a beneficiary. At the end of the term of the trust, the trust principal is paid to a not-for-profit organization.

charity care The term used in the health care industry to describe a situation in which services are provided to a patient without the expectation of receiving payment. FASB characterizes charity care patients as those with a demonstrated inability to pay at the time of treatment. Revenue is not recognized for charity care.

codification A listing of GASB or FASB pronouncements organized by topic. In contrast to a chronological listing in the *GASB (FASB) Original Pronouncements.*

cognizant agency Under the Single Audit Act and amendments, an agency that deals with the auditee, as representative of all federal agencies. Is assigned by the U.S. Office of Management and Budget (q.v.) for auditees with more than $50 million in federal awards.

collection Under both FASB and GASB standards, collections are works of art, historical treasures, etc., that are (1) held for public exhibition, education, or research in furtherance of public service, other than financial gain; (2) protected, kept unencumbered, cared for and preserved; and (3) subject to an organizational policy that requires the proceeds from sales of collection items to be used to acquire other items for collections or used to preserve existing items. Collections may or may not be capitalized and depreciated.

committed fund balance A classification of fund balance reported in governmental-type funds to indicate net resources of the fund that the governing body has specified for particular use. To be classified as committed, the resources should have been designated through ordinance or resolution by the government's highest level of authority.

component unit Separate governmental unit, agency, or nonprofit corporation that, pursuant to the criteria in the GASB *Codification,* Section 2100, is combined with other component units and the primary government to constitute the reporting entity (q.v.).

Comprehensive Annual Financial Report (CAFR) A governmental unit's official annual report prepared and published as a matter of public record. In addition to the basic financial statements (q.v.) and required supplementary information, the CAFR should contain introductory material, schedules to demonstrate compliance, and statistical tables specified in the GASB *Codification.*

consumption method Refers to method used to recognize expenditures for governmental funds (q.v.) in which an expenditure (q.v.) is recognized when inventory is consumed. Similar to the method of expense recognition used by commercial organizations.

contingencies Term used by both GASB and FASB. Something must happen (for example a matching requirement) before a revenue (expense) can be recognized. For GASB, an eligibility requirement.

contractual adjustment Also called *explicit price-concession.* Term used in the health care industry to describe discounts provided to third-party payors (insurance companies, Medicare, and Medicaid). It is the difference between the standard rate charged by a health care entity for a service and the reimbursement rate. Patient service revenues are reported net of these contractual adjustments.

cost-sharing multiple-employer defined benefit pension plan Statewide pension plan in which separate account balances are not maintained for each participating employer. Contrast with *agent multiple-employer defined benefit pension plan.*

current financial resources measurement focus Measurement focus used for governmental funds that measures current financial resources, not fixed assets and long-term debt. Contrast with *economic resources measurement focus* (q.v.).

current refunding A bond refunding (q.v.) in which new debt is issued, and the proceeds are used to call in the existing debt. Contrast with *advance refunding* (q.v.).

custodial funds Funds used to account for fiduciary activities other than those reported in pension trust funds, investment trust funds, and private purpose trust funds. These include activities where a trust agreement is not in effect. An example would be a county tax custodial fund, where the county collects property taxes on behalf of towns located within the county.

D

debt limit Maximum amount of gross or net debt that is legally permitted.

debt margin Difference between the amount of the debt limit (q.v.) and the net amount of outstanding indebtedness subject to the limitation.

debt service fund Fund established to report financial resources that are restricted, committed, or assigned for the payment of interest and principal on tax-supported long-term debt.

deductions GASB term for fiduciary fund financial reporting, replacing the term *expenses*. Deductions are reported on the accrual basis.

defeased In an advanced refunding (q.v.) where proceeds are placed in an escrow account pending the call date or maturity date of the existing debt, the old debt is considered not to exist and to be replaced by the existing debt.

deferred inflows of resources These are balance sheet accounts with credit balances, similar to liabilities. However, these items do not represent obligations and are therefore not liabilities. The most common example in a governmental fund is deferred taxes. Only items specifically identified in GASB standards may be reported as deferred inflows.

deferred outflows of resources These are balance sheet accounts with debit balances but are not assets. Deferred outflows rarely appear in governmental funds but arise most commonly in accrual-based statements. Only items specifically identified in GASB standards may be reported as deferred outflows.

deferred serial bonds Serial bonds (q.v.) in which the first installment does not fall due for two or more years from the date of issue.

defined benefit (pension or retirement) plan Retirement plan in which the benefit is defined, normally as a percentage multiplied by a retiree's salary and by the number of years worked.

defined contribution (pension or retirement) plans Retirement plans in which the amount to be paid at retirement is based on employee and employer contributions and investment income.

derived tax revenues One of the four classes of nonexchange transactions established by GASB. Examples are sales taxes and income taxes.

discrete presentation Method of reporting financial data of component units (q.v.) in a column or columns separate from the financial data of the primary government (q.v.). Contrast with *blending*.

E

economic resources measurement focus Term used by GASB to indicate measurement focus for government-wide, proprietary fund, and fiduciary fund statements. The economic resources measurement focus measures all economic resources, including fixed assets and long-term debt. Contrast with *current financial resources measurement focus* (q.v.).

eligibility requirements Term used by GASB that describes certain conditions or events that must be met before a nonexchange revenue can be recognized. The four eligibility requirements are (1) required characteristics of recipients, (2) time requirements, (3) reimbursements, and (4) contingencies.

encumbrances The estimated amount of purchase orders, contracts, or salary commitments chargeable to an appropriation. A budgetary account recognized in governmental-type funds.

endowment Exist when a donor contributes resources that are to be invested rather than expended. The income from endowments may or may not be *restricted* (q.v.).

enterprise fund Fund used in state and local government accounting. Established to finance and account for the acquisition, operation, and maintenance of services that are entirely or predominantly self-supporting by user charges; or for which the governing body of the governmental unit has decided periodic determination of revenues earned, expenses incurred, and/or net income is appropriate. Government-owned utilities and hospitals are ordinarily accounted for by enterprise funds.

escheat property Private property that reverts to government ownership upon the death of the owner if there are no legal claimants or heirs.

estimated other financing sources Amounts of financial resources estimated to be received or accrued during a period by a governmental or similar type fund from interfund transfers or from the proceeds of noncurrent debt issuances. Budgetary account.

estimated other financing uses Amounts of financial resources estimated to be disbursed or accrued during a period by a governmental or similar type fund for transfer to other funds. Budgetary account.

estimated revenues Budgetary account providing an estimate of the revenues that will be recognized during an accounting period by a governmental fund, such as the General Fund.

expendable Resources, where focus is on the receipt and expenditure of resources; for example, modified accrual accounting. See *nonexpendable.*

expended Term describing outflow of resources (or increase in liabilities) associated with receipt of goods or services. Especially used in budgetary accounting, e.g., when an appropriation (q.v.) is expended.

expenditures Recorded when liabilities are incurred pursuant to authority given in an appropriation (q.v.). Designates the cost of goods delivered or services received, whether paid or unpaid, including current items, provision for interest and debt retirement, and capital outlays. Used for governmental funds of governmental units.

F

Federal Accounting Standards Advisory Board (FASAB) Standards-setting body that promulgates federal government accounting and financial reporting standards.

fiduciary funds Any fund held by a governmental unit in a fiduciary capacity, ordinarily as agent or trustee. Also called *trust and custodial funds.* Four categories exist: custodial funds, pension trust funds, investment trust funds, and private-purpose trust funds.

Financial Accounting Foundation (FAF) Parent organization of the Financial Accounting Standards Board (FASB) and the Governmental Accounting Standards Board (GASB). Responsible for overall policy direction, raising funds, and selecting board members, but not for setting standards.

Financial Accounting Standards Board (FASB) Independent seven-member body designated to set accounting and financial reporting standards for commercial entities and nongovernmental not-for-profit entities.

financial audits Under Government Auditing Standards (q.v.), type of governmental audit that provides assurance about the fairness of financial statements.

financial reporting entity Primary government and all related component units, if any, combined in accordance with the GASB *Codification* Sec. 2100 constituting the governmental reporting entity.

fiscal entity Where assets are set aside, for example in a fund, for specific purposes. See *accounting entity.*

Form 990 Tax form information return filed by most tax-exempt organizations under Section 501(c)(3) (q.v.) of the Internal Revenue Code.

full faith and credit Pledge of the general taxing power for the payment of debt obligations. General obligation bonds are backed by the full faith and credit of a given governmental unit.

functional classification Grouping of expenditures on the basis of the principal purposes for which they are made. Examples in government are public safety, public health, and public welfare. Examples in not-for-profit organizations are the various programs, fund-raising, management and general, and membership development.

fund accounting Accounting system organized on the basis of funds, each of which is considered a separate accounting entity. The operations of each fund are accounted for with a separate set of self-balancing accounts that comprise its assets, liabilities, fund equity, revenues, and expenditures, or expenses, as appropriate.

fund balance Term used for governmental funds (q.v.) representing the difference between assets and liabilities. Fund balance may be restricted, committed, assigned for various purposes, or unassigned. (q.v.).

G

general capital (or fixed) assets Capital assets of a governmental unit that are not accounted for by a proprietary or fiduciary fund.

General Fund Fund used to account for all transactions of a governmental unit that are not accounted for in another fund.

general long-term debt Long-term debt legally payable from general revenues and backed by the full faith and credit of a governmental unit.

general obligation bonds Bonds for whose payment the full faith and credit of the issuing body is pledged. More commonly, but not necessarily, considered to be those payable from taxes and other general revenues (q.v.). In some states, called *tax-supported* bonds.

Generally Accepted Accounting Principles (GAAP) Body of accounting and financial reporting standards as defined by Rule 203 of the American Institute of Certified Public Accountants (AICPA). "Level A" GAAP is set by the FASB, the GASB, and the FASAB.

Generally Accepted Auditing Standards (GAAS) Standards prescribed by the American Institute of Certified Public Accountants to provide guidance for planning, conducting, and reporting audits by Certified Public Accountants.

Government Accountability Office (GAO) Legislative branch agency of the federal government that prepares *Government Auditing Standards* (q.v.); responsible for auditing the U.S. government consolidated statements and selective agencies.

Government Auditing Standards (GAS) Auditing standards set forth by the Comptroller General of the United States to provide guidance for federal auditors and state and local governmental auditors and public accountants who audit federal organizations, programs, activities, and functions. Also referred to as *Generally Accepted Government Auditing Standards (GAGAS).*

government-mandated nonexchange transactions One of the four classes of nonexchange transactions established by GASB. Example would be a grant to a school district to carry out a mandated state program.

Governmental Accounting Standards Board (GASB) Independent agency established under the Financial Accounting Foundation in 1984 to set accounting and financial reporting standards for state and local governments and for governmentally related not-for-profit organizations.

governmental funds Generic classification used by the GASB to refer to all funds other than proprietary and fiduciary. Includes the General Fund, special revenue funds, capital projects funds, debt service funds, and permanent funds.

I

implicit price concessions Exist when a heath care entity has a customary business practice of accepting less than their stated charges for medical treatment. Patient service revenues are reported net of implicit price concessions.

interfund loans and advances Interfund transaction where one fund provides a short-term loan or a long-term advance to another. Type of reciprocal interfund transaction (q.v.). One fund recognizes a receivable and the other a liability.

interfund reimbursements Type of interfund transaction in which one fund reimburses another for expenditures already incurred. One fund recognizes an expenditure or expense; the other reduces an expenditure or expense.

interfund services provided and used Interfund transaction in which one fund provides service to another. Type of reciprocal interfund transaction (q.v.). One fund recognizes a revenue, and the other fund recognizes an expenditure or expense. Replaces the term *quasi-external transaction.*

interfund transactions GASB term to describe transactions between funds. Four types of interfund transactions exist. Reciprocal interfund transactions (q.v.) include interfund loans and advances (q.v.) and interfund services provided and used (q.v.). Nonreciprocal interfund transactions include interfund transfers (q.v.) and reimbursements (q.v.).

interfund transfers Type of interfund transaction in which one fund transfers resources to another, without an exchange transaction. One fund recognizes an Other Financing Source (q.v.) (or Transfer In) and the other fund recognizes an Other Financing Use (q.v.) (or Transfer Out).

internal service fund Fund established to finance and account for services and commodities furnished by a designated department or agency to other departments and agencies within a single governmental unit or to other governmental units. Type of proprietary fund.

interpretations Documents issued by the GASB (q.v.), FASB (q.v.), and FASAB (q.v.) that provide guidance regarding previously issued statements (q.v.).

investing activities Cash flow statement category required by both FASB and GASB. FASB and GASB have differing content requirements for this category. FASB includes cash inflows and outflows associated with the acquisition and sale of long-term assets, including capital assets. GASB includes inflows and outflows associated with the acquisition and sale of investments and interest or dividends received on investments.

investment trust fund Fiduciary fund that accounts for the external portion of investment pools governed by a trust agreement in which the sponsoring government is the trustee.

IRS 457 Deferred Compensation Plans Tax deferred plans allowed by law to be offered by state and local governmental units. In some cases, reported as Pension Trust Funds.

L

lapse As applied to appropriations, denotes the automatic termination of an appropriation. As applied to encumbrances, denotes the termination of an encumbrance (q.v.) at the end of a fiscal year.

low-risk auditee Auditee determined by an auditor who is auditing under the Single Audit Act (q.v.) to have met certain criteria, permitting the auditor to examine a smaller percentage of the federal funds received by the entity being audited.

M

major funds Major funds must be displayed in the basic statements for governmental and proprietary funds. Funds are considered major when both of the following conditions exist: (1) total assets, liabilities, revenues, or expenditures/expenses of that individual governmental or enterprise fund constitute 10 percent of the governmental or enterprise activity; and (2) total assets, liabilities, revenues, or expenditures/expenses are 5 percent of the governmental and enterprise category.

measurable One of two conditions (along with available) that must be met before a revenue can be recognized under the modified accrual basis of accounting. The amount must be subject to reliable measurement.

measurement focus Nature of the resources, claims against resources, and flows of resources that are measured and reported by a fund or other entity. For example, governmental funds measure and report current financial resources, whereas proprietary and fiduciary funds measure and report economic resources.

modified accrual basis of accounting Basis of accounting required for use by governmental funds (q.v.) in which revenues are recognized in the period in which they become available and measurable, and expenditures are recognized at the time a liability is incurred, except for principal and interest on long-term debt, which are recorded when due.

N

National Association of College and University Business Officers (NACUBO) Association of college and university financial vice presidents, controllers, budget officials, and other finance officers that produces and distributes the *Financial Accounting and Reporting Manual for Higher Education* (q.v.).

net assets with donor restrictions Residual equity account used by private not-for-profit organizations to indicate resources have been restricted by an outside donor for purpose, time, or fixed asset acquisition.

net assets without donor restrictions Residual equity account used by private not-for-profit organizations that includes board-designated amounts and other resources, such as unrestricted contributions, revenues from providing services, and unrestricted income from investments.

net investment in capital assets The portion of net position (q.v.) representing the excess of capital assets (net of accumulated depreciation) over debt associated with the acquisition of capital assets.

net pension liability The difference between the total pension liability and the net position of the pension fund reported in the Statement of Fiduciary Net Position.

nonaudit services Under Government Auditing Standards (q.v.), gathering, providing, or explaining information requested by decision makers or providing advice or assistance to management officials.

noncapital financing activities Cash flow statement category required by GASB. Includes cash flows from financing not related to capital acquisition, including borrowing and transfers to and from other funds and interest on noncapital borrowings.

nonexchange transactions Transactions that are not the result of arm's-length exchange between two parties that are bargaining for the best position. Contrasted with exchange transactions, such as sales and services for user charges. Examples are taxes and contributions. Imposed nonexchange transactions are not derived from underlying transactions but are commonly derived from the assessed value of property.

nonreciprocal interfund transactions Type of interfund transaction where one fund receives resources without an expectation that they will be repaid or exchanged for goods or services. Includes interfund transfers and interfund reimbursements. The interfund equivalent of nonexchange transactions (q.v.).

nonspendable fund balance A classification offund balance reported in governmental-type funds to indicate net resources of the fund that cannot be spent. Nonspendable resources include inventories, prepaid items, and the corpus of permanent funds.

not-for-profit organization An entity that possesses the following characteristics: (1) receives significant resources from donors who do not expect equivalent value in return; (2) operates for purposes other than to provide goods or services at a profit; and (3) lacks an identifiable individual or group of individuals who hold a legally enforceable residual claim. Entities that fall outside this definition include all investor-owned enterprises and other organizations that provide economic benefits to the owners, members, or participants.

notes to the financial statements Required part of the basic financial statements for state and local governments. Includes a summary of significant accounting policies and other required and optional disclosures.

O

object As used in expenditure classification, applies to the article purchased or the service obtained (as distinguished from the results obtained from expenditures). Examples are personal services, contractual services, materials, and supplies.

Office of Management and Budget, U.S. (OMB) Executive agency of the federal government responsible for the preparation of the executive budget proposal and for the form and content of agency financial statements. The director is one of the principals (q.v.) that approves the recommendations of the Financial Accounting Standards Advisory Board (FASAB) (q.v.).

operating activities Cash flow statement category required by both FASB and GASB. Includes receipts from customers, payments to suppliers and employees, etc.

operating lease A lease whose initial term is less than 12 months. These leases do not result in the recording of a lease liability.

other financing sources Operating statement classification in which financial inflows other than revenues are reported; for example, proceeds of general obligation bonds and transfers in.

other financing uses Operating statement classification in which financial outflows other than expenditures are reported; for example, operating transfers out.

other not-for-profit organizations Term describing category of not-for-profit organizations. Includes all but *voluntary health and welfare organizations* (q.v.), colleges and universities, and health care organizations.

oversight agency Under the Single Audit Act and amendments, agency that deals with entities being audited as a result of receiving federal funds, as representative of all federal agencies. Agency with the most dollars expended by the auditee assumes the role.

P

pension (or other employee benefit) trust fund One of the fiduciary fund types. Accounts for pension and other employee benefit plans when the governmental unit is trustee.

performance audits Under Government Auditing Standards (q.v.), an independent assessment of the performance and management of a program against objective criteria.

performance indicator Used in the *Health Care Guide* (q.v.) to describe a measure of operations (equivalent to operating income). It is required to be presented in the Statement of Operations (q.v.) by the *Health Care Guide.*

permanent fund Governmental fund that is restricted so that only earnings, not principal, may be expended, for purposes that benefit the government and its citizenry.

perpetual trust held by a third party Similar to a split-interest (q.v.) agreement in which trust assets are held by a third party but the income is to go to a not-for-profit organization.

pooled (life) income fund Split-interest agreement described in AICPA *Not-for-Profit Guide* (q.v.) in which several life income agreements are pooled together. A life income fund represents a situation where all of the income is paid to a donor or beneficiary during his or her lifetime.

primary government State government or general-purpose local government. Also, special-purpose government that has a separately elected governing body, is legally separate, and is fiscally independent of other state or local governments.

principals The director of the Office of Management and Budget (q.v.), the secretary of the Treasury (q.v.), and the comptroller general of the United States (q.v.). These three individuals review standards passed by the FASAB (q.v.) and, unless they object, those standards become GAAP (q.v.).

private organizations Organizations and entities that are not owned or controlled by any governments. They include for-profit and not-for-profit organizations. In contrast to *public organizations.*

private-purpose trust fund Funds used to report fiduciary activities governed by trust arrangements (other than pension and investment trust funds) under which principal and income benefit individuals, private organizations, or other governments.

proceeds of bonds (or long-term notes) Account used in governmental accounting for governmental funds to indicate the issuance of long-term debt. Considered an "other financing source." (q.v.)

program expense ratio The most common financial ratio used to evaluate not-for-profit organizations. It is computed as program services expenses divided by total expenses.

proprietary accounts Accounts used by federal agencies in the accrual basis financial statements, as distinguished from budgetary accounts (q.v.).

proprietary funds One of the major fund classifications of governmental accounting, the others being governmental (q.v.) and fiduciary (q.v.). Sometimes referred to as *income determination or commercial-type funds.* Includes enterprise funds and internal service funds.

public charity Churches, schools, hospitals, governmental units, and publicly supported charities and certain other entities. Distinguished from private foundations, which are subject to different tax rules.

Public Employee Retirement Systems (PERS) Organizations that collect retirement and other employee benefit contributions from government employers and employees, manage assets, and make payments to qualified retirees, beneficiaries, and disabled employees.

public organizations Organizations owned or controlled by a government, including government authorities and enterprises. In contrast to *private organizations.*

purchases method Refers to method used to recognize expenditures for governmental funds (q.v.) in which an expenditure (q.v.) is recognized when inventory is acquired.

R

reciprocal interfund transactions Type of interfund transaction including interfund loans and advances (q.v.) and interfund services provided and used (q.v.). The interfund equivalent of exchange transactions (q.v.).

reimbursements An eligibility requirement imposed by GASB. A nonexchange revenue (or expense) cannot be recognized until the resources are expended, when a grant or contribution makes this requirement. Also see *interfund reimbursements.*

required characteristics of recipients An eligibility requirement imposed by GASB. A nonexchange revenue (or expense) cannot be recognized unless the recipient government meets the characteristics specified by the provider.

required supplementary information (RSI) Information required by GASB to be reported along with basic financial statements. Includes MD&A (q.v.) and, when applicable, budgetary comparison schedules, schedules related to pension plans, and information about infrastructure assets using the modified format.

restricted fund balance A classification of fund balance reported in governmental-type funds to indicate net resources of the fund that are subject to constraints imposed by external parties or law.

restricted net position The portion of governmental activities (government-wide) or proprietary fund resources that is restricted by donors, grantors, creditors, other governments, laws or regulations, or legislation.

revenue bonds Bonds whose principal and interest are payable exclusively from earnings of a public enterprise.

revenues Additions to fund financial resources other than from interfund transfers (q.v.) and debt issue proceeds. Examples include taxes and charges for services.

S

service efforts and accomplishments (SEA) Conceptualization of the resources consumed (inputs), tasks performed (outputs), and goals attained (outcomes), and the relationships among these items in providing services in selected areas (e.g., police protection, solid waste garbage collection, and elementary and secondary education).

special item Classification by GASB in financial statements to indicate that a revenue, expense, gain, or loss is either unusual or infrequent and within the control of management.

special revenue fund Fund used to report resources from specific taxes or other earmarked revenue sources that are restricted or committed to finance particular functions or activities of government.

split-interest agreement Agreement between a donor and a not-for-profit organization in which the donor (or beneficiary) and the organization "split" the income and/or principal of the gift. Examples are charitable lead trusts (q.v.) and charitable remainder trusts (q.v.).

statement of activities (not-for-profit accounting) One of the three statements required for not-for-profit organizations by FASB *Statement 117*. Requirements are to show revenues, expenses, gains, losses, and reclassifications (q.v.) and to show the change in net assets by net asset class (unrestricted, temporarily restricted, permanently restricted).

statement of cash flows Required basic statement for proprietary funds for governmental units and for public colleges and universities. Also required statement for nongovernmental not-for-profit organizations.

statement of changes in fiduciary net position Required basic statement for fiduciary funds. Reported by fund type.

Statement of Federal Financial Accounting Concepts (SFFACs) Concepts statements passed by the FASAB that provide objectives of accounting and financial reporting for the federal government. They do not have the authoritative status of statements.

statement of fiduciary net position Required basic statement for fiduciary funds where assets less liabilities equals net position. Reported by fund type.

statement of financial position Required basic statement that reports assets, liabilities, and net assets of a not-for-profit organization.

statement of operations Required by the *Health Care Guide* (q.v.) to be prepared by all health care organizations. The Statement reflects changes among unrestricted net assets and must include a performance indicator (q.v.).

Statements Issued by the GASB (q.v.), FASB (q.v.), and FASAB (q.v.) outlining accounting principles for those entities under each board's jurisdiction. Constitutes GAAP (q.v.). Also principal financial presentations of governments and not-for-profit organizations.

T

technical bulletins Issued by the staffs of the standards-setting bodies and approved by the boards, providing additional information regarding questions and answers that might be addressed by those bodies.

time requirements An eligibility requirement imposed by GASB. A nonexchange revenue (or expense) cannot be recognized until the time specified by the donor, grantor, or contributor for expenditure.

total pension liability The portion of the actuarial present value of projected benefit payments that is attributable to past periods of employee service.

transfers As used in state and local government accounting, the shifting of resources from one category to another. In fund reporting, the transfer of resources from one fund to another. In government-wide reporting, the transfer of resources from one type of activity to another, such as from governmental activities to business-type activities.

Treasury, U.S. Department of the Federal executive branch agency; prepares Consolidated Financial Statements of the federal government. One of the "principals" that approves FASAB standards of financial reporting for the federal government.

trust fund Fund consisting of resources received and held by the governmental unit as trustee, to be expended or invested in accordance with the conditions of the trust. In governmental accounting, includes investment trust (q.v.), private-purpose Trust (q.v.), and pension and other employee benefit trust (q.v.).

U

unassigned fund balance A classification of fund balance reported in governmental-type funds. This is the residual fund balance category for the General Fund and is used to report negative fund balances in other governmental funds.

unmodified opinion Audit report in which the auditor states that the financial statements are "fairly presented" and comply with GAAP.

Unrelated Business Income Tax (UBIT) Tax that applies to business income of otherwise tax-exempt not-for-profit entities. Determined by relationship to exempt purpose and other criteria.

unrestricted net position The portion of a governmental unit or proprietary fund that is unrestricted by donors, grantors, creditors, laws or regulations, or legislation. This is the net position account for resources that are not reported in one of the other two residual equity classifications (Net Investment in Capital Assets or Restricted Net Position).

V

voluntary health and welfare organizations Not-for-profit organizations formed for the purpose of performing voluntary services for various segments of society. They are tax exempt, supported by the public, and operate on a not-for-profit basis.

voluntary nonexchange transactions One of the four classes of nonexchange transactions established by GASB. Examples are contributions and grants for restricted purposes, but which purposes are not mandated independent of the grant.

Index